NEGOTIATING ACADEMIC LITERACIES
Teaching and Learning Across Languages and Cultures

NEGOTIATING ACADEMIC LITERACIES
Teaching and Learning Across Languages and Cultures

Edited by

Vivian Zamel
University of Massachusetts Boston

Ruth Spack
Tufts University

LEA LAWRENCE ERLBAUM ASSOCIATES, PUBLISHERS
1998 Mahwah, New Jersey   London

Lawrence Erlbaum Associates, Inc., Publishers
10 Industrial Avenue
Mahwah, New Jersey 07430-2262

Cover design by Kathryn Houghtaling Lacey

Library of Congress Cataloging-in-Publication Data

Zamel, Vivian.
    Negotiating academic literacies : teaching and
learning across languages and cultures / edited by
Vivian Zamel, Ruth Spack.
        p.   cm.
    Includes bibliographical references.
    ISBN 0-8058-2998-9 (pbk. : alk. paper)
    1.   English language—Rhetoric—Study and
teaching. 2. English language—Study and teaching—Foreign speakers. 3. Academic writing—Study and teaching. 4. Multicultural
education. I. Spack, Ruth. II. Title.
PE1404.Z33 1998
808'.042'07—dc21   98-13599
                                              CIP

Printed in the United States of America
10 9 8 7 6 5 4 3

Contents

Preface

In *Negotiating Academic Literacies*, we bring together different voices from a range of publications and fields and unite them in pursuit of an understanding of how academic ways of knowing are acquired. Such an understanding is critical, we believe, given the extent to which the growing diversity in U.S. postsecondary institutions is challenging assumptions and terms that once seemed straightforward. For example, it is no longer possible to assume that there is one type of literacy in the academy. Academic literacy, which once denoted simply the ability to read and write college-level texts, now must embrace multiple approaches to knowledge. Hence, our use of the term academic *literacies*. College classrooms have become sites where different languages and cultures intersect, including the various discourses of students, teachers, and researchers. In our experience, the result of this interaction, even when (perhaps because) it involves struggle and conflict, is most often intellectual growth, for these different languages and cultures build on and give shape to one another.

As teachers and researchers, we have discovered that this perspective on language and culture applies not only to students who are still in the process of acquiring English but also to learners who find themselves in an academic situation that exposes them to a new set of expectations. We view this situation as a new culture, or rather, as various cultures, for when students travel from one classroom to another, they find that each has its unique conventions, concepts, and terms. At the same time that each classroom culture brings with it a particular language and set of assumptions, like all cultures it is inevitably shaped by the interaction of students, teacher, and texts. Collectively, classroom experiences across the curriculum require that students become fluent in multiple ways of reading and writing. In other words, students are expected to be conversant in a variety of academic literacies.

The principles we embrace to achieve an understanding of how students acquire literacies are drawn from research on second language acquisition. Fundamental to our understanding of language acquisition is the notion that language is acquired when it is viewed not as an end in itself, but rather as a means for understanding and constructing knowledge. Students who are actively engaged in work that they view as purposeful grow as language learners. As we investigate and reflect on the experiences of students both within our own classrooms and beyond, we understand that every teacher's role involves helping students negotiate meaning. To fulfill this academy-wide responsibility for language acquisition, we believe that higher education needs a pedagogical model that enables all faculty to transform and enrich the culture of the academy.

We can begin by taking into account and building on students' previous knowledge as they move into various areas of study and are introduced to new languages and approaches. It is important to emphasize here that we do not view academic literacies as substitutions for students' own ways of knowing. Rather, we value students' previous knowledge as an essential resource, one that enables the acquisition of unfamiliar terms and concepts. Given the opportunity to make connections between what they already know and what they are being asked to learn, students can take ownership of subject matter. Because they are in the process of acquisition, students' attempts at learning may, of course, fall short. We perceive these incomplete or imperfect attempts as reflections of an interlanguage, a linguistic term used here to represent the transitional but logical stage of a learner's growing understanding of language as well as subject matter. We have come to appreciate interlanguage as the mark of the kind of risk taking that is necessary in order for learning to take place. The process of acquisition is fostered through ongoing experiences and therefore is long-term and evolving. Through trial and error and by hypothesis testing, learners progress through various, somewhat predictable stages as they slowly achieve closer and closer approximations of the language and culture they are studying. Thus, students benefit from frequent opportunities to test out their ideas, receive instructive feedback, and revise their work. And because knowledge acquisition is socially generated, students can also benefit from collaboration with one another as they are challenged to make sense of their work. We want to stress that these principles are not simply accommodations that address the growing diversity of students within our institutions. They are fundamental to the teaching of all students.

Teaching that engages and challenges learners in meaningful work, is responsive to risk taking, encourages collaboration, revises its approaches purposefully, and anticipates the long-term and ongoing nature of learning is good pedagogy for everyone.

In addition to re-envisioning the way we promote academic literacies, we need to reconsider the way academic discourse is typically conceptualized. What is often viewed as a universal approach to knowledge does not always resonate with students' previous experiences. This is especially the case when students' assumptions about academic discourse—influenced by the ways in which their individual, cultural, and educational histories interact—are brought to bear on the expectations of the classrooms they are entering. Thus, for example, they may not produce writing that fits our preconceived models. But we can learn from what they do create. Students' alternative and often unpredictable approaches to academic work make us aware of the contingent nature of reading and writing. Their texts and interpretations can challenge us to recognize our own rhetorical prejudices and to reconceptualize our perspectives on academic discourse. This is a mutually enriching process.

We understand that reconstructing discourse practices is not a neutral undertaking. The same is true of acquiring new discourse practices, a process that goes to the heart of one's sense of self. Because students' ways with language are inextricably linked with who they are (as is true for all of us), when they attempt to adopt new literacy practices, they are, in effect, trying on social and cultural identities that may feel disorienting. Such shifts in identity are understandably difficult. One way to enable students to find their way in the academy, we believe, is for us to accept wider varieties of expression, to embrace multiple ways of communicating. That is exactly what we are asking students to do.

It may be obvious by now that we believe that the conditions that foster learning in students apply as well to the learning of teachers and researchers. Transforming ourselves, acquiring fluency and expertise in our work—these are not smooth, finite processes. Rather, they require recurring opportunities to undertake reflective inquiry, to struggle with ideas, to consult with colleagues, to test out new theories and reconsider earlier ones, to use writing to explore and interpret, to take risks in our teaching and researching, and to examine our goals and practices in light of students' experiences. This transformative work necessarily involves questioning what we do, what we are asking students to acquire, and what colleagues in our institution and in our discipline expect of us and of students. Ultimately, then, not only students but also teachers and researchers must inevitably engage in the ongoing process of negotiating academic literacies.

SELECTION OF READINGS

The chapters in this volume consist of previously published pieces that have informed, influenced, challenged, and defined our own theory and practice. Reflecting our interest in promoting collaboration across the curriculum, the works here are situated in several different fields—including composition studies, literature, applied linguistics, English as a second language, history, education, and anthropology—and originally appeared in a range of publications. Collectively, the authors raise important philosophical questions and they consider practical classroom applications. They complicate the nature of our work by revealing that the complex processes of learning, teaching, and researching are messy and contingent and thus are not amenable to neat and coherent representations. Acquiring discourses of and within the academy is necessarily a dynamic process of negotiation, involving both adaptation and resistance, and involving both teachers and students. Hence, the title of this book. It is the very nature of this process and the challenges that it poses for us that made it particularly appropriate to cast the title in terms that suggest that the enterprises that engage our thinking are ongoing: Negotiat*ing*, Teach*ing*, Learn*ing*.

ORGANIZATION OF THE READINGS

In organizing the readings for this volume, we chose to present the chapters chronologically, on the basis of publication dates, so as to avoid creating or suggesting any kind of hierarchy. Presenting the chapters in this way also gives readers some sense of the historical context in which discussions about academic literacy have evolved. We recognize, of course, that organizational choices of this sort reflect our own perspective and we anticipate that there are multiple ways in which to read the articles in this volume, generating a number of thematic possibilities. We therefore invite readers to conceptualize an organizational framework that seems most beneficial and instructive.

HISTORICAL OVERVIEW OF THE READINGS

Beginning in the 1970s, major changes occurred in the academy with the establishment of more open admissions policies, creating a need for new ways to think not only about the students who enter the classroom but also about the instructors who are assigned to teach them.

- In "Diving In," Mina Shaughnessy argues that students are not the only ones who need to learn and then proposes a developmental scale for teachers that begins with "guarding the tower"—the effort to keep "remedial" students out of the academy—and ends with "diving in," a courageous stance in which teachers "remediate" themselves.

- In "The Language of Exclusion," Mike Rose suggests that educators can begin to transform deeply held beliefs about student writers by revising the very language used to characterize writing instruction, language that constructs students as illiterate and deficient.
- Writing from the perspective of one who has suffered from such demoralizing characterizations as a colonized Jamaican in a land dominated by anglocentrism, Michelle Cliff describes how academic writing silenced her and how she recaptured her own history in "A Journey into Speech."

The desire to close the gap between students' language and the language of the academy and between first-language literacies and second-language literacies drove much of the debate about teaching and learning across cultures.

- In "Between Students' Language and Academic Discourse," Eleanor Kutz offers a pedagogical model for enabling students to find a middle ground to add to—rather than substitute for—their own personal, social, cultural, and historical backgrounds.
- Such a transformative model inevitably led to the question, "What Is Literacy?" which James Paul Gee answers by analyzing the differences among various discourses that students practice at home and at school and the ways in which these discourses are acquired.

The two chapters that follow provide unique examples of how these apparently conflicting discourses can mold a person's identity and ultimately contribute to growth in reading and writing.

- Barbara Mellix recounts the emotional toll of moving "From Outside, In" as she learns how and when to speak "black English and standard English" and finally to take control of written language.
- In "From Silence to Words," Min-zhan Lu relates a constructive identity struggle between a Chinese-language self and an English-language self, both formed in China, as she learned a Communist discourse in school and a Western discourse at home.

Because there was great pressure to prepare a diverse student body to do the work of the academy, one issue that fostered discussion was the question of whether English faculty should teach the writing of the other academic disciplines.

- Pointing to the complexity of disciplinary knowledge—and the need for immersion in a discipline in order for acquisition to take place—Ruth Spack cautions that we need to be realistic about the role composition programs can play in the process of "Initiating ESL Students into the Academic Discourse Community."
- In his critique of discipline-specific writing instruction, Kurt Spellmeyer searches for "A Common Ground" between what students bring to the academy and what the academy ultimately expects of them as he examines the personal nature of all writing.

As more and more students for whom English is an additional language entered the academy, the question of whether students can or should be taught to conform to U.S. rhetoric or allowed to transform U.S. rhetoric was addressed.

- In "The Classroom and the Wider Culture," Fan Shen reveals the cross-cultural implications of writing instruction as he describes how his Chinese cultural background shaped his approaches to writing in English in the United States and how, in turn, writing in English redefined his sense of self.
- Acknowledging that multiple rhetorical traditions exist, and faced with the task of "Evaluating Second Language Essays in Regular Composition Classes," Robert Land and Catherine Whitley argue for writing assessment that recognizes and values the alternative rhetorics that students bring to the academy.

Academic discourse itself began to be challenged by scholars in several fields, including composition, literature, English as a second language, and history.

- In "Reflections on Academic Discourse," Peter Elbow questions what academic discourse represents, even wonders whether it actually exists, as he makes a case for the kind of "nonacademic" writing he chooses to teach.
- Mary Louise Pratt, revealing how texts that do not fit conventional definitions of academic writing are ignored by Western scholars, calls for the inclusion of "Arts of the Contact Zone" that reflect the way cultures actually engage and interact with one another and in the process create culture and language anew.
- Also "Questioning Academic Discourse," Vivian Zamel argues that ESL programs should not exist to serve the interests of an academy that discourages and silences students but rather should foster genuine intellectual work that allows students to construct knowledge actively.

- In "Dancing with Professors: The Trouble with Academic Prose," Patricia Nelson Limerick expresses concern that graduate students, too, are silenced by the dull writing style they are forced to adopt and exhorts her colleagues to abandon their written models of pompousness and pedantry.

The connection between English language acquisition and power in the larger society has raised questions about whose voices should be heard, whose ideas should count, and whose English should be taught.

- Recognizing that language is linked to power, Lisa Delpit, in "The Politics of Teaching Literate Discourse," calls for a pedagogy that simultaneously teaches "mainstream" discourse and creates a place for African American and other voices that traditionally have been drowned out.
- Writing out of her own background experience as a member of an isolated mountain community, Linda Blanton illustrates in "Discourse, Artifacts, and the Ozarks" what can happen when academic discourse makes room for writers' histories and stories.
- In "The Ownership of English," Henry Widdowson calls attention to the fact that an exclusive minority of people determine what constitutes "standard English" and argues that, given the varieties of English outside as well as within the academy, we need to ask whose English is the standard against which we measure students' acquisition of literacy.

Twenty years after Mina Shaughnessy invited us to dive in, we still need to be reminded that not only the students but also teachers and the academy itself can benefit from transformed and transformative world views.

- Borrowing Mina Shaughnessy's description of students, Vivian Zamel recognizes that teachers, too, feel like "Strangers in Academia" and envisions potential solutions in collaborative work among faculty across the curriculum that focuses on ways in which language is actually acquired.
- Exposing a paradoxical Western tradition that privileges originality and creativity yet emphasizes a fixed canon of disciplinary knowledge, Alastair Pennycook invites us to reflect on the hypocrisy and double standards that obtain in the academy when we freely engage in the process of "Borrowing Others' Words."
- Focusing on the issue of identity vis-à-vis race, class, gender, culture, religion, language, and sexual orientation, Ruth Spack analyzes the complex role teachers and scholars play in the world of academic

multiculturalism as she examines "The (In)visibility of the Person(al) in Academe."

- Acknowledging the limitations of research that attempts to analyze and represent language and culture on the basis of conventional academic frameworks, Norma González argues for the legitimacy of "Blurred Voices" in the investigations we undertake.

REFLECTING ON THE READINGS

These readings have proven productive for our thinking precisely because they complicate the ways in which we see language, literacy, and culture and thus push us to interrogate what we do and why. They have challenged us to acknowledge the tensions and uncertainties in our work, to reconsider our assumptions and practices, and ultimately to engage in a generative and exciting process of reflection and inquiry. And so we have included here the kinds of questions that we bring to our reading of these articles and that the articles, in turn, raise about our thinking. We invite readers to choose whichever of the following questions offer the most fruitful direction for reflection and, of course, to generate other questions for further exploration.

1. How does this essay contribute to, raise questions about, or change my understanding of academic literacies?

- What new knowledge do I bring to my understanding of language acquisition?
- What new knowledge do I bring to my understanding of culture(s)?
- How do I now define literacy?
- What have I learned about how students learn?
- What have I learned about how teachers (can) teach?
- What have I learned about how researchers (can) research?
- How do I now envision the relationship between teaching and learning?
- Which aspects of language acquisition theory make sense in light of what I know about students' reading and writing processes?
- What knowledge and understanding do I now bring to the reading and evaluating of students' texts?
- How can or should I revise the language I use to describe students, their academic work, and the standards of the academy?

2. How does this essay enrich my understanding of any other chapter(s) in the book?

- How does this essay contribute to my understanding of a work written earlier?
- How does this piece contribute to my understanding of a work written subsequently?
- To what extent does the theoretical perspective of this essay provide a framework for my understanding of an individual writer's personal experience described in another essay?
- To what extent does this writer's own experience provide a framework for my understanding of an abstract theory delineated in another essay?
- How does this writer's perspective on literacy (in a first or second language) contribute to my understanding of another writer's perspective on literacy (in a first or second language)?
- How does an issue of identity discussed in this essay (for example, vis-à-vis language, culture, race, or class) contribute to my understanding of a theory or experience discussed in another essay?

3. How should I deal with the tensions and contradictions among different writers' ideas?

- How might I reconcile such contradictions?
- If I cannot reconcile certain contradictions, which writer's argument makes more sense to me, and why?
- What do the contradictions suggest about the theory and practice of teaching and learning across languages and cultures?
- What do the contradictions suggest about the process of undertaking research across languages and cultures?

4. How does this essay contribute to or raise questions about my own ongoing development?

- What have I learned about myself as a learner?
- What have I learned about myself as a teacher?
- What have I learned about myself as a writer?
- What have I learned about myself as a researcher?

5. How does this essay contribute to, raise questions about, or change my understanding of my various roles within my own institution?

- How do I now envision my relationship to faculty within my own department?
- How do I now envision my relationship to faculty outside my own department?

- How does my own area of interest or expertise relate to other disciplines within the institution?
- How might I redefine my role in light of what I have read?
- How might I share my (new) understanding of academic literacies with various members of the academic community?

6. How are the ideas in this essay connected to or in conflict with the world outside the academy?

- What have I read or seen lately that deals with a topic similar to the one discussed in the essay?
- How similarly or differently are these ideas represented in print media, visual media, or public forums?
- How might I be able to influence the way these ideas are represented outside the academy?

7. Overall, how can this historical overview productively guide my approach to teaching, learning, and research?

Chapter 1

Diving In:
An Introduction
to Basic Writing

Mina P. Shaughnessy

Basic writing, alias remedial, developmental, pre-baccalaureate, or even handicapped English, is commonly thought of as a writing course for young men and women who have many things wrong with them. Not only do medical metaphors dominate the pedagogy (*remedial, clinic, lab, diagnosis,* and so on), but teachers and administrators tend to discuss basic-writing students much as doctors tend to discuss their patients, without being tinged by mortality themselves and with certainly no expectations that questions will be raised about the state of *their* health.

Yet such is the nature of instruction in writing that teachers and students cannot easily escape one another's maladies. Unlike other courses, where exchanges between teacher and student can be reduced to as little as one or two objective tests a semester, the writing course requires students to write things down regularly, usually once a week, and requires teachers to read what is written and then write things back and every so often even talk directly with individual students about the way they write.

This system of exchange between teacher and student has so far yielded much more information about what is wrong with students than about what is wrong with teachers, reinforcing the notion that students, not teachers, are the people in education who must do the changing. The phrase "catching up," so often used to describe the progress of BW students, is illuminating here, suggesting as it does that the only person who must

College Composition and Communication, 1976

move in the teaching situation is the student. As a result of this view, we are much more likely in talking about teaching to talk about students, to theorize about *their* needs and attitudes or to chart *their* development and ignore the possibility that teachers also change in response to students, that there may in fact be important connections between the changes teachers undergo and the progress of their students.

I would like, at any rate, to suggest that this is so, and since it is common these days to "place" students on developmental scales, saying they are eighth-graders or fifth-graders when they read and even younger when they write or that they are stalled some place on Piaget's scale without formal propositions, I would further like to propose a developmental scale for teachers, admittedly an impressionistic one, but one that fits the observations I have made over the years as I have watched traditionally prepared English teachers, including myself, learning to teach in the open-admissions classroom.

My scale has four stages, each of which I will name with a familiar metaphor intended to suggest what lies at the center of the teacher's emotional energy during that stage. Thus I have chosen to name the first stage of my developmental scale GUARDING THE TOWER, because during this stage the teacher is in one way or another concentrating on protecting the academy (including himself) from the outsiders, those who do not seem to belong in the community of learners. The grounds for exclusion are various. The mores of the times inhibit anyone's openly ascribing the exclusion to genetic inferiority, but a few teachers doubtless still hold to this view.

More often, however, the teacher comes to the basic-writing class with every intention of preparing his students to write for college courses, only to discover, with the first batch of essays, that the students are so alarmingly and incredibly behind any students he has taught before that the idea of their ever learning to write acceptably for college, let alone learning to do so in one or two semesters, seems utterly pretentious. Whatever the sources of their incompetence—whether rooted in the limits they were born with or those that were imposed upon them by the world they grew up in—the fact seems stunningly, depressingly obvious: they will never "make it" in college unless someone radically lowers the standards.

The first pedagogical question the teacher asks at this stage is therefore not "How do I teach these students?" but "What are the consequences of flunking an entire class?" It is a question that threatens to turn the class into a contest, a peculiar and demoralizing contest for both student and teacher, since neither expects to win. The student, already conditioned to the idea that there is something wrong with his English and that writing is a device for magnifying and exposing this deficiency, risks as little as possible on the page, often straining with what he does write to approximate the academic style and producing in the process what might better be called "written Anguish" rather than English—sentences whose subjects are crowded out by such phrases as "it is my conviction that" or "on the contrary to my opinion," inflections that belong to no variety of English, standard or non-standard, but grow out of the writer's attempt to be correct, or words whose idiosyncratic spellings reveal not simply an increase in the number of conventional misspellings but new orders of difficulty with the correspondences between spoken and written English. Meanwhile, the teacher assumes that he must not only hold out for the same product he held out for in the past but teach unflinchingly in the same way as before, as if any pedagogical adjustment to the needs of students were a kind of cheating. Obliged because of the exigencies brought on by open admissions to serve his time in the defense of the academy, he does if not his best, at least his duty, setting forth the material to be mastered, as if he expected students to learn it, but feeling grateful when a national holiday happens to fall on a basic-writing day and looking always for ways of evading conscription next semester.

But gradually, student and teacher are drawn into closer range. They are obliged, like emissaries from opposing camps, to send messages back and forth. They meet to consider each other's words and separate to study them in private. Slowly, the teacher's preconceptions of his students begin to give way here and there. It now appears that, in some instances at least, their writing, with its rudimentary errors and labored style, has belied their intelligence and individuality. Examined at a closer range, the class now appears to have at least some members in it who might, with hard work, eventually "catch up." And it is the intent of reaching these students that moves the teacher into the second stage of development—which I will name CONVERTING THE NATIVES.

As the image suggests, the teacher has now admitted at least some to the community of the educable. These learners are perceived, however, as empty vessels, ready to be filled with new knowledge. Learning is thought of not so much as a constant and often troubling reformulation of the world so as to encompass new knowledge but as a steady flow of truth into a void. Whether the truth is delivered in lectures or modules, cassettes or computers, circles or squares, the teacher's purpose is the same: to carry the technology of advanced literacy to the inhabitants of an underdeveloped country. And so confident is he of the reasonableness and allure of what he is presenting, it does not occur to him to consider the competing logics and values and habits that may be influencing his students, often in ways that they themselves are unaware of.

Sensing no need to relate what he is teaching to what his students know, to stop to explore the contexts within which the conventions of academic discourse have developed, and to view these conventions in patterns large enough to encompass what students do know about language already, the teacher becomes a mechanic of the sentence, the paragraph, and the essay.

Drawing usually upon the rules and formulas that were part of his training in composition, he conscientiously presents to his students flawless schemes for achieving order and grammaticality and anatomizes model passages of English prose to uncover, beneath brilliant, unique surfaces, the skeletons of ordinary paragraphs.

Yet too often the schemes, however well meant, do not seem to work. Like other simplistic prescriptions, they illuminate for the moment and then disappear in the melee of real situations, where paradigms frequently break down and thoughts will not be regimented. S's keep reappearing or disappearing in the wrong places; regular verbs shed their inflections and irregular verbs acquire them; tenses collide; sentences derail; and whole essays idle at one level of generalization.

Baffled, the teacher asks, "How is it that these young men and women whom I have personally admitted to the community of learners cannot learn these simple things?" Until one day, it occurs to him that perhaps these simple things—so transparent and compelling to him—are not in fact simple at all, that they only appear simple to those who already know them, that the grammar and rhetoric of formal written English have been shaped by the irrationalities of history and habit and by the peculiar restrictions and rituals that come from putting words on paper instead of into the air, that the sense and nonsense of written English must often collide with the spoken English that has been serving students in their negotiations with the world for many years. The insight leads our teacher to the third stage of his development, which I will name SOUNDING THE DEPTHS, for he turns now to the careful observation not only of his students and their writing but of himself as writer and teacher, seeking a deeper understanding of the behavior called writing and of the special difficulties his students have in mastering the skill. Let us imagine, for the sake of illustration, that the teacher now begins to look more carefully at two common problems among basic writers—the problem of grammatical errors and the problem of undeveloped paragraphs.

Should he begin in his exploration of error not only to count and name errors but to search for patterns and pose hypotheses that might explain them, he will begin to see that while his lessons in the past may have been "simple," the sources of the error he was trying to correct were often complex. The insight leads not inevitably or finally to a rejection of all rules and standards, but to a more careful look at error, to the formulation of what might be called a "logic" of errors that serves to mark a pedagogical path for teacher and student to follow.

Let us consider in this connection the "simple" *s* inflection on the verb, the source of a variety of grammatical errors in BW papers. It is, first, an alien form to many students whose mother tongues inflect the verb differently or not at all. Uniformly called for, however, in all verbs in the third person singular present indicative of standard English, it would seem to be a highly predictable or stable form and therefore one easily remembered. But note the grammatical concepts the student must grasp before he can apply the rule: the concepts of person, tense, number, and mood. Note that the *s* inflection is an atypical inflection within the modern English verb system. Note too how often it must seem to the student that he hears the stem form of the verb after third person singular subjects in what sounds like the present, as he does for example whenever he hears questions like "Does *she want* to go?" or "Can the *subway stop?*" In such sentences, the standard language itself reinforces the student's own resistance to the inflection.

And then, beyond these apparent unpredictabilities within the standard system, there is the influence of the student's own language or dialect, which urges him to ignore a troublesome form that brings no commensurate increase in meaning. Indeed, the very *s* he struggles with here may shift in a moment to signify plurality simply by being attached to a noun instead of a verb. No wonder then that students of formal English throughout the world find this inflection difficult, not because they lack intelligence or care but because they think analogically and are linguistically efficient. The issue is not the capacity of students finally to master this and the many other forms of written English that go against the grain of their instincts and experience but the priority this kind of problem ought to have in the larger scheme of learning to write and the willingness of students to mobilize themselves to master such forms at the initial stages of construction.

Somewhere between the folly of pretending that errors don't matter and the rigidity of insisting that they matter more than anything, the teacher must find his answer, searching always under pressure for short cuts that will not ultimately restrict the intellectual power of his students. But as yet, we lack models for the maturation of the writing skill among young, native-born adults and can only theorize about the adaptability of other models for these students. We cannot say with certainty just what progress in writing ought to look like for basic-writing students, and more particularly how the elimination of error is related to their over-all improvement.

Should the teacher then turn from problems of error to his students' difficulties with the paragraphs of academic essays, new complexities emerge. Why, he wonders, do they reach such instant closure on their ideas, seldom moving into even one subordinate level of qualification but either moving on to a new topic sentence or drifting off into reverie and anecdote until the point of the essay has been dissolved? Where is that attitude of "suspended conclusion" that Dewey called thinking, and what can one infer about their intellectual competence from such behavior?

Before consigning his students to some earlier stage of mental development, the teacher at this stage begins to look more closely at the task

even in the '70s,
how testing affects
learners

he is asking students to perform. Are they aware, for example, after years of right/wrong testing, after the ACT's and the GED's and the OAT's, after straining to memorize what they read but never learning to doubt it, after "psyching out" answers rather than discovering them, are they aware that the rules have changed and that the rewards now go to those who can sustain a play of mind upon ideas—teasing out the contradictions and ambiguities and frailties of statements?

Or again, are the students sensitive to the ways in which the conventions of talk differ from those of academic discourse? Committed to extending the boundaries of what is known, the scholar proposes generalizations that cover the greatest possible number of instances and then sets about supporting his case according to the rules of evidence and sound reasoning that govern his subject. The spoken language, looping back and forth between speakers, offering chances for groping and backing up and even hiding, leaving room for the language of hands and faces, of pitch and pauses, is by comparison generous and inviting. The speaker is not responsible for the advancement of formal learning. He is free to assert opinions without a display of evidence or recount experiences without explaining what they "mean." His movements from one level of generality to another are more often brought on by shifts in the winds of conversation rather than by some decision of his to be more specific or to sum things up. For him the injunction to "be more specific" is difficult to carry out because the conditions that lead to specificity are usually missing. He may not have acquired the habit of questioning his propositions, as a listener might, in order to locate the points that require amplification or evidence. Or he may be marooned with a proposition he cannot defend for lack of information or for want of practice in retrieving the history of an idea as it developed in his own mind.

Similarly, the query "What is your point?" may be difficult to answer because the conditions under which the student is writing have not allowed for the slow generation of an orienting conviction, that underlying sense of the direction he wants his thinking to take. Yet without this conviction, he cannot judge the relevance of what comes to his mind, as one sentence branches out into another or one idea engenders another, gradually crowding from his memory the direction he initially set for himself.

Or finally, the writer may lack the vocabulary that would enable him to move more easily up the ladder of abstraction and must instead forge out of a non-analytical vocabulary a way of discussing thoughts about thoughts, a task so formidable as to discourage him, as travelers in a foreign land are discouraged, from venturing far beyond bread-and-butter matters.

From such soundings, our teacher begins to see that teaching at the remedial level is not a matter of being simpler but of being more profound, of not only starting from "scratch" but also determining where "scratch" is. The experience of studenthood is the experience of being just so far over one's head that it is both realistic and essential to work at surviving. But by underestimating the sophistication of our students and by ignoring the complexity of the tasks we set before them, we have failed to locate in precise ways where to begin and what follows what.

But I have created a fourth stage in my developmental scheme, which I am calling DIVING IN in order to suggest that the teacher who has come this far must now make a decision that demands professional courage—the decision to remediate himself, to become a student of new disciplines and of his students themselves in order to perceive both their difficulties and their incipient excellence. "Always assume," wrote Leo Strauss to the teacher, "that there is one silent student in your class who is by far superior to you in head and in heart." This assumption, as I have been trying to suggest, does not come easily or naturally when the teacher is a college teacher and the young men and women in his class are labeled remedial. But as we come to know these students better, we begin to see that the greatest barrier to our work with them is our ignorance of them and of the very subject we have contracted to teach. We see that we must grope our ways into the turbulent disciplines of semantics and linguistics for fuller, more accurate data about words and sentences; we must pursue more rigorously the design of developmental models, basing our schemes less upon loose comparisons with children and more upon case studies and developmental research of the sort that produced William Perry's impressive study of the intellectual development of Harvard students; we need finally to examine more closely the nature of speaking and writing and divine the subtle ways in which these forms of language both support and undo each other.

The work is waiting for us. And so irrevocable now is the tide that brings the new students into the nation's college classrooms that it is no longer within our power, as perhaps it once was, to refuse to accept them into the community of the educable. They are here. DIVING IN is simply deciding that teaching them to write well is not only suitable but challenging work for those who would be teachers and scholars in a democracy.

Chapter 2

The Language of Exclusion: Writing Instruction at the University

Mike Rose

"How many '*minor* errors' are acceptable?"

"We must try to isolate and define those *further* skills in composition . . ."

". . . we should provide a short remedial course to patch up any deficiencies."

"Perhaps the most striking feature of this campus' siege against illiteracy . . ."

"One might hope that, after a number of years, standards might be set in the high schools which would allow us to abandon our own defensive program."

These snippets come from University of California and California state legislative memos, reports, and position papers and from documents produced during a recent debate in UCLA's Academic Senate over whether a course in our freshman writing sequence was remedial. Though these quotations—and a half dozen others I will use in this essay—are local, they represent a kind of institutional language about writing instruction in American higher education. There are five ideas about writing implicit in these comments: Writing ability is judged in terms of the presence of error and can thus be quantified. Writing is a skill or a tool rather than a discipline. A number of our students lack this skill and must be remediated. In fact, some percentage of our students are, for all intents and purposes, illiterate.

Our remedial efforts, while currently necessary, can be phased out once the literacy crisis is solved in other segments of the educational system.

This kind of thinking and talking is so common that we often fail to notice that it reveals a reductive, fundamentally behaviorist model of the development and use of written language, a problematic definition of writing, and an inaccurate assessment of student ability and need. This way of talking about writing abilities and instruction is woven throughout discussions of program and curriculum development, course credit, instructional evaluation, and resource allocation. And, in various ways, it keeps writing instruction at the periphery of the curriculum.

It is certainly true that many faculty and administrators would take issue with one or more of the above notions. And those of us in writing would bring current thinking in rhetoric and composition studies into the conversation. (Though we often—perhaps uncomfortably—rely on terms like "skill" and "remediation.") Sometimes we successfully challenge this language or set up sensible programs in spite of it. But all too often we can do neither. The language represented in the headnotes of this essay reveals deeply held beliefs. It has a tradition and a style, and it plays off the fundamental tension between the general education and the research missions of the American university. The more I think about this language and recall the contexts in which I've heard it used, the more I realize how caught up we all are in a political-semantic web that restricts the way we think about the place of writing in the academy. The opinions I have been describing are certainly not the only ones to be heard. But they are strong. Influential. Rhetorically effective. And profoundly exclusionary. Until we seriously rethink it, we will misrepresent the nature of writing, misjudge our students' problems, and miss any chance to effect a true curricular change that will situate writing firmly in the undergraduate curriculum.

Let us consider the college writing course for a moment. Freshman composition originated in 1874 as a Harvard response to the poor writing of *upper* classmen, spread rapidly, and became and remained the most consistently required course in the American curriculum. Upper division writing courses have a briefer and much less expansive history, but they are currently receiving a good deal of institutional energy and support. It would be hard to think of an ability more desired than the ability to write. Yet, though writing courses are highly valued, even enjoying a boom, they are also viewed with curious eyes. Administrators fund them—often generously—but academic senates worry that the boundaries between high school and college are eroding, and worry as well that the considerable investment of resources in such courses will drain money from the research enterprise. They deny some of the courses curricular status by tagging them remedial, and their members secretly or not-so-secretly wish the courses could be moved to community colleges. Scientists and social scientists underscore the importance of effective writing, yet find it difficult—if not impossible—to restructure their own courses of study to encourage and support writing. More than a few humanists express such difficulty as well. English departments hold onto writing courses but consider the work intellectually second-class. The people who teach writing are more often than not temporary hires; their courses are robbed of curricular continuity and of the status that comes with tenured faculty involvement. And the instructors? Well, they're just robbed.

The writing course holds a very strange position in the American curriculum. It is within this setting that composition specialists must debate and defend and interminably evaluate what they do. And how untenable such activity becomes if the very terms of the defense undercut both the nature of writing and the teaching of writing, and exclude it in various metaphorical ways from the curriculum. We end up arguing with words that sabotage our argument. The first step in resolving such a mess is to consider the language institutions use when they discuss writing. What I want to do in this essay is to look at each of the five notions presented earlier, examine briefly the conditions that shaped their use, and speculate on how it is that they misrepresent and exclude. I will conclude by entertaining a less reductive and exclusionary way to think—and talk—about writing in the academy.

BEHAVIORISM, QUANTIFICATION, AND WRITING

A great deal of current work in fields as diverse as rhetoric, composition studies, psycholinguistics, and cognitive development has underscored the importance of engaging young writers in rich, natural language use. And the movements of the last four decades that have most influenced the teaching of writing—life adjustment, liberal studies, and writing as process—have each, in their very different ways, placed writing pedagogy in the context of broad concerns: personal development and adjustment, a rhetorical-literary tradition, the psychology of composing. It is somewhat curious, then, that a behaviorist approach to writing, one that took its fullest shape in the 1930s and has been variously and severely challenged by the movements that followed it, remains with us as vigorously as it does. It is atomistic, focusing on isolated bits of discourse, error centered, and linguistically reductive. It has a style and a series of techniques that influence pedagogy, assessment, and evaluation. We currently see its influence in workbooks, programmed instruction, and many formulations of behavioral objectives, and it gets most of its airplay in remedial courses. It has staying power. Perhaps we can better understand its resilience if we briefly survey the history that gives it its current shape.

When turn-of-the-century educational psychologists like E. L. Thorndike began to study the teaching of writing, they found a Latin and Greek-influenced school grammar that was primarily a set of prescriptions for conducting socially acceptable discourse, a list of the arcane do's and don'ts of usage for the ever-increasing numbers of children—many from lower classes and immigrant groups—entering the educational system. Thorndike and his colleagues also found reports like those issuing from the Harvard faculty in the 1890s which called attention to the presence of errors in handwriting, spelling, and grammar in the writing of the university's entering freshmen. The twentieth-century writing curriculum, then, was focused on the particulars of usage, grammar, and mechanics. Correctness became, in James Berlin's words, the era's "most significant measure of accomplished prose" (*Writing Instruction in Nineteenth-Century American Colleges* [Carbondale: Southern Illinois University Press, 1984], p. 73).

Such particulars suited educational psychology's model of language quite well: a mechanistic paradigm that studied language by reducing it to discrete behaviors and that defined language growth as the accretion of these particulars. The stress, of course, was on quantification and measurement. ("Whatever exists at all exists in some amount," proclaimed Thorndike.[1]) The focus on error—which is eminently measurable—found justification in a model of mind that was ascending in American academic psychology. Educators embraced the late Victorian faith in science.

Thorndike and company would champion individualized instruction and insist on language practice rather than the rote memorization of rules of grammar that characterized nineteenth-century pedagogy. But they conducted their work within a model of language that was tremendously limited, and this model was further supported and advanced by what Raymond Callahan has called "the cult of efficiency," a strong push to apply to education the principles of industrial scientific management (*Education and the Cult of Efficiency* [Chicago: University of Chicago Press, 1962]). Educational gains were defined as products, and the output of products could be measured. Pedagogical effectiveness—which meant cost-effectiveness—could be determined with "scientific" accuracy. This was the era of the educational efficiency expert. (NCTE even had a Committee on Economy of Time in English.) The combination of positivism, efficiency, and skittishness about correct grammar would have a profound influence on pedagogy and research.

This was the time when workbooks and "practice pads" first became big business. Their success could at least partly be attributed to the fact that they were supported by scientific reasoning. Educational psychologists had demonstrated that simply memorizing rules of grammar and usage had

---

[1]Quoted in Lawrence A. Cremin, *The Transformation of the School: Progressivism in American Education* (New York: Alfred A. Knopf, 1961), p. 185.

no discernible effect on the quality of student writing. What was needed was application of those rules through practice provided by drills and exercises. The theoretical underpinning was expressed in terms of "habit formation" and "habit strength," the behaviorist equivalent of learning— the resilience of an "acquired response" being dependent on the power and number of reinforcements. The logic was neat: specify a desired linguistic behavior as precisely as possible (e.g., the proper use of the pronouns "he" and "him") and construct opportunities to practice it. The more practice, the more the linguistic habit will take hold. Textbooks as well as workbooks shared this penchant for precision. One textbook for teachers presented a unit on the colon.[2] A text for students devoted seven pages to the use of a capital letter to indicate a proper noun.[3] This was also the time when objective tests—which had been around since 1890— enjoyed a sudden rebirth as "new type" tests. And they, of course, were precision incarnate. The tests generated great enthusiasm among educators who saw in them a scientific means accurately and fairly to assess student achievement in language arts as well as in social studies and mathematics. Ellwood Cubberley, the dean of the School of Education at Stanford, called the development of these "new type" tests "one of the most significant movements in all our educational history."[4] Cubberley and his colleagues felt they were on the threshold of a new era.

Research too focused on the particulars of language, especially on listing and tabulating error. One rarely finds consideration of the social context of error, or of its cognitive-developmental meaning—that is, no interpretation of its significance in the growth of the writer. Instead one finds W. S. Guiler tallying the percentages of 350 students who, in misspelling "mortgage," erred by omitting the "t" vs. those who dropped the initial "g."[5] And one reads Grace Ransom's study of students' "vocabularies of errors"—a popular notion that any given student has a more or less stable set of errors he or she commits. Ransom showed that with drill and practice, students ceased making many of the errors that appeared on pretests (though, unfortunately for the theory, a large number of new errors appeared in their post-tests).[6] One also reads Luella Cole Pressey's assertion that "everything needed for about 90 per cent of the writing students do . . . appears to involve only some 44 different rules of English composition."

---

[2]Arthur N. Applebee, *Tradition and Reform in the Teaching of English: A History* (Urbana, Ill.: National Council of Teachers of English, 1974), pp. 93–94.

[3]P. G. Perrin, "The Remedial Racket," *English Journal,* 22 (1933), 383.

[4]From Cubberley's introduction to Albert R. Lang, *Modern Methods in Written Examinations* (Boston: Houghton Mifflin, 1930), p. vii.

[5]"Background Deficiencies," *Journal of Higher Education,* 3 (1932), 371.

[6]"Remedial Methods in English Composition," *English Journal,* 22 (1933), 749–754.

And therefore, if mastery of the rules is divided up and allocated to grades 2 through 12, "there is an average of 4.4 rules to be mastered per year."[7]

Such research and pedagogy was enacted to good purpose, a purpose stated well by H. J. Arnold, Director of Special Schools at Wittenberg College:

> [Students'] disabilities are specific. The more exactly they can be located, the more promptly they can be removed. . . . It seems reasonably safe to predict that the elimination of the above mentioned disabilities through adequate remedial drill will do much to remove students' handicaps in certain college courses. ("Diagnostic and Remedial Techniques for College Freshmen," *Association of American Colleges Bulletin*, 16 [1930], pp. 271–272)

The trouble, of course, is that such work is built on a set of highly questionable assumptions: that a writer has a relatively fixed repository of linguistic blunders that can be pinpointed and then corrected through drill, that repetitive drill on specific linguistic features represented in isolated sentences will result in mastery of linguistic (or stylistic or rhetorical) principles, that bits of discourse bereft of rhetorical or conceptual context can form the basis of curriculum and assessment, that good writing is correct writing, and that correctness has to do with pronoun choice, verb forms, and the like.

Despite the fact that such assumptions began to be challenged by the late 30s,[8] the paraphernalia and the approach of the scientific era were destined to remain with us. I think this trend has the staying power it does for a number of reasons, the ones we saw illustrated in our brief historical overview. It gives a method—a putatively objective one—to the strong desire of our society to maintain correct language use. It is very American in its seeming efficiency. And it offers a simple, understandable view of complex linguistic problems. The trend seems to reemerge with most potency in times of crisis: when budgets crunch and accountability looms or, particularly, when "nontraditional" students flood our institutions.[9] A reduction of

---

[7]"Freshmen Needs in Written English," *English Journal*, 19 (1930), 706.

[8]I would mislead if I did not point out that there were cautionary voices being raised all along, though until the late 1930s they were very much in the minority. For two early appraisals, see R. L. Lyman, *Summary of Investigations Relating to Grammar, Language, and Composition* (Chicago: University of Chicago Press, 1924), and especially P. G. Perrin, "The Remedial Racket," *English Journal*, 22 (1933), 382–388.

[9]Two quotations. The first offers the sort of humanist battle cry that often accompanies reductive drill, and the second documents the results of such an approach. Both are from NCTE publications.

"I think . . . that the chief objective of freshman English (at least for the first semester and low or middle—but not high—sections) should be ceaseless, brutal drill on mechanics, with exercises and themes. Never mind imagination, the soul, literature, for at least one semester, but pray for literacy and fight for it" (A University of Nebraska professor quoted with approval in Oscar James Campbell, *The Teaching of College English* [New York: Appleton-Century, 1934], pp. 36–37).

complexity has great appeal in institutional decision making, especially in difficult times: a scientific-atomistic approach to language, with its attendant tallies and charts, nicely fits an economic/political decision-making model. When in doubt or when scared or when pressed, count.

And something else happens. When student writing is viewed in this particularistic, pseudo-scientific way, it gets defined in very limited terms as a narrow band of inadequate behavior separate from the vastly complex composing that faculty members engage in for a living and delve into for work and for play. And such perception yields what it intends: a behavior that is stripped of its rich cognitive and rhetorical complexity. A behavior that, in fact, looks and feels basic, fundamental, atomistic. A behavior that certainly does not belong in the university.

ENGLISH AS A SKILL

As English, a relatively new course of study, moved into the second and third decades of this century, it was challenged by efficiency-obsessed administrators and legislators. Since the teaching of writing required tremendous resources, English teachers had to defend their work in utilitarian terms. One very successful defense was their characterization of English as a "skill" or "tool subject" that all students had to master in order to achieve in almost any subject and to function as productive citizens. The defense worked, and the utility of English in schooling and in adult life was confirmed for the era.

The way this defense played itself out, however, had interesting ramifications. Though a utilitarian defense of English included for many the rhetorical/conceptual as well as the mechanical/grammatical dimensions of language, the overwhelming focus of discussion in the committee reports and the journals of the 1920s and 1930s was on grammatical and mechanical error. The narrow focus was made even more narrow by a fetish for "scientific" tabulation. One could measure the degree to which students mastered their writing skill by tallying their mistakes.

"Members of the Task Force saw in many classes extensive work in traditional schoolroom grammar and traditional formal English usage. They commonly found students with poor reading skills being taught the difference between *shall* and *will* or pupils with serious difficulties in speech diagramming sentences. Interestingly, observations by the Task Force reveal far more extensive teaching of traditional grammar in this study of language programs for the disadvantaged than observers saw in the National Study of High School English Programs, a survey of comprehensive high schools known to be achieving important results in English with college-bound students able to comprehend the abstractions of such grammar" (Richard Corbin and Muriel Crosby, *Language Programs for the Disadvantaged* [Urbana, Ill.: NCTE, 1965], pp. 121–122).

We no longer use the phrase "tool subject," and we have gone a long way in the last three decades from error tabulation toward revitalizing the rhetorical dimension of writing. But the notion of writing as a skill is still central to our discussions and our defenses: we have writing skills hierarchies, writing skills assessments, and writing skills centers. And necessary as such a notion may seem to be, I think it carries with it a tremendous liability. Perhaps the problem is nowhere more clearly illustrated than in this excerpt from the UCLA Academic Senate's definition of a university course:

> A university course should set forth an integrated body of knowledge with primary emphasis on presenting principles and theories rather than on developing skills and techniques.

If "skills and techniques" are included, they must be taught "primarily as a means to learning, analyzing, and criticizing theories and principles." There is a lot to question in this definition, but for now let us limit ourselves to the distinction it establishes between a skill and a body of knowledge. The distinction highlights a fundamental tension in the American university: between what Laurence Veysey labels the practical-utilitarian dimension (applied, vocational, educationalist) and both the liberal culture and the research dimensions—the latter two, each in different ways, elevating appreciation and pure inquiry over application (*The Emergence of the American University* [Chicago: University of Chicago Press, 1965]). To discuss writing as a skill, then, is to place it in the realm of the technical, and in the current, research-ascendant American university, that is a kiss of death.

Now it is true that we commonly use the word *skill* in ways that suggest a complex interweaving of sophisticated activity and rich knowledge. We praise the interpretive skills of the literary critic, the diagnostic skills of the physician, the interpersonal skills of the clinical psychologist. Applied, yes, but implying a kind of competence that is more in line with obsolete definitions that equate skill with reason and understanding than with this more common definition (that of the *American Heritage Dictionary*): "An art, trade, or technique, particularly one requiring use of the hands or body." A skill, particularly in the university setting, is, well, a tool, something one develops and refines and completes in order to take on the higher-order demands of purer thought. Everyone may acknowledge the value of the skill (our senate praised our course to the skies as it removed its credit), but it is valuable as the ability to multiply or titrate a solution or use an index or draw a map is valuable. It is absolutely necessary but remains second-class. It is not "an integrated body of knowledge" but a technique, something acquired differently from the way one acquires knowledge—from drill, from practice, from procedures that conjure up the hand and the eye but not the mind. Skills are discussed as separable, distinct, circumscribable activities; thus we talk of subskills, levels of skills, sets of skills. Again writing is defined by abilities one can quantify and connect as opposed to the dynamism and organic vitality one associates with thought.

Because skills are fundamental tools, basic procedures, there is the strong expectation that they be mastered at various preparatory junctures in one's educational career and in the places where such tools are properly crafted. In the case of writing, the skills should be mastered before one enters college and takes on higher-order endeavors. And the place for such instruction—before or after entering college—is the English class. Yes, the skill can be refined, but its fundamental development is over, completed via a series of elementary and secondary school courses and perhaps one or two college courses, often designated remedial. Thus it is that so many faculty consider upper-division and especially graduate-level writing courses as de jure remedial. To view writing as a skill in the university context reduces the possibility of perceiving it as a complex ability that is continually developing as one engages in new tasks with new materials for new audiences.

If the foregoing seems a bit extreme, consider this passage from our Academic Senate's review of UCLA Writing Programs:

> . . . it seems difficult to see how *composition*—whose distinctive aspect seems to be the transformation of language from thought or speech to hard copy— represents a distinct further step in shaping cogitation. There don't seem to be persuasive grounds for abandoning the view that composition is still a *skill* attendant to the attainment of overall linguistic competence.

The author of the report, a chemist, was reacting to some of our faculty's assertions about the interweaving of thinking and writing; writing for him is more or less a transcription skill.

So to reduce writing to second-class intellectual status is to influence the way faculty, students, and society view the teaching of writing. This is a bitter pill, but we in writing may have little choice but to swallow it. For, after all, is not writing simply different from "integrated bodies of knowledge" like sociology or biology? Is it? Well, yes and no. There are aspects of writing that would fit a skills model (the graphemic aspects especially). But much current theory and research are moving us to see that writing is not simply a transcribing skill mastered in early development. Writing seems central to the shaping and directing of certain modes of cognition, is integrally involved in learning, is a means of defining the self and defining reality, is a means of representing and contextualizing information (which has enormous political as well as conceptual and archival importance), and is an activity that develops over one's lifetime. Indeed it is worth pondering whether many of the "integrated bodies of knowledge" we study, the disciplines we practice, would have ever developed in the way they did and reveal the knowledge they do if writing did not exist. Would history or philosophy or economics exist as we know them? It is not simply that the work of such disciplines is recorded in writing, but that writing is intimately involved in the nature of their inquiry. Writing is not just a skill with which one can present or analyze knowledge. It is essential to the very existence of certain kinds of knowledge.

REMEDIATION

Since the middle of the last century, American colleges have been establishing various kinds of preparatory programs and classes within their halls to maintain enrollments while bringing their entering students up to curricular par.[10] One fairly modern incarnation of this activity is the "remedial class," a designation that appears frequently in the education and language arts journals of the 1920s.[11] Since that time remedial courses have remained very much with us: we have remedial programs, remedial sections, remedial textbooks, and, of course, remedial students. Other terms with different twists (like "developmental" and "compensatory") come and go, but "remedial" has staying power. Exactly what the adjective "remedial" means, however, has never quite been clear. To remediate seems to mean to correct errors or fill in gaps in a person's knowledge. The implication is that the material being studied should have been learned during prior education but was not. Now the reasons why it was not could vary tremendously: they could rest with the student (physical impairment, motivational

---

[10]In 1894, for example, over 40% of entering freshmen came from the preparatory divisions of the institutions that enrolled them. And as late as 1915—a time when the quantity and quality of secondary schools had risen sufficiently to make preparatory divisions less necessary—350 American colleges still maintained their programs. See John S. Brubacher and Willis Rudy, *Higher Education in Transition: A History of American Colleges and Universities, 1636–1976*, 3rd ed. (New York: Harper & Row, 1976), pp. 241 ff., and Arthur Levine, *Handbook on Undergraduate Curriculum* (San Francisco: Jossey-Bass, 1981), pp. 54 ff.

[11]Several writers point to a study habits course initiated at Wellesley in 1894 as the first modern remedial course in higher education (K. Patricia Cross, *Accent on Learning* [San Francisco: Jossey-Bass, 1979], and Arthur Levine, *Handbook on Undergraduate Curriculum*). In fact, the word "remedial" did not appear in the course's title and the course was different in kind from the courses actually designated "remedial" that would emerge in the 1920s and 30s. (See Cross, pp. 24–25, for a brief discussion of early study skills courses.) The first use of the term "remedial" in the context I am discussing was most likely in a 1916 article on the use of reading tests to plan "remedial work" (Nila Banton Smith, *American Reading Instruction* [Newark, Delaware: International Reading Association, 1965], p. 191). The first elementary and secondary level remedial courses in reading were offered in the early 1920s; remedial courses in college would not appear until the late 20s.

problems, intelligence), the family (socio-economic status, stability, the support of reading-writing activities), the school (location, sophistication of the curriculum, adequacy of elementary or secondary instruction), the culture or subculture (priority of schooling, competing expectations and demands), or some combination of such factors. What "remedial" means in terms of curriculum and pedagogy is not clear either. What is remedial for a school like UCLA might well be standard for other state or community colleges, and what is considered standard during one era might well be tagged remedial in the next.

It is hard to define such a term. The best definition of remedial I can arrive at is a highly dynamic, contextual one: The function of labelling certain material remedial in higher education is to keep in place the hard fought for, if historically and conceptually problematic and highly fluid, distinction between college and secondary work. "Remedial" gains its meaning, then, in a political more than a pedagogical universe.

And the political dimension is powerful—to be remedial is to be substandard, inadequate, and, because of the origins of the term, the inadequacy is metaphorically connected to disease and mental defect. It has been difficult to trace the educational etymology of the word "remedial," but what I have uncovered suggests this: Its origins are in law and medicine, and by the late nineteenth century the term fell pretty much in the medical domain and was soon applied to education. "Remedial" quickly generalized beyond the description of students who might have had neurological problems to those with broader, though special, educational problems and then to those normal learners who are not up to a particular set of standards in a particular era at particular institutions. Here is some history.

Most of the enlightened work in the nineteenth century with the training of special populations (the deaf, the blind, the mentally retarded) was conducted by medical people, often in medical settings. And when young people who could hear and see and were of normal intelligence but had unusual—though perhaps not devastating—difficulties began to seek help, they too were examined within a medical framework. Their difficulties had to do with reading and writing—though mostly reading—and would today be classified as learning disabilities. One of the first such difficulties to be studied was dyslexia, then labelled "congenital word blindness."

In 1896 a physician named Morgan reported in the pages of *The British Medical Journal* the case of a "bright and intelligent boy" who was having great difficulty learning to read. Though he knew the alphabet, he would spell some words in pretty unusual ways. He would reverse letters or drop them or write odd combinations of consonants and vowels. Dr. Morgan examined the boy and had him read and write. The only diagnosis that made sense was one he had to borrow and analogize from the cases of stroke victims, "word blindness," but since the child had no history of cerebral trauma, Morgan labelled his condition "*congenital* word blindness" (W. Pringle Morgan, "A Case of Congenital Word Blindness," *The British Medical Journal*, 6, Part 2 [1896], 1378). Within the next two decades a number of such cases surfaced; in fact another English physician, James Hinshelwood, published several books on congenital word blindness.[12] The explanations were for the most part strictly medical, and, it should be noted, were analogized from detectable cerebral pathology in adults to conditions with no detectable pathology in children.

In the 1920s other medical men began to advance explanations a bit different from Morgan's and Hinshelwood's. Dr. Samuel Orton, an American physician, posed what he called a "cerebral physiological" theory that directed thinking away from trauma analogues and toward functional explanations. Certain areas of the brain were not defective but underdeveloped and could be corrected through "remedial effort." But though he posed a basically educational model for dyslexia, Dr. Orton's language should not be overlooked. He spoke of "brain habit" and the "handicap" of his "physiological deviates."[13] Though his theory was different from that of his forerunners, his language, significantly, was still medical.

As increasing access to education brought more and more children into the schools, they were met by progressive teachers and testing experts interested in assessing and responding to individual differences. Other sorts of reading and writing problems, not just dyslexia, were surfacing, and increasing numbers of teachers, not just medical people, were working with the special students. But the medical vocabulary—with its implied medical model—remained dominant. People tried to *diagnose* various *disabilities, defects, deficits, deficiencies,* and *handicaps,* and then tried to *remedy* them.[14] So one starts to see all sorts of reading/writing problems clustered together and addressed with this language. For example, William S. Gray's important monograph, *Remedial Cases in Reading: Their Diagnosis and Treatment* (Chicago: University of Chicago Press, 1922), listed as "specific causes of failure in reading" inferior learning capacity, congenital word blindness, poor auditory memory, defective vision, a narrow span of recognition, ineffective eye movements, inadequate training in phonetics, inadequate attention to the content, an inadequate speaking vocabulary, a small meaning vocabulary, speech defects, lack of interest, and timidity. The remedial

---

[12]*Letter-, Word-, and Mind-Blindness* (London: Lewis, 1902); *Congenital Word-Blindness* (London: Lewis, 1917).

[13]"The 'Sight Reading' Method of Teaching Reading, as a Source of Reading Disability," *Journal of Educational Psychology*, 20 (1929), 135–143.

[14]There were, of course, some theorists and practitioners who questioned medical-physiological models, Arthur Gates of Columbia Teacher's College foremost among them. But even those who questioned such models—with the exception of Gates—tended to retain medical language.

paradigm was beginning to include those who had troubles as varied as bad eyes, second-language interference, and shyness.[15]

It is likely that the appeal of medical-remedial language had much to do with its associations with scientific objectivity and accuracy—powerful currency in the efficiency-minded 1920s and 30s. A nice illustration of this interaction of influences appeared in Albert Lang's 1930 textbook, *Modern Methods in Written Examinations* (Boston: Houghton Mifflin, 1930). The medical model is quite explicit:

> teaching bears a resemblance to the practice of medicine. Like a successful physician, the good teacher must be something of a diagnostician. The physician by means of a general examination singles out the individuals whose physical defects require a more thorough testing. He critically scrutinizes the special cases until he recognizes the specific troubles. After a careful diagnosis he is able to prescribe intelligently the best remedial or corrective measures. (p. 38)

By the 1930s the language of remediation could be found throughout the pages of publications like *English Journal*, applied now to writing (as well as reading and mathematics) and to high school and college students who had in fact learned to write but were doing so with a degree of error thought unacceptable. These were students—large numbers of them—who were not unlike the students who currently populate our "remedial" courses: students from backgrounds that did not provide optimal environmental and educational opportunities, students who erred as they tried to write the prose they thought the academy required, second-language students. The semantic net of "remedial" was expanding and expanding.

There was much to applaud in this focus on writing. It came from a progressive era desire to help *all* students progress through the educational system. But the theoretical and pedagogical model that was available for "corrective teaching" led educators to view writing problems within a medical-remedial paradigm. Thus they set out to diagnose as precisely as possible the errors (defects) in a student's paper—which they saw as symptomatic of equally isolable defects in the student's linguistic capacity—and devise drills and exercises to remedy them. (One of the 1930s nicknames for

---

[15]There is another layer to this terminological and conceptual confusion. At the same time that remediation language was being used ever more broadly by some educators, it maintained its strictly medical usage in other educational fields. For example, Annie Dolman Inskeep has only one discussion of "remedial work" in her book *Teaching Dull and Retarded Children* (New York: Macmillan, 1926), and that discussion has to do with treatment for children needing health care: "Children who have poor teeth, who do not hear well, or who hold a book when reading nearer than eight inches to the eyes or further away than sixteen. . . . Nervous children, those showing continuous fatigue symptoms, those under weight, and those who are making no apparent bodily growth" (p. 271).

remedial sections was "sick sections." During the next decade they would be tagged "hospital sections.") Such corrective teaching was, in the words of H. J. Arnold, "the most logical as well as the most scientific method" ("Diagnostic and Remedial Techniques for College Freshmen," p. 276).

These then are the origins of the term, remediation. And though we have, over the last fifty years, moved very far away from the conditions of its origins and have developed a richer understanding of reading and writing difficulties, the term is still with us. A recent letter from the senate of a local liberal arts college is sitting on my desk. It discusses a "program in remedial writing for . . . [those] entering freshmen suffering from severe writing handicaps." We seem entrapped by this language, this view of students and learning. Dr. Morgan has long since left his office, but we still talk of writers as suffering from specifiable, locatable defects, deficits, and handicaps that can be localized, circumscribed, and remedied. Such talk reveals an atomistic, mechanistic-medical model of language that few contemporary students of the use of language, from educators to literary theorists, would support. Furthermore, the notion of remediation, carrying with it as it does the etymological wisps and traces of disease, serves to exclude from the academic community those who are so labelled. They sit in scholastic quarantine until their disease can be diagnosed and remedied.

ILLITERACY

In a recent meeting on graduation requirements, a UCLA dean referred to students in remedial English as "the truly illiterate among us." Another administrator, in a memorandum on the potential benefits of increasing the number of composition offerings, concluded sadly that the increase "would not provide any assurance of universal literacy at UCLA." This sort of talk about illiteracy is common. We hear it from college presidents, educational foundations, pop grammarians, and scores of college professors like the one who cried to me after a recent senate meeting, "All I want is a student who can write a simple declarative sentence!" We in the academy like to talk this way.[16] It is dramatic and urgent, and, given the current concerns about illiteracy in the United States, it is topical. The trouble is, it is wrong. Perhaps we can better understand the problems with such labelling if we leave our colleagues momentarily and consider what it is that literacy means.

To be literate means to be acquainted with letters or writings. But exactly how such acquaintance translates into behavior varies a good deal over

---

[16]For a sometimes humorous but more often distressing catalogue of such outcries, see Harvey A. Daniels, *Famous Last Words* (Carbondale: Southern Illinois University Press, 1983), especially pp. 31–58.

time and place. During the last century this country's Census Bureau defined as literate anyone who could write his or her name. These days the government requires that one be able to read and write at a sixth-grade level to be *functionally* literate: that is, to be able to meet—to a minimal degree—society's reading and writing demands. Things get a bit more complex if we consider the other meanings "literacy" has acquired. There are some specialized uses of the term, all fairly new: computer literacy, mathematical literacy, visual literacy, and so on. Literacy here refers to an acquaintance with the "letters" or elements of a particular field or domain. And there are also some very general uses of the term. Cultural literacy, another new construction, is hard to define because it is so broad and so variously used, but it most often refers to an acquaintance with the humanistic, scientific, and social scientific achievements of one's dominant culture. Another general use of the term, a more traditional one, refers to the attainment of a liberal education, particularly in belles-lettres. Such literacy, of course, is quite advanced and involves not only an acquaintance with a literary tradition but interpretive sophistication as well.

Going back over these definitions, we can begin by dismissing the newer, specialized uses of "literacy." Computer literacy and other such literacies are usually not the focus of the general outcries we have been considering. How about the fundamental definition as it is currently established? This does not seem applicable either, for though many of the students entering American universities write prose that is grammatically and organizationally flawed, with very few exceptions they can read and write at a sixth-grade level. A sixth-grade proficiency is, of course, absurdly inadequate to do the work of higher education, but the definition still stands. By the most common measure the vast majority of students in college are literate. When academics talk about illiteracy they are saying that our students are "without letters" and cannot "write a simple declarative sentence." And such talk, for most students in most segments of higher education, is inaccurate and misleading.

One could argue that though our students are literate by common definition, a significant percentage of them might not be if we shift to the cultural and belletristic definitions of literacy or to a truly functional-contextual definition: that is, given the sophisticated, specialized reading and writing demands of the university—and the general knowledge they require—then it might be appropriate to talk of a kind of cultural illiteracy among some percentage of the student body. These students lack knowledge of the achievements of a tradition and are not at home with the ways we academics write about them. Perhaps this use of illiteracy is more warranted than the earlier talk about simple declarative sentences, but I would still advise caution. It is my experience that American college students tend to have learned more about western culture through their twelve years of schooling than their papers or pressured classroom responses demonstrate. (And, of course, our immigrant students bring with them a different cultural knowledge that we might not tap at all.) The problem is that the knowledge these students possess is often incomplete and fragmented and is not organized in ways that they can readily use in academic writing situations. But to say this is not to say that their minds are cultural blank slates.

There is another reason to be concerned about inappropriate claims of illiteracy. The term illiteracy comes to us with a good deal of semantic baggage, so that while an appropriately modified use of the term may accurately denote, it can still misrepresent by what it suggests, by the traces it carries from earlier eras. The social historian and anthropologist Shirley Brice Heath points out that from the mid-nineteenth century on, American school-based literacy was identified with "character, intellect, morality, and good taste . . . literacy skills co-occurred with moral patriotic character."[17] To be literate is to be honorable and intelligent. Tag some group illiterate, and you've gone beyond letters; you've judged their morals and their minds.

Please understand, it is not my purpose here to whitewash the very real limitations a disheartening number of our students bring with them. I dearly wish that more of them were more at home with composing and could write critically better than they do. I wish they enjoyed struggling for graceful written language more than many seem to. I wish they possessed more knowledge about humanities and the sciences so they could write with more authority than they usually do. And I wish to God that more of them read novels and poems for pleasure. But it is simply wrong to leap from these unrequited desires to claims of illiteracy. Reading and writing, as any ethnographic study would show, are woven throughout our students' lives. They write letters; some keep diaries. They read about what interests them, and those interests range from rock and roll to computer graphics to black holes. Reading, for many, is part of religious observation. They carry out a number of reading and writing acts in their jobs and in their interactions with various segments of society. Their college preparatory curriculum in high school, admittedly to widely varying degrees, is built on reading, and even the most beleaguered schools require some kind of writing. And many of these students read and even write in languages other than English. No, these students are not illiterate, by common definition, and if the more sophisticated definitions apply, they sacrifice their accuracy by all they imply.

Illiteracy is a problematic term. I suppose that academics use it because it is rhetorically effective (evoking the specter of illiteracy to an audience

---

[17]"Toward an Ethnohistory of Writing in American Education," in Marcia Farr Whiteman, ed., *Writing: The Nature, Development, and Teaching of Written Communication*, Vol. 1 (Hillsdale, N.J.: Erlbaum, 1981), 35–36.

of peers, legislators, or taxpayers can be awfully persuasive) or because it is emotionally satisfying. It gives expression to the frustration and disappointment in teaching students who do not share one's passions. As well, it affirms the faculty's membership in the society of the literate. One reader of this essay suggested to me that academics realize the hyperbole in their illiteracy talk, do not really mean it to be taken, well, literally. Were this invariably true, I would still voice concern over such exaggeration, for, as with any emotionally propelled utterance, it might well be revealing deeply held attitudes and beliefs, perhaps not unlike those discussed by Heath. And, deeply felt or not, such talk in certain political and decision-making settings can dramatically influence the outcomes of deliberation.

The fact remains that cries of illiteracy substitute a fast quip for careful analysis. Definitional accuracy here is important, for if our students are in fact adult illiterates, then a particular, very special curriculum is needed. If they are literate but do not read much for pleasure, or lack general knowledge that is central to academic inquiry, or need to write more than they do and pay more attention to it than they are inclined to, well, then these are very different problems. They bring with them quite different institutional commitments and pedagogies, and they locate the student in a very different place in the social-political makeup of the academy. Determining that place is crucial, for where but in the academy would being "without letters" be so stigmatizing?

THE MYTH OF TRANSIENCE

I have before me a report from the California Postsecondary Education commission called *Promises to Keep*. It is a comprehensive and fair-minded assessment of remedial instruction in the three segments of California's public college and university system. As all such reports do, *Promises to Keep* presents data on instruction and expenses, discusses the implications of the data, and calls for reform. What makes the report unusual is its inclusion of an historical overview of preparatory instruction in the United States. It acknowledges the fact that such instruction in some guise has always been with us. In spite of its acknowledgement, the report ends on a note of optimism characteristic of similar documents with less historical wisdom. It calls for all three segments of the higher education system to "implement . . . plans to reduce remediation" within five years and voices the hope that if secondary education can be improved, "within a very few years, the state and its institutions should be rewarded by . . . lower costs for remediation as the need for remediation declines." This optimism in the face of a disconfirming historical survey attests to the power of what I will call the myth of transience. Despite the accretion of crisis reports, the belief persists in the American university that if we can just do *x* or *y*, the problem will be solved—in five years, ten years, or a generation—and higher education will be able to return to its real work. But entertain with me the possibility that such peaceful reform is a chimera.

Each generation of academicians facing the characteristic American shifts in demographics and accessibility sees the problem anew, laments it in the terms of the era, and optimistically notes its impermanence. No one seems to say that this scenario has gone on for so long that it might not be temporary. That, in fact, there will probably *always* be a significant percentage of students who do not meet some standard. (It was in 1841, not 1985, that the president of Brown complained, "Students frequently enter college almost wholly unacquainted with English grammar ..." [Frederick Rudolph, *Curriculum: A History of the American Undergraduate Course of Study* (San Francisco: Jossey-Bass, 1978), p. 88].) The American higher educational system is constantly under pressure to expand, to re-define its boundaries, admitting, in turn, the sons of the middle class, and later the daughters, and then the American poor, the immigrant poor, veterans, the racially segregated, the disenfranchised. Because of the social and educational conditions these groups experienced, their preparation for college will, of course, be varied. Add to this the fact that disciplines change and society's needs change, and the ways society determines what it means to be educated change.

All this works itself rather slowly into the pre-collegiate curriculum. Thus there will always be a percentage of students who will be tagged substandard. And though many insist that this continued opening of doors will sacrifice excellence in the name of democracy, there are too many economic, political, and ethical drives in American culture to restrict higher education to a select minority. (And, make no mistake, the history of the American college and university from the early nineteenth century on could also be read as a history of changes in admissions, curriculum, and public image in order to keep enrollments high and institutions solvent.[18] The research institution as we know it is made possible by robust undergraduate enroll-ments.) Like it or not, the story of American education has been and will in all likelihood continue to be a story of increasing access. University of Nashville President Philip Lindsley's 1825 call echoes back and forth across our history: "The farmer, the mechanic, the manufacturer, the merchant, the sailor, the soldier ... must be educated" (Frederick Rudolph, *The American College and University: A History* [New York: Vintage, 1962], p. 117).

---

[18]Of turn-of-the-century institutions, Laurence Veysey writes: "Everywhere the size of enrollments was closely tied to admission standards. In order to assure themselves of enough students to make a notable "splash," new institutions often opened with a welcome to nearly all comers, no matter how ill prepared; this occurred at Cornell, Stanford, and (to a lesser degree) at Chicago" (*The Emergence of the American University*, p. 357).

Why begrudge academics their transience myth? After all, each generation's problems are new to those who face them, and people faced with a
problem need some sense that they can solve it. Fair enough. But it seems
to me that this myth brings with it a powerful liability. It blinds faculty
members to historical reality and to the dynamic and fluid nature of the
educational system that employs them. Like any golden age or utopian myth,
the myth of transience assures its believers that the past was better or that
the future will be.[19] The turmoil they are currently in will pass. The source
of the problem is elsewhere; thus it can be ignored or temporarily dealt with
until the tutors or academies or grammar schools or high schools or families
make the changes they must make. The myth, then, serves to keep certain
fundamental recognitions and thus certain fundamental changes at bay. It
is ultimately a conservative gesture, a way of preserving administrative and
curricular status quo.

And the myth plays itself out against complex social-political dynamics.
One force in these dynamics is the ongoing struggle to establish admissions
requirements that would protect the college curriculum, that would, in fact,
define its difference from the high school course of study. Another is the
related struggle to influence, even determine, the nature of the high school
curriculum, "academize" it, shape it to the needs of the college (and the
converse struggle of the high school to declare its multiplicity of purposes,
college preparation being only one of its mandates). Yet another is the
tension between the undergraduate, general education function of the
university vs. its graduate, research function. To challenge the myth is to
vibrate these complex dynamics; thus it is that it is so hard to dispel. But I
would suggest that it must be challenged, for though some temporary
"remedial" measures are excellent and generously funded, the presence of
the myth does not allow them to be thought through in terms of the whole
curriculum and does not allow the information they reveal to reciprocally
influence the curriculum. Basic modifications in educational philosophy,
institutional purpose, and professional training are rarely considered. They
do not need to be if the problem is temporary. The myth allows the final
exclusionary gesture: The problem is not ours in any fundamental way; we
can embrace it if we must, but with surgical gloves on our hands.

There may be little anyone can do to change the fundamental tension in
the American university between the general educational mission and the

---

[19]An appropriate observation here comes from Daniel P. and Lauren B. Resnick's critical
survey of reading instruction and standards of literacy: "there is little to go back to in terms
of pedagogical method, curriculum, or school organization. The old tried and true
approaches, which nostalgia prompts us to believe might solve current problems, were
designed neither to achieve the literacy standard sought today nor to assure successful literacy
for everyone ... there is no simple past to which we can return" ("The Nature of Literacy:
An Historical Exploration," *Harvard Educational Review*, 47 [1977], 385).

research mission, or to remove the stigma attached to application. But there is something those of us involved in writing can do about the language that has formed the field on which institutional discussions of writing and its teaching take place.

We can begin by affirming a rich model of written language development and production. The model we advance must honor the cognitive and emotional and situational dimensions of language, be psycholinguistic as well as literary and rhetorical in its focus, and aid us in understanding what we can observe as well as what we can only infer. When discussions and debates reveal a more reductive model of language, we must call time out and reestablish the terms of the argument. But we must also rigorously examine our own teaching and see what model of language lies beneath it. What linguistic assumptions are cued when we face freshman writers? Are they compatible with the assumptions that are cued when we think about our own writing or the writing of those we read for pleasure? Do we too operate with the bifurcated mind that for too long characterized the teaching of "remedial" students and that is still reflected in the language of our institutions?

Remediation. It is time to abandon this troublesome metaphor. To do so will not blind us to the fact that many entering students are not adequately prepared to take on the demands of university work. In fact, it will help us perceive these young people and the work they do in ways that foster appropriate notions about language development and use, that establish a framework for more rigorous and comprehensive analysis of their difficulties, and that do not perpetuate the raree show of allowing them entrance to the academy while, in various symbolic ways, denying them full participation.

Mina Shaughnessy got us to see that even the most error-ridden prose arises from the confrontation of inexperienced student writers with the complex linguistic and rhetorical expectations of the academy. She reminded us that to properly teach writing to such students is to understand "the intelligence of their mistakes."[20] She told us to interpret errors rather than circle them, and to guide these students, gradually and with wisdom, to be more capable participants within the world of these conventions. If we fully appreciate her message, we see how inadequate and limiting the remedial model is. Instead we need to define our work as transitional or as initiatory, orienting, or socializing to what David Bartholomae and Patricia Bizzell call the academic discourse community.[21] This redefinition is

---

[20]*Errors and Expectations* (New York: Oxford University Press, 1977), p. 11.

[21]David Bartholomae, "Inventing the University," in Mike Rose, ed., *When a Writer Can't Write: Studies in Writer's Block and Other Composing Process Problems* (New York: Guilford, 1985); Patricia Bizzell, "College Composition: Initiation into the Academic Discourse Community," *Curriculum Inquiry*, 12 (1982), 191–207.

not just semantic sleight-of-hand. If truly adopted, it would require us to reject a medical-deficit model of language, to acknowledge the rightful place of all freshmen in the academy, and once and for all to replace loose talk about illiteracy with more precise and pedagogically fruitful analysis. We would move from a mechanistic focus on error toward a demanding curriculum that encourages the full play of language activity and that opens out onto the academic community rather than sequestering students from it.

A much harder issue to address is the common designation of writing as a skill. We might begin by considering more fitting terms. Jerome Bruner's "enabling discipline" comes to mind. It does not separate skill from discipline and implies something more than a "tool subject" in that to enable means to make possible. But such changes in diction might be little more than cosmetic.

If the skills designation proves to be resistant to change, then we must insist that writing is a very unique skill, not really a tool but an ability fundamental to academic inquiry, an ability whose development is not fixed but ongoing. If it is possible to go beyond the skills model, we could see a contesting of the fundamental academic distinction between integrated bodies of knowledge and skills and techniques. While that distinction makes sense in many cases, it may blur where writing is concerned. Do students really *know* history when they learn a "body" of facts, even theories, or when they act like historians, thinking in certain ways with those facts and theories? Most historians would say the latter. And the academic historian (vs. the chronicler or the balladeer) conducts inquiry through writing; it is not just an implement but is part of the very way of doing history.

It is in this context that we should ponder the myth of transience. The myth's liability is that it limits the faculty's ability to consider the writing problems of their students in dynamic and historical terms. Each academic generation considers standards and assesses the preparation of its students but seems to do this in ways that do not call the nature of the curriculum of the time into question. The problem ultimately lies outside the academy. But might not these difficulties with writing suggest the need for possible far-ranging changes within the curriculum as well, changes that *are* the proper concern of the university? One of the things I think the myth of transience currently does is to keep faculty from seeing the multiple possibilities that exist for incorporating writing throughout their courses of study. Profound reform could occur in the much-criticized lower-division curriculum if writing were not seen as only a technique and the teaching of it as by and large a remedial enterprise.

The transmission of a discipline, especially on the lower-division level, has become very much a matter of comprehending information, committing it to memory, recalling it, and displaying it in various kinds of "objective" or short-answer tests. When essay exams are required, the prose all too often becomes nothing more than a net in which the catch of individual bits of knowledge lie. Graders pick through the essay and tally up the presence of key phrases. Such activity trivializes a discipline; it reduces its methodology, grounds it in a limited theory of knowledge, and encourages students to operate with a restricted range of their cognitive abilities. Writing, on the other hand, assumes a richer epistemology and demands fuller participation. It requires a complete, active, struggling engagement with the facts and principles of a discipline, an encounter with the discipline's texts and the incorporation of them into one's own work, the framing of one's knowledge within the myriad conventions that help define a discipline, the persuading of other investigators that one's knowledge is legitimate. So to consider the relationship between writing and disciplinary inquiry may help us decide what is central to a discipline and how best to teach it. The university's research and educational missions would intersect.

Such reform will be difficult. True, there is growing interest in writing adjuncts and discipline-specific writing courses, and those involved in writing-across-the-curriculum are continually encouraging faculty members to evaluate the place of writing in their individual curricula. But wide-ranging change will occur only if the academy redefines writing for itself, changes the terms of the argument, sees instruction in writing as one of its central concerns.

Academic senates often defend the labelling of a writing course as remedial by saying that they are defending the integrity of the baccalaureate, and they are sending a message to the high schools. The schools, of course, are so beleaguered that they can barely hear those few units ping into the bucket. Consider, though, the message that would be sent to the schools and to the society at large if the university embraced—not just financially but conceptually—the teaching of writing: if we gave it full status, championed its rich relationship with inquiry, insisted on the importance of craft and grace, incorporated it into the heart of our curriculum. What an extraordinary message that would be. It would affect the teaching of writing as no other message could.

Chapter 3

A Journey into Speech

Michelle Cliff

The first piece of writing I produced, beyond a dissertation on intellectual game-playing in the Italian Renaissance, was entitled "Notes on Speech-lessness," published in *Sinister Wisdom*, no. 5. In it I talked about my iden-tification with Victor, the wild boy of Aveyron, who, after his rescue from the forest and wildness by a well-meaning doctor of Enlightenment Europe, became "civilized," but never came to speech. I felt, with Victor, that my wildness had been tamed—that which I had been taught was my wildness.

My dissertation was produced at the Warburg Institute, University of London, and was responsible for giving me an intellectual belief in myself that I had not had before, while at the same time distancing me from who I am, almost rendering me speechless about who I am. At least I believed in the young woman who wrote the dissertation—still, I wondered who she was and where she had come from.

I could speak fluently, but I could not reveal. I immersed myself in the social circles and academies of Siena, Florence, Urbino, as well as Venice, creating a place for myself there, and describing this ideal world in eloquent linear prose.

When I began, finally, partly through participation in the feminist move-ment, to approach myself as a subject, my writing was jagged, nonlinear, almost shorthand. The "Notes on Speechlessness" were indeed notes, writ-ten in snatches on a nine-to-five job. I did not choose the noteform con-

Preface to *The Land of Look Behind: Poetry & Prose*, 1985

sciously; a combination of things drew me to it. An urgency for one thing. I also felt incompetent to construct an essay in which I would describe the intimacies, fears, and lies I wrote of in "Speechlessness." I felt my thoughts, things I had held within for a lifetime, traversed so wide a terrain, had so many stops and starts, apparent nonsequiturs, that an essay—with its cold-blooded dependence on logical construction, which I had mastered practically against my will—could not work. My subject could not respond to that form, which would have contradicted the idea of speechlessness. This tender approach to myself within the confines and interruptions of a forty-hour-a-week job and against a history of forced fluency was the beginning of a journey into speech.

To describe this journey further, I must begin at the very beginning, with origins, and the significance of these origins. How they have made me the writer I am.

I originate in the Caribbean, specifically on the island of Jamaica, and although I have lived in the United States and in England, I travel as a Jamaican. It is Jamaica that forms my writing for the most part, and which has formed for the most part, myself. Even though I often feel what Derek Walcott expresses in his poem "The Schooner *Flight*": "I had no nation now but the imagination." It is a complicated business.

Jamaica is a place halfway between Africa and England, to put it simply, although historically one culture (guess which one) has been esteemed and the other denigrated (both are understatements)—at least among those who control the culture and politics of the island—the Afro-Saxons. As a child among these people, indeed of these people, as one of them, I received the message of anglocentrism, of white supremacy, and I internalized it. As a writer, as a human being, I have had to accept that reality and deal with its effect on me, as well as finding what has been lost to me from the darker side, and what may be hidden, to be dredged from memory and dream. And it *is* there to be dredged. As my writing delved longer and deeper into this part of myself, I began to dream and imagine. I was able to clearly envision Nanny, the leader of a group of guerrilla fighters known as the Windward Maroons, as she is described: an old Black woman naked except for a necklace made from the teeth of whitemen. I began to love her.

It is a long way from the court of Urbino to Nanny the Coromantyn[1] warrior.

One of the effects of assimilation, indoctrination, passing into the anglocentrism of British West Indian culture is that you believe absolutely in the hegemony of the King's English and in the form in which it is meant

---

[1]Coromantyn, or Coromantee, was used by the British in Jamaica to describe slaves from the Gold Coast of Africa, especially slaves who spoke Akan.

to be expressed. Or else your writing is not literature; it is folklore, and folklore can never be art. Read some poetry by West Indian writers—some, not all—and you will see what I mean. You have to dissect stanza after extraordinarily anglican stanza for Afro-Caribbean truth; you may never find the latter. But this has been our education. The anglican ideal—Milton, Wordsworth, Keats—was held before us with an assurance that we were unable, and would never be enabled, to compose a work of similar correctness. No reggae spoken here.

To write as a complete Caribbean woman, or man for that matter, demands of us retracing the African part of ourselves, reclaiming as our own, and as our subject, a history sunk under the sea, or scattered as potash in the canefields, or gone to bush, or trapped in a class system notable for its rigidity and absolute dependence on color stratification. On a past bleached from our minds. It means finding the artforms of these of our ancestors and speaking in the *patois* forbidden us. It means realizing our knowledge will always be wanting. It means also, I think, mixing in the forms taught us by the oppressor, undermining his language and co-opting his style, and turning it to our purpose. In my current work-in-progress, a novel, I alternate the King's English with *patois*, not only to show the class background of characters, but to show how Jamaicans operate within a split consciousness. It would be as dishonest to write the novel entirely in *patois* as to write entirely in the King's English. Neither is the novel a linear construction; its subject is the political upheavals of the past twenty years. Therefore, I have mixed time and incident and space and character and also form to try to mirror the historical turbulence.

For another example, included in this volume is a long poem, actually half-poem, half-prose, in which I imagine the visit of Botha of South Africa to the heads of western Europe in the summer of 1984. I wrote this as a parody of Gilbert and Sullivan because their work epitomizes salient aspects of the British Empire which remain vibrant. And because as a child I was sick to death of hearing "I am the very model of a modern major general." I enjoyed writing this, playing with rhyme and language—it was like spitting into their cultural soup.

We are a fragmented people. My experience as a writer coming from a culture of colonialism, a culture of Black people riven from each other, my struggle to get wholeness from fragmentation while working within fragmentation, producing work which may find its strength in its depiction of fragmentation, through form as well as content, is similar to the experience of other writers whose origins are in countries defined by colonialism.

Ama Ata Aidoo, the Ghanaian writer, in her extraordinary book, *Our Sister Killjoy or Reflections from a Black-Eyed Squint*,[2] plots this fragmentation,

---

[2] NOK Publishers, Lagos and New York, 1979.

and shows how both the demand and solace of the so-called mother country can claim us, while we long for our homeland and are shamed for it and ourselves at the same time. The form Aidoo uses to depict this dilemma of colonial peoples—part prose, fictional and epistolary, part poetry—illustrates the fragmentation of the heroine and grasps the fury of the heroine, living in Europe but drawn back to Ghana, knowing she can never be European. She will only be a been-to; that is, one who has been to the mother country. *Our Sister Killjoy* affected me directly, not just because like Aidoo's heroine I was a been-to. I was especially drawn by the way in which Aidoo expresses rage against colonialism—crystallized for her by the white-man she calls the "Christian Doctor" throughout, excising Black African hearts to salvage white South African lives. In her expression of the rage she feels her prose breaks apart sharply into a staccato poetry—direct, short, brilliantly bitter—as if measured prose would disintegrate under her fury.

I wanted that kind of directness in my writing, as I came into closer contact with my rage, and a realization that rage could fuel and shape my work. As a light-skinned colonial girlchild, both in Jamaica and in the Jamaican milieu of my family abroad, rage was the last thing expected of me.

After reading Aidoo I knew I wanted to tell exactly how things were, what had been done, to us and by us, without muddying the issue with conventional beauty, avoiding becoming trapped in the grace of language for its own sake, which is always seductive.

In *Claiming an Identity They Taught Me to Despise*, a piece published before I read Aidoo, halfway between poetry and prose, as I am halfway between Africa and England, patriot and expatriate, white and Black, I felt my use of language and imagery had sometimes masked what I wanted to convey. It seemed sometimes that the reader was able to ignore what I was saying while admiring the way in which it was said.

And yet, *Claiming* is an honest self-portrait of who I was at the time. Someone who was unable, for the most part, to recapture the native language of Jamaica, and who relied on the King's English and European allusions, but who wrote from a feminist consciousness and a rapidly evolving consciousness of colonialism, and a knowledge of self-hatred. Someone who also dreamed in Latin—as I did and as I recorded in the title section, included here. *Claiming*'s strengths, I think, are in the more intimate, private places of the piece, which I constructed much as the "Notes on Speechlessness" are constructed. Shorthand—almost—as memory and dream emerge; fast, at once keen, at once incomplete. I was also, in those sections, laboring under the ancient taboos of the assimilated: don't tell outsiders anything real about yourself. Don't reveal *our* secrets to *them*. Don't make us seem foolish, or oppressed. Write it quickly before someone catches you. Before you catch yourself.

After reading *Our Sister Killjoy*, something was set loose in me, I directed rage outward rather than inward, and I was able to write a piece called "If I Could Write This in Fire I Would Write This in Fire." In it I let myself go, any thought of approval for my words vanished; I strung together myth, dream, historical detail, observation, as I had done before, but I added native language, tore into the indoctrination of the colonizer, surprised myself with the violence of my words.

That piece of writing led to other pieces, collected in this volume, in which I try to depict personal fragmentation and describe political reality, according to the peculiar lens of the colonized.

Chapter 4

Between Students' Language and Academic Discourse: Interlanguage as Middle Ground

Eleanor Kutz

In 1972 the Executive Committee of the Conference on College Composition and Communication passed a resolution asserting the Students' Right to their Own Language. The resolution was adopted as policy by the larger body of CCCC in 1974 and has, presumably, provided a foundation for our work on the teaching of writing over these past eleven years. Yet, in the final session of the 1985 Minneapolis CCCC, "Academic Discourse and the Individual Imagination," a debate in which Patricia Bizzell and Bruce Herzberg argued for the primacy of academic discourse and Lil Brannon and Cy Knoblauch for that of the individual imagination in our writing courses, the ultimate disagreement between the two sides, each of which was working to empower students through their use of language, came to rest on this very issue. The real question, as stated by Pat Bizzell in her closing remarks, and echoed in audience response, was whether, if we start with the student's own language, we will ever get to academic discourse.

The question is an important one, and it makes visible a reef on which much of our work still founders. While politically we may affirm students' right to their own language, in our real concern for students and for their success in the academy we show our lack of faith in that position and return to argue for the primacy of academic discourse in our teaching, an argument that lends itself to misuse by traditionalists who have never accepted the premises of the 1972 resolution. We want to validate our stu-

College English, 1986

dents as people and language users, but we also want to teach them to use language in ways that support academic success, ways they do not know when they enter our classes. We fear that validating their present language will lead them to believe anything goes, when we know that in the university and the world beyond there are rigid conventions, not only for correct usage, but for genre, style, and diverse other features they must use to be successful. Further, we know that many conventions of academic discourse are not arbitrary prescriptions, but have evolved as the clearest way to express the thinking done in various disciplines—even as a heuristic for that thinking.

I would suggest that between the poles of "everything goes" and of rigidly applied rules of academic discourse, there is a middle ground. And this middle ground is not just a shaky bridge but is firm and continuous and solid and rests on much of the real work of our profession and related disciplines over the last eleven years.

The idea that upholding students' right to their own language really means "everything goes" can be countered by a look at the premises on which the 1972 resolution was based, premises drawn from recent work in linguistics, and can then be restated as "everything goes somewhere." My colleague Neal Bruss, himself a linguist, asserts that the most important concept for the rest of us in English departments to understand from contemporary linguistics is style shifting. As stated in the resolution's background document, "every speaker of a language has a tremendous range of versatility, constantly making subtle changes to meet various situations" (6). We all shift through a wide range of styles appropriate to different contexts, and we all have sufficient mastery of those styles to allow us to function effectively within them.[1] What we are really asking students to do as they enter the university is not to replace one way of speaking or writing with another, but to add yet another style to their existing repertoire. Fully understanding and accepting the concept of style shifting should lead us to accept not only the students' right to their own language but also the validity of the style "academic discourse" within its particular domain—academia.

The corollary to "everything goes somewhere" is "academic discourse goes in academia." All of us would, I think, agree on these revised statements of position and concur that they do in fact represent a middle ground between reifying the absolutes of either students' right to their own language or academic discourse. But we are still left with the question of how to negotiate between them, of how to implement our understanding that both statements are true.

---

[1] For a discussion of style-shifting as part of the necessary conceptual framework for our teaching, see Labov.

Brannon and Knoblauch resist any approach that might focus on "formal shells rather than on modes of thinking and learning in different domains" and would place emphasis in composition courses on writing as learning as opposed to formal constraints. In reviewing Maimon et al., *Writing in the Arts and Sciences*, they note that the authors claim the heuristic potential of writing as a way of learning, but see this claim negated by the emphasis on convention: "Writing to learn is subtly displaced by an extensive discussion of how learning is to be acceptably displayed" (468). Brannon and Knoblauch do not deny that disciplinary generic conventions can have heuristic value, but suggest that only the external form of those conventions is likely to be abstracted for an extra-disciplinary composition course. Rather than attend to formal constraints, citing Ann Berthoff's muffin tin metaphor, they would focus on "meaning-making" and on open-ended forms of writing such as the dialectical notebook, which push intellectual involvement and development by establishing a genuine intellectual dialogue between teacher and student.

Bizzell, on the other hand, in her essay review of writing across the curriculum texts, dismisses what she refers to as "authentic voice" pedagogy, represented in that review by *Four Worlds of Writing* (Lauer et al.), but applicable to the approach of Brannon and Knoblauch, and approves Maimon et al.'s focus on academic discourse conventions and their attempts to demystify these conventions while initiating students into them. She sees questions about students' right to their own language as "subsumed, in *Writing in the Arts and Sciences*, in questions about students' intellectual engagement in the academic disciplines" (205). She goes on to suggest that a dialectical relationship exists between the mind of the individual and the conventions of the community, and she draws an analogy between her position and the work of Paulo Freire, seeing the acquisition of formal academic discourse as providing the distance and perspective needed for "critical consciousness."

The argument here becomes circular. Bizzell approves emphasis on disciplinary forms as a route to Freirean critical consciousness, while Brannon and Knoblauch disavow Maimon's focus on disciplinary forms and espouse Berthoffian "meaning-making." But Berthoff, herself an ardent espouser of Freirean analysis and pedagogy, proposes dialectical notebooks instead of formal muffin tins as the way for students to achieve this same critical consciousness.[2]

Perhaps the "academic discourse" pedagogy does subsume the concerns about students' right to their own language that are more explicitly supported in what Bizzell dismisses as the "authentic voice" pedagogy. Perhaps

---

[2]See, for example, selections from Freire's *Education for Critical Consciousness* in Berthoff, *The Making of Meaning* (159–72).

pedagogy that focuses on meaning before form does lead to richer formal presentations of that meaning. And perhaps both approaches can lead to the empowering of students through the development of critical conscious-ness. (I think that each of the persons cited above, though not necessarily all who would be classified or would classify themselves with them, does attempt to encompass all of these concerns.) What, then, accounts for the schism?

The argument could be reduced to one of form versus content. Yet both sides would agree that it is not possible to have, in the end, a rich and meaningful piece of writing that is not at the same time both deeply and individually insightful and formally crafted. The disagreement really is about how to proceed as we begin teaching students to produce such writing. To resolve it we must answer three questions: 1) How do people learn to use written language effectively? 2) What is the most effective way to foster this learning? and 3) How can we determine that this learning is taking place? In other words, we need to draw on theories of language learning, to develop pedagogies, and to devise appropriate methods of assessment.

In seeking to answer these questions in my teaching of basic writers, I have turned first to language acquisition theory, particularly as applied to adult learners of second languages. For such language learners, as for children learning their native language, language use is systematic (gov-erned by rules of an internal grammar, though not of the grammar of a standard language), creative (rules are generated to fit new data), and responsive (grammar is generated and refined as needed for making sense of the language that learners hear and for communicating effectively with other language users). Stephen Krashen has proposed a model that dis-tinguishes between learning and acquisition. He applies the term acquisi-tion to unconscious and intuitive responses to language in meaningful contexts (that is, through natural language use). And he would apply the term learning only to the conscious application of rules in response to overt instruction, instruction that most researchers see as having little influence on the acquisition of communicative competence in a language.

Within languages, as Labov reminds us, a speaker's overall linguistic competence must be distinguished from that speaker's performance in any particular set of circumstances (9). (And it should be, in part, measured by the speaker's range of styles—a range that is greater for speakers of non-standard dialects than for speakers of standard English.) If that per-formance takes place under stressful circumstances it is likely to include more features from an earlier stage of language development; if it takes place within the classroom its features are likely to differ from those of the learner's real communicative efforts (and will often be restricted and give us inadequate information about the learner's real language compe-tence) (see Corder 69).

What application does all of this have to the teaching of writing? For our students, standard English and the standard forms of academic discourse are a new style, a new dialect, in a sense, a new language. They will not learn that new language effectively from the application of rules of grammar[3] or from the application of discourse models, just as children will not attend to language features that seem to conflict with the meaning they intend.[4] All of these language learners will, however, learn out of communicative need, in real contexts in which language is pushed by meaning.

Establishing those real contexts is a matter of pedagogy. Writing across the curriculum programs are one answer to the problem of meaningful context. But to the extent that such programs focus on identifying and teaching generic features apart from the real work demanded in the discipline, they can have only limited success in developing a real intellectual need for the forms they teach. I share Brannon and Knoblauch's concern here, that a writing across the curriculum emphasis within a standard composition course is not the same as writing within or in conjunction with a disciplinary course, as well as their preference for creating meaningful contexts for developing cognitive and writing skills that can then be applied by the student to the generic demands of other courses. At the same time, I understand Bizzell's fear that a pedagogy which does not expose students to the kind of discourse they must ultimately produce will not move them toward such production. (Many researchers into child language acquisition have now rejected the hypothesis that the language of the mother is appropriately syntactically simplified in ways which provide ideal input for the child's acquisition, arguing, on the contrary, that if a child is to acquire a grammar that will incorporate all of the features of adult language, that grammar can be generated only from a model that contains all of those features (see Wexler 308).

Team-teaching with members of other disciplines provides one way to integrate both the writing as learning approach of Brannon and Knoblauch, with its "open-ended investigative dialogue," and the initiation of students into the disciplinary discourse conventions of Maimon's writing in the disciplines. With my colleague Suzy Groden, I have developed a team-taught six-credit Freshman Studies Seminar that combines an introduction to the concepts and methodology of historical and cultural studies with a freshman writing course for students coming out of basic writing. The seminar is designed to enable students to learn to ask questions the way a historian or anthropologist asks questions, to think historically and gain insight into what can be gained by taking a comparative perspective on human behavior, to gather data, formulate hypotheses, draw conclu-

---

[3]For a thorough discussion of why this is so, see Hartwell.
[4]On the relationship between form and meaning in child language acquisition, see Wexler.

sions and undertake a research project in a way a practitioner of these disciplines might. Writing in this context becomes part of a process of perceiving and understanding experience within particular frameworks and expressing that understanding. Most students, as they begin to study history, expect it to be a series of events they must memorize, and they see the job of the historian as one of accurately identifying these events. It surprises them to discover that the historian engages in a process of selection and interpretation that is intrinsically subjective and constructive and can never be a perfectly accurate representation of "just the facts." Thus to teach students about the character of historical knowledge and thought, we introduce them to ways of understanding and interpreting that lie at the root of writing as well.

In this course students begin by developing the skills needed for precise observation and description, then work on categorization, comparison, and differentiation. They are asked to interpret, generalize, find implications, develop hypotheses, and discover analogies. As they master these processes, and as they read the observations and hypotheses of anthropologists, the facts and interpretations of historians, they make their own observations and generalizations from them. As they learn to list and categorize and compare and contrast to draw meaning from what they observe or read, they also learn to use writing to record these processes and to express the meanings they discover. As they learn how to move back and forth from specific example to general concept, to describe and categorize as steps toward analyzing and interpreting, they learn the structural principles that increase both their need and their ability to write prose in which details are articulated. At this point they begin to perceive writing as an active, personal, and constructive process. Such writing within a discipline, then, goes beyond the "content-free" writing process heuristics that, though based on sound research into writers' strategies for constructing meaning, can be applied merely as recipes. It also goes beyond the potentially empty formalism of a product-orientation to writing across the curriculum which relies on readings from a discipline as models for student writing about that discipline; the thinking processes underlying work within a particular discipline are often not evident from the final document produced, and reliance on them as models can artificially limit the student's own thinking about that discipline in the way strictly product-oriented approaches to composition have. An integrated approach works with the fundamental thinking processes basic to all writing within all disciplines, while recognizing that work within a particular discipline rests on particular models and procedures that must also be understood.

Within this process of writing to learn within a discipline, students begin to master the conventional forms not only of disciplinary genres but of standard English. Here too their learning is pushed by exposure to meaningful texts, and by the need to communicate. To the extent that the patterns of conventional usage are logical and meaning-based, they will be acquired as other language is acquired, unconsciously and intuitively from exposure to examples. To the extent that the power and precision of particular words affects communication, the use of those words will be refined. (Where, however, a convention of usage is unrelated to meaning, it is unlikely to be noted.) Of course, new errors will appear as the student tries out new terms and more complex sentence structures as a means of expressing new concerns and awareness. But a classroom environment that encourages risk-taking, that rewards experimentation with new forms versus the production of error-free papers, will, in the long run, stimulate the greatest gains in the student's acquisition of the language of academic discourse. Finally, style shifting is inevitable. The same factor that interferes with the linguist's attempt to gain accurate data from a speaker's dialect, ensures that the individual student who enters the dominant culture of the university will gradually acquire its conventions: "Whenever a speaker of a nonstandard dialect is in a subordinate position to a speaker of a standard dialect, the rules of his grammar will shift in an unpredictable manner towards the standard" (Labov 11).

There are of course other pedagogical alternatives to interdisciplinary team-teaching that combine beginning with and validating the student's current language, pushing the development of language and thought in meaningful contexts, and initiating students into academic discourse conventions. Within individual sections of basic writing courses I have built on the generic strengths that students bring with their oral language, particularly their use of narrative, not simply to begin with what is "easiest," as composition texts based on rhetorical modes have done, but to begin where most students already show significant competence and to show them how that competence can be extended and applied to academic writing. After telling of an incident in their own early experiences, they read *The Diary of a Young Girl* and see that Anne Frank tells about particular events in her life, that something makes them significant. They begin to use evidence from the diary to support hypotheses about Anne's development and values. Having told of their own experiences and then having "read" Anne's life, having used the evidence of the diary to interpret that life, and having seen it in relation to a framework which makes it meaningful, they begin to conceive of a framework of their own, to see what gives their own lives meaning, what has made them see particular events that they have told about as significant. They begin to practice the kind of critical perspective on their own lives that Freire (and Bizzell and Berthoff) see as a fundamental value of formal education. Along the way they read some twentieth century German history and reflect on the ways such information alters their reading and understanding. They read the communiques written by Nazi commanders in The Netherlands back to their superiors in Germany and compare the depersonalized language, the concern with numbers and completing a task, to Anne's very personal response to news of each new round-up and deportation. (Here the urge to read closely, to find answers in the documents, comes from the students themselves. Comparison and contrast are not empty forms to be filled but ways of finding meaning in what seems incomprehensible.)

And the students write: nightly responses to their reading; responses to their responses (and to my responses to them); short in-class writings on particular sentences and paragraphs in the texts they read; weekly essays (using the original sense of try or attempt) in which they try out their ideas in relation to a particular question and which we discuss in writing workshops.

Over the semester, the students develop skills in interpretation and use of evidence, in doing work that ultimately, but not narrowly, fits into academic genres and rhetorical formats (I name them only after they have used them), and they see how these formats emerge from the attempt to reach real understandings and solve real problems. Finally, as they read another work of autobiography and try to find a framework that encompasses not only their own experience but the experiences of two other people, they take a significant step beyond direct comparison to the more complex act of synthesizing three or more things.

Others have developed courses and programs with similar means and goals. David Bartholomae and Mariolina Salvatore in the Basic Reading and Writing Program at the University of Pittsburgh have created an expanded, six-credit intensive course that builds on the kind of reflectivity in reading and writing described above. Mike Rose has reported on The Freshman Preparatory Program at UCLA, a program that focuses on global discourse strategies, to be taught as speculative strategies for examining the reality of academic work. Both of these programs are fundamentally developmental in design, building in careful sequence from students' present abilities while making constant connections with and applications to the discourse of the university. My point is that there is much pedagogical middle ground here that validates students' own language, combines writing with learning, and introduces students to academic discourse through a semester or year of carefully designed developmental courses in which the need to use such discourse is fueled by course content and assignments.

In such pedagogies, a way of assessing students' entering language skills, measuring their progress, and evaluating their final writing is needed. The method of assessment must be responsive to the overall developmental orientation of the pedagogy; to look down from a pinnacle of generically appropriate, elaborated, and wholly standard academic discourse to the valley of students' present language use is to reject completely the spirit of the 1972 resolution, and to discount all we know about language acquisition and style shifting. Our standards for perfect or "A" papers of whatever format must not provide the measure. We need instead an assessment tool that allows us to see and appreciate the extensive language competencies our students, however basic their writing skills, bring to our classrooms, and that helps us focus on the development of new competencies rather than on what they do not yet know.

Here again I have turned to research in second language acquisition, which draws from the students' present language use, insights into the language patterns of that particular learner, or into language learners in general, rather than dismissing the learners' language as merely a wrong version of the target language. Error analysis, as a descriptive rather than prescriptive approach to error, provides a methodology for determining why a student makes a particular grammatical error and has been a potentially valuable borrowing from this field, one that could have altered the prescriptive drilling of standard forms which still comprises much of basic writing texts.[5] Unfortunately, however, error analysis in the composition classroom has generally served to simply keep the focus on error.

The present language system of a second language learner with reference to the target language has been called an approximative system, or interlanguage. Like error analysis, the study of interlanguage looks at the learner's present language use. However, while error analysis looks back from the perspective of the entire target language in comparing the learner's present output with the end goal, the study of interlanguage is "interested in the relationship of what has been taught *so far* with the learner's knowledge at that same point," providing a prospective rather than retrospective comparison (Corder 57). The student's production provides evidence of the student's acquisition of new language skills, and allows us to see a relationship between what has been taught and what the student can do.

Among my students, the characteristics of interlanguage that seem applicable to the intermediate mastery of written discourse (and beginning mastery of academic written discourse), are these:

1. Interlanguage contains features that do not occur in either the first or the target language. This gives me a framework in which to consider the aberrant forms, in both syntax and diction, that appear in the papers of student writers.
2. An interlanguage's unique features are developmental, representing necessary stages in the acquisition process. Convoluted syntax and malformed or misused words ("instinctions," The boy "ornated" the

---

[5]See Richards. David Bartholomae, in "The Study of Error," explores the implications of error analysis for the teaching of first language basic writing.

Christmas tree) represent important steps toward the incorporation of new forms into the writer's repertoire.

3. Interlanguage is systematic, rule-governed, and predictable (though transitional). ("Instinctions" is the misapplication of the rule for forming an abstract noun from a verb by adding "-tion." This student's systematic approach to word formation is seen in the creation of similar forms in other instances—"conflictions.")

4. Although interlanguage is not correct from the point of view of the target language, it is a valid linguistic system and allows its user to communicate competently, though sometimes only for particular functions, in restricted contexts. (The meaning of "The boy ornated the Christmas tree" is clear.)

5. While some features represent errors, they are a necessary part of constructing and testing hypotheses about the new language.

6. Interlanguage looks beyond error to the whole language production of the learner. It is particularly important to see the work of basic writers in the context of what they can produce.

7. The interlanguage of each person at any moment is unique, though there are common patterns. This means that our analysis and pedagogy must be sensitive to those differences while taking advantage of the commonalities that will allow effective classroom teaching.

8. Interlanguage is characterized by a return to abandoned features when the learner encounters new or stressful discourse demands. This explains why students frequently fail dismally in another class on writing assignments similar to those they have handled successfully in Basic Writing.

Interlanguage provides a conceptual framework for seeing student writing as a stage in a developmental process, for seeing what is there as opposed to what isn't, for seeing the individual differences, and for seeing common patterns also as a way of seeing variations.

By applying the concept of interlanguage to the intermediate stage of written language production represented in the texts of student writers, and by extending the process of systematic examination of those texts providing the basis of error analysis, it is possible to assess the multiple features of student writing that lie below the surface of the text, an assessment appropriate to the developmental, rather than remedial, teaching of writing. "Interlanguage analysis" allows another perspective from which to view student texts, and to see the strategies and knowledge the writer is using, in order to elicit and build on these in future assignments.

Identifying discourse features and the stages of their development has helped to shift my perspective and to respond in constructive ways to student writing. The following paper was the first out-of-class writing of the semester in the Freshman Studies Seminar described above. It was written in response to an assignment to observe, take notes on, and write about someone working. The writer, a student for whom English was a second language but who was educated in regular classrooms in the Boston Public Schools, was extremely reluctant to turn in this assignment, claiming that he couldn't write. I had already been trying to apply the principles of error analysis to my reading of student texts. But it was this paper, with its obvious competencies, that pushed me to find a way to look systematically at the multiple and various features of a student's discourse.

> The ill interest to work is shared among everyone in this working place near lunch break and breaks, especially end of the day break. They pass the time with breakaways to the Rest Room, for 10 to 15 minutes, or slowing down the production. Those who weren't interested in putting in a good 8 hour day got even lazier when it was close to break time. They keep moving about lazily and sometimes doing nothing but trying to entertaining themselves until it was time to stop working.
>
> Among those blue collars worker's who didn't I found not contribute much sweating eye-brow, to their paycheck was a man who looked like a chinese and Hispanic cross-breed. In my opinion, A misfit, attempting to go straight, and earn an honest living. He's a short sleezy bearded Fatu look-a-like, much taller though.
>
> He started the morning in a fearly desent pace. But as the day lingered, his enthusiasm desapated to a point where he just goes around, 5 minutes here and there bringing up conversation, Making time go by faster. finally after finishing, He proceeded to the second phase of his duties. At this point of the working day He starts doing his carefree thing. He slowly drags a misplaced piece of lumber, dusts of his wrangler, blows dust off his plastic shoe, He casually goes to the Rest Room for 15 minutes, stops and talks a little with his pal. All of a sudden, It's close to lunch break. He takes a leisure walk around the plant, trying to look busy while the boss is looking. It's lunch break.
>
> He comes back starts the second half of the day as loosely as he finished. And continues to work in that lagedazical pace, until it's time to clean-up, taking his time. does what he can do in that depressing pace. he checks his watch; it's almost time to leave. He picks what he swept, dusts off and joins his friend until the whistle blew. Another dollar another day.

Beneath the surface of this error-laden text lies the work of a writer already in many ways competent. The text is *fluent*, as measured not simply by overall length but by the extended sentences and paragraphs that show the expansion and extension of each idea. It is *coherent*, focusing on one worker who is representative of the larger group, and unified, with effective closure, ending not only with the end of the observation but with a statement which sums up the attitude implied by this worker's activities: "Another dollar another day."

In terms of *logical structuring*, an initial, generalizing assertion is made ("the ill interest to work is shared among everyone in this working place"), and then supported with the specific example of this worker. The ordering principle here is one of simple chronology, but temporal connectives are not the explicit "first, second" which one would expect at this level: they are far more subtle and implicit: "as the day lingered," "At this point of the working day." The paragraphs represent clear units of thought.

The opening passage places the reader in a context (*autonomy*). While the workplace is not specifically named (and that ambiguity effectively allows the reader to associate what follows with any number of workplaces), a general frame is established before focusing on one particular worker. Individual statements are expanded and *elaborated*: "At this point of the working day He starts doing his carefree thing. He slowly drags a misplaced piece of lumber, dusts of his wrangler, blows dust off his plastic shoe." And they contain effective and imbedded modification: "He's a short sleezy bearded Fatu look-a-like" instead of "he is short and sleezy and looks like Fatu." And overall *sentence complexity* is demonstrated by other imbeddings: "Among those blue collars worker's who didn't I found not contribute much sweating eye-brow, to their paycheck was a man . . ." This is the paper of an already skilled language user, who will be able to transfer much of that skill to the mastery of academic discourse.

After identifying the features of academic discourse that I will try to develop in students' writing during the semester, I now look for evidence of the presence, not the absence, of these features in the early assignments, so that I can build on these strengths. This student's strengths in making generalizations and supporting them with richly detailed evidence, with seeing relationships and imbedding those relationships within syntactic structures provided the foundation for academic argumentation. A dialogue journal provided an opportunity for the student to practice such argumentation while receiving real responses, questions, and objections, and to experiment with syntactic structures that would clarify relationships among parts, and with words that would pinpoint his meaning. Succeeding assignments supported the same development more formally by asking students to build from data (gathered from observations and from readings) to hypotheses and then to return to the data for proof. With freedom to work through and examine a position, the student lost the inhibitions that kept him from writing because he "wasn't any good," and at midterm he turned in a sensitive five page analysis of the central conflict in *The Chosen*. After a careful and detailed explication of this conflict as it appears throughout the text the essay concludes:

With all his [Danny's] genius, his father raised him in a state of unassurance. He couldn't make his own mind up, what was best, psychology or his religion. The system which was going to make him a sound human being couldn't help him come to a decision.

While new problems of diction or syntax emerged as this student struggled with the complexity of his ideas, most of the errors of the early papers (sentence boundaries, tense) disappeared without direct remediation under the deluge of reading and writing.[6] And by rechecking the features I had identified in the beginning I was able to keep my own focus on his real progress, and not despair, as I had in the past, at each new syntactic knot or experimental bit of undigested academese.[7] I could allow him to work from his own language while learning that of the university, and what I had found harder, to see the language in the middle, the interlanguage, as evidence of the kind of learning that it in fact represented.

WORKS CITED

Bartholomae, David. "The Study of Error." *CCC* 31 (1980): 253–69.

———. "Teaching Basic Writing: An Alternative to Basic Skills." *Journal of Basic Writing* 2.2 (1979): 85–109.

Berthoff, Ann E. *The Making of Meaning.* Montclair, NJ: Boynton/Cook, 1981.

Bizzell, Patricia. "College Composition: Initiation into the Academic Discourse Community." *Curriculum Inquiry* 12 (1982): 191–207.

Corder, S. Pit. *Error Analysis and Interlanguage.* Oxford: Oxford UP, 1981.

Freire, Paulo. *Education for Critical Consciousness.* New York: Seabury, 1973.

Hartwell, Patrick. "Grammar, Grammars, and the Teaching of Grammar." *College English* 47 (1985): 105–27.

Knoblauch, C. H., and Lil Brannon. "Writing as Learning Through the Curriculum." *College English* 45 (1983): 465–74.

Krashen, Stephen. *Second Language Acquisition and Second Language Learning.* Oxford: Pergamon, 1981.

Labov, William. *The Study of Non-Standard English.* Urbana: NCTE, 1968.

Lauer, Janice, Gene Montague, Andrea Lunsford, and Janet Emig. *Four Worlds of Writing.* 2nd ed. New York: Harper, 1985.

Richards, Jack C., ed. *Error Analysis: Perspectives on Second Language Acquisition.* London: Longman, 1974.

Rose, Mike. "Remedial Writing Courses: A Critique and a Proposal." *College English* 45 (1983): 109–28.

---

[6]Krashen discusses the importance of such intake, which he defines as input that is understood and that is "a little beyond" the learner's present level of competence, 102 ff.

[7]I have refined the features of this analysis to reflect the work underlying a paper which links these characteristics of linguistic development to those of intellectual development. S. Groden, E. Kutz, V. Zamel, ms. in preparation.

Salvatore, Mariolina. "Reading and Writing a Text: Correlations between Reading and Writing." *College English* 45 (1983): 657–66.

"Students' Right to Their Own Language." *CCC* 25 (1974): 1–32.

Wexler, Kenneth. "A Principle Theory for Language Acquisition." *Language Acquisition: The State of the Art*. Eds. Eric Wanner and Lila Gleitman. Cambridge, Eng.: Cambridge UP, 1982. 288–318.

Chapter 5

What Is Literacy?

James Paul Gee

It is a piece of folk wisdom that part of what linguists do is define words. In over a decade as a linguist, however, no one, until now, has asked me to define a word. So my first try: what does "literacy" mean? It won't surprise you that we have to define some other words first. So let me begin my giving a technical meaning to an old term which, unfortunately, already has a variety of other meanings. The term is "discourse." I will use the word as a count term ("a discourse," "discourses," "many discourses"), not as a mass term ("discourse," "much discourse"). By "a discourse" I will mean:

> a socially accepted association among ways of using language, of thinking, and of acting that can be used to identify oneself as a member of a socially meaningful group or "social network."

Think of discourse as an "identity kit" which comes complete with the appropriate costume and instructions on how to act and talk so as to take on a particular role that others will recognize. Let me give an example: Being "trained" as a linguist meant that I learned to speak, think and act like a linguist, and to recognize others when they do so. Now actually matters are not that simple: the larger discourse of linguistics contains many subdiscourses, different socially accepted ways of being a linguist. But the master discourse is not just the sum of its parts, it is something

---

also over and above them. Every act of speaking, writing and behaving a linguist does as a linguist is meaningful only against the background of the whole social institution of linguistics, and that institution is made up of concrete things like people, books and buildings; abstract things like bodies of knowledge, values, norms and beliefs; mixtures of concrete and abstract things like universities, journals and publishers; as well as a shared history and shared stories. Some other examples of discourses: being an American or a Russian, being a man or a woman, being a member of a certain socio-economic class, being a factory worker or a boardroom executive, being a doctor or a hospital patient, being a teacher, an administrator, or a student, being a member of a sewing circle, a club, a street gang, a lunchtime social gathering, or a regular at a local watering hole.

There are a number of important points that one can make about discourses, none of which, for some reason, are very popular to Americans, though they seem to be commonplace in European social theory (Belsey, 1980; Eagleton, 1983; Jameson, 1981; Macdonell, 1986; Thompson, 1984):

1. Discourses are inherently "ideological." They crucially involve a set of values and viewpoints in terms of which one must speak and act, at least while being in the discourse; otherwise one doesn't count as being in it.

2. Discourses are resistant to internal criticism and self-scrutiny since uttering viewpoints that seriously undermine them defines one as being outside them. The discourse itself defines what counts as acceptable criticism. Of course, one can criticize a particular discourse from the viewpoint of another one (e.g., psychology criticizing linguistics). But what one cannot do is stand outside all discourse and criticize any one or all of them—that would be like trying to repair a jet in flight by stepping outside it.

3. Discourse-defined positions from which to speak and behave are not, however, just defined internal to a discourse, but also as standpoints taken up by the discourse in its relation to other, ultimately opposing, discourses. The discourse of managers in an industry is partly defined by their opposition to analogous points in the discourse of workers (Macdonell, 1986: 1–7). The discourse we identify with being a feminist is radically changed if all male discourses disappear.

4. Any discourse concerns itself with certain objects and puts forward certain concepts, viewpoints and values at the expense of others. In doing so it will marginalize viewpoints and values central to other discourses (Macdonell, 1986: 1–7). In fact, a discourse can call for one to accept values in conflict with other discourses one is a member of—for example, the discourse used in literature departments used to marginalize popular literature and women's writings. Further, women readers of Hemingway, for instance, when acting as "acceptable readers" by the standards of the discourse of literary criticism, might find themselves complicit with values

which conflict with those of various other discourses they belong to as women (Culler, 1982: 43–64).

5. Finally, discourses are intimately related to the distribution of social power and hierarchical structure in society. Control over certain discourses can lead to the acquisition of social goods (money, power, status) in a society. These discourses empower those groups who have the least conflicts with their other discourses when they use them. For example, many academic, legalistic and bureaucratic discourses in our society contain a moral subdiscourse that sees "right" as what is derivable from general abstract principles. This can conflict to a degree with a discourse about morality that appears to be more often associated with women than men in terms of which "wrong" is seen as the disruption of social networks, and "right" as the repair of those networks (Gilligan, 1982). Or, to take another example, the discourse of literary criticism was a standard route to success as a professor of literature. Since it conflicted less with the other discourses of white, middle class men than it did with those of women, men were empowered by it. Women were not, as they were often at cross-purposes when engaging in it. Let us call discourses that lead to social goods in a society "dominant discourses" and let us refer to those groups that have the fewest conflicts when using them as "dominant groups." Obviously these are both matters of degree and change to a certain extent in different contexts.

It is sometimes helpful to say that it is not individuals who speak and act, but rather historically and socially defined discourses speak to each other through individuals. The individual instantiates, gives body to, a discourse every time he acts or speaks and thus carries it, and ultimately changes it, through time. Americans tend to be very focused on the individual, and thus often miss the fact that the individual is simply the meeting point of many, sometimes conflicting, socially and historically defined discourses.

The crucial question is: how does one come by the discourses that he controls? And here it is necessary, before answering the question, to make an important distinction, a distinction that does not exist in non-technical parlance, but one which is important to a linguist: a distinction between "acquisition" and "learning" (Krashen, 1982, 1985; Krashen & Terrell, 1983). I will distinguish these two as follows:

Acquisition is a process of acquiring something subconsciously by exposure to models and a process of trial and error, without a process of formal teaching. It happens in natural settings which are meaningful and functional in the sense that the acquirer knows that he needs to acquire the thing he is exposed to in order to function and the acquirer in fact wants to so function. This is how most people come to control their first language.

Learning is a process that involves conscious knowledge gained through teaching, though not necessarily from someone officially designated a teacher. This teaching involves explanation and analysis, that is, breaking down the thing to be learned into its analytic parts. It inherently involves attaining, along with the matter being taught, some degree of meta-knowledge about the matter.

Much of what we come by in life, after our initial enculturation, involves a mixture of acquisition and learning. However, the balance between the two can be quite different in different cases and different at different stages in the process. For instance, I initially learned to drive a car by instruction, but thereafter acquired, rather than learned, most of what I know. Some cultures highly value acquisition and so tend simply to expose children to adults modeling some activity and eventually the child picks it up, picks it up as a gestalt, rather than as a series of analytic bits (Scollon & Scollon, 1981; Heath, 1983). Other cultural groups highly value teaching and thus break down what is to be mastered into sequential steps and analytic parts and engage in explicit explanation. There is an up side and a down side to both that can be expressed as follows: "we are better at what we acquire, but we consciously know more about what we have learned." For most of us, playing a musical instrument, or dancing, or using a second language are skills we attained by some mixture of acquisition and learning. But it is a safe bet that, over the same amount of time, people are better at these activities if acquisition predominated during that time. The point can be made using second language as the example: most people aren't very good at attaining a second language in any very functional way through formal instruction in a classroom. That's why teaching grammar is not a very good way of getting people to control a language. However, people who have acquired a second language in a natural setting don't thereby make good linguists, and some good linguists can't speak the languages they learned in a classroom. What is said here about second languages is true, I believe, of all of what I will later refer to as "secondary discourses": acquisition is good for performance, learning is good for meta-level knowledge (cf. Scribner & Cole, 1981). Acquisition and learning are thus, too, differential sources of power: acquirers usually beat learners at performance, learners usually beat acquirers at talking about it, that is, at explication, explanation, analysis and criticism.

Now what has this got to do with literacy? First, let me point out that it renders the common sense understanding of literacy very problematic. Take the notion of a "reading class." I don't know if they are still prevalent, but when I was in grammar school we had a special time set aside each day for "reading class" where we would learn to read. Reading is at the very least the ability to interpret print (surely not just the ability to call out the names of letters), but an interpretation of print is just a viewpoint on a set of symbols, and viewpoints are always embedded in a discourse. Thus, while many different discourses use reading, even in opposing ways, and while there could well be classes devoted to these discourses, reading outside such a discourse or class would be truly "in a vacuum," much like our repairman above trying to repair the jet in flight by jumping out the door. Learning to read is always learning some aspect of some discourse. One can trivialize this insight to a certain degree by trivializing the notion of interpretation (of printed words), until one gets to reading as calling out the names of letters. Analogously, one can deepen the insight by taking successively deeper views of what interpretation means. But, there is also the problem with "reading class," that it stresses learning and not acquisition. To the extent that reading as both decoding and interpretation is a performance, learning stresses the production of poor performers. If we wanted to stress acquisition we would have to expose children to reading and this would always be to expose them to a discourse whose name would never be "Reading" (at least until the student went to the university and earned a degree called "Reading"). To the extent that it is important to have meta-level skills in regard to language, reading class as a place of learning rather than of acquisition might facilitate this, but it is arguable that a reading class would hardly be the best place to do this. While reading classes like mine might not be around any more, it encapsulated the common sense notion of literacy as "the ability to read and write" (intransitively), a notion that is nowhere near as coherent as it at first sounds.

Now I will approach a more positive connection between a viable notion of literacy and the concepts we have dealt with above. All humans, barring serious disorder, get one form of discourse free, so to speak, and this through acquisition. This is our socio-culturally determined way of using our native language in face-to-face communication with intimates (intimates are people with whom we share a great deal of knowledge because of a great deal of contact and similar experiences). This is sometimes referred to as "the oral mode" (Gee, 1986b)—it is the birth right of every human and comes through the process of primary socialization within the family as this is defined within a given culture. Some small, so-called "primitive," cultures function almost like extended families (though never completely so) in that this type of discourse is usable in a very wide array of social contacts. This is due to the fact that these cultures are small enough to function as a "society of intimates" (Givon, 1979). In modern technological and urban societies which function as a "society of strangers," the oral mode is more narrowly useful. Let us refer then to this oral mode, developed in the primary process of enculturation, as the "primary discourse." It is important to realize that even among speakers of English there are socio-culturally different primary discourses. For example, lower socio-economic black children use English to make sense of their experience differently than do middle class children; they have a different primary discourse (Gee, 1985; 1986a; Michaels, 1981;

1985). And this is not due merely to the fact that they have a different dialect of English. So-called "Black Vernacular English" is, on structural grounds, only trivially different from standard English by the norms of linguists accustomed to dialect differences around the world (Labov, 1972). Rather, these children use language, behavior, values and beliefs to give a different shape to their experience.

Beyond the primary discourse, however, are other discourses which crucially involve social institutions beyond the family (or the primary socialization group as defined by the culture), no matter how much they also involve the family. These institutions all share the factor that they require one to communicate with non-intimates (or to treat intimates as if they were not intimates). Let us refer to these as "secondary institutions" (such as schools, workplaces, stores, government offices, businesses, churches, etc.). Discourses beyond the primary discourse are developed in association with and by having access to and practice with these secondary institutions. Thus, we will refer to them as "secondary discourses." These secondary discourses all build on, and extend, the uses of language we acquired as part of our primary discourse, and they may be more or less compatible with the primary discourses of different social groups. It is, of course, a great advantage when the secondary discourse is compatible with your primary one. But all these secondary discourses involve uses of language, either written or oral, or both, that go beyond our primary discourse no matter what group we belong to. Let's call those uses of language in secondary discourses which go beyond the uses of language stemming from our primary discourse "secondary uses of language." Telling your mother you love her is a primary use of language, telling your teacher you don't have your homework is a secondary use. It can be noted, however, that sometimes people must fall back on their primary uses of language in inappropriate circumstances when they fail to control the requisite secondary use.

Now we can get to what I believe is a useful definition of literacy:

literacy is control of secondary uses of language (i.e., uses of language in secondary discourses)

Thus, there are as many applications of the word "literacy" as there are secondary discourses, which is many. We can define various types of literacy as follows:

dominant literacy is control of a secondary use of language used in what I called above a "dominant discourse"

powerful literacy is control of a secondary use of language used in a secondary discourse that can serve as a meta-discourse to critique the primary discourse or other secondary discourses, including dominant discourses

What do I mean by "control" in the above definitions? I mean some degree of being able to "use," to "function" with, so "control" is a matter of degree. "Mastery" I define as "full and effortless control." In these terms I will state a principle having to do with acquisition which I believe is true:

> Any discourse (primary or secondary) is for most people most of the time only mastered through acquisition, not learning. Thus, literacy is mastered through acquisition, not learning, that is, it requires exposure to models in natural, meaningful, and functional settings, and teaching is not liable to be very successful—it may even initially get in the way. Time spent on learning and not acquisition is time not well spent if the goal is mastery in performance.

There is also a principle having to do with learning that I think true:

> One cannot critique one discourse with another one (which is the only way to seriously criticize and thus change a discourse) unless one has meta-level knowledge in both discourses. And this meta-knowledge is best developed through learning, though often learning applied to a discourse one has to a certain extent already acquired. Thus, powerful literacy, as defined above, almost always involves learning, and not just acquisition.

The point is that acquisition and learning are means to quite different goals, though in our culture we very often confuse these means and thus don't get what we thought and hoped we would.

Let me just briefly mention some practical connections of the above remarks. Mainstream middle class children often look like they are learning literacy (of various sorts) in school. But, in fact, I believe much research shows they are acquiring these literacies through experiences in the home both before and during school, as well as by the opportunities school gives them to practice what they are acquiring (Wells, 1985; 1986a, b). The learning they are doing, provided it is tied to good teaching, is giving them not the literacies, but meta-level cognitive and linguistic skills that they can use to critique various discourses throughout their lives. However, we all know that teaching is not by any means always that good—though it should be one of our goals to see to it that it is. Children from non-main-stream homes often do not get the opportunities to acquire dominant secondary discourses, for example those connected with the school, prior to school in their homes, due to the lack of access their parents have to these secondary discourses. Thus, when coming to school they cannot practice what they haven't yet got and they are exposed mostly to a process of learning and not acquisition. Since little acquisition thereby goes on, they often cannot use this learning-teaching to develop meta-level skills since this requires some degree of acquisition of secondary discourses to use in the critical process. Further, research pretty clearly shows that many school-based secondary discourses conflict with the values and viewpoints in some non-mainstream children's primary discourses and other community-based secondary discourses (e.g., stemming from religious institutions) (Heath, 1983; Cook-Gumperz, 1986; Gumperz, 1982).

While the above remarks may all seem rather theoretical, they do in fact lead to some obvious practical suggestions for directions future research and intervention efforts ought to take. As far as I can see some of these are as follows:

1. Settings which focus on acquisition, not learning, should be stressed if the goal is to help non-mainstream children attain mastery of literacies. This is certainly not liable to be a traditional classroom setting (let alone my "reading class"), but rather natural and functional environments, which may or may not happen to be inside a school.

2. We should realize that teaching and learning are connected with the development of meta-level cognitive and linguistic skills. They will work better if we explicitly realize this and build this realization into our curricula. Further, they must be ordered and integrated with acquisition in viable ways if they are to have any effect other than obstruction.

3. Mainstream children are actually using much of the teaching-learning they get not to learn but to acquire, by practicing developing skills. We should thus honor this practice effect directly and build on it, rather than leave it as a surreptitious and indirect by-product of teaching-learning.

4. Learning should lead to the ability for all children—mainstream and non-mainstream—to critique their primary discourses and secondary discourses, including dominant secondary discourses. This requires exposing children to a variety of alternative primary discourses and secondary ones (not necessarily so that they acquire them, but so that they learn about them). It also requires realizing explicitly that this is what good teaching and learning is good at. We rarely realize that this is where we fail mainstream children just as much as non-mainstream ones.

5. We must take seriously that no matter how good our schools become, both as environments where acquisition can go on (so involving meaningful and functional settings) and where learning can go on, the non-mainstream child will always have more conflicts in using and thus mastering dominant secondary discourses, since they conflict more seriously with his primary discourse and community-based secondary ones. This is precisely what it means (by my definitions above) to be "non-mainstream." This does not mean we should give up. It also does not mean merely that research and intervention efforts must have sensitivity to these conflicts built into them, though it certainly does mean this. It also requires, I believe, that we must also stress research and intervention efforts that facilitate the development of wider and more humane concepts of mastery and its connections to

gate-keeping. We must remember that conflicts, while they do very often detract from standard sorts of full mastery, can give rise to new sorts of mastery. This is commonplace in the realm of art. We must make it commonplace in society at large.

REFERENCES

Belsey, C. (1980). *Critical Practice.* London: Methuen.

Cook-Gumperz, J., Ed. (1986). *The Social Construction of Literacy.* Cambridge: Cambridge University Press.

Culler, J. (1982). *On Deconstruction: Theory and Criticism after Structuralism.* Ithaca, NY: Cornell University Press.

Eagleton, T. (1983). *Literary Theory: An Introduction.* Minneapolis: University of Minnesota Press.

Gee, J. P. (1985). The narrativization of experience in the oral mode, *Journal of Education, 167,* 9–35.

Gee, J. P. (1986a). Units in the production of discourse, *Discourse Processes, 9,* 391–422.

Gee, J. P. (1986b). Orality and literacy: From the *Savage Mind* to *Ways with Words, TESOL Quarterly, 20,* 719–746.

Gilligan, C. (1982). *In a Different Voice.* Cambridge: Harvard University Press.

Givon, T. (1979). *On Understanding Grammar.* New York: Academic Press.

Gumperz, J. J., Ed. (1982). *Language and Social Identity.* Cambridge: Cambridge University Press.

Heath, S. B. (1983). *Ways with Words: Language, Life, and Work in Communities and Classrooms.* Cambridge: Cambridge University Press.

Jameson, F. (1981). *The Political Unconscious: Narrative as a Socially Symbolic Act.* Ithaca, NY: Cornell University Press.

Krashen, S. (1982). *Principles and Practice in Second Language Acquisition.* Hayward, CA: Alemany Press.

Krashen, S. (1985). *Inquiries and Insights.* Hayward, CA: Alemany Press.

Krashen, S. & Terrell, T. (1983). *The Natural Approach: Language Acquisition in the Classroom.* Hayward, CA: Alemany Press.

Labov, W. (1972). *Language in the Inner City.* Philadelphia: University of Pennsylvania Press.

Macdonell, D. (1986). *Theories of Discourse: An Introduction.* Oxford: Basil Blackwell.

Michaels, S. (1981). "Sharing time": Children's narrative styles and differential access to literacy, *Language in Society, 10,* 423–442.

Michaels, S. (1985). Hearing the connections in children's oral and written discourse, *Journal of Education, 167,* 36–56.

Scollon, R. & Scollon, S. B. K. (1981). *Narrative, Literacy, and Face in Inter-ethnic Communication.* Norwood, NJ: Ablex.

Scribner, S. & Cole, M. (1981). *The Psychology of Literacy.* Cambridge: Harvard University Press.

Thompson, J. B. (1984). *Studies in the Theory of Ideology.* Berkeley and Los Angeles: University of California Press.

Wells, G. (1985). "Preschool literacy-related activities and success in school," in D. R. Olson, N. Torrance, & A. Hildyard, eds. *Literacy, Language, and Learning.* Cambridge: Cambridge University Press.

Wells, G. (1986a). "The language experience of five-year-old children at home and at school" in J. Cook-Gumperz, ed. *The Social Construction of Literacy.* Cambridge: Cambridge University Press.

Wells, G. (1986b). *The Meaning Makers: Children Learning Language and Using Language to Learn.* New York: Heinemann.

From Outside, In

Barbara Mellix

Two years ago, when I started writing this paper, trying to bring order out of chaos, my ten-year-old daughter was suffering from an acute attack of boredom. She drifted in and out of the room complaining that she had nothing to do, no one to "be with" because none of her friends were at home. Patiently I explained that I was working on something special and needed peace and quiet, and I suggested that she paint, read, or work with her computer. None of these interested her. Finally, she pulled up a chair to my desk and watched me, now and then heaving long, loud sighs. After two or three minutes (nine or ten sighs), I lost my patience. "Looka here, Allie," I said, "you too old for this kinda carryin' on. I done told you this is important. You wronger than dirt to be in here haggin' me like this and you know it. Now git on outta here and leave me off before I put my foot all the way down."

I was at home, alone with my family, and my daughter understood that this way of speaking was appropriate in that context. She knew, as a matter of fact, that it was almost inevitable; when I get angry at home, I speak some of my finest, most cherished black English. Had I been speaking to my daughter in this manner in certain other environments, she would have been shocked and probably worried that I had taken leave of my sense of propriety.

The Georgia Review, 1987

Like my children, I grew up speaking what I considered two distinctly different languages—black English and standard English (or as I thought of them then, the ordinary everyday speech of "country" coloreds and "proper" English)—and in the process of acquiring these languages, I developed an understanding of when, where, and how to use them. But unlike my children, I grew up in a world that was primarily black. My friends, neighbors, minister, teachers—almost everybody I associated with every day—were black. And we spoke to one another in our own special language: *That sho is a pretty dress you got on. If she don' soon leave me off I'm gon tell her head a mess. I was so mad I could'a pissed a blue nail. He all the time trying to low-rate somebody. Ain't that just about the nastiest thing you ever set ears on?*

Then there were the "others," the "proper" blacks, transplanted relatives and one-time friends who came home from the city for weddings, funerals, and vacations. And the whites. To these we spoke standard English. "Ain't?" my mother would yell at me when I used the term in the presence of "others." "You *know* better than that." And I would hang my head in shame and say the "proper" word.

I remember one summer sitting in my grandmother's house in Greeley-ville, South Carolina, when it was full of the chatter of city relatives who were home on vacation. My parents sat quietly, only now and then volun-teering a comment or answering a question. My mother's face took on a strained expression when she spoke. I could see that she was being careful to say just the right words in just the right way. Her voice sounded thick, muffled. And when she finished speaking, she would lapse into silence, her proper smile on her face. My father was more articulate, more aggres-sive. He spoke quickly, his words sharp and clear. But he held his proud head higher, a signal that he, too, was uncomfortable. My sisters and brothers and I stared at our aunts, uncles, and cousins, speaking only when prompted. Even then, we hesitated, formed our sentences in our minds, then spoke softly, shyly.

My parents looked small and anxious during those occasions, and I waited impatiently for our leave-taking when we would mock our relatives the moment we were out of their hearing. "Reeely," we would say to one another, flexing our wrists and rolling our eyes, "how dooo you stan' this heat? Chile, it just too hy*ooo*-mid for words." Our relatives had made us feel "country," and this was our way of regaining pride in ourselves while getting a little revenge in the bargain. The words bubbled in our throats and rolled across our tongues, a balming.

As a child I felt this same doubleness in uptown Greeleyville where the whites lived. "Ain't that a pretty dress you're wearing!" Toby, the town policeman, said to me one day when I was fifteen. "Thank you very much," I replied, my voice barely audible in my own ears. The words felt wrong in my mouth, rigid, foreign. It was not that I had never spoken that phrase before—it was common in black English, too—but I was extremely conscious that this was an occasion for proper English. I had taken out my English and put it on as I did my church clothes, and I felt as if I were wearing my Sunday best in the middle of the week. It did not matter that Toby had not spoken grammatically correct English. He was white and could speak as he wished. I had something to prove. Toby did not.

Speaking standard English to whites was our way of demonstrating that we knew their language and could use it. Speaking it to standard-English-speaking blacks was our way of showing them that we, as well as they, could "put on airs." But when we spoke standard English, we acknowledged (to ourselves and to others—but primarily to ourselves) that our customary way of speaking was inferior. We felt foolish, embarrassed, somehow diminished because we were ashamed to be our real selves. We were reserved, shy in the presence of those who owned and/or spoke *the* language.

My parents never set aside time to drill us in standard English. Their forms of instruction were less formal. When my father was feeling particularly expansive, he would regale us with tales of his exploits in the outside world. In almost flawless English, complete with dialogue and flavored with gestures and embellishment, he told us about his attempt to get a haircut at a white barbershop; his refusal to acknowledge one of the town merchants until the man addressed him as "Mister"; the time he refused to step off the sidewalk uptown to let some whites pass; his airplane trip to New York City (to visit a sick relative) during which the stewardesses and porters—recognizing that he was a "gentleman"—addressed him as "Sir." I did not realize then—nor, I think, did my father—that he was teaching us, among other things, standard English and the relationship between language and power.

My mother's approach was different. Often, when one of us said, "I'm gon wash off my feet," she would say, "And what will you walk on if you wash them off?" Everyone would laugh at the victim of my mother's "proper" mood. But it was different when one of us children was in a proper mood. "You think you are so superior," I said to my oldest sister one day when we were arguing and she was winning. "Superior!" my sister mocked. "You mean I'm acting 'biggidy'?" My sisters and brothers sniggered, then joined in teasing me. Finally, my mother said, "Leave your sister alone. There's nothing wrong with using proper English." There was a half-smile on her face. I had gotten "uppity," had "put on airs" for no good reason. I was at home, alone with the family, and I hadn't been prompted by one of my mother's proper moods. But there was also a proud light in my mother's eyes; her children were learning English very well.

Not until years later, as a college student, did I begin to understand our ambivalence toward English, our scorn of it, our need to master it, to own and be owned by it—an ambivalence that extended to the public-school classroom. In our school, where there were no whites, my teachers taught standard English but used black English to do it. When my grammar-school teachers wanted us to write, for example, they usually said something like, "I want y'all to write five sentences that make a statement. Anybody git done before the rest can color." It was probably almost those exact words that led me to write these sentences in 1953 when I was in the second grade:

> The white clouds are pretty.
> There are only 15 people in our room.
> We will go to gym.
> We have a new poster.
> We may go out doors.

Second grade came after "Little First" and "Big First," so by then I knew the implied rules that accompanied all writing assignments. Writing was an occasion for proper English. I was not to write in the way we spoke to one another: The white clouds pretty; There ain't but 15 people in our room; We going to gym; We got a new poster; We can go out in the yard. Rather I was to use the language of "other": clouds *are*, there *are*, we *will*, we *have*, we *may*.

My sentences were short, rigid, perfunctory, like the letters my mother wrote to relatives:

> Dear Papa,
> How are you? How is Mattie? Fine I hope. We are fine. We will come to see you Sunday. Cousin Ned will give us a ride.
> > Love,
> > Daughter

The language was not ours. It was something from outside us, something we used for special occasions.

But my coloring on the other side of that second-grade paper is different. I drew three hearts and a sun. The sun has a smiling face that radiates and envelops everything it touches. And although the sun and its world are enclosed in a circle, the colors I used—red, blue, green, purple, orange, yellow, black—indicate that I was less restricted with drawing and coloring than I was with writing standard English. My valentines were not just red. My sun was not just a yellow ball in the sky.

By the time I reached the twelfth grade, speaking and writing standard English had taken on new importance. Each year, about half of the newly graduated seniors of our school moved to large cities—particularly in the North—to live with relatives and find work. Our English teacher constantly corrected our grammar: "Not 'ain't,' but 'isn't.' " We seldom wrote papers, and even those few were usually plot summaries of short stories. When our teacher returned the papers, she usually lectured on the importance of using standard English: "I *am*; you *are*; he, she, or it *is*," she would say, writing on the chalkboard as she spoke. "How you gon git a job talking about 'I is,' or 'I isn't' or 'I ain't'?"

In Pittsburgh, where I moved after graduation, I watched my aunt and uncle—who had always spoken standard English when in Greeleyville—switch from black English to standard English to a mixture of the two, according to where they were or who they were with. At home and with certain close relatives, friends, and neighbors, they spoke black English. With those less close, they spoke a mixture. In public and with strangers, they generally spoke standard English.

In time, I learned to speak standard English with ease and to switch smoothly from black to standard or a mixture, and back again. But no matter where I was, no matter what the situation or occasion, I continued to write as I had in school:

> Dear Mommie,
> How are you? How is everybody else? Fine I hope. I am fine. So are Aunt and Uncle. Tell everyone I said hello. I will write again soon.
> > Love,
> > Barbara

At work, at a health insurance company, I learned to write letters to customers. I studied form letters and letters written by co-workers, memorizing the phrases and the ways in which they were used. I dictated:

> Thank you for your letter of January 5. We have made the changes in your coverage you requested. Your new premium will be $150 every three months. We are pleased to have been of service to you.

In a sense, I was proud of the letters I wrote for the company: they were proof of my ability to survive in the city, the outside world—an indication of my growing mastery of English. But they also indicate that writing was still mechanical for me, something that didn't require much thought.

Reading also became a more significant part of my life during those early years in Pittsburgh. I had always liked reading, but now I devoted more and more of my spare time to it. I read romances, mysteries, popular novels. Looking back, I realize that the books I liked best were simple, unambiguous: good versus bad and right versus wrong with right rewarded and wrong punished, mysteries unraveled and all set right in the end. It was how I remembered life in Greeleyville.

Of course I was romanticizing. Life in Greeleyville had not been so very uncomplicated. Back there I had been—first as a child, then as a young woman with limited experience in the outside world—living in a relatively closed-in society. But there were implicit and explicit principles that guided our way of life and shaped our relationships with one another and the people outside—principles that a newcomer would find elusive and baffling. In Pittsburgh, I had matured, become more experienced: I had worked at three different jobs, associated with a wider range of people, married, had children. This new environment with different prescripts for living required that I speak standard English much of the time, and slowly, imperceptibly, I had ceased seeing a sharp distinction between myself and "others." Reading romances and mysteries, characterized by dichotomy, was a way of shying away from change, from the person I was becoming.

But that other part of me—that part which took great pride in my ability to hold a job writing business letters—was increasingly drawn to the new developments in my life and the attending possibilities, opportunities for even greater change. If I could write letters for a nationally known business, could I not also do something better, more challenging, more important? Could I not, perhaps, go to college and become a school teacher? For years, afraid and a little embarrassed, I did no more than imagine this different me, this possible me. But sixteen years after coming north, when my youngest daughter entered kindergarten, I found myself unable—or unwilling—to resist the lure of possibility. I enrolled in my first college course: Basic Writing, at the University of Pittsburgh.

For the first time in my life, I was required to write extensively about myself. Using the most formal English at my command, I wrote these sentences near the beginning of the term:

> One of my duties as a homemaker is simply picking up after others. A day seldom passes that I don't search for a mislaid toy, book, or gym shoe, etc. I change the Ty-D-Bol, fight "ring around the collar," and keep our laundry smelling "April fresh." Occasionally, I settle arguments between my children and suggest things to do when they're bored. Taking telephone messages for my oldest daughter is my newest (and sometimes most aggravating) chore. Hanging the toilet paper roll is my most insignificant.

My concern was to use "appropriate" language, to sound as if I belonged in a college classroom. But I felt separate from the language—as if it did not and could not belong to me. I couldn't think and feel genuinely in that language, couldn't make it express what I thought and felt about being a housewife. A part of me resented, among other things, being judged by such things as the appearance of my family's laundry and toilet bowl, but in that language I could only imagine and write about a conventional housewife.

For the most part, the remainder of the term was a period of adjustment, a time of trying to find my bearings as a student in a college composition class, to learn to shut out my black English whenever I composed, and to prevent it from creeping into my formulations; a time for trying to grasp the language of the classroom and reproduce it in my prose; for trying to talk about myself in that language, reach others through it. Each experience of writing was like standing naked and revealing my imperfection, my "otherness." And each new assignment was another chance to make myself over in language, reshape myself, make myself "better" in my rapidly changing image of a student in a college composition class.

But writing became increasingly unmanageable as the term progressed, and by the end of the semester, my sentences sounded like this:

> My excitement was soon dampened, however, by what seemed like a small voice in the back of my head saying that I should be careful with my long awaited opportunity. I felt frustrated and this seemed to make it difficult to concentrate.

There is a poverty of language in these sentences. By this point, I knew that the clichéd language of my Housewife essay was unacceptable, and I generally recognized trite expressions. At the same time, I hadn't yet mastered the language of the classroom, hadn't yet come to see it as belonging to me. Most notable is the lifelessness of the prose, the apparent absence of a person behind the words. I wanted those sentences—and the rest of the essay—to convey the anguish of yearning to, at once, become something more and yet remain the same. I had the sensation of being split in two, part of me going into a future the other part didn't believe possible. As that person, the student writer at that moment, I was essentially mute. I could not—in the process of composing—use the language of the old me, yet I couldn't imagine myself in the language of "others."

I found this particularly discouraging because at midsemester I had been writing in a much different way. Note the language of this introduction to an essay I had written then, near the middle of the term:

> Pain is a constant companion to the people in "Footwork." Their jobs are physically damaging. Employers are insensitive to their feelings and in many cases add to their problems. The general public wounds them further by treating them with disgrace because of what they do for a living. Although the workers are as diverse as they are similar, there is a definite link between them. They suffer a great deal of abuse.

The voice here is stronger, more confident, appropriating terms like "physically damaging," "wounds them further," "insensitive," "diverse"—terms I couldn't have imagined using when writing about my own experience—and shaping them into sentences like, "Although the workers are as diverse as they are similar, there is a definite link between them." And there is the sense of a personality behind the prose, someone who sympathizes with the workers: "The general public wounds them further by treating them with disgrace because of what they do for a living."

What caused these differences? I was, I believed, explaining other people's thoughts and feelings, and I was free to move about in the language of "others" so long as I was speaking *of* others. I was unaware that I was transforming into my best classroom language my own thoughts and feelings about people whose experiences and ways of speaking were in many ways similar to mine.

The following year, unable to turn back or to let go of what had become something of an obsession with language (and hoping to catch and hold the sense of control that had eluded me in Basic Writing), I enrolled in a research writing course. I spent most of the term learning how to prepare for and write a research paper. I chose sex education as my subject and spent hours in libraries, searching for information, reading, taking notes. Then (not without messiness and often-demoralizing frustration) I organized my information into categories, wrote a thesis statement, and composed my paper—a series of paraphrases and quotations spaced between carefully constructed transitions. The process and results felt artificial, but as I would later come to realize I was passing through a necessary stage. My sentences sounded like this:

> This reserve becomes understandable with examination of who the abusers are. In an overwhelming number of cases, they are people the victims know and trust. Family members, relatives, neighbors and close family friends commit seventy-five percent of all reported sex crimes against children, and parents, parent substitutes and relatives are the offenders in thirty to eighty percent of all reported cases.[12] While assault by strangers does occur, it is less common, and is usually a single episode.[13] But abuse by family members, relatives and acquaintances may continue for an extended period of time. In cases of incest, for example, children are abused repeatedly for an average of eight years.[14] In such cases, "the use of physical force is rarely necessary because of the child's trusting, dependent relationship with the offender. The child's cooperation is often facilitated by the adult's position of dominance, an offer of material goods, a threat of physical violence, or a misrepresentation of moral standards."[15]

The completed paper gave me a sense of profound satisfaction, and I read it often after my professor returned it. I know now that what I was pleased with was the language I used and the professional voice it helped me maintain. "Use better words," my teacher had snapped at me one day after reading the notes I'd begun accumulating from my research, and slowly I began taking on the language of my sources. In my next set of notes, I used the word "vacillating"; my professor applauded. And by the time I composed the final draft, I felt at ease with terms like "overwhelming number of cases," "single episode," and "reserve," and I shaped them into sentences similar to those of my "expert" sources.

If I were writing the paper today, I would of course do some things differently. Rather than open with an anecdote—as my teacher suggested— I would begin simply with a quotation that caught my interest as I was researching my paper (and which I scribbled, without its source, in the margin of my notebook): "Truth does not do so much good in the world as the semblance of truth does evil." The quotation felt right because it captured what was for me the central idea of my essay—an idea that emerged gradually during the making of my paper—and expressed it in a way I would like to have said it. The anecdote, a hypothetical situation I invented to conform to the information in the paper, felt forced and insincere because it represented—to a great degree—my teacher's understanding of the essay, *her* idea of what in it was most significant. Improving upon my previous experiences with writing, I was beginning to think and feel in the language I used, to find my own voices in it, to sense that how one speaks influences how one means. But I was not yet secure enough, comfortable enough with the language to trust my intuition.

Now that I know that to seek knowledge, freedom, and autonomy means always to be in the concentrated process of becoming—always to be venturing into new territory, feeling one's way at first, then getting one's balance, negotiating, accommodating, discovering one's self in ways that previously defined "others"—I sometimes get tired. And I ask myself why I keep on participating in this highbrow form of violence, this slamming against perplexity. But there is no real futility in the question, no hint of that part of the old me who stood outside standard English, hugging to herself a disabling mistrust of a language she thought could not represent a person with her history and experience. Rather, the question represents a person who feels the consequence of her education, the weight of her possibilities as a teacher and writer and human being, a voice in society. And I would not change that person, would not give back the good burden that accompanies my growing expertise, my increasing power to shape myself in language and share that self with "others."

"To speak," says Frantz Fanon, "means to be in a position to use a certain syntax, to grasp the morphology of this or that language, but it means above all to assume a culture, to support the weight of a civilization."[1] To write means to do the same, but in a more profound sense. However, Fanon also says that to achieve mastery means to "get" in a position of power, to "grasp," to "assume." This, I have learned—both as a student and subsequently as a teacher—can involve tremendous emotional and

---

[1] *Black Skin, White Masks* (1952; rpt. New York: Grove Press, 1967), pp. 17–18.

psychological conflict for those attempting to master academic discourse. Although as a beginning student writer I had a fairly good grasp of ordinary spoken English and was proficient at what Labov calls "code-switching" (and what John Baugh in *Black Street Speech* terms "style shifting"), when I came face to face with the demands of academic writing, I grew increasingly self-conscious, constantly aware of my status as a black and a speaker of one of the many black English vernaculars—a traditional outsider. For the first time, I experienced my sense of doubleness as something menacing, a built-in enemy. Whenever I turned inward for salvation, the balm so available during my childhood, I found instead this new fragmentation which spoke to me in many voices. It was the voice of my desire to prosper, but at the same time it spoke of what I had relinquished and could not regain: a safe way of being, a state of powerlessness which exempted me from responsibility for who I was and might be. And it accused me of betrayal, of turning away from blackness. To recover balance, I had to take on the language of the academy, the language of "others." And to do that, I had to learn to imagine myself a part of the culture of that language, and therefore someone free to manage that language, to take liberties with it. Writing and rewriting, practicing, experimenting, I came to comprehend more fully the generative power of language. I discovered—with the help of some especially sensitive teachers—that through writing one can continually bring new selves into being, each with new responsibilities and difficulties, but also with new possibilities. Remarkable power, indeed. I write and continually give birth to myself.

Chapter 7

From Silence to Words:
Writing as Struggle

Min-zhan Lu

> *Imagine that you enter a parlor. You come late. When you arrive, others have long preceded you, and they are engaged in a heated discussion. . . . You listen for a while, until you decide that you have caught the tenor of the argument; then you put in your oar. Someone answers; you answer him; another comes to your defense; another aligns himself against you, to either the embarrassment or gratification of your opponent, depending upon the quality of your ally's assistance. However, the discussion is interminable. The hour grows late, you must depart. And you do depart, with the discussion still vigorously in progress.*
> —Kenneth Burke (*The Philosophy of Literary Form*)

> *Men are not built in silence, but in word, in work, in action-reflection.*
> —Paulo Freire (*Pedagogy of the Oppressed*)

My mother withdrew into silence two months before she died. A few nights before she fell silent, she told me she regretted the way she had raised me and my sisters. I knew she was referring to the way we had been brought up in the midst of two conflicting worlds—the world of home, dominated by the ideology of Western humanistic tradition, and the world of a society dominated by Mao Tse-tung's Marxism. My mother had devoted her life to our education, an education she knew had made us suffer political persecution during the Cultural Revolution. I wanted to find a way to convince her that, in spite of the persecution, I had benefited from the education she had worked so hard to give me. But I was silent. My understanding of my education was so dominated by memories of confusion and frustration that I was unable to reflect on what I could have gained from it.

This paper is my attempt to fill up that silence with words, words I didn't have then, words that I have since come to by reflecting on my earlier experience as a student in China and on my recent experience as a composition teacher in the United States. For in spite of the frustration and confusion I experienced growing up caught between two conflicting worlds, the conflict ultimately helped me to grow as a reader and writer. Constantly having to switch back and forth between the discourse of home and that of school made me sensitive and self-conscious about the struggle I experienced every time I tried to read, write, or think in either discourse. Eventually, it led me to search for constructive uses for such struggle.

From early childhood, I had identified the differences between home and the outside world by the different languages I used in each. My parents had wanted my sisters and me to get the best education they could conceive of—Cambridge. They had hired a live-in tutor, a Scot, to make us bilingual. I learned to speak English with my parents, my tutor, and my sisters. I was allowed to speak Shanghai dialect only with the servants. When I was four (the year after the Communist Revolution of 1949), my parents sent me to a local private school where I learned to speak, read, and write in a new language—Standard Chinese, the official written language of New China.

In those days I moved from home to school, from English to Standard Chinese to Shanghai dialect, with no apparent friction. I spoke each language with those who spoke the language. All seemed quite "natural"— servants spoke only Shanghai dialect because they were servants; teachers spoke Standard Chinese because they were teachers; languages had different words because they were different languages. I thought of English as my family language, comparable to the many strange dialects I didn't speak but had often heard some of my classmates speak with their families. While I was happy to have a special family language, until second grade I didn't feel that my family language was any different than some of my classmates' family dialects.

My second grade homeroom teacher was a young graduate from a missionary school. When she found out I spoke English, she began to practice her English on me. One day she used English when asking me to run an errand for her. As I turned to close the door behind me, I noticed the puzzled faces of my classmates. I had the same sensation I had often experienced when some stranger in a crowd would turn on hearing me speak English. I was more intensely pleased on this occasion, however, because suddenly I felt that my family language had been singled out from the family languages of my classmates. Since we were not allowed to speak any dialect other than Standard Chinese in the classroom, having my teacher speak

English to me in class made English an official language of the classroom. I began to take pride in my ability to speak it.

This incident confirmed in my mind what my parents had always told me about the importance of English to one's life. Time and again they had told me of how my paternal grandfather, who was well versed in classic Chinese, kept losing good-paying jobs because he couldn't speak English. My grandmother reminisced constantly about how she had slaved and saved to send my father to a first-rate missionary school. And we were made to understand that it was my father's fluent English that had opened the door to his success. Even though my family had always stressed the importance of English for my future, I used to complain bitterly about the extra English lessons we had to take after school. It was only after my homeroom teacher had "sanctified" English that I began to connect English with my education. I became a much more eager student in my tutorials.

What I learned from my tutorials seemed to enhance and reinforce what I was learning in my classroom. In those days each word had one meaning. One day I would be making a sentence at school: "The national flag of China is red." The next day I would recite at home, "My love is like a red, red rose." There seemed to be an agreement between the Chinese "red" and the English "red," and both corresponded to the patch of color printed next to the word. "Love" was my love for my mother at home and my love for my "motherland" at school; both "loves" meant how I felt about my mother. Having two loads of homework forced me to develop a quick memory for words and a sensitivity to form and style. What I learned in one language carried over to the other. I made sentences such as, "I saw a red, red rose among the green leaves," with both the English lyric and the classic Chinese lyric—red flower among green leaves—running through my mind, and I was praised by both teacher and tutor for being a good student.

Although my elementary schooling took place during the fifties, I was almost oblivious to the great political and social changes happening around me. Years later, I read in my history and political philosophy textbooks that the fifties were a time when "China was making a transition from a semi-feudal, semi-capitalist, and semi-colonial country into a socialist country," a period in which "the Proletarians were breaking into the educational territory dominated by Bourgeois Intellectuals." While people all over the country were being officially classified into Proletarians, Petty-bourgeois, National-bourgeois, Poor-peasants, and Intellectuals, and were trying to adjust to their new social identities, my parents were allowed to continue the upper middle-class life they had established before the 1949 Revolution because of my father's affiliation with British firms. I had always felt that my family was different from the families of my classmates, but I didn't perceive society's view of my family until the summer vacation before I entered high school.

First, my aunt was caught by her colleagues talking to her husband over the phone in English. Because of it, she was criticized and almost labeled a Rightist. (This was the year of the Anti-Rightist movement, a movement in which the Intellectuals became the target of the "socialist class-struggle.") I had heard others telling my mother that she was foolish to teach us English when Russian had replaced English as the "official" foreign language. I had also learned at school that the American and British Imperialists were the arch-enemies of New China. Yet I had made no connection between the arch-enemies and the English our family spoke. What happened to my aunt forced the connection on me. I began to see my parents' choice of a family language as an anti-Revolutionary act and was alarmed that I had participated in such an act. From then on, I took care not to use English outside home and to conceal my knowledge of English from my new classmates.

Certain words began to play important roles in my new life at the junior high. On the first day of school, we were handed forms to fill out with our parents' class, job, and income. Being one of the few people not employed by the government, my father had never been officially classified. Since he was a medical doctor, he told me to put him down as an Intellectual. My homeroom teacher called me into the office a couple of days afterwards and told me that my father couldn't be an Intellectual if his income far exceeded that of a Capitalist. He also told me that since my father worked for Foreign Imperialists, my father should be classified as an Imperialist Lackey. The teacher looked nonplussed when I told him that my father couldn't be an Imperialist Lackey because he was a medical doctor. But I could tell from the way he took notes on my form that my father's job had put me in an unfavorable position in his eyes.

The Standard Chinese term "class" was not a new word for me. Since first grade, I had been taught sentences such as, "The Working class are the masters of New China." I had always known that it was good to be a worker, but until then, I had never felt threatened for not being one. That fall, "class" began to take on a new meaning for me. I noticed a group of Working-class students and teachers at school. I was made to understand that because of my class background, I was excluded from that group.

Another word that became important was "consciousness." One of the slogans posted in the school building read, "Turn our students into future Proletarians with socialist consciousness and education!" For several weeks we studied this slogan in our political philosophy course, a subject I had never had in elementary school. I still remember the definition of "socialist consciousness" that we were repeatedly tested on through the years: "Socialist consciousness is a person's political soul. It is the consciousness of the Proletarians represented by Marxist Mao Tse-tung thought. It takes expression in one's action, language, and lifestyle. It is the task of every

Chinese student to grow up into a Proletarian with a socialist consciousness so that he can serve the people and the motherland." To make the abstract concept accessible to us, our teacher pointed out that the immediate task for students from Working-class families was to strengthen their socialist consciousnesses. For those of us who were from other class backgrounds, the task was to turn ourselves into Workers with socialist consciousnesses. The teacher never explained exactly how we were supposed to "turn" into Workers. Instead, we were given samples of the ritualistic annual plans we had to write at the beginning of each term. In these plans, we performed "self-criticism" on our consciousnesses and made vows to turn ourselves into Workers with socialist consciousnesses. The teacher's division between those who did and those who didn't have a socialist consciousness led me to reify the notion of "consciousness" into a thing one possesses. I equated this intangible "thing" with a concrete way of dressing, speaking, and writing. For instance, I never doubted that my political philosophy teacher had a socialist consciousness because she was from a steelworker's family (she announced this the first day of class) and was a Party member who wore grey cadre suits and talked like a philosophy textbook. I noticed other things about her. She had beautiful eyes and spoke Standard Chinese with such a pure accent that I thought she should be a film star. But I was embarrassed that I had noticed things that ought not to have been associated with her. I blamed my observation on my Bourgeois consciousness.

At the same time, the way reading and writing were taught through memorization and imitation also encouraged me to reduce concepts and ideas to simple definitions. In literature and political philosophy classes, we were taught a large number of quotations from Marx, Lenin, and Mao Tse-tung. Each concept that appeared in these quotations came with a definition. We were required to memorize the definitions of the words along with the quotations. Every time I memorized a definition, I felt I had learned a word: "The national red flag symbolizes the blood shed by Revolutionary ancestors for our socialist cause"; "New China rises like a red sun over the eastern horizon." As I memorized these sentences, I reduced their metaphors to dictionary meanings: "red" meant "Revolution" and "red sun" meant "New China" in the "language" of the Working class. I learned mechanically but eagerly. I soon became quite fluent in this new language.

As school began to define me as a political subject, my parents tried to build up my resistance to the "communist poisoning" by exposing me to the "great books"—novels by Charles Dickens, Nathaniel Hawthorne, Emily Brontë, Jane Austen, and writers from around the turn of the century. My parents implied that these writers represented how I, their child, should read and write. My parents replaced the word "Bourgeois" with the word "cultured." They reminded me that I was in school only to learn math and science. I needed to pass the other courses to stay in school, but I was not to let the "Red doctrines" corrupt my mind. Gone were the days when I could innocently write, "I saw the red, red rose among the green leaves," collapsing, as I did, English and Chinese cultural traditions. "Red" came to mean Revolution at school, "the Commies" at home, and adultery in *The Scarlet Letter.* Since I took these symbols and metaphors as meanings natural to people of the same class, I abandoned my earlier definitions of English and Standard Chinese as the language of home and the language of school. I now defined English as the language of the Bourgeois and Standard Chinese as the language of the Working class. I thought of the language of the Working class as someone else's language and the language of the Bourgeois as my language. But I also believed that, although the language of the Bourgeois was my real language, I could and would adopt the language of the Working class when I was at school. I began to put on and take off my Working class language in the same way I put on and took off my school clothes to avoid being criticized for wearing Bourgeois clothes.

In my literature classes, I learned the Working-class formula for reading. Each work in the textbook had a short "Author's Biography": "X X X, born in 19-- in the province of X X, is from a Worker's family. He joined the Revolution in 19--. He is a Revolutionary realist with a passionate love for the Party and Chinese Revolution. His work expresses the thoughts and emotions of the masses and sings praise to the prosperous socialist construction on all fronts of China." The teacher used the "Author's Biography" as a yardstick to measure the texts. We were taught to locate details in the texts that illustrated these summaries, such as words that expressed Workers' thoughts and emotions or events that illustrated the Workers' lives.

I learned a formula for Working-class writing in the composition classes. We were given sample essays and told to imitate them. The theme was always about how the collective taught the individual a lesson. I would write papers about labor-learning experiences or school-cleaning days, depending on the occasion of the collective activity closest to the assignment. To make each paper look different, I dressed it up with details about the date, the weather, the environment, or the appearance of the Master-worker who had taught me "the lesson." But as I became more and more fluent in the generic voice of the Working-class Student, I also became more and more self-conscious about the language we used at home.

For instance, in senior high we began to have English classes ("to study English for the Revolution," as the slogan on the cover of the textbook said), and I was given my first Chinese-English dictionary. There I discovered the English version of the term "class-struggle." (The Chinese characters for a school "class" and for a social "class" are different.) I had often used the English word "class" at home in sentences such as, "So and so has class," but I had not connected this sense of "class" with "class-struggle."

Once the connection was made, I heard a second layer of meaning every time someone at home said a person had "class." The expression began to mean the person had the style and sophistication characteristic of the Bourgeoisie. The word lost its innocence. I was uneasy about hearing that second layer of meaning because I was sure my parents did not hear the word that way. I felt that therefore I should not be hearing it that way either. Hearing the second layer of meaning made me wonder if I was losing my English.

My suspicion deepened when I noticed myself unconsciously merging and switching between the "reading" of home and the "reading" of school. Once I had to write a report on *The Revolutionary Family*, a book about an illiterate woman's awakening and growth as a Revolutionary through the deaths of her husband and all her children for the cause of the Revolution. In one scene the woman deliberated over whether or not she should encourage her youngest son to join the Revolution. Her memory of her husband's death made her afraid to encourage her son. Yet she also remembered her earlier married life and the first time her husband tried to explain the meaning of the Revolution to her. These memories made her feel she should encourage her son to continue the cause his father had begun.

I was moved by this scene. "Moved" was a word my mother and sisters used a lot when we discussed books. Our favorite moments in novels were moments of what I would now call internal conflict, moments which we said "moved" us. I remember that we were "moved" by Jane Eyre when she was torn between her sense of ethics, which compelled her to leave the man she loved, and her impulse to stay with the only man who had ever loved her. We were also moved by Agnes in *David Copperfield* because of the way she restrained her love for David so that he could live happily with the woman he loved. My standard method of doing a book report was to model it on the review by the Publishing Bureau and to dress it up with detailed quotations from the book. The review of *The Revolutionary Family* emphasized the woman's Revolutionary spirit. I decided to use the scene that had moved me to illustrate this point. I wrote the report the night before it was due. When I had finished, I realized I couldn't possibly hand it in. Instead of illustrating her Revolutionary spirit, I had dwelled on her internal conflict, which could be seen as a moment of weak sentimentality that I should never have emphasized in a Revolutionary heroine. I wrote another report, taking care to illustrate the grandeur of her Revolutionary spirit by expanding on a quotation in which she decided that if the life of her son could change the lives of millions of sons, she should not begrudge his life for the cause of Revolution. I handed in my second version but kept the first in my desk.

I never showed it to anyone. I could never show it to people outside my family, because it had deviated so much from the reading enacted by the jacket review. Neither could I show it to my mother or sisters, because I was ashamed to have been so moved by such a "Revolutionary" book. My parents would have been shocked to learn that I could like such a book in the same way they liked Dickens. Writing this book report increased my fear that I was losing the command over both the "language of home" and the "language of school" that I had worked so hard to gain. I tried to remind myself that if I could still tell when my reading or writing sounded incorrect, then I had retained my command over both languages. Yet I could no longer be confident of my command over either language because I had discovered that when I was not careful—or even when I was—my reading and writing often surprised me with its impurity. To prevent such impurity, I became very suspicious of my thoughts when I read or wrote. I was always asking myself why I was using this word, how I was using it, always afraid that I wasn't reading or writing correctly. What confused and frustrated me most was that I could not figure out why I was no longer able to read or write correctly without such painful deliberation.

I continued to read only because reading allowed me to keep my thoughts and confusion private. I hoped that somehow, if I watched myself carefully, I would figure out from the way I read whether I had really mastered the "languages." But writing became a dreadful chore. When I tried to keep a diary, I was so afraid that the voice of school might slip in that I could only list my daily activities. When I wrote for school, I worried that my Bourgeois sensibilities would betray me.

The more suspicious I became about the way I read and wrote, the more guilty I felt for losing the spontaneity with which I had learned to "use" these "languages." Writing the book report made me feel that my reading and writing in the "language" of either home or school could not be free of the interference of the other. But I was unable to acknowledge, grasp, or grapple with what I was experiencing, for both my parents and my teachers had suggested that, if I were a good student, such interference would and should not take place. I assumed that once I had "acquired" a discourse, I could simply switch it on and off every time I read and wrote as I would some electronic tool. Furthermore, I expected my readings and writings to come out in their correct forms whenever I switched the proper discourse on. I still regarded the discourse of home as natural and the discourse of school alien, but I never had doubted before that I could acquire both and switch them on and off according to the occasion.

When my experience in writing conflicted with what I thought should happen when I used each discourse, I rejected my experience because it contradicted what my parents and teachers had taught me. I shied away from writing to avoid what I assumed I should not experience. But trying to avoid what should not happen did not keep it from recurring whenever I had to write. Eventually my confusion and frustration over these recurring experiences compelled me to search for an explanation: how and why had I failed to learn what my parents and teachers had worked so hard to teach me?

I now think of the internal scene for my reading and writing about *The Revolutionary Family* as a heated discussion between myself, the voices of home, and those of school. The review on the back of the book, the sample student papers I came across in my composition classes, my philosophy teacher—these I heard as voices of one group. My parents and my home readings were the voices of an opposing group. But the conversation between these opposing voices in the internal scene of my writing was not as polite and respectful as the parlor scene Kenneth Burke had portrayed (see epigraph). Rather, these voices struggled to dominate the discussion, constantly incorporating, dismissing, or suppressing the arguments of each other, like the battles between the hegemonic and counter-hegemonic forces described in Raymond Williams' *Marxism and Literature* (108–14).

When I read *The Revolutionary Family* and wrote the first version of my report, I began with a quotation from the review. The voices of both home and school answered, clamoring to be heard. I tried to listen to one group and turn a deaf ear to the other. Both persisted. I negotiated my way through these conflicting voices, now agreeing with one, now agreeing with the other. I formed a reading out of my interaction with both. Yet I was afraid to have done so because both home and school had implied that I should speak in unison with only one of these groups and stand away from the discussion rather than participate in it.

social reader response

My teachers and parents had persistently called my attention to the intensity of the discussion taking place on the external social scene. The story of my grandfather's failure and my father's success had from my early childhood made me aware of the conflict between Western and traditional Chinese cultures. My political education at school added another dimension to the conflict: the war of Marxist-Maoism against them both. Yet when my parents and teachers called my attention to the conflict, they stressed the anxiety of having to live through China's transformation from a semi-feudal, semi-capitalist, and semi-colonial society to a socialist one. Acquiring the discourse of the dominant group was, to them, a means of seeking alliance with that group and thus of surviving the whirlpool of cultural currents around them. As a result, they modeled their pedagogical practices on this utilitarian view of language. Being the eager student, I adopted this view of language as a tool for survival. It came to dominate my understanding of the discussion on the social and historical scene and to restrict my ability to participate in that discussion.

To begin with, the metaphor of language as a tool for survival led me to be passive in my use of discourse, to be a bystander in the discussion. In Burke's "parlor," everyone is involved in the discussion. As it goes on through history, what we call "communal discourses"—arguments specific to particular political, social, economic, ethnic, sexual, and family groups—form, re-form and transform. To use a discourse in such a scene is to participate in the argument and to contribute to the formation of the discourse. But when I was growing up, I could not take on the burden of such an active role in the discussion. For both home and school presented the existent conventions of the discourse each taught me as absolute laws for my action. They turned verbal action into a tool, a set of conventions produced and shaped prior to and outside of my own verbal acts. Because I saw language as a tool, I separated the process of producing the tool from the process of using it. The tool was made by someone else and was then acquired and used by me. How the others made it before I acquired it determined and guaranteed what it produced when I used it. I imagined that the more experienced and powerful members of the community were the ones responsible for making the tool. They were the ones who participated in the discussion and fought with opponents. When I used what they made, their labor and accomplishments would ensure the quality of my reading and writing. By using it, I could survive the heated discussion. When my immediate experience in writing the book report suggested that knowing the conventions of school did not guarantee the form and content of my report, when it suggested that I had to write the report with the work and responsibility I had assigned to those who wrote book reviews in the Publishing Bureau, I thought I had lost the tool I had earlier acquired.

Another reason I could not take up an active role in the argument was that my parents and teachers contrived to provide a scene free of conflict for practicing my various languages. It was as if their experience had made them aware of the conflict between their discourse and other discourses and of the struggle involved in reproducing the conventions of any discourse on a scene where more than one discourse exists. They seemed convinced that such conflict and struggle would overwhelm someone still learning the discourse. Home and school each contrived a purified space where only one discourse was spoken and heard. In their choice of textbooks, in the way they spoke, and in the way they required me to speak, each jealously silenced any voice that threatened to break the unison of the scene. The homogeneity of home and of school implied that only one discourse could and should be relevant in each place. It led me to believe I should leave behind, turn a deaf ear to, or forget the discourse of the other when I crossed the boundary dividing them. I expected myself to set down one discourse whenever I took up another just as I would take off or put on a particular set of clothes for school or home.

Despite my parents' and teachers' attempts to keep home and school discrete, the internal conflict between the two discourses continued whenever I read or wrote. Although I tried to suppress the voice of one discourse in the name of the other, having to speak aloud in the voice I had just silenced each time I crossed the boundary kept both voices active in my mind. Every "I think . . ." from the voice of home or school brought forth a "However . . ." or a "But . . ." from the voice of the opponents. To identify with the voice of home or school, I had to negotiate through the conflicting voices of both by restating, taking back, qualifying my thoughts. I was unconsciously doing so when I did my book report. But I could not use the interaction comfortably and constructively. Both my parents and my teachers had implied that my job was to prevent that interaction from happening. My sense of having failed to accomplish what they had taught silenced me.

To use the interaction between the discourses of home and school constructively, I would have to have seen reading or writing as a process in which I worked my way towards a stance through a dialectical process of identification and division. To identify with an ally, I would have to have grasped the distance between where he or she stood and where I was positioning myself. In taking a stance against an opponent, I would have to have grasped where my stance identified with the stance of my allies. Teetering along the "wavering line of pressure and counter-pressure" from both allies and opponents, I might have worked my way towards a stance of my own (Burke, *A Rhetoric of Motives* 23). Moreover, I would have to have understood that the voices in my mind, like the participants in the parlor scene, were in constant flux. As I came into contact with new and different groups of people or read different books, voices entered and left. Each time I read or wrote, the stance I negotiated out of these voices would always be at some distance from the stances I worked out in my previous and my later readings or writings.

I could not conceive such a form of action for myself because I saw reading and writing as an expression of an established stance. In delineating the conventions of a discourse, my parents and teachers had synthesized the stance they saw as typical for a representative member of the community. Burke calls this the stance of a "god" or the "prototype"; Williams calls it the "official" or "possible" stance of the community. Through the metaphor of the survival tool, my parents and teachers had led me to assume I could automatically reproduce the official stance of the discourse I used. Therefore, when I did my book report on *The Revolutionary Family*, I expected my knowledge of the official stance set by the book review to ensure the actual stance of my report. As it happened, I began by trying to take the official stance of the review. Other voices interrupted. I answered back. In the process, I worked out a stance approximate but not identical to the official stance I began with. Yet the experience of having to labor to realize my knowledge of the official stance or to prevent myself from wandering away from it frustrated and confused me. For even though I had been actually reading and writing in a Burkean scene, I was afraid to participate actively in the discussion. I assumed it was my role to survive by staying out of it.

Not long ago, my daughter told me that it bothered her to hear her friend "talk wrong." Having come to the United States from China with little English, my daughter has become sensitive to the way English, as spoken by her teachers, operates. As a result, she has amazed her teachers with her success in picking up the language and in adapting to life at school. Her concern to speak the English taught in the classroom "correctly" makes her uncomfortable when she hears people using "ain't" or double negatives, which her teacher considers "improper." I see in her the me that had eagerly learned and used the discourse of the Working class at school. Yet while I was torn between the two conflicting worlds of school and home, she moves with seeming ease from the conversation she hears over the dinner table to her teacher's words in the classroom. My husband and I are proud of the good work she does at school. We are glad she is spared the kinds of conflicts between home and school I experienced at her age. Yet as we watch her becoming more and more fluent in the language of the classroom, we wonder if, by enabling her to "survive" school, her very fluency will silence her when the scene of her reading and writing expands beyond that of the composition classroom.

For when I listen to my daughter, to students, and to some composition teachers talking about the teaching and learning of writing, I am often alarmed by the degree to which the metaphor of a survival tool dominates their understanding of language as it once dominated my own. I am especially concerned with the way some composition classes focus on turning the classroom into a monological scene for the students' reading and writing. Most of our students live in a world similar to my daughter's, somewhere between the purified world of the classroom and the complex world of my adolescence. When composition classes encourage these students to ignore those voices that seem irrelevant to the purified world of the classroom, most students are often able to do so without much struggle. Some of them are so adept at doing it that the whole process has for them become automatic.

However, beyond the classroom and beyond the limited range of these students' immediate lives lies a much more complex and dynamic social and historical scene. To help these students become actors in such a scene, perhaps we need to call their attention to voices that may seem irrelevant to the discourse we teach rather than encourage them to shut them out. For example, we might intentionally complicate the classroom scene by bringing into it discourses that stand at varying distances from the one we teach. We might encourage students to explore ways of practicing the

Ideas for Teaching

conventions of the discourse they are learning by negotiating through these conflicting voices. We could also encourage them to see themselves as responsible for forming or transforming as well as preserving the discourse they are learning.

As I think about what we might do to complicate the external and internal scenes of our students' writing, I hear my parents and teachers saying: "Not now. Keep them from the wrangle of the marketplace until they have acquired the discourse and are skilled at using it." And I answer: "Don't teach them to 'survive' the whirlpool of crosscurrents by avoiding it. Use the classroom to moderate the currents. Moderate the currents, but teach them from the beginning to struggle." When I think of the ways in which the teaching of reading and writing as classroom activities can frustrate the development of students, I am almost grateful for the overwhelming complexity of the circumstances in which I grew up. For it was this complexity that kept me from losing sight of the effort and choice involved in reading or writing with and through a discourse.

WORKS CITED

Burke, Kenneth. *The Philosophy of Literary Form: Studies in Symbolic Action.* 2nd ed. Baton Rouge: Louisiana State UP, 1967.

————. *A Rhetoric of Motives.* Berkeley: U of California P, 1969.

Freire, Paulo. *Pedagogy of the Oppressed.* Trans. M. B. Ramos. New York: Continuum, 1970.

Williams, Raymond. *Marxism and Literature.* New York: Oxford UP, 1977.

Chapter 8

Initiating ESL Students into the Academic Discourse Community: How Far Should We Go?

Ruth Spack

Within the last decade, numerous approaches to the teaching of writing in programs for ESL college students have been tried, and much discussion has focused on the most appropriate approach to adopt (see the *TESOL Quarterly* Forum contributions of Horowitz, 1986c/Liebman-Kleine, 1986/Horowitz, 1986b/Hamp-Lyons, 1986/Horowitz, 1986a; Reid, 1984b/Spack, 1985a/Reid, 1985; Reid, 1984a/Zamel, 1984). Though a misleading process/product, or process-centered/content-based, dichotomy has characterized the debate, ESL writing researchers and teachers have generally agreed that the goal of college-level second language (L2) writing programs is to prepare students to become better academic writers.

However, the achievement of this goal is complicated by at least two major factors. One is that we have not yet satisfactorily determined, despite numerous surveys, what academic writing is, an issue that this article examines. The other is that there is most often a large gap between what students bring to the academic community and what the academic community expects of them.

In the case of native English-speaking basic writers—academically disadvantaged students who have achieved only very modest standards of high school literacy—Bizzell (1982) points out that the students' social situation and previous training may hamper their ability to succeed in the academy. In other words, their problems with academic writing may not lie in a lack of innate ability but rather in the social and cultural factors that influence composing. The gap is even wider for ESL students who can be classified as basic writers, for it includes L2 linguistic and cultural differences. Even for ESL students who are highly literate in their native language, a similar gap exists: The students' lack of L2 linguistic and cultural knowledge can stand in the way of academic success.

It is clearly the obligation of the ESL college-level writing teacher, whether teaching basic writers or highly literate students, to find a way to narrow the gap. As Bizzell (1982) suggests, we must help students master the language and culture of the university; the role of the university writing teacher is to initiate students into the academic discourse community. The issue of concern in this article is the means through which we should fulfill our role.

My concern stems from what I perceive to be a disturbing trend in L2 writing instruction, a trend that has been influenced both by the Writing Across the Curriculum (WAC) movement in first language (L1) writing instruction and the English for specific purposes (ESP) movement in L2 instruction. This trend toward having teachers of English, including teachers of freshman composition, teach students to write in disciplines other than English may lead many in the composition field to assign papers that they are ill-equipped to handle. The purpose of this article is to remind teachers of English that we are justified in teaching general academic writing and to argue that we should leave the teaching of writing in the disciplines to the teachers of those disciplines.

DEFINING ACADEMIC WRITING

Determining what academic writing is and what ESL students need to know in order to produce it has not been an easy task for researchers and teachers. In fact, a number of L2 writing instructors, including this author, have tried several different approaches, faithfully following textbook guidelines. Early ESL writing textbooks were largely workbooks that fostered controlled composition and that did not satisfy students' need to learn how to produce their own body of work for their other university courses. Later efforts to have students create their own academic texts often resulted in absurd assignments that students could not logically fulfill. For example, one textbook (Bander, 1978) suggested that science students begin with a topic sentence such as "The importance of oxygen to mankind cannot be overstated" and that humanities students show how "the revolutions that took place in France, the United States, and Russia resulted in major changes in those countries" (p. 30). (This, according to the book, could be done in one paragraph!)

ESL writing textbooks began at this time to be modeled after textbooks for native speakers (NSs) of English, which emphasized the rhetorical patterns researchers claimed were commonly found in American academic prose. These books ask students to write whole pieces of discourse by imitating models (which are, paradoxically, often excerpts rather than whole pieces of discourse) and to describe, compare, classify, define, and determine the cause and effect of everything from religion to Chinese food.

Though still popular with many teachers, this approach has been called into question in both L2 and L1 fields because "starting from given patterns and asking students to find topics and produce essays to fit them is a reversal of the normal writing process" (Shih, 1986, p. 622) and turns attention away from the meaningful act of communication in a social context (Connors, 1981). Furthermore, a recent (though admittedly limited) survey of actual writing assignment handouts given to university students by teachers in courses other than writing (Horowitz, 1986d) reveals that these assignments do not ask students to start from patterns and produce essays to fit them. If further research bears this out, it will be safe to say that this pattern-centered approach is not suitable for a program that emphasizes academic writing.

In response to some of this criticism, and again following the model of NS writing textbooks, the ESL field has begun to publish textbooks that emphasize the cognitive process of writing. This approach is based on the research of composition specialists who have drawn on the theories of cognitive psychologists and psycholinguists to explore the mental procedures writers use to communicate ideas (see, for example, the L1 research of Flower & Hayes, 1977, 1981; the L2 research of Lay, 1982; Raimes, 1985; Zamel, 1982, 1983). The thrust of these ESL textbooks (see, for example, Hartfiel, Hughey, Warmuth, & Jacobs, 1985) is to teach students systematic thinking and writing skills so that they can use their own composing strategies effectively to explore ideas. Emphasis is on self-generated topics, with thematically organized readings usually, but not always, acting as springboards for ideas.

Yet the writing produced in such courses has not been universally accepted as academic, even though it takes place in the academy. Much of the writing is based solely on students' personal experiences or interests. Although this provides students with a drive to learn to write by focusing on what really matters to them, it has its drawbacks. As Bazerman (1980) points out, in emphasizing the writer's independent self, teachers ignore the fact that writing is "not contained entirely in the envelope of experience, native thought, and personal motivation to communicate" (p. 657).

I would argue that since the personal essay as a genre informs the discipline known as English literature, this kind of writing can be considered academic. It also serves as a vehicle for reflection and self-expression for specialists in many other fields, including science (e.g., Cole, 1985), medicine (e.g., Thomas, 1983), and engineering (e.g., Petroski, 1986). And the personal essay plays a role in students' future academic success: When they apply for transfer, for scholarships, or to graduate school, they are asked to write on personal topics in order to sell themselves and presumably to display their writing skills. Still, there is no evidence that the skills learned in this kind of writing adequately provide students with the tools they need to produce the academic writing required in other courses.

Although the cognitive process approach is admired because of its emphasis on writing as a learning process and its development of useful, teachable skills, MacDonald (1987) reveals its limitations: Its L1 research (e.g., Flower & Hayes, 1977, 1981) is based on only one kind of writing, which MacDonald describes as "composing with an undefined problem, with the writer forced to create a problem for him- or herself . . . a kind of composing traditionally associated with English departments—whether interpretations of literature or personal essays" (p. 328). Other kinds of writing, such as scientific or social science writing, which have different demands and constraints, are ignored. Raimes's (1985) L2 research, based on students' personal experience essays, has been challenged on similar grounds (Horowitz, 1986c).

A further criticism of a process approach that promotes student-generated meaning and form is that it does not acknowledge that "most writing for academic classes is in response to a specific assignment or prompt" (Johns, 1986, p. 253). Shaughnessy (1977), Bizzell (1982), and Rose (1985) therefore claim that it does not prepare students to grapple with the challenges of academic life but rather postpones their confrontation with the "complex linguistic and rhetorical expectations of the academy" (Rose, 1985, p. 357).

Bizzell (1982) argues that to succeed in their university studies, students need critical training and recommends a "social-contextual approach" that "demystifies the institutional structure of knowledge" (p. 196). Researchers and textbook writers, Bizzell contends, need to focus on the conventions of academic discourse, emphasizing the relationship between discourse, community, and knowledge. In finding ways to "demystify" academic discourse, ESP researchers have been at the forefront of genre analysis, identifying and analyzing "key genres, such as Case Studies in Business, Legislative documents in Law, lab reports in Science, disease-descriptions in Medicine and Agriculture" (Swales, 1986, p. 18).

L1 and L2 researchers have conducted a number of surveys to determine what writing tasks are actually assigned across academic disciplines. Horowitz (1986d) has found fault with some of the studies (Bridgeman & Carlson, 1984; Johns, 1981, 1985; Kroll, 1979; Ostler, 1980), which, he points out, "beg the question" of what the tasks are: "Instead of trying to discover and classify university writing tasks—a logical prior endeavor—they began with a set of preconceived classifications, forcing on the respondents the particular scheme used in each survey" (p. 448). The surveys of Behrens (1980), Rose (1983), and Horowitz (1986d) take a more ethnographic view, creating classifications after examining the data. Nevertheless, the Horowitz survey has been criticized on the grounds that it is a limited study (only 38 of the 750 faculty members who were contacted responded; only 54 writing assignments were collected) (Raimes, 1987) and that it ignores the context in which the tasks were assigned (Zamel, 1987).

Until we collect more assignments, interview the teachers to learn the purposes of the assigned tasks, observe the courses in which the tasks are assigned, examine the resulting student essays, and analyze the teacher responses to and evaluations of these papers, we cannot truly understand the nature of the academic writing students are asked to produce. Furthermore, we should not forget that it is important to take a critical look at these assignments. Having seen numerous examples of writing assignments for other courses, I suspect that one reason so few faculty members responded to Horowitz is that they may have been reluctant to show English teachers their own poorly written or poorly designed texts. The fact that papers assigned by teachers in other disciplines are different from those assigned in freshman composition classes—the finding of several surveys—does not necessarily mean that the former are superior.

Still, it is impossible and perhaps foolish to ignore the implications of the surveys: The writing students do in courses other than English composition is rarely dependent solely on their own general knowledge base. Rather, "students will be confronted with either academic or professional writing tasks that surface in relation to *texts* of various kinds (literary, historical, psychological, legal, managerial) or *data* (computer, laboratory-testing, statistical, chemical)" (Scheiber, 1987, p. 15). These assignments are viewed as a means of promoting understanding of the content presented in subject-matter courses (Shih, 1986). Furthermore, writing academic papers involves the recursive processes of drafting, revising, and editing (Shih, 1986). Therefore, writing teachers can comfortably design process-centered courses around text-based or data-based tasks in which written language acts as a medium for learning something else. What that something else should be is the focus of this article.

TEACHING WRITING IN THE DISCIPLINES

Until fairly recently, students wrote the various kinds of papers listed above only in classes other than English, with the obvious exception of essays related to literary texts. But there has been a growing tendency in both

L1 and L2 composition instruction to add the responsibility of teaching writing in other disciplines to the other responsibilities of English department writing programs. It is beyond the scope of this article to examine all the reasons for this trend; only two of the influences are touched on in this section: Writing Across the Curriculum, an L1 movement, and English for specific or academic purposes, an L2 movement.

Writing Across the Curriculum

For a number of years, faculty have complained about weaknesses in students' ability to produce papers of high quality in subject-area courses—weaknesses attributed in part to a loosening of standards in the academy and in part to the change in the student population in the 1960s and 1970s from a somewhat elitist, homogeneous group to an academically underprepared group representing diverse cultures and educational backgrounds. Partly in response to this concern, a movement known as Writing Across the Curriculum, modeled on a British program, took hold in colleges and universities in the 1970s, its purpose to restore writing to its central place in the curricula of institutions of learning (Maimon, 1984). Though there have been several WAC models, they have shared the goal of encouraging instructors in all disciplines to make writing an inevitable part of the teaching and learning process in their courses. In faculty development seminars teachers of English have collaborated with subject-area instructors so that the latter can learn more about writing.

But WAC programs have not always met with success (Russell, 1987). Obstacles such as "increased teaching loads, large classes, administrative responsibilities, lack of collegial support, pressures to research, publish, write grants and the like" (Fulwiler, 1984, p. 119) on teachers in other disciplines have caused some to refuse the extra burden of introducing the writing process into their courses. Furthermore, the lack of understanding on the part of English department faculty of the processes involved in writing essays that are neither personal nor interpretive has led to counterproductive faculty workshops (Applebee, 1986; Fulwiler, 1984). Collaborative faculty workshops have only recently begun to focus on the processes and strategies involved in scientific, technical, and social science writing, perhaps because researchers have only recently begun studying the writing processes of scientists (see Gilbert & Mulkay, 1984; Myers, 1985; and, for a discussion of these and other studies, Swales, 1987), engineers (Selzer, 1983), and social scientists (Becker, 1986).

Faculty development seminars now bring teachers of English together with subject-area instructors not only so that the latter can learn more about writing, but also so that the former can learn more about the subject area (Dick & Esch, 1985). In writing and planning linked courses with colleagues, the English composition teacher's general goal of strengthening students' writing skills is becoming the more specific goal of training students to handle the tasks of the other disciplines. This goal had led today to the creation of programs such as that at Beaver College (described in Maimon, Belcher, Hearn, Nodine, & O'Connor, 1981), which are built on the foundation of a cross-disciplinary, required freshman composition course. L1 textbooks designed for use in such English composition courses include instructions for writing in other disciplines—case studies in the social sciences, laboratory reports in the natural sciences, and so on (e.g., Bazerman, 1985; Maimon et al., 1981).

English for Specific Purposes/English for Academic Purposes

At approximately the same time the WAC movement was gaining prominence in L1 writing instruction, the ESP movement had taken hold in the field of L2 acquisition. ESP programs arose as a "practical alternative to the 'general' orientation of language teaching: cultural and literary emphases, education for life" (Maher, 1986, p. 113). Taking as its focus science and technology—the fields with the heaviest concentrations of international students—ESP creates courses, taught by English language teachers, whose aim is generally to fulfill the practical needs of L2 learners and specifically to produce technicians and technocrats who are proficient in English (Coffey, 1984). Collaboration, or team teaching, between the language instructor and the instructor in the other discipline is the preferred method of instruction but is possible "only where there is a high level of goodwill and mutual interest and understanding" (Coffey, 1984, p. 9).

When the students' needs consist of "the quick and economical use of the English language to pursue a course of academic study" (Coffey, 1984, p. 3), English for academic purposes (EAP) is offered. The incorporation of writing into the EAP curriculum, however, necessitates collaboration with the instructor in the other discipline, following what Shih (1986) calls the "adjunct model" of many university composition programs for native students. But the development of such programs for ESL students has been slow, and Shih recommends that we learn from existing programs:

> The potential contributions and possible limitations of the adjunct-course approach for ESL programs in general, and for preparing ESL students to handle university writing tasks in particular, remain to be evaluated. What is needed, minimally, is cooperation from subject-area instructors and ESL faculty willingness to step into subject-area classrooms and keep up with class events. For ESL instructors seeking to set up adjunct courses, the experiences of composition adjunct programs already in place for native students are a rich source of information. (p. 640)

The next section of this article examines studies of these NS programs and discusses the implications of the researchers' findings.

STUDIES OF WRITING PROGRAMS
IN THE DISCIPLINES AND THEIR IMPLICATIONS

Several L1 programs have been instituted to introduce students to the methods of inquiry in various disciplines. In typical programs, English teachers have collaborated with teachers in other disciplines, such as biology (Wilkinson, 1985), psychology (Faigley & Hansen, 1985), and sociology (Faigley & Hansen, 1985), linking the compositions to subject matter in the other course. Investigations of these programs reveal some obvious advantages: Students learn new forms of writing which as professionals they might need; they have more time to write, since there is less reading due to the fact that one subject matter is employed for two courses; and their discussions of student papers are more informative, since knowledge is shared among class members.

However, the disadvantages of such a program are equally, if not more, significant, as Wilkinson (1985) and others show, and should be of great concern to the English teacher. First of all, it is difficult for a writing course to have a carefully planned pedagogical or rhetorical rationale when it is dependent on another content course; furthermore, the timing of assignments is not always optimal. Second, the program can raise false expectations among the faculty as well as among the students. English faculty, even when they collaborate with content teachers, find they have little basis for dealing with the content. They therefore find themselves in the uncomfortable position of being less knowledgeable than their students. Students likewise can resent finding themselves in a situation in which their instructor cannot fully explain or answer questions about the subject matter. Faigley and Hansen (1985) observed collaborative courses in which completely different criteria for evaluation were applied to students' papers by the two teachers because the English teacher did not recognize when a student failed to demonstrate adequate knowledge of a discipline or showed a good grasp of new knowledge.

The same phenomenon can hold true in L2 writing instruction. Pearson (1983) finds that "the instructor cannot always conveniently divorce the teaching of form from the understanding of content" (pp. 396–397). This drawback is often mentioned only in passing in articles recommending that English teachers use technical and scientific materials they are not familiar with (see Hill, Soppelsa, & West, 1982). But the lack of control over content on the part of English teachers who teach in the other disciplines is a serious problem. This concern is reflected in a state-of-the-art article on English for medical purposes (EMP):

A sense of insecurity and uncertainty can sometimes be observed amongst EMP teachers regarding their effective roles as lay persons teaching 'medical English' among medical professionals. . . .

Occasionally, the specialist informant, who is co-opted on to a teaching programme, harbours suspicions about the language teacher's motives. Consider the view of the *DUODECIM* [Finnish Medical Society] team of doctors: 'We believe that it is essential to have teachers *entirely at home* in medicine and English and who have some experience in writing and lecturing' (Collan, 1974:629), and 'Too few teachers combine enough experience in the use of the English language in general and knowledge of the specialty in particular' (Lock et al., 1975:cover). 'Is the teacher trying to teach my subject?' 'What if s/he gets the medical bits wrong and misleads the learners?' (Maher, 1986, p. 138)

In spite of these drawbacks, some investigators claim that it is possible for an English teacher to conduct a course that focuses on writing in a particular discipline if the teacher learns how a discipline creates and transmits knowledge. This is accomplished by examining the kinds of issues a discipline considers important, why certain methods of inquiry and not others are sanctioned, how the conventions of a discipline shape text in that discipline, how individual writers represent themselves in a text, how texts are read and disseminated within the discipline, and how one text influences subsequent texts (Faigley & Hansen, 1985; Herrington, 1985).

This exploration, of course, would involve a great deal of commitment, as anyone who has studied a particular field or discipline knows. Specialists in second language instruction, for example, have spent years acquiring the knowledge and understanding that enable them to recognize the issues that dominate discussion in the field (e.g., communicative competence), the methods of inquiry employed (e.g., ethnography), the structure of manuscripts focusing on those issues (e.g., the *TESOL Quarterly* format), the names associated with various issues (e.g., Krashen/Input Hypothesis; Carrell/schema theory; Zamel/writing process), and the impact a given article might have on thinking and research in the field.

It seems that only the rare individual teacher can learn another discipline, for each discipline offers a different system for examining experience, a different angle for looking at subject matter, a different kind of thinking (Maimon et al., 1981). Furthermore, whereas the transmission of a discipline within content courses primarily requires that students comprehend, recall, and display information in examinations, writing in the disciplines

requires a complete, active, struggling engagement with the facts and principles of a discipline, an encounter with the discipline's texts and the incorporation of them into one's own work, the framing of one's knowledge within the myriad conventions that help define a discipline, the persuading of other investigators that one's knowledge is legitimate. (Rose, 1985, p. 359)

The teaching of writing in a discipline, then, involves even more specialized knowledge and skills than does the teaching of the subject matter itself.

The difficulty of teaching writing in another discipline is compounded when we realize that within each discipline, such as the social sciences, there are subdisciplines, each with its own set of conventions. Reflection on personal events, for example, is considered legitimate evidence in sociology and anthropology, but not in behavioral psychology (Rose, 1983). Even within the subdisciplines, such as anthropology, there are other subdisciplines with their own sets of conventions. The articles of physical anthropologists, for example, resemble those of natural scientists, whereas those of cultural anthropologists sometimes resemble those of literary scholars (Faigley & Hansen, 1985).

To further complicate matters, no discipline is static. In virtually all academic disciplines there is controversy concerning the validity of approaches, controversy that nonspecialists are usually unaware of until it is covered in the popular media (see, for example, Silk, 1987, for a discussion of the recent debate between political and anthropological historians). In addition, the principles of reasoning in a discipline may change over time, even in science, which is affected by the emergence of new mathematical techniques, new items of apparatus, and even new philosophical precepts (Yearley, 1981). Formal scientific papers, then, though often considered final statements of facts, are primarily contributions to scientific debate (Yearley, 1981).

And although we may be able to read and study texts from other disciplines, analyze genres, and thereby learn writing styles and conventions to teach our students, we should also be aware of any critical stance in relation to the texts. For example, Woodford (1967), editor of a scholarly scientific research journal, has mocked the state of scientific writing:

> The articles in our journals—even the journals with the highest standards—are, by and large, poorly written. Some of the worst are produced by the kind of author who consciously pretends to a "scientific scholarly" style. He takes what should be lively, inspiring, and beautiful and, in an attempt to make it seem dignified, chokes it to death with stately abstract nouns; next, in the name of scientific impartiality, he fits it with a complete set of passive constructions to drain away any remaining life's blood or excitement; then he embalms the remains in molasses of polysyllable, wraps the corpse in an impenetrable veil of vogue words, and buries the stiff old mummy with much pomp and circumstance in the most distinguished journal that will take it. (p. 743)

Woodford argues that this kind of writing is damaging to the students who read it. In his experience as a teacher of graduate students of science, he has found that it adversely affects students' ability to read, write, and think well. (English teachers, who traditionally have seen themselves as purveyors of effective prose, might do well to wonder why they should present such poorly written texts to their students.)

Even studying a finished product—whether well written or not—cannot prepare English teachers to teach students how writers in other disciplines write. A written product such as a scientific report is merely a representation of a research process, which is finally summarized for peers; it is not a representation of a writing process. To teach writing, writing teachers should teach the writing process; and to teach the writing process, they should know how to write. But English teachers are not necessarily equipped to write in other disciplines. Testimony to this truth appears in the ESP literature:

> In the author's experience, every attempt to write a passage, however satisfactory it seemed on pedagogic grounds, was promptly vetoed by the Project's scientific adviser because a technical solecism of some kind had been committed. The ESP writer, however experienced, simply does not know when a mistake of this kind is being committed. (Coffey, 1984, p. 8)

To learn to write in any discipline, students must become immersed in the subject matter; this is accomplished through reading, lectures, seminars, and so on. They learn by participating in the field, by doing, by sharing, and by talking about it with those who know more. They can also learn by observing the process through which professional academic writers produce texts or, if that is not possible, by studying that process in the type of program recommended by Swales (1987) for teaching the research paper to nonnative-speaking graduate students. They will learn most efficiently from teachers who have a solid grounding in the subject matter and who have been through the process themselves.

I do not deny that programs that instruct students to write in other disciplines can work. But a review of the L1 literature (e.g., Herrington, 1985) and the L2 literature (e.g., Swales, 1987) on successful programs reveals that the teachers are themselves immersed in the discipline. For example, Herrington's (1985) study is an observation of senior-level engineering courses taught by engineering faculty. And Swales's list of publications reveals a background in scientific discourse dating back at least to 1970.

ACADEMIC WRITING TASKS
FOR ESL COLLEGE STUDENTS

English teachers cannot and should not be held responsible for teaching writing in the disciplines. The best we can accomplish is to create programs in which students can learn general inquiry strategies, rhetorical principles, and tasks that can transfer to other course work. This has been our traditional role, and it is a worthy one. The materials we use should be those we can fully understand. The writing projects we assign and evaluate should be those we are capable of doing ourselves. The remainder of this article is devoted to practical suggestions for incorporating academic writing into an English composition course designed for ESL undergraduates, without the need for linking the course with another subject-area program.

Working With Data

According to a number of surveys discussed earlier, students are often asked to work with data, either as observers or as participants. These experiences can become a part of the writing class instruction. In the L1 literature, Hillocks (1984, 1986) recommends that we engage students in a process of examining various kinds of data—either objects such as shells or photographs, or sets of information such as arguments. Students can be led to formulate and test explanatory generalizations, observe and report significant details, and generate criteria for contrasting similar phenomena.

Such programs have been shown to work in L2 writing classes. Zamel (1984) has reported on a class project in which students read published interviews with workers, then conducted and wrote up their own interviews, and later compared the data. Likewise, students have become amateur ethnographers, observing and evaluating the language in their communities (Zamel, 1986). Such tasks can produce writing that is "rich and original" (Zamel, 1984, p. 202).

But since composing in a second language is an enormously complex undertaking and because "it seems that this complexity has more to do with the constraints imposed by the writing task itself than with linguistic difficulties" (Zamel, 1984, p. 198), students need consistent teacher input in the observation and interviewing processes. They also need regular in-class collaborative workshops so that they can comment on and raise questions about each other's writing.

Writing From Other Texts

Though training in observation and interviewing can undoubtedly be useful in students' academic careers, perhaps the most important skill English teachers can engage students in is the complex ability to write from other texts, a major part of their academic writing experience. Students' "intellectual socialization may be accomplished not only by interacting with people, but also by encountering the writing of others" (Bizzell, 1986, p. 65). As Bazerman (1980) says, "we must cultivate various techniques of absorbing, reformulating, commenting on, and using reading" if we want to prepare our students to "enter the written exchanges of their chosen disciplines and the various discussions of personal and public interest" (p. 658).

L1 and L2 research shows the interdependent relationship between reading and writing processes (see Krashen, 1984; Petrosky, 1982; Salvatori, 1983; Spack, 1985b): Both processes focus on the making of meaning; they share the "act of constructing meaning from words, text, prior knowledge, and feelings" (Petrosky, 1982, p. 22). To become better writers, then, students need to become better readers.

Intelligent response to reading, Bazerman (1980) reminds us, begins with an accurate understanding of a text—not just the facts and ideas, but also what the author is trying to achieve. But this is not easy for second language readers. Even advanced, highly literate students struggle in a way that their NS counterparts do not. First, there are linguistic difficulties. Overcoming them is not simply a matter of learning specialists' language because often the more general use of language causes the greatest problem, as one of my freshman students pointed out in a working journal (mechanical errors corrected):

> During the last few days I had to read several (about 150) pages for my psychology exam. I had great difficulties in understanding the material. There are dozens, maybe hundreds of words I'm unfamiliar with. It's not the actual scientific terms (such as "repression," "schizophrenia," "psychosis," or "neurosis") that make the reading so hard, but it's descriptive and elaborating terms (e.g., "to coax," "gnawing discomfort," "remnants," "fervent appeal"), instead. To understand the text fully, it often takes more than an hour to read just ten pages. And even then I still didn't look up all the words I didn't understand. It is a very frustrating thing to read these kinds of texts, because one feels incredibly ignorant and stupid.

And there are cultural barriers, best expressed by another student (mechanical errors corrected):

> My last essay was about bowing in the Japanese culture. After discussing my first draft with my classmates, Ramy and Luis, I felt I could get about half of the message across. But I found it interesting that both of them were stuck at the part where I mentioned Buddhism. I was interested because I saw a similarity with my own experience; i.e., I am always stuck when any essay mentions Christianity. I am not Buddhist or Shintoist, but Japanese culture is so much influenced by those religions that it is almost impossible to talk about Japan without them. The problem is that many concepts associated with these religions are nonexistent in Christian-influenced society (Western society). I do not know how to explain something which does not exist in the English-speaking world in the English language. And I do not know how to understand something that never existed in my frame of reference. To me it is almost as hard as solving complicated math problems.

Given the complexity of reading in a second language, it is necessary for L2 writing teachers to become familiar with theories and techniques of L2 reading instruction (see, for example, Dubin, Eskey, & Grabe, 1986) if they are to guide their students to become better academic writers.

Some of those techniques are already part of L1 and L2 composition instruction. Marginal notes, note taking, working journals (see Spack & Sadow, 1983), and response statements (Petrosky, 1982) can train students to discover and record their own reactions to a text. Exercises that focus on the processes of summarizing, paraphrasing, and quoting can encourage precise understanding of an author's style and purpose. But these techniques should not be ends unto themselves. Rather, paraphrase, summary, and quotation become part of students' texts as they incorporate key ideas and relevant facts from their reading into their own writing. In this way, students can develop informed views on the issues they pursue, building on what has already been written.

Readings can be content based, grouped by themes, and can be expressive or literary as well as informative. They can be drawn from a specific field, if the area of study is one that the instructor is well versed in, or from several fields, if the articles are written by professionals for a general audience. Although these articles may not be considered academic since they were not written for academic/professional audiences, they can give students an understanding of how writers from different disciplines approach the same subject. Most important, they allow instructors to avoid placing themselves in the awkward position of presenting materials they do not fully understand. But whatever readings are chosen, teachers of ESL students should always consider the background knowledge that readers are expected to bring to written texts (e.g., knowledge of American history, recognition of the publications in which the texts originally appeared, discernment of organizational formats, etc.) and help their students establish a frame of reference that will facilitate comprehension (Dubin et al., 1986).

Writing tasks should build upon knowledge students already possess but should also be designed to allow new learning to occur. Students can initially write about their own experiences or views, then read, discuss, and respond informally in writing to the assigned readings. They can next be assigned the task of evaluating, testing the truth of, or otherwise illuminating the texts. Students can be directed to compare the ideas discussed in one or more of the readings with their own experiences, or they can be asked to agree or disagree or take a mixed position toward one of the readings. Making specific references to the readings, they can develop ideas by giving examples, citing experiences, and/or providing evidence from other texts on the subject.

By sequencing assignments, the teacher can move the students away from a primarily personal approach to a more critical approach to the readings. The goal should not be regurgitation of others' ideas, but the development of an independent viewpoint. Students can develop the ability to acknowledge the points of view of others but still "question and critique established authorities in a field of knowledge" (Coles & Wall, 1987, p. 299). This is a particularly important skill for foreign students, many of whom are "products of educational systems where unquestioning acceptance of books and teachers as the ultimate authority is the norm" (Horowitz & McKee, 1984, p. 5).

Yet other assignments, such as research projects utilizing the library and perhaps data from interviews and/or observations, can ask students to evaluate and synthesize material from a number of sources in order to establish a perspective on a given subject or area of controversy. Like the assignments discussed above, this type of assignment allows for demonstration of knowledge and prompts the "independent thinking, researching, and learning" (Shih, 1986, p. 621) often required when students write for their other university courses. Such an assignment also builds on skills students have already practiced: reading, note taking, summarizing, paraphrasing, quoting, evaluating, comparing, agreeing/disagreeing, and so on.

These skills are transferable to many writing tasks that students will be required to perform in other courses when they write for academic audiences. The content will vary from course to course, and the format will vary from discipline to discipline and within disciplines, depending on the particular constraints of individual assignments and the particular concerns of individual teachers. But students should have a fairly good sense of how to focus on a subject, provide evidence to support a point or discovery, and examine the implications of the material discussed.

The Process of Academic Writing

Although it might appear at first glance that asking students to write from other texts—a common writing assignment before research on the composing process gained prominence—is a throwback to traditional teaching methods, that is far from the case. The kinds of writing assignments described above take place within the context of a process-centered approach, with students employing appropriate inquiry strategies, planning, drafting, consulting, revising, and editing.

The students' papers become teaching tools of the course. An assigned paper is not a test of their ability to follow prescribed rules of writing, but a chance to examine and organize, and then reexamine and reorganize, their thinking. Because more than one draft is read, it is not a matter of "better luck next time," but "try again until you have communicated your ideas clearly." Students can be trained to respond productively to each other's work-in-progress; thus, they can learn how collaboration among scholars evolves. These experiences in collaborative learning help students become "socialized into the academic community" (Maimon, 1983, p. 122).

Student-teacher interaction is almost always necessary, at least initially, for learning to take place. Over time, students internalize various routines and procedures and "take greater responsibility for controlling the progress of an assigned task" (Applebee, 1986, p. 110). But first, teacher feedback on drafts guides students toward producing a more tightly organized, well-focused paper that fulfills the assignment. The final product of this effort shows them what effective writing should look like. Their own good work becomes a model for future academic papers, including essay examinations. The writing classroom is the place where students are given the time to learn how to write.

With each assignment, learning can be structured so that students are provided with useful strategies for fulfilling the task at hand. Assignments can be given in such a way that students understand from the beginning what the task requires and what its evaluative criteria will be (Herrington, 1981). Students can be helped to " 'deconstruct' the assignment prompt" (Johns, 1986, p. 247). After they have done some informal writing, including invention techniques (Spack, 1984), they can be given a variety of suggestions on how to organize an academic paper that makes reference to another author's work. For example, they can be told what might go in the beginning (a summary of the author's article and an identification of the particular issue the student will respond to), middle (ideas and examples presented in logical order, never wandering from the central issue and frequently referring back to the reading), and ending (discussion of the implications of what has just been written).

The constraints of the form are meant to benefit, not hamper, the students' writing. Knowledge of what usually comes at the beginning, in the middle, and at the end of such discourse can give students another writing strategy or cognitive framework. However, rigid adherence to specific formulas is counterproductive. Students, especially those who were trained in a different culture and who are now enriched by a second culture, can create texts that may not follow explicit guidelines but that are still effective.

Indeed, Lu's (1987) discussion of her experience in writing is an example of this phenomenon. Caught between the rigid, imitative forms required at school in China and the inner-directed approach for the at-home English instruction given by her Westernized parents, she wrote a book report that was not acceptable to either her school instructors (because she sentimentally focused on the internal conflict of a character) or her at-home instructors (because she praised a "Revolutionary" book). Yet the essay was a highly original text.

As Coe (1987) points out, an understanding of the purpose of form—to enable writers to communicate accurately and effectively to readers—can "empower students to understand, use, and even invent new forms for new purposes" (p. 26). So, respect for form is encouraged—and necessary if students are to succeed in certain other courses—but flexibility is built into the course to encourage students to respect the composing process as well.

CONCLUSION

It is ironic that the pressure on ESL/English teachers to teach the writing of other disciplines is manifesting itself at precisely the time when influential technological institutes such as the Massachusetts Institute of Technology are funding programs to increase student exposure to the humanities in an effort to produce more well-rounded, open-minded students. The English composition course is and should be a humanities course: a place where students are provided the enrichment of reading and writing that provoke thought and foster their intellectual and ethical development.

This approach includes exploratory writing tasks that deal with making sense of thoughts and experiences. As Rose (1983) reminds us, "making meaning for the self, ordering experience, establishing one's own relation to it is what informs any serious writing" (p. 118). It also includes expository writing tasks that direct students to take an evaluative and analytical stance toward what they read. Each of these processes "makes a crucial contribution to the whole of intellectual activity" (Zeiger, 1985, p. 457).

Students will mature as writers as they receive invaluable input from numerous classroom experiences and from teachers who are conversant in other disciplines. To initiate students into the academic discourse community, we do not have to change our orientation completely, assign tasks we ourselves cannot master, or limit our assignments to prescribed, rule-governed tasks. We can instead draw on our own knowledge and abilities as we strengthen and expand the knowledge and abilities of our students.

REFERENCES

Applebee, A.N. (1986). Problems in process approaches: Toward a reconceptualization of process instruction. In A.R. Petrosky & D. Bartholomae (Eds.), *The teaching of writing* (pp. 95–113). Chicago: The National Society for the Study of Education.

Bander, R.G. (1978). *American English rhetoric.* New York: Holt, Rinehart & Winston.

Bazerman, C. (1980). A relationship between reading and writing: The conversational model. *College English, 41,* 656–661.

Bazerman, C. (1985). *The informed writer: Using sources in the disciplines* (2nd ed.). Boston: Houghton Mifflin.

Becker, H.S. (1986). *Writing for social scientists.* Chicago: University of Chicago Press.

Behrens, L. (1980). Meditations, reminiscences, polemics: Composition readers and the service course. *College English, 41,* 561–570.

Bizzell, P. (1982). College composition: Initiation into the academic discourse community. *Curriculum Inquiry, 12,* 191–207.

Bizzell, P. (1986). Composing processes: An overview. In A.R. Petrosky & D. Bartholomae (Eds.), *The teaching of writing* (pp. 49–70). Chicago: The National Society for the Study of Education.

Bridgeman, B., & Carlson, S.B. (1984). Survey of academic writing tasks. *Written Communication, 1,* 247–280.

Coe, R.M. (1987). An apology for form; or, who took the form out of the process? *College English, 49,* 13–28.

Coffey, B. (1984). ESP—English for specific purposes [State-of-the-art article]. *Language Teaching: The International Abstracting Journal for Language Teachers and Applied Linguists, 17,* 2–16.

Cole, K.C. (1985). *Sympathetic vibrations: Reflections on physics as a way of life.* New York: Bantam.

Coles, N., & Wall, S.V. (1987). Conflict and power in the reader-responses of adult basic writers. *College English, 49,* 298–314.

Connors, R.J. (1981). The rise and fall of the modes of discourse. *College Composition and Communication, 32,* 444–455.

Dick, J.A.R., & Esch, R.M. (1985). Dialogues among disciplines: A plan for faculty discussions of writing across the curriculum. *College Composition and Communication, 36,* 178–182.

Dubin, F., Eskey, D.E., & Grabe, W. (1986). *Teaching second language reading for academic purposes.* Reading, MA: Addison-Wesley.

Faigley, L., & Hansen, K. (1985). Learning to write in the social sciences. *College Composition and Communication, 36,* 140–149.

Flower, L.S., & Hayes, J.R. (1977). Problem-solving strategies and the writing process. *College English, 39,* 449–461.

Flower, L., & Hayes, J.R. (1981). A cognitive process theory of writing. *College Composition and Communication, 32,* 365–387.

Fulwiler, T. (1984). How well does writing across the curriculum work? *College English, 46,* 113–125.

Gilbert, G.N., & Mulkay, M. (1984). *Opening Pandora's box: A sociological analysis of scientists' discourse.* Cambridge: Cambridge University Press.

Hamp-Lyons, L. (1986). No new lamps for old yet, please [in The Forum]. *TESOL Quarterly, 20,* 790–796.

Hartfiel, V.F., Hughey, J.B., Wormuth, D.R., & Jacobs, H.L. (1985). *Learning ESL composition.* Rowley, MA: Newbury House.

Herrington, A.J. (1981). Writing to learn: Writing across the disciplines. *College English, 43,* 379–387.

Herrington, A.J. (1985). Classrooms as forums for reasoning and writing. *College Composition and Communication, 36,* 404–413.

Hill, S.S., Soppelsa, B.F., & West, G.K. (1982). Teaching ESL students to read and write experimental-research papers. *TESOL Quarterly, 16,* 333–347.

Hillocks, G., Jr. (1984). What works in teaching composition: A meta-analysis of experimental treatment studies. *American Journal of Education, 93,* 133–170.

Hillocks, G., Jr. (1986). *Research on written composition: New directions for teaching.* Urbana, IL: National Conference on Research in English/ERIC Clearinghouse on Reading and Communication Skills.

Horowitz, D.M. (1986a). The author responds to Hamp-Lyons . . . [in The Forum]. *TESOL Quarterly, 20,* 796–797.

Horowitz, D.M. (1986b). The author responds to Leibman-Kleine . . . [in The Forum]. *TESOL Quarterly, 20,* 788–790.

Horowitz, D. (1986c). Process, not product: Less than meets the eye [in The Forum]. *TESOL Quarterly, 20,* 141–144.

Horowitz, D.M. (1986d). What professors actually require: Academic tasks for the ESL classroom. *TESOL Quarterly, 20,* 445–462.

Horowitz, D.M., & McKee, M.B. (1984). Methods for teaching academic writing. *TECFORS, 7,* 5–11.

Johns, A.M. (1981). Necessary English: A faculty survey. *TESOL Quarterly, 15,* 51–57.

Johns, A.M. (1985). Academic writing standards: A questionnaire. *TECFORS, 8,* 11–14.

Johns, A.M. (1986). Coherence and academic writing: Some definitions and suggestions for teaching. *TESOL Quarterly, 20,* 247–265.

Krashen, S.D. (1984). *Writing: Research, theory and applications.* Oxford: Pergamon Press.

Kroll, B. (1979). A survey of the writing needs of foreign and American college freshmen. *English Language Teaching Journal, 33,* 219–227.

Lay, N.D.S. (1982). Composing processes of adult ESL learners: A case study. *TESOL Quarterly, 16,* 406.

Leibman-Kleine, J. (1986). In defense of teaching process in ESL composition [in The Forum]. *TESOL Quarterly, 20,* 783–788.

Lu, M. (1987). From silence to words: Writing as struggle. *College English, 49,* 437–448.

MacDonald, S.P. (1987). Problem definition in academic writing. *College English, 49,* 315–331.

Maher, J. (1986). English for medical purposes. [State-of-the-art article]. *Language Teaching: The International Abstracting Journal for Language Teachers and Applied Linguists, 19,* 112–145.

Maimon, E.P. (1983). Maps and genres: Exploring connections in the arts and sciences. In W.B. Horner (Ed.), *Composition and literature: Bridging the gaps* (pp. 110–125). Chicago: University of Chicago Press.

Maimon, E.P. (1984). *Writing across the curriculum: Knowledge and acknowledgment in an educated community.* Unpublished manuscript.

Maimon, E.P., Belcher, G.L., Hearn, G.W., Nodine, B.F., & O'Connor, F.B. (1981). *Writing in the arts and sciences.* Boston: Little, Brown.

Myers, G. (1985). Texts as knowledge claims: The social construction of two biology articles. *Social Studies of Science, 15,* 593–630.

Ostler, S.E. (1980). A survey of academic needs for advanced ESL. *TESOL Quarterly, 14,* 489–502.

Pearson, S. (1983). The challenge of Mai Chung: Teaching technical writing to the foreign-born professional in industry. *TESOL Quarterly, 17,* 383–399.

Petroski, H. (1986). *Beyond engineering: Essays and other attempts to figure without equations.* New York: St. Martin's Press.

Petrosky, A.R. (1982). From story to essay: Reading and writing. *College English, 46,* 19–36.

Raimes, A. (1985). What unskilled ESL students do as they write: A classroom study of composing. *TESOL Quarterly, 19,* 229–258.

Raimes, A. (1987, April). *Why write? Perspectives in purpose and pedagogy.* Paper presented at the 21st Annual TESOL Convention, Miami Beach.

Reid, J. (1984a). Comments on Vivian Zamel's "The composing processes of advanced ESL students: Six case studies" [in The Forum]. *TESOL Quarterly, 18,* 149–153.

Reid, J. (1984b). The radical outliner and the radical brainstormer: A perspective on composing processes [in The Forum]. *TESOL Quarterly, 18,* 529–534.

Reid, J. (1985). The author responds . . . [in The Forum]. *TESOL Quarterly, 19,* 398–400.

Rose, M. (1983). Remedial writing courses: A critique and a proposal. *College English, 45,* 109–126.

Rose, M. (1985). The language of exclusion: Writing instruction at the university. *College English, 47,* 341–359.

Russell, D.R. (1987). Writing across the curriculum and the communications movement: Some lessons from the past. *College English, 38,* 184–194.

Salvatori, M. (1983). Reading and writing a text: Correlations between reading and writing. *College English, 45,* 657–666.

Scheiber, H.J. (1987). Toward a text-based pedagogy in the freshman composition course—with two process-oriented writing tasks. *Freshman English News, 15,* 15–18.

Selzer, J. (1983). The composing processes of an engineer. *College Composition and Communication, 34,* 178–187.

Shaughnessy, M. (1977). *Errors and expectations.* New York: Oxford University Press.

Shih, M. (1986). Content-based approaches to teaching academic writing. *TESOL Quarterly, 20,* 617–648.

Silk, M. (1987, April 19). The hot history department. *The New York Times Magazine,* pp. 41, 43, 46–47, 50, 56, 62, 64.

Spack, R. (1984). Invention strategies and the ESL college composition student. *TESOL Quarterly, 18,* 649–670.

Spack, R. (1985a). Comments on Joy Reid's "The radical outliner and the radical brainstormer: A perspective on composing processes" [in The Forum]. *TESOL Quarterly, 19,* 396–398.

Spack, R. (1985b). Literature, reading, writing, and ESL: Bridging the gaps. *TESOL Quarterly, 19,* 703–725.

Spack, R., & Sadow, C. (1983). Student-teacher working journals in ESL composition. *TESOL Quarterly, 17,* 575–593.

Swales, J. (1986). A genre-based approach to language across the curriculum. In M. Tickoo (Ed.), *Language across the curriculum* (pp. 10–22). Singapore: RELC.

Swales, J. (1987). Utilizing the literatures in teaching the research paper. *TESOL Quarterly, 21,* 41–68.

Thomas, L. (1983). *The youngest science: Notes of a medicine-watcher.* New York: Viking Press.

Wilkinson, A.M. (1985). A freshman writing course in parallel with a science course. *Composition and Communication, 36,* 160–165.

Woodford, F.P. (1967). Sounder thinking through clearer writing. *Science, 156,* 743–745.

Yearley, S. (1981). Textual persuasion: The role of social accounting in the construction of scientific arguments. *Philosophy of Social Sciences, 11,* 409–435.

Zamel, V. (1982). Writing: The process of discovering meaning. *TESOL Quarterly, 16,* 195–209.

Zamel, V. (1983). The composing processes of advanced ESL students: Six case studies. *TESOL Quarterly, 17,* 165–187.

Zamel, V. (1984). In search of the key: Research and practice in composition. In J. Handscombe, R.A. Orem, & B.P. Taylor (Eds.), *On TESOL '83* (pp. 195–207). Washington, DC: TESOL.

Zamel, V. (1986, March). *From process to product.* Paper presented at the 20th Annual TESOL Convention, Anaheim, CA.

Zamel, V. (1987). *Teaching composition: Toward a pedagogy of questions.* Unpublished manuscript.

Zeiger, W. (1985). The exploratory essay: Enfranchising the spirit of inquiry in college composition. *College English, 47,* 454–466.

A Common Ground:
The Essay in the Academy

Kurt Spellmeyer

> *. . . the objectivity of dialectical cognition needs not less subjectivity, but more.*
> —T. W. Adorno (*Negative Dialectics*)

In his essay "Of the Education of Children," Montaigne recalls an encounter with two scholars who, on the road to Orleans, were followed closely by a third traveler, La Rochefoucauld:

> One of my men inquired of the first of these teachers who was the gentleman that came behind him. He, not having seen the retinue that was following him, and thinking that my man was talking about his companion, replied comically: "He is not a gentleman; he is a grammarian, and I am a logician." (125)

If the essay as a distinct genre begins with Montaigne, it also begins as an assault upon the scholasticism he alludes to in this passage. Through his account of the two self-absorbed pedants, Montaigne makes light of the conception of knowledge that distinguishes so exactly between the grammarian and the logician, and he introduces, as an alternative to such distinctions, the example of La Rochefoucauld, the "gentleman," by which he does not mean a member of the ruling class, but instead the questioner whose pursuit of understanding has carried him beyond the limitations of the customary.

College English, 1989

The new system of education proposed by Montaigne in his essay is designed to repair precisely that fragmentation of experience—into grammar, logic, theology, rhetoric, and so forth—which characterized scholastic discourse, and which arose from still another fragmentation, between the "high" language of court and college and the "low" language of the street and the home. Unlike Montaigne's two erudite travelers, a person of genuine sophistication, a person like La Rochefoucauld, surmounts these divisions because he measures them against an experiential unity no single discipline can encompass. Indeed, Montaigne repeatedly warns that the conventional branches of learning, because they are by nature specialized and mutually exclusive, obscure not only the complexity of real life, but also the coherence. As an antidote to the tautological circularity which is a danger for all discourse, he commends the test of personal experience. "Let" the student "be asked for an account not merely of the words of his lesson, but of its sense and substance, and let him judge the profit he has made by the testimony not of his memory, but of his life" (110).

In contrast to Bacon, who reacted to the fragmentation of scholastic learning with the call for a unifying system, his "Great Instauration," Montaigne's real concern is not knowledge proper, but the relationship between individuals and the conventions by which their experience is defined and contained. To philosophers in the Middle Ages, the "world of experience" was simply an inferior copy of a purely intellectual reality, a reality mirrored more clearly in language than in sensation. Thus, in the *Monologion*, Anselm of Canterbury affirms that the Word "is not the likeness of created things" but their "true Existence" (45). As a demonstration of the process by which language, rather than determining the shape of experience, is shaped through the interaction of self and world, Montaigne's new genre, the essay, breaks irreparably the connection between words and "true Existence." The essay serves to dramatize the situation of the writer who moves beyond the familiar to bring language into closer accord with life. Against the systematic impersonality of scholastic tradition, Montaigne defends the central position of the author-as-speaker, at once subject and object in discourse. And yet, the final purpose of the author's new and central role is not narcissistic introspection, but the very opposite; Montaigne's entire program for the reform of education is intended to encourage a "personal worldliness" or "personal outwardness" that his learned contemporaries, the logician and the grammarian, would certainly have dismissed as a contradiction, an impossibility. For them, the rigor of scholarly discourse owed to its exclusionary purity—its abstractness, its power of discrimination. For Montaigne, convention was literally con-vention, a "coming together" of dissonant perspectives in order to restore the lived world, at the risk of imprecision and incongruity. If other, later essayists were not always as willing to endure this risk, or to acknowledge so frankly its importance to their success, the form of the essay nonetheless demands a self-conscious formlessness, a con-vention through contravention.

Although it has persisted from Montaigne's day until our own, and in spite of its continued popularity outside the university, the exploratory, contravening essay has become increasingly peripheral. At Rutgers, for instance, we offer classes in film studies, detective fiction, and the literature of fantasy, but there is no course devoted exclusively to the reading and writing of essays except for freshman English. Even in this setting, the essay's usefulness has been questioned by those who argue that the traditional "composition," with its intrusive authorial presence and its tolerance of indirection, fails to prepare students for the writing they must do when they leave our classes and go on to psychology, or political science, or philosophy where, it is commonly alleged, they cannot write from their own experience. Despite Bacon, Addison and Steele, Lamb, Hazlitt, Newman, Carlyle—the list is already long enough, I think, to make my point—anthologists and scholars tend to see the universe of literary discourse as a triumvirate composed of poetry, drama, and "prose," either fiction or "nonfiction." The universe of academic discourse includes virtually every form of institutionalized writing taught outside of freshman English, from lab reports to ethnographies. In the context of literary prose, the essay is too specialized; in comparison to writing in the disciplines, not specialized enough.

I suspect, however, that this neglect of the essay as an object of study in its own right reflects an unstated distrust of the form among professors of literature, and more recently, among teachers of writing, because it departs so radically in its rhetorical strategies and epistemological assumptions from its more prestigious, authoritative counterparts. The essay stands apart from both poetry and prose fiction, as well as from other forms of academic writing, in its emphasis upon the actual situation of the writer, and thus upon the personal nature, the "situatedness," of all writing. Consider these two passages, the first from an essay by Zora Neale Hurston, the second from a work of literary criticism:

I am colored but I offer nothing in the way of extenuating circumstances except the fact that I am the only Negro in the United States whose grandfather on the mother's side was *not* an Indian chief.

I remember the very day that I became colored. Up to my thirteenth year I lived in the little Negro town of Eatonville, Florida. It is exclusively a colored town. The only white people I knew passed through the town going to or coming from Orlando. (152)

Dickens is, then, opposed to any change in the political and economic structure of society, and places his hopes for amelioration in a change of heart, mind and soul in those who possess power, who will then disseminate the fruits of change over the lower echelons of society. Dickens's ideal State would be one of "benevolent and genial anarchy."

> This is an insecure basis from which to launch a critique of society, and
> its insecurity becomes all the more obvious when we look outside *Hard Times*
> to Dickens's journalism of the same period. (Lodge 147)

From its inception with Montaigne, the essay purports to disclose the
reflections of an actual person in response to actual events, or to the
reflections and beliefs of other people. Hurston's essay, in which she
examines the influence of race and history upon self-definition, begins
with a radical personalization of the problem, not with "being colored"
but with "I am colored." In his discussion of *Hard Times*, David Lodge
employs the opposite rhetorical strategy, a strategy of ostensible detachment from his own situation as a writer. Speaking from—or rather, for—the
institution of literary study, Lodge's critique possesses an authority that
Hurston's essay cannot claim, despite its aggressive promotion of private
insight over public commonplace. And yet, however faithfully Lodge may
hold to the method of his discipline, his assessment of Dickens remains
no less a "rationalization," in Kenneth Burke's terms, than Hurston's "I
am colored"; no less, that is, a "set of motives belonging to a specific
orientation" (Burke 23).

By disguising authorial fallibility and bias, as well as the uncertainty of
discourse itself, more "serious" forms of writing typically perpetuate an
unequal relationship between the writer and the audience, and between
the writer and the subject under scrutiny—Lodge in judgment of Dickens'
politics, for example. The literary critic, the philosopher, the political scientist, and to some degree even the novelist, tender versions of experience
in which their own ordeal of uncertainty, the ordeal that every writer
endures, and from which no one ever escapes, has unfolded beforehand,
behind the scenes, and it is the reader who must catch up in order to be
instructed. By contrast, the essay foregrounds the speaker's movement
from presentation to representation, from experience as "fact" to experience invested more fully with personal, and with social, meaning. Disal-
lowing the pose of objectivity through which experts maintain their privileged status as "knowers," the essay dramatizes a process of appropriation
concealed by other genres, a process never wholly methodical or disinterested. An essayist, such as Hurston in the passage above, does not speak
for Reason, History, or the Heav'nly Muse. Rather, she speaks as an individual in the uncertainty typified by Montaigne's own motto, "Que sais-je?"
Even when the essayist has reached a tentative decision and begins to write
with an intention to persuade, the obligation to persuade reaffirms her
equality with the audience, and sharply marks the limits of her reliability.

Because the essay is the genre that acknowledges most openly the tentative, recursive, and conversational nature of discourse, its loss of prestige
among teachers of writing is a predictable, though unnecessary, consequence of their legitimate dissatisfaction with writer-based, process-cen-

tered modes of instruction. As critics of the process model have persuasively argued, a purely psychological account of writing—of what happens to writers while they compose—ignores the methodological contexts that distinguish one form of discourse from another. By dutifully following the stages of a supposedly universal "writing process," our students may produce prose acceptable to the teacher in English 101, but these same dutiful students will meet with less success in history or philosophy unless they are taught to recognize the conventions of each discipline. Indeed, students trained to look within themselves when they compose may be less alert to discourse conventions that those who have received no training at all, and less prepared to comply with the expectations of a real academic audience.

And yet, while teachers committed to a heuristics of process misconstrued the writer's situatedness by denying the historicity of language and audience, I believe that many teachers today have misconstrued this situatedness in the very opposite way, by insisting that the right to speak must be learned—or perhaps more accurately, earned—through what is essentially the effacement of subjectivity. Ironically, this suspicion of personal writing may have originated in the efforts of theorists like Ann Berthoff to reassert the sovereignty of the writer. As she contends in *The Making of Meaning*, "Despite the talk of process and the active choices of an engaged composer, the new rhetorics, like the old rhetorics they claim to supplant, conceive of a world 'out there' that is to be manipulated by the writer" (102). Breaking with the notion of a fixed world "out there"—breaking with what it is, in effect, a naive material determinism—Berthoff contends that the constitutive powers of language and the imagination allow the writer to create meaning rather than simply to discover it. But this critique of material determinism, if pushed to an extreme that Berthoff herself never intended, can also be used to defend an equally naive and constricting linguistic determinism: the view that people who do not share the same words cannot share the same world.

Supporters of this position maintain that the study of discourse conventions, the structure of an argument in philosophy, or the uses of evidence in political science, furnishes the beginner with a content as well as a context, both defined by the "rules" of the discipline. In "Cognition, Convention, and Certainty," for example, Patricia Bizzell claims that

> we cannot look at reality in an unfiltered way—"reality" only makes sense when organized by the interpretive conventions of a discourse community. Students often complain that they have nothing to say, whereas "real-world" writers almost never do, precisely because real-world writers are writing for discourse communities. (232)

Berthoff suggests that the conventions of a community or tradition retain their significance only when they are perpetually reinterpreted by individuals struggling with the complexity of experience, but Bizzell explicitly condemns "debilitating individualism" as the primary obstacle to effective writing because she assumes that language determines, in advance of experience, the meaning of "real-world" events. Whereas Berthoff advocates critical thinking, through a conjunction of disparate perspectives—convention with experience, the past with the present—Bizzell insists upon the primacy of systematic thinking, from within the boundaries of a single community. Although she advocates a program of instruction that will make the student's presuppositions "more clearly a matter of conscious commitment, instead of unconscious conformity," her conception of meaning as discipline-specific prevents her from valorizing a comparable reassessment of our own, institutional presuppositions (238–39). In this sense, Bizzell's most recent article, "Arguing about Literacy," must be seen as a significant departure from her earlier work, a departure arising from growing misgivings about the tacit demand for "submission" in the pedagogy of interpretive communities (150).

While I agree that meaning can never be detached from its social context, I suspect that the prevailing tradition of discipline-specific writing instruction encourages both conformity and submission by failing to recognize in discourse what Bakhtin calls "heteroglossia." If, as he argues, every language without exception "represents the co-existence of socio-ideological contradictions between the present and the past" and "between different socio-ideological groups in the present"—if, in other words, discourse communities are not the monolithic unities that Bizzell suggests, but "heteroglot from top to bottom"—then student-writers cannot become more accomplished by ignoring their situatedness. Because languages "intersect" with one another on many levels at the same time, entry into a community of discourse must begin, not with a renunciation of the "home language" or "home culture," but with those points of commonality that expose the alien within the familiar, the familiar within the alien (Bakhtin 291). By characterizing each discourse as essentially monological, the pedagogy of community conventions prevents novice writers from discovering, in their own commitments, the areas of concern they already share with us.

On the assumption that instruction in writing must start with the inculcation of a properly systematic way of thinking, one widely-used textbook, *The Informed Writer*, opens with this observation:

> Will Roger's famous quip, "All I know is what I read in the newspapers," has great truth. Most of what we learn about the world—events in the distant past or in distant countries, the collisions of subatomic particles or of corporate finance, the secrets of the beginnings of the world or of another person's mind—is filtered through written communication. Even when we learn things directly, we perceive and interpret that experience through attitudes influenced by the words of others. (Bazerman 3)

The author of the passage, Charles Bazerman, later characterizes writing as a conversation between students and the writers who have preceded them, but the students' actual role in the conversation is negligible:

> The first two parts of this book have treated you as consumers of knowledge—active, thoughtful, evaluative, selective consumers, but consumers nonetheless. You have learned to take knowledge in, understand it, and respond to it. You have learned how to discover the personal meaning and importance in texts. You have learned to evaluate and think about texts. And you have learned to make original statements using your reading. (329)

Inexperienced writers become more experienced by "consuming" or internalizing a discourse; only after it has been thoroughly consumed, and I presume "digested" through formal analysis, is the writer entitled to make "original statements." But originality has no place in Bazerman's pedagogy. During a student's "conversation" with the assigned readings, his or her private responses are largely irrelevant because the merit of any statement will be decided solely by the standards of public knowledge. Not only does Bazerman contrast personal values to "the way the world actually is," but he urges the student-writer to "go beyond . . . feelings or internal conviction to develop the kind of argument and evidence others will accept" (329). While most teachers would agree that understanding and originality require a familiarity with discourse conventions, the admonition to suppress feelings and beliefs for the sake of public approval encourages an attitude of calculating alienation, the antithesis of Herbert Marcuse's notion of "praxis in the 'realm of freedom,' " praxis that does not require submission to "an 'alien' objectivity" (31).

The proponents of discourse-specific writing typically invoke the ethos of "empowerment"—of breaking down longstanding distinctions between student-writers and "real" writers—but their sense of the term is often synonymous with pragmatic accommodation. Among textbooks which encourage accommodation as a preliminary to empowerment, the *reductio ad absurdum* may well be *Asking the Right Questions*, by M. Neil Browne and Stuart M. Keeley:

> We think you would rather *choose* for yourself what to absorb and what to ignore. To make this choice you must read with a special attitude—a question-asking attitude. Such a thinking style requires *active* input from *you.* (2)

"Active input," however, should not be confused with personal input. In responding to what they read, students have only two choices, "absorbing" the text or "ignoring" it, but neither approach allows them the liberty of reading and speaking from their own perspectives about the perspectives of others. Neither allows them to initiate a Bakhtinian dialogue, at once "double-voiced" and "internally persuasive" (325, 342). Like Bazerman and Bizzell, Browne and Keeley adopt the filter as an analogue for the interposition of discourse between the writer and his or her experience, and their remarks to student-readers demonstrate the fundamental circularity of the language-as-filter model:

> The inadequacies in what someone says will not "leap out" at you. You must be an *active* searcher. You do this by *asking questions*. The best search strategy is a critical-questioning strategy. Throughout this book we will be giving you the critical questions to ask. A powerful advantage of these questions is that they permit you to ask revealing questions even when you know very little about the topic being discussed. (5)

If the topic cannot be understood on its own terms without the "revealing questions" of an intervening filter, then the questions themselves are immune to the test of experience because they decisively control the nature of experience. Strictly speaking, Browne and Keeley's "active searcher" investigates the filter rather than the topic, in the best tradition of scholastic tautology. Rather than preceding the writer's encounter with an issue, authentically critical questioning should arise from this encounter in such a manner that the status of both the writer and the issue will be redefined. No matter how often they may urge students to ask questions in a dialogical manner, Browne and Keeley's model of inquiry is antidialogical because it severs language, not only from the contexts that give an issue its importance, but also from the intentionality described by Bakhtin as a "living impulse toward the object" (292).

By emphasizing the institutional rigidity of discourse while ignoring the ability of language to transcend the boundaries of one particular community or another, these new formalists have returned us to Montaigne's encounter at Orleans. A writer can think like a psychologist, or like an economist, but is there really no more inclusive or expansive way of thinking "from the outside"—the dialogical thinking which Montaigne enacts in his characteristic shifts of perspective, from Dante to Plato to Xenophon, from the sayings of Cicero to "Paluel or Pompey, those fine dancers of my time" (112)? As Adorno observes in "The Essay as Form," Montaigne succeeded in discrediting the "delusion that the *ordo idearum* (order of ideas) should be the *ordo rerum* (order of things)." Through a discourse that transgresses the propriety of discrete communities and challenges "the unconditional priority of method" itself, Montaigne points to a greater experiential and linguistic commonality (158). And if he is correct in his belief that such a commonality cannot be recovered except through transgression, then the rejection of individualism—and with it, the essay—as an obstacle to both discourse and community eliminates the only common ground which remains to the university.

Responding to his contemporaries within the academy, Montaigne opposed the assertion that any particular language, community, or worldview could define absolutely the boundaries of human experience. "In comparison with most men," he affirms, "few things touch me, or, to put it better, hold me; for it is right that things should touch us, provided they do not possess us. I take great care to augment by study and reasoning this privilege of insensibility, which is naturally well advanced in me. . . . One must moderate oneself between hatred of pain and love of pleasure" (766–67). Without an ability to resist the coercive power of authoritative language by cultivating a sociable insensibility to what is known, presupposed, and accepted, our students will never be able to make the "conscious commitments" the discourse-community theorists applaud. Montaigne may describe his writing as a process of self-questioning, but this self-questioning presumes that the refinement of knowledge begins with his own perspectives and presuppositions, and not with their "disciplined" suppression. Instead of abandoning the practice of writing from the outside, teachers should recognize that English 101, with its tolerance for essayistic introspection and digression, is probably the last opportunity most students will ever have to discover the relationship of mutual implication, a relationship fundamental to all writing, between the self and the cultural heritage within which selfhood has meaning. To put it in the simplest terms, we do not deny the socially-constituted nature of either learning or identity when we ask our students to write from their own situations, but I believe that it is both dishonest and disabling to pretend that writing, no matter how formal or abstract, is not created by persons, from within the contexts—historical, social, intellectual, institutional—of their lived experience. Whatever may have been the case in freshman classes fifteen years ago, writing from experience is not limited to summer vacations, first dates, or greatest embarrassments: the discussion of issues, events, and texts is also, inescapably, personal writing. It seems to me that the discourse-community theorists have mistaken the pose of objectivity, the approved dissimulation exemplified by David Lodge's assessment of Dickens, for an absence of personal commitment in the creation of a text. From the appearance of impersonality in the final product of writing, they have inferred that the process itself is impersonal.

Whatever sense of community we may associate with "higher education," our students inhabit a universe of discourse so fragmented that the allure of an impersonal knowledge, an automatic knowledge, becomes nearly irresistible. In response to this fragmentation, teachers may decide, with Elaine Maimon, to "deemphasize the informal essay and adopt a more sophisticated, multidisciplinary approach," an approach that will familiarize beginners with the "modes of behavior" characteristic of "successful practitioners" in particular fields (2–3). But however "sophisticated" this approach may be, it cannot make the universe of academic discourse any less divided, nor will it guarantee any greater consistency between the students' world and the world of their teachers, since learning a mode of behavior does not ensure an understanding of the values implicit within it. Still less does Maimon's approach invite a reasoned critique of such implicit values. By reifying the prevailing configuration of knowledge, by accepting this configuration as a fait accompli and supporting the narrow vocationalism which has created it, proponents of discipline-specific writing may spare themselves the recalcitrance of "Science majors who were," in Maimon's words, "force-fed James Joyce," but they also discourage these same science majors from thinking that might culminate in necessary social change. Because the choice of a discipline is for most students a reflection of presuppositions which discipline-specific instruction leaves virtually unchallenged, I suggest that we teach freshman writing, not by attempting to simulate the lab report or the ethnography, but by calling attention to the writer's situatedness, a situatedness the essay takes as its central concern—not, perhaps, the freshman essay in its often-degraded variants, but the essay as literary tradition represents it, and as we should teach it in our classes.

Whereas the defenders of a process-based pedagogy have failed to account for the differences between styles, the proponents of discipline-specific writing have overlooked what is in fact universal to all discourse. Although it may be true in an abstract sense that tradition determines what we write, from the perspective of the writer moved by Bakhtin's "living impulse" there is no way to allow conventions of discourse to guide the hand that holds the pen—who would not welcome such a guiding hand, when composing is so difficult and precarious? No matter how adept a writer becomes, the activity of writing always entails a radical loss of certainty. Not only have the discourse theorists confused product with process, but they have conflated writing as a demonstration of understanding—after a writer has worked through his or her uncertainty—with writing as a means of achieving understanding, an achievement that demands the willingness to surrender instrumental control. As Hans-Georg Gadamer observes, understanding in the encounter with a text begins as an effort to reconstruct the experience of questioning from which the text has arisen (333–34). Asked to write on a new and difficult reading, such as Walker Percy's essay "The Loss of the Creature," many freshmen will probably follow only a portion of his argument; perhaps they will miss his point altogether on the first try. But for the ones who succeed in entering Percy's world, the effort to understand will assume the form of a search for equivalents: to reconstruct the motives behind Percy's text, these students must start by re-reading the "text" of their own experience from the standpoint of the question that Percy has posed, even while the question itself remains to some degree unclear.

Like Montaigne, Gadamer believes that the learner's presuppositions are the ground from which he or she views the world, and therefore the achievement of understanding requires, not the suspension of these presuppositions in some pretended neutrality, but a reaffirmation of the self, at first against the question and then within it. Balancing the past against the present, dialogical language allows us to "rise above the pressure of what comes to meet us in the world"—the pressure of racism, for example, in Zora Neale Hurston's essay—and to declare our participation in the making of that world (402). When we ask our students to respond to an assigned text, we should not be too surprised, therefore, if they misread the text in order to make its question more fully a part of their own concerns. In Gadamer's situational hermeneutics, this misreading is not evidence of inattentiveness or lack of discipline, but an indispensable preliminary to a more coherent interpretation. Only after the first misreading, when a disjunction has emerged—between the world as our students thought it to be, and the world as others have represented it—will they be able to initiate the dialogue through which a new selfhood can be fashioned in response to the text, a text that will also be refashioned after each transformation of the self.

Initially, the strangeness of an unfamiliar point of view compels readers to look back at the events of their own lives, but once their understanding of these events has begun to change as a result of surveying them from a new perspective, they find that the text has opened up commensurately. Gadamer concludes from this dialogical process that understanding is never objective but always disclosure of "the conversation that we ourselves are" (340). And if the dialogue continues long enough, it will move toward what he terms a "fusion of horizons," a fusion of worlds, public and private. I believe this progression from disjunction to dialogue and fusion—like Montaigne's progression from insensibility to considered engagement— can be realized most completely within the transgressive form of the essay, and I am convinced the students who learn to use writing as a way of thinking dialogically achieve in the process a heightened awareness of their situation, an awareness which allows them to overcome past misunderstandings without at the same time disowning the past.

Although the discourse theorists imply that student-writers today have become too independent, too ready to contravene the traditional, I find the very opposite to be true. Trained in the high schools to filter, absorb, and digest, they typically lack any sense of inquiry as a conversation. The following excerpt, from a paper submitted in an entry-level sociology course, is typical in this respect:

> The modern world in which we live is a complex and fast-moving one.
> Modern societies are plagued by reoccurring, extensive social problems.
> Although there exist many serious problems, the one which demands im-

mediate examination and resolution is that of suicide among youths. Children are taking their own lives with an alarming frequency. Whatever the reasons may be for these tragedies, an emphasis must be placed upon preventing them rather than analyzing them after they have occurred.

In this work, *Suicide: A Study in Sociology*, Emile Durkheim studies the various causes associated with suicide. He categorizes the different types of suicide into four basic groups: egoistic, anomic, altruistic, and fatalistic. All four of these classifications can be applied to the growing problem of youth suicide in society. . . .

The classification of egoistic suicide can be applied to the problem of child suicide. It is not uncommon for children, particularly adolescents, to feel "left out." A child may become so hopelessly depressed, that he feels as if he has no worth. . . .

Superficially, this passage is the work of an advanced student-writer, insofar as it closely approximates the ideal of systematic, impersonal, "academic" discourse. And yet, despite this apparent sophistication, the discussion strikes me as ultimately unsuccessful because its impersonality is not simply a rhetorical posture, but evidence of a pervasive absence of commitment. Although he works hard to enter the discourse community, to comply with its rules and fulfill its expectations, the author has nothing of his own to say. A young man who must have felt "left out" more than once in his life, and who may even have contemplated suicide at some point, he obscures his situatedness from the beginning, by treating "youths" in the first paragraph as a synonym for "children." While he has read the assigned material and has learned some of the conventions most typical of Durkheim's own prose, whenever there is an opportunity to make a real discovery, to venture beyond the assigned reading into the realm of implication, through assent, disagreement, or the consideration of examples, he retreats again into summary.

This retreat is most obvious in the final paragraphs of the essay when, having ended a lengthy, three-page recapitulation of Durkheim, the writer goes on to offer a number of terse suggestions—suggestions that his teacher intended to be the focus of the assignment—for addressing the problem of teenage suicides:

There are many ways in which society could help to reduce the number of suicides among youths. For example, the answer may lie in the home. Parents and other family members must stick together in order to give one another support and encouragement. This would make a child feel as if he has worth as a brother, sister, or child as the case may be. . . . Another way for children to feel needed or wanted is to become a member of some sort of team, group or club. This could be done in or out of school. . . .

Children can find a sense of worth through religion. A lack of religious values is one of the main reasons for the high suicide rates in modern countries. Religion gives people a purpose and direction, and it gives children reasons for suffering and hardship in the world.

It would also be beneficial to develop various rap sessions and big brother and sister programs in the community. Often children do not feel they can talk to their parents, and these would provide other outlets.

The previous suggestions are ways in which the tragedies of suicide among youths can be prevented and perhaps stopped completely one day.

With each paragraph growing shorter than the preceding one, the writer attempts to slip, as unobtrusively as possible, out of his text, and out of his own situation, before he has revealed too much of himself, as though any revelation of personality would violate the decorum of academic writing. Virtually all of the putative examples that he offers—a team, a group, a club—are not examples in any real sense, but disembodied types, often allusions to more detailed illustrations from Durkheim. Even in his discussion of family relationships, the writer presents us with a perfectly generic family, in which the members can be counted on to "stick together" and to offer one another the appropriate support in every situation. Rather than exploring solutions as the assignment requires, he abandons the problem. And by attempting to exclude subjectivity from his discussion, he also forestalls any consideration of Durkheim's personality and motives, although the reconstruction of Durkheim's situation might have started him on the way to a more engaged reading.

In *Suicide* Durkheim makes any number of assertions which readily invite dispute, but the text dominates the student-writer so completely that his response could not be more deferential, or more perfunctory. His passivity is especially remarkable in view of the paper's first paragraph, where he announces, "Whatever the reasons may be for these tragedies, an emphasis must be placed upon preventing them rather than analyzing them after they have occurred." Following this initial resolution to appropriate the issue for his own purposes, he devotes three pages out of four to exactly the kind of analysis he eschews. Despite his respectfulness toward Durkheim, or perhaps because of it, he has also failed to understand the rhetorical implications of *Suicide*, which is intended to be, as the subtitle indicates, a "Study of Sociology," a demonstration of sociological method. In contrast to the student's disembodied examples, Durkheim's prose is densely furnished with supporting illustrations, which allow him to examine related forms of behavior in order to identify the cultural institutions that promote these forms: such is the method of "study" he intends his work to demonstrate. Fittingly enough, the student's proposals to reduce suicide are directed toward institutions also—the home, the group or club, the church, the community. But he cannot decide what to say about these institutions. To say something more, he would need to ask why they currently fail to discourage suicide. And to ask that question, he would need to adopt a critical attitude toward his own family, group, church, and community. They are, after all, the only institutions that he knows in detail, and the only ones against which he could test Durkheim's argument and method. His unwillingness to allow personal experience to intrude upon what he perceives as the objectivity of academic discourse finally prevents him from coming to understand such discourse.

By contrast, the student-writer whose work I have excerpted in the passage below has submitted an essay which, although far less conventional in its organization, goes beyond summary to an active interpretation of the assigned reading, Sartre's "What Is Existentialism"—interpretation in its root sense, as a "going between" two distinct positions—and to a use of Sartre's text as a way of reseeing her own values and assumptions. For comparison to the first student, I have chosen a writer who stands still further outside the circle of expertise, to whom an essay on Sartre might seem at first an impossible task:

> I have kept a pet rat for the past two and a half years. Not wanting to be separated from my friend Mickey (the name I gave him), I decided to bring him to school to live with me [sic]. He remained his usual happy and healthy self for about three months. However, he suddenly became ill and deteriorated rapidly before my eyes. His sunken eyes and overall crippled state worried me to the point of a panic-like state. Quickly I consulted several people about what I could do to help my pet. Sadly, each one confirmed my fear that it was too late for Mickey to be saved.
>
> First, I called our family vet whose opinion I respected highly; he told me that Mickey would probably not regain his former good health, but that I could bring him in to be examined if I liked. My second call was to the pet store where I had gotten my rat in the first place. . . . Unfortunately, the man I talked with responded in a rather ignorant way, telling me that rats usually lived to be about 2 or 3 years old. . . .
>
> Discarding this man's advice as worthless, I called my friend Chris figuring that he would offer me the most accurate guidance about Mickey. Chris has been raising rats for more than ten years, and has witnessed every aspect of their lives in captivity just about. After questioning me about the details of the symptoms, Chris told me that my pet was dying because of a cancerous tumor and could not be saved. Once I was able to locate the actual tumor under Chris's tutelage, I realized that Mick had a tangible, real disease and that it was up to me alone to end his pain. . . .
>
> Jean-Paul Sartre tells us in his essay "Existentialism" that making a decision when faced with a moral issue is not so easy or personal as we may think it is: "To choose to be this or that is to affirm at the same time the value of what we choose." Furthermore, according to Sartre, any choice we make involving morals will affect not only ourselves directly but also all of humanity in general. When we are facing such an ethical decision, no matter how trivial it may seem to us, "we always choose the good, and nothing can be good for us without being good for all." One would not admire an image of Man as a cruel, inhumane beast. Ironically, it would be more humane and kind to kill Mickey to end his suffering. . . . Mickey was not born asking

to be raised in a cage as a pet. He was not responsible for his taming nor for his fatal affliction. I had taken him and put him into a cage, and now I had to decide if he should be left alone to suffer just so that I could cling to the hope that he may get better and I could avoid having to mourn the loss of my pet.

Surely one of the most obvious features of this paper—aside from the juxtaposition of Sartre's sophisticated analysis against a narrative so thoroughly naive—is the omission of any reference to Sartre himself until the second page. Instead of beginning with a summary of Sartre's position, the writer holds him in abeyance (Gadamer would say that she rises above the pressures of Sartre's world) in order to consider the text of her own experience in a new light. As she explores this text, her text, she begins to notice points of correspondence between her decisions about Mickey the rat and Sartre's existential ethics. Retrospectively she realizes that her own behavior could be explained in existential terms, and in arriving at this recognition she offers two mutually sustaining interpretations: an interpretation of her text in terms of Sartre's, and an interpretation of Sartre's text in terms of an ethical crisis in her own life. As Gadamer suggests, it is impossible to achieve one without the other, even if conventions sometimes require a writer to conceal the personal engagement which is, after all, what it means to have an attitude, or an opinion, or a perspective (see 340–41).

While the bathetic quality of the account of Mickey's death would probably be conspicuous to a student more familiar with academic discourse, this bathos is simply a measure of the writer's distance from our world, a distance that will not diminish—not diminish in fact, although it might in appearance—if she learns to imitate the language of the academy without gaining an ability to use that language on her own behalf. In spite of her initial situation of disadvantage, the form of the essay enables her to appropriate a territory which has become unmistakably Sartre's, the territory of "existence and essence," of "good faith" and "bad faith," of "condemnation to freedom." Whereas suicide and sociology, in the first student essay, belong exclusively to Durkheim, the writer of this second paper has begun to perceive that the area of meaning defined by Sartre is not strictly Sartre's, or strictly her own, but a common ground. However unsophisticated her account may seem to us, she employs narrative incident just as Sartre does, to furnish practical illustrations of philosophic principles: to a significant degree she has recognized, beyond the particulars of Sartre's argument, the way his argument operates rhetorically. If she continues to use writing in this fashion, as the means of discovering an enlarging horizon that every discourse can open to her view, she will gradually enter the community of "knowers" while retaining her own voice in the process. But if we demand from the start a demonstration of conventional proficiency, without the moments of naivete and indirection that are essential to any legitimate conversation, our students will remain outsiders, unempowered in our world and unaware of the forces which have created theirs. Although I recognize that the second writer is not ready to leave freshman English behind, I consider her essay to be a significant achievement, an essential first step in her progress toward work that is more complex intellectually, more self-conscious stylistically.

The essay on Durkheim, on the other hand, requires extensive revision, which I would initiate by urging its author to bring himself into the conversation, possibly in a preliminary "working paper" on the destructive forces in his life and the lives of his friends. Once he has completed this working paper, I might ask him to discuss what he supposes to be the most likely causes of teenage suicide, and to make a case either for or against its inevitability. Only after he has placed himself within the context of Durkheim's question will he be prepared to understand the significance of Durkheim's analysis. To the degree that this writer still imagines an anonymous, expert language which can protect him from uncertainty, he remains, for all his formal proficiency, a beginner. Like Foucault's persona at the opening of the *Discourse on Language*, he "would have preferred to be enveloped in words," a "happy wreck" carried along by the flow of language, instead of recovering a voice, and a self, through struggle in the "risky world of discourse" (215–16). Precisely because discourse is risky in the manner that Foucault describes, the writers we most admire, "academic" writers by any standard, are typically those who have learned to reinstate their voices within the language of a discipline: or rather, they have learned to enter a discipline by finding their own voices. Durkheim and Sartre are both examples; Burke is another, Gadamer another, and certainly Foucault.

For Montaigne, the various traditions of learning are no more than compartments within a larger intersubjectivity. Not in any one of these compartments, nor in all of them together, can we "recognize ourselves from the proper angle," but only in the irreducible complexity of the "great world" (116). Insisting upon a meaning fully resident in the text, teachers in the period of New Criticism tyrannized over student-readers by concealing, albeit inadvertently, the sources of their classroom authority, which did not arise from greater attention to words on a page, but from a formidable knowledge of literature, of history, of philosophy, of "life." By reifying discourse communities as teachers reified texts a generation ago, we dis-empower our students in yet another way: whereas before they were expected only to look to an author's language, their task now is more complicated and more intimidating, to speak about such language in terms of extra-textual conventions with which they are almost always unfamiliar. And post-structuralist teachers, with a knowledge of these invisible conventions, wield an authority that would probably have embarrassed their New-

Critical predecessors. The alternative, I believe, is to permit our students to bring their extra-textual knowledge to bear upon every text we give them, and to provide them with strategies for using this knowledge to undertake a conversation which belongs to us all.

WORKS CITED

Adorno, T. W. "The Essay as Form." Trans. Bob Hullot-Kentor and Frederic Will. *New German Critique* 32 (1984): 151–71.

———. *Negative Dialectics.* Trans. E. B. Ashton. New York: Continuum, 1987.

Anselm of Canterbury. *Monologion. Anselm of Canterbury.* Ed. and trans. Jasper Hopkins and Herbert Richardson. Vol. 1. Toronto: Mellen, 1974. 1–86. 4 vols. 1974–76.

Bakhtin, M. M. *The Dialogic Imagination.* Trans. Caryl Emerson and Michael Holquist. Ed. Michael Holquist. Austin: U of Texas P, 1981.

Bazerman, Charles. *The Informed Writer: Using Sources in the Disciplines.* 2nd ed. Boston: Houghton, 1985.

Berthoff, Ann. *The Making of Meaning: Metaphors, Models, and Maxims for Writing Teachers.* Upper Montclair, NJ: Boynton, 1981.

Bizzell, Patricia. "Arguing about Literacy." *College English* 50 (1988): 141–53.

———. "Cognition, Convention, and Certainty: What We Need to Know about Writing." *Pre/Text* 3 (1982): 213–43.

Browne, M. Neil, and Stuart M. Keeley. *Asking the Right Questions.* Englewood Cliffs: Prentice, 1981.

Burke, Kenneth. *Permanence and Change: An Anatomy of Purpose.* 2nd ed. Berkeley: U of California P, 1954.

Foucault, Michel. *The Archaeology of Knowledge and the Discourse on Language.* New York: Pantheon, 1972.

Gadamer, Hans-Georg. *Truth and Method.* London: Sheed, 1975. New York: Crossroad, 1986.

Hurston, Zora Neale. *I Love Myself When I Am Laughing.* New York: Feminist P, 1979.

Lodge, David. *Language of Fiction: Essays in Criticism and Verbal Analysis of the English Novel.* New York: Columbia UP, 1966.

Maimon, Elaine P., et al. *Instructors Manual: Writing in the Arts and Sciences.* Cambridge, MA: Winthrop, 1981.

Marcuse, Herbert. "On the Philosophical Foundation of the Concept of Labor in Economics." *Telos* 16 (1973): 9–37.

Montaigne, Michel. *The Complete Works of Montaigne.* Ed. and trans. Donald M. Frame. Stanford: Stanford UP, 1958.

Chapter 10

The Classroom and the Wider Culture: Identity as a Key to Learning English Composition

Fan Shen

One day in June 1975, when I walked into the aircraft factory where I was working as an electrician, I saw many large-letter posters on the walls and many people parading around the workshops shouting slogans like "Down with the word 'I'!" and "Trust in masses and the Party!" I then remembered that a new political campaign called "Against Individualism" was scheduled to begin that day. Ten years later, I got back my first English composition paper at the University of Nebraska–Lincoln. The professor's first comments were: "Why did you always use 'we' instead of 'I'?" and "Your paper would be stronger if you eliminated some sentences in the passive voice." The clashes between my Chinese background and the requirements of English composition had begun. At the center of this mental struggle, which has lasted several years and is still not completely over, is the prolonged, uphill battle to recapture "myself."

In this paper I will try to describe and explore this experience of reconciling my Chinese identity with an English identity dictated by the rules of English composition. I want to show how my cultural background shaped—and shapes—my approaches to my writing in English and how writing in English redefined—and redefines—my *ideological* and *logical* identities. By "ideological identity" I mean the system of values that I acquired (consciously and unconsciously) from my social and cultural background. And by "logical identity" I mean the natural (or Oriental) way I

College Composition and Communication, 1989

organize and express my thoughts in writing. Both had to be modified or redefined in learning English composition. Becoming aware of the process of redefinition of these different identities is a mode of learning that has helped me in my efforts to write in English, and, I hope, will be of help to teachers of English composition in this country. In presenting my case for this view, I will use examples from both my composition courses and literature courses, for I believe that writing papers for both kinds of courses contributed to the development of my "English identity." Although what I will describe is based on personal experience, many Chinese students whom I talked to said that they had had the same or similar experiences in their initial stages of learning to write in English.

IDENTITY OF THE SELF: IDEOLOGICAL AND CULTURAL

Starting with the first English paper I wrote, I found that learning to compose in English is not an isolated classroom activity, but a social and cultural experience. The rules of English composition encapsulate values that are absent in, or sometimes contradictory to, the values of other societies (in my case, China). Therefore, learning the rules of English composition is, to a certain extent, learning the values of Anglo-American society. In writing classes in the United States I found that I had to reprogram my mind, to redefine some of the basic concepts and values that I had about myself, about society, and about the universe, values that had been imprinted and reinforced in my mind by my cultural background, and that had been part of me all my life.

Rule number one in English composition is: Be yourself. (More than one composition instructor has told me, "Just write what *you* think.") The values behind this rule, it seems to me, are based on the principle of protecting and promoting individuality (and private property) in this country. The instruction was probably crystal clear to students raised on these values, but, as a guideline of composition, it was not very clear or useful to me when I first heard it. First of all, the image or meaning that I attached to the word "I" or "myself" was, as I found out, different from that of my English teacher. In China, "I" is always subordinated to "We"—be it the working class, the Party, the country, or some other collective body. Both political pressure and literary tradition require that "I" be somewhat hidden or buried in writings and speeches; presenting the "self" too obviously would give people the impression of being disrespectful of the Communist Party in political writings and boastful in scholarly writings. The word "I" has often been identified with another "bad" word, "individualism," which has become a synonym for selfishness in China. For a long time the words "self" and "individualism" have had negative connotations in my mind, and the negative force of the words naturally extended to the field of literary studies. As a result, even if I had brilliant ideas, the "I" in my papers always had to show some modesty by not competing with or trying to stand above the names of ancient and modern authoritative figures. Appealing to Mao or other Marxist authorities became the required way (as well as the most "forceful" or "persuasive" way) to prove one's point in written discourse. I remember that in China I had even committed what I can call "reversed plagiarism"—here, I suppose it would be called "forgery"—when I was in middle school: willfully attributing some of my thoughts to "experts" when I needed some arguments but could not find a suitable quotation from a literary or political "giant."

Now, in America, I had to learn to accept the words "I" and "Self" as something glorious (as Whitman did), or at least something not to be ashamed of or embarrassed about. It was the first and probably biggest step I took into English composition and critical writing. Acting upon my professor's suggestion, I intentionally tried to show my "individuality" and to "glorify" "I" in my papers by using as many "I's" as possible—"I think," "I believe," "I see"—and deliberately cut out quotations from authorities. It was rather painful to hand in such "pompous" (I mean immodest) papers to my instructors. But to an extent it worked. After a while I became more comfortable with only "the shadow of myself." I felt more at ease to put down *my* thoughts without looking over my shoulder to worry about the attitudes of my teachers or the reactions of the Party secretaries, and to speak out as "bluntly" and "immodestly" as my American instructors demanded.

But writing many "I's" was only the beginning of the process of redefining myself. Speaking of redefining myself is, in an important sense, speaking of redefining the word "I." By such a redefinition I mean not only the change in how I envisioned myself, but also the change in how *I* perceived the world. The old "I" used to embody only one set of values, but now it had to embody multiple sets of values. To be truly "myself," which I knew was a key to my success in learning English composition, meant *not to be my Chinese self* at all. That is to say, when I write in English I have to wrestle with and abandon (at least temporarily) the whole system of ideology which previously defined me in myself. I had to forget Marxist doctrines (even though I do not see myself as a Marxist by choice) and the Party lines imprinted in my mind and familiarize myself with a system of capitalist/bourgeois values. I had to put aside an ideology of collectivism and adopt the values of individualism. In composition as well as in literature classes, I had to make a fundamental adjustment: if I used to examine society and literary materials through the microscopes of Marxist dialectical materialism and historical materialism, I now had to learn to look through the microscopes the other way around, i.e., to learn to look at and understand the world from the point of view of "idealism." (I must add here that there are American professors who use a Marxist approach in their teaching.)

The word "idealism," which affects my view of both myself and the universe, is loaded with social connotations, and can serve as a good example of how redefining a key word can be a pivotal part of redefining my ideological identity as a whole.

To me, idealism is the philosophical foundation of the dictum of English composition: "Be yourself." In order to write good English, I knew that I had to be myself, which actually meant not to be my Chinese self. It meant that I had to create an English self and be *that* self. And to be that English self, I felt, I had to understand and accept idealism the way a Westerner does. That is to say, I had to accept the way a Westerner sees himself in relation to the universe and society. On the one hand, I knew a lot about idealism. But on the other hand, I knew nothing about it. I mean I knew a lot about idealism through the propaganda and objections of its opponent, Marxism, but I knew little about it from its own point of view. When I thought of the word "materialism"—which is a major part of Marxism and in China has repeatedly been "shown" to be the absolute truth—there were always positive connotations, and words like "right," "true," etc., flashed in my mind. On the other hand, the word "idealism" always came to me with the dark connotations that surround words like "absurd," "illogical," "wrong," etc. In China "idealism" is depicted as a ferocious and ridiculous enemy of Marxist philosophy. Idealism, as the simplified definition imprinted in my mind had it, is the view that the material world does not exist; that all that exists is the mind and its ideas. It is just the opposite of Marxist dialectical materialism which sees the mind as a product of the material world. It is not too difficult to see that idealism, with its idea that mind is of primary importance, provides a philosophical foundation for the Western emphasis on the value of individual human minds, and hence individual human beings. Therefore, my final acceptance of myself as of primary importance—an importance that overshadowed that of authority figures in English composition—was, I decided, dependent on an acceptance of idealism.

My struggle with idealism came mainly from my efforts to understand and to write about works such as Coleridge's *Literaria Biographia* and Emerson's "Over-Soul." For a long time I was frustrated and puzzled by the idealism expressed by Coleridge and Emerson—given their ideas, such as "I think, therefore I am" (Coleridge obviously borrowed from Descartes) and "the transparent eyeball" (Emerson's view of himself)—because in my mind, drenched as it was in dialectical materialism, there was always a little voice whispering in my ear, "You are, therefore you think." I could not see how human consciousness, which is not material, could create apples and trees. My intellectual conscience refused to let me believe that the human mind is the primary world and the material world secondary. Finally, I had to imagine that I was looking at a world with my head upside down. When I imagined that I was in a new body (born with the head upside down) it was easier to forget biases imprinted in my subconsciousness about idealism, the mind, and my former self. Starting from scratch, the new inverted self—which I called my "English Self" and into which I have transformed myself—could understand and *accept*, with ease, idealism as "the truth" and "himself" (i.e., my English Self) as the "creator" of the world.

Here is how I created my new "English Self." I played a "game" similar to ones played by mental therapists. First I made a list of (simplified) features about writing associated with my old identity (the Chinese Self), both ideological and logical, and then beside the first list I added a column of features about writing associated with my new identity (the English Self). After that I pictured myself getting out of my old identity, the timid, humble, modest Chinese "I," and creeping into my new identity (often in the form of a new skin or a mask), the confident, assertive, and aggressive English "I." The new "Self" helped me to remember and accept the different rules of Chinese and English composition and the values that underpin these rules. In a sense, creating an English Self is a way of reconciling my old cultural values with the new values required by English writing, without losing the former.

An interesting structural but not material parallel to my experiences in this regard has been well described by Min-zhan Lu in her important article, "From Silence to Words: Writing as Struggle" (*College English* 49 [April 1987]: 437–48). Min-zhan Lu talks about struggles between two selves, an open self and a secret self, and between two discourses, a mainstream Marxist discourse and a bourgeois discourse her parents wanted her to learn. But her struggle was different from mine. Her Chinese self was severely constrained and suppressed by mainstream cultural discourse, but never interfused with it. Her experiences, then, were not representative of those of the majority of the younger generation who, like me, were brought up on only one discourse. I came to English composition as a Chinese person, in the fullest sense of the term, with a Chinese identity already fully formed.

IDENTITY OF THE MIND: ILLOGICAL AND ALOGICAL

In learning to write in English, besides wrestling with a different ideological system, I found that I had to wrestle with a logical system very different from the blueprint of logic at the back of my mind. By "logical system" I mean two things: the Chinese way of thinking I used to approach my theme or topic in written discourse, and the Chinese critical/logical way to develop a theme or topic. By English rules, the first is illogical, for it is the opposite of the English way of approaching a topic; the second is alogical (non-logical), for it mainly uses mental pictures instead of words as a critical vehicle.

The Illogical Pattern. In English composition, an essential rule for the logical organization of a piece of writing is the use of a "topic sentence." In Chinese composition, "from surface to core" is an essential rule, a rule which means that one ought to reach a topic gradually and "systematically" instead of "abruptly."

The concept of a topic sentence, it seems to me, is symbolic of the values of a busy people in an industrialized society, rushing to get things done, hoping to attract and satisfy the busy reader very quickly. Thinking back, I realized that I did not fully understand the virtue of the concept until my life began to rush at the speed of everyone else's in this country. Chinese composition, on the other hand, seems to embody the values of a leisurely paced rural society whose inhabitants have the time to chew and taste a topic slowly. In Chinese composition, an introduction explaining how and why one chooses this topic is not only acceptable, but often regarded as necessary. It arouses the reader's interest in the topic little by little (and this is seen as a virtue of composition) and gives him/her a sense of refinement. The famous Robert B. Kaplan "noodles" contrasting a spiral Oriental thought process with a straight-line Western approach ("Cultural Thought Patterns in Inter-Cultural Education," *Readings on English as a Second Language*, Ed. Kenneth Croft, 2nd ed., Winthrop, 1980, 403–10) may be too simplistic to capture the preferred pattern of writing in English, but I think they still express some truth about Oriental writing. A Chinese writer often clears the surrounding bushes before attacking the real target. This bush-clearing pattern in Chinese writing goes back two thousand years to Kong Fuzi (Confucius). Before doing anything, Kong says in his *Luen Yu* (*Analects*), one first needs to call things by their proper names (expressed by his phrase "Zheng Ming" 正名). In other words, before touching one's main thesis, one should first state the "conditions" of composition: how, why, and when the piece is being composed. All of this will serve as a proper foundation on which to build the "house" of the piece. In the two thousand years after Kong, this principle of composition was gradually formalized (especially through the formal essays required by imperial examinations) and became known as "Ba Gu," or the eight-legged essay. The logic of Chinese composition, exemplified by the eight-legged essay, is like the peeling of an onion: layer after layer is removed until the reader finally arrives at the central point, the core.

Ba Gu still influences modern Chinese writing. Carolyn Matalene has an excellent discussion of this logical (or illogical) structure and its influence on her Chinese students' efforts to write in English ("Contrastive Rhetoric: An American Writing Teacher in China," *College English* 47 [November 1985]: 789–808). A recent Chinese textbook for composition lists six essential steps (factors) for writing a narrative essay, steps to be taken in this order: time, place, character, event, cause, and consequence (*Yuwen Jichu Zhishi Liushi Jiang* [*Sixty Lessons on the Basics of the Chinese Language*], Ed. Beijing Research Institute of Education, Beijing Publishing House, 1981, 525–609). Most Chinese students (including me) are taught to follow this sequence in composition.

The straightforward approach to composition in English seemed to me, at first, illogical. One could not jump to the topic. One had to walk step by step to reach the topic. In several of my early papers I found that the Chinese approach—the bush-clearing approach—persisted, and I had considerable difficulty writing (and in fact understanding) topic sentences. In what I deemed to be topic sentences, I grudgingly gave out themes. Today, those papers look to me like Chinese papers with forced or false English openings. For example, in a narrative paper on a trip to New York, I wrote the forced/false topic sentence, "A trip to New York in winter is boring." In the next few paragraphs, I talked about the weather, the people who went with me, and so on, before I talked about what I learned from the trip. My real thesis was that one could always learn something even on a boring trip.

The Alogical Pattern. In learning English composition, I found that there was yet another cultural blueprint affecting my logical thinking. I found from my early papers that very often I was unconsciously under the influence of a Chinese critical approach called the creation of "yijing," which is totally nonWestern. The direct translation of the word "yijing" is: yi, "mind or consciousness," and jing, "environment." An ancient approach which has existed in China for many centuries and is still the subject of much discussion, yijing is a complicated concept that defies a universal definition. But most critics in China nowadays seem to agree on one point, that yijing is the critical approach that separates Chinese literature and criticism from Western literature and criticism. Roughly speaking, yijing is the process of creating a pictorial environment while reading a piece of literature. Many critics in China believe that yijing is a creative process of inducing oneself, while reading a piece of literature or looking at a piece of art, to create mental pictures, in order to reach a unity of nature, the author, and the reader. Therefore, it is by its very nature both creative and critical. According to the theory, this nonverbal, pictorial process leads directly to a higher ground of beauty and morality. Almost all critics in China agree that yijing is not a process of logical thinking—it is not a process of moving from the premises of an argument to its conclusion, which is the foundation of Western criticism. According to yijing, the process of criticizing a piece of art or literary work has to involve the process of creation on the reader's part. In yijing, verbal thoughts and pictorial thoughts are one. Thinking is conducted largely in pictures and then "transcribed" into words. (Ezra Pound once tried to capture the creative aspect of yijing in poems such as "In a Station of the Metro." He also tried to capture the critical aspect of it in his theory of imagism and vorticism, even though he did not know the term "yijing.") One characteristic of the yijing approach to criticism, therefore, is that it often includes a description of the created mental pictures on the part of the reader/critic and his/her mental attempt to bridge (unite) the literary work, the pictures, with ultimate beauty and peace.

In looking back at my critical papers for various classes, I discovered that I unconsciously used the approach of yijing, especially in some of my earlier papers when I seemed not yet to have been in the grip of Western logical critical approaches. I wrote, for instance, an essay entitled "Wordsworth's Sound and Imagination: The Snowdon Episode." In the major part of the essay I described the pictures that flashed in my mind while I was reading passages in Wordsworth's long poem, *The Prelude.*

> I saw three climbers (myself among them) winding up the mountain in silence "at the dead of night," absorbed in their "private thoughts." The sky was full of blocks of clouds of different colors, freely changing their shapes, like oily pigments disturbed in a bucket of water. All of a sudden, the moonlight broke the darkness "like a flash," lighting up the mountain tops. Under the "naked moon," the band saw a vast sea of mist and vapor, a silent ocean. Then the silence was abruptly broken, and we heard the "roaring of waters, torrents, streams/Innumerable, roaring with one voice" from a "blue chasm," a fracture in the vapor of the sea. It was a joyful revelation of divine truth to the human mind: the bright, "naked" moon sheds the light of "higher reasons" and "spiritual love" upon us; the vast ocean of mist looked like a thin curtain through which we vaguely saw the infinity of nature beyond; and the sounds of roaring waters coming out of the chasm of vapor cast us into the boundless spring of imagination from the depth of the human heart. Evoked by the divine light from above, the human spring of imagination is joined by the natural spring and becomes a sustaining source of energy, feeding "upon infinity" while transcending infinity at the same time. . . .

Here I was describing my own experience more than Wordsworth's. The picture described by the poet is taken over and developed by the reader. The imagination of the author and the imagination of the reader are thus joined together. There was no "because" or "therefore" in the paper. There was little *logic.* And I thought it was (and it is) criticism. This seems to me a typical (but simplified) example of the yijing approach. (Incidentally, the instructor, a kind professor, found the paper interesting, though a bit "strange.")

In another paper of mine, "The Note of Life: Williams's 'The Orchestra'," I found myself describing my experiences of pictures of nature while reading William Carlos Williams's poem "The Orchestra." I "painted" these fleeting pictures and described the feelings that seemed to lead me to an understanding of a harmony, a "common tone," between man and nature. A paragraph from that paper reads:

> The poem first struck me as a musical fairy tale. With rich musical sounds in my ear, I seemed to be walking in a solitary, dense forest on a spring morning. No sound from human society could be heard. I was now sitting under a giant pine tree, ready to hear the grand concert of Nature. With the sun slowly rising from the east, the cello (the creeping creek) and the clarinet (the rustling pine trees) started with a slow overture. Enthusiastically the violinists (the twittering birds) and the French horn (the mumbling cow) "interpose[d] their voices," and the bass (bears) got in at the wrong time. The orchestra did not stop, they continued to play. The musicians of Nature do not always play in harmony. "Together, unattuned," they have to seek "a common tone" as they play along. The symphony of Nature is like the symphony of human life: both consist of random notes seeking a "common tone." For the symphony of life
>
> > Love is that common tone
> > shall raise his fiery head
> > and sound his note.

Again, the logical pattern of this paper, the "pictorial criticism," is illogical to Western minds but "logical" to those acquainted with yijing. (Perhaps I should not even use the words "logical" and "think" because they are so conceptually tied up with "words" and with culturally-based conceptions, and therefore very misleading if not useless in a discussion of yijing. Maybe I should simply say that yijing is neither illogical nor logical, but alogical.)

I am not saying that such a pattern of "alogical" thinking is wrong—in fact some English instructors find it interesting and acceptable—but it is very non-Western. Since I was in this country to learn the English language and English literature, I had to abandon Chinese "pictorial logic," and to learn Western "verbal logic."

IF I HAD TO START AGAIN

The change is profound: through my understanding of new meanings of words like "individualism," "idealism," and "I," I began to accept the underlying concepts and values of American writing, and by learning to use "topic sentences" I began to accept a new logic. Thus, when I write papers in English, I am able to obey all the general rules of English composition. In doing this I feel that I am writing through, with, and because of a new identity. I welcome the change, for it has added a new dimension to me and to my view of the world. I am not saying that I have entirely lost my Chinese identity. In fact I feel that I will never lose it. Any time I write in Chinese, I resume my old identity, and obey the rules of Chinese composition such as "Make the 'I' modest," and "Beat around the bush before attacking the central topic." It is necessary for me to have such a Chinese identity in order to write authentic Chinese. (I have seen people who, after learning to write in English, use English logic and sentence patterning to write Chinese. They produce very awkward Chinese texts.) But when I write in English, I imagine myself slipping into a new "skin," and I let the "I" behave much more aggressively and knock the topic right on the head. Being conscious of these different identities has helped me to reconcile different systems of values and logic, and has played a pivotal role in my learning to compose in English.

Looking back, I realize that the process of learning to write in English is in fact a process of creating and defining a new identity and balancing it with the old identity. The process of learning English composition would have been easier if I had realized this earlier and consciously sought to compare the two different identities required by the two writing systems from two different cultures. It is fine and perhaps even necessary for American composition teachers to teach about topic sentences, paragraphs, the use of punctuation, documentation, and so on, but can anyone design exercises sensitive to the ideological and logical differences that students like me experience—and design them so they can be introduced at an early stage of an English composition class? As I pointed out earlier, the traditional advice "Just be yourself" is not clear and helpful to students from Korea, China, Vietnam, or India. From "Be yourself" we are likely to hear either "Forget your cultural habit of writing" or "Write as you would write in your own language." But neither of the two is what the instructor meant or what we want to do. It would be helpful if he or she pointed out the different cultural/ideological connotations of the word "I," the connotations that exist in a group-centered culture and an individual-centered culture. To sharpen the contrast, it might be useful to design papers on topics like "The Individual vs. The Group: China vs. America" or "Different 'I's' in Different Cultures."

Carolyn Matalene mentioned in her article (789) an incident concerning American businessmen who presented their Chinese hosts with gifts of cheddar cheese, not knowing that the Chinese generally do not like cheese. Liking cheddar cheese may not be essential to writing English prose, but being truly accustomed to the social norms that stand behind ideas such as the English "I" and the logical pattern of English composition—call it "compositional cheddar cheese"—is essential to writing in English. Matalene does not provide an "elixir" to help her Chinese students like English "compositional cheese," but rather recommends, as do I, that composition teachers not be afraid to give foreign students English "cheese," but to make sure to hand it out slowly, sympathetically, and fully realizing that it tastes very peculiar in the mouths of those used to a very different cuisine.

Chapter 11

Evaluating Second Language Essays in Regular Composition Classes: Toward a Pluralistic U.S. Rhetoric

Robert E. Land, Jr.
Catherine Whitley

How we go about empowering English as a second language (ESL) students when they enter regular college composition classes in the United States is determined by our response to two questions: What do we wish them to be empowered to do, and for whom are they being empowered? Our first response to these questions (a traditional, nominal one) is that we wish ESL students to acquire enough facility with standard written English (SWE) to succeed in school and in the workplace for their own benefit and, second, especially in the case of the large numbers of ESL students who are immigrants to this country, for the benefit of our society. To achieve these goals, we need to emphasize grammatical and syntactic correctness and, certainly at the college level where students are called upon to use written communication in a variety of disciplines and for a variety of purposes, we need to emphasize the larger rhetorical conventions of academic writing. Although, as Raimes (1986) notes, we have problems of implementation even in separate ESL classes, we have at hand the means of establishing programs to meet these goals.

Our nominal goal of helping students avoid linguistic disenfranchisement seems, at first glance, both pragmatic and responsible. However, the prevalent methods of evaluating writing—especially in classes where ESL students compete directly with native speakers (NSs) and where instructors

Richness in Writing: Empowering ESL Students, 1989

have little or no training in teaching second language (L2) learners—suggest that we don't wish ESL students to attain only a "facility" with written English; instead, we expect them to become entirely fluent in English, a goal different in nature and implication from our purported one. The discrepancy between our purported and apparent goals for instructing ESL students emerges in our standards of evaluation as a hidden agenda—that is, an agenda that is rarely made known to the students whose writing is being evaluated and one that is seldom clear to the evaluator (see Sommers, 1982; Zamel, 1985). Thus, even when an ESL writer produces an error-free composition in English, a hidden agenda leads the evaluator to find fault with other formal features. Our research (Land and Whitley, 1986) suggests that the text features influencing English NS readers most negatively are the ESL students' patterns of organization, patterns established in what Purves (1986) calls "rhetorical communities" where ESL students learned their native language. At present, our understanding of the cultural determination of rhetorical patterns is limited, although investigations like those by Purves (1986), Hinds (1983), and Kaplan (1983) are extending these limits. We probably know too little about the mechanisms of our own preferred rhetorical patterns, let alone about those that ESL students bring with them, to establish programs aimed at reifying "ours" by isolating and eliminating "theirs" from their written English. But even if such knowledge were available, our efforts at making ESL students entirely fluent would almost certainly fail.

To be truly "fluent," our ESL students would have to be able to produce essays in English that were not only grammatically and syntactically, but also rhetorically indistinguishable from those written by their NS peers. But, as Haugen (1986) points out, even writers who are isolated for years from their first language (L1) culture produce texts in their L2 which carry noticeable L1 features; and most of our ESL students maintain strong associations with members of their L1 rhetorical communities. The distinct world views of these communities influence members' thoughts, actions, and, consequently, their patterns of communication for many generations (see, e.g., Giordano, 1976; Havighurst, 1978; McGoldrick, 1982). "English only" movements and literacy crises notwithstanding, we can neither legislate nor educate away culturally determined rhetorical differences in writing.

To enable ESL students to write English with "facility," we should, of course, pay special attention to teaching the linguistic conventions of SWE. We may also be able to teach them how to use some of SWE's rhetorical conventions. But such instruction may not be an end in itself. In the United States, SWE rhetorical conventions generally emphasize strong sentence-to-sentence connections, resulting in "linear" prose (see Kaplan, 1966), and a deductive logical arrangement that satisfies what Lakoff and Johnson (1980) call our "objectivist myth." But there are many patterns of cohesion, other logics, other myths through which views of the world may be constructed (see Knoblauch and Brannon, 1984). In teaching SWE rhetorical conventions, we are teaching students to reproduce in a mechanical fashion our preferred vehicle of understanding.

As MacCannell and MacCannell (1982) note, "culture that reproduces itself as a series of endless mirrorings, yet adds nothing to either the original 'natural culture' or the original 'image' of it, is literally the death of culture" (p. 28). Elsewhere they stress that "the heart of cultural evolution . . . begins with a production and proceeds to a reproduction that is not a simple doubling but a reflection at a higher power" (p. 26). In this view, we are encouraging our ESL students to contribute to the death of our culture: Their textual productions are simply to mirror, in their use of our rhetorical tradition, an experience that might be entirely foreign to them. We are not asking ESL writers to add to our culture from their own storehouses of experience; the sense is that our culture has reached the end of its evolution: There's nothing more to add. Trying to teach ESL students to reproduce SWE rhetoric may be not only likely to fail, but even if it were to be successful, it would be a pyrrhic victory.

Thus, we must change the way we read, respond to, and evaluate ESL writers' work at all stages of its development. If we fail to do so, our composition courses will be as retributive as they are instructive. If we wish to admit rhetorical concerns openly to our system of evaluation (thus unmasking the hidden agenda), if we believe that concerns of "correctness," content, and rhetoric are inseparable, then we must learn to recognize, value, and foster the alternative rhetorics that the ESL student brings to our language. In this chapter, we argue for such an approach, one that will not only empower students to succeed in school and at work, but will also free them to incorporate their own forms of logic into their writing, to the potential benefit of our language and culture.

RHETORICAL DIFFERENCES

No one who has ever read through a stack of compositions written by native and nonnative speakers needs to consult research to confirm that there are differences. Differences in the number of surface errors made by ESL students are obvious to teachers and have been well documented by researchers (Ahrens, 1984; Fein, 1980; Kroll, 1983). But error is not the only difference between texts written by ESL students and their NS peers. Even with error removed from all essays, researchers (McGirt, 1984; Whitley,

1984) have found that NS readers give higher scores to papers of NSs than to those written by ESL students. Clearly, other important differences exist.

Most of the research designed to find these important differences has focused on patterns of organization. Some of this research, following the work of Halliday and Hasan (1976), has focused on contrasting cohesive ties and drawing conclusions about textual cohesion from analysis of the ties, or from global measures of cohesion, or both (Connor, 1984; Land & Whitley, 1986; Lindsay, 1984; Scarcella, 1984). Along with more general investigations of differences (Hinds, 1983; Kaplan, 1966; Purves, 1986), these studies taken as a whole demonstrate fairly clearly that ESL writers connect their ideas differently than do NS writers. They demonstrate as well that these differences in organization are, at least in part, the result of ESL students' membership in distinct rhetorical communities and not necessarily the result of inadequate mastery of U.S. English. Finally, they demonstrate that these organizational differences are partly responsible for ESL students' essays being judged by NS readers as inferior to native speakers' essays.

One of the questions we have asked in our research (Land & Whitley, 1986) is whether or not the L1 status of readers would affect their perceptions of batches of student essays sampled from freshman composition classes where about half the students were nonnative speakers of English. We found, predictably, that U.S.-born NS readers rated the papers of ESL writers lower than the papers of NS students. But we also found that readers whose L1 was not English (our sample included native speakers of German, Spanish, and Japanese) rated essays from both ESL and NS students as being of about equal quality. Data from analytic rating scales revealed that the differences in perceptions of quality were probably the result of differences in perceptions of organization: The U.S.-born NS readers marked down ESL essays for what they perceived as problems of organization; readers whose L1 was not English did not mark down ESL texts for organization. In this respect our results mirror the language-specific research of Hinds (1983), who found that native English speaking readers rated the organization of English translations of Japanese newspaper articles lower than Japanese speaking readers rated the originals.

From our results we concluded that either our English NNS readers have lax standards and can't tell a poorly organized essay from a well organized one or they can accommodate to more kinds of rhetorical patterns than can NS readers. Because both groups of readers agreed on the ratings of NS essays, and because both groups were sampled from our pool of experienced teachers of freshman writing, we opted for the second conclusion. We believe that our bilingual and multilingual readers' experience with different kinds of texts used in different cultures allow them to adapt to and value writing that employs varying rhetorical organizations.

READERS READING

Any reader confronting any text faces it with a preconceived set of expectations; as Iser (1976/1978) and Carrell (1982) note, the reader comes to a text armed with the sum of previous reading experiences. The reader and the text interact in the process of reading. The wandering viewpoint is a means of describing the way in which the reader is present in the text. This presence is at a point where memory and expectation converge, and the resultant dialectic movement brings about a continual modification of memory and an increasing complexity of expectation. These processes depend on the reciprocal spotlighting of the perspectives, which provide interrelated backgrounds for one another. The interaction between these backgrounds provokes the reader into synthesizing activity (Iser, 1976/1978). The expectations of a teacher of writing in the United States would be based upon the grammatical, syntactic, and rhetorical conventions of SWE, expectations which the student essay should trigger and bring into play, thus beginning the dialectic movement. For instance, the presence of an identifiable, analytic thesis sentence signals a certain rhetorical pattern and allows the reader to begin building a set of expectations specific to that particular text. The reader remembers the thesis, moves on, and expects to find its promise fulfilled.

Because ESL readers seem to find organization in ESL texts—texts that NS readers judge to be poorly organized—perhaps they have a wider and more varied set of expectations when they come to a text, expectations resulting from a wider and more varied reading experience. As Purves (1986) has shown, "good" student writers from different countries (students selected by their own instructors as being exemplary), when asked to write an essay on the same topic, write those essays in different rhetorical modes that vary in stance, descriptive quality, and levels of abstraction and concreteness. He notes that "the fact that the compositions come from 'good' students suggests that these students have learned and are applying the norms of their rhetorical community" (Purves, 1986, p. 43); these students have learned to conform to the expectations of the community in which they find themselves. Likewise, the ESL readers have negotiated between the norms of their native communities and the one in which they find themselves; these readers recognized the SWE patterns of organization in the NS essays.

If every time we face a student paper we do so with the expectations of SWE firmly in mind, and we expect to find a linear, deductive argument, our experience of reading ESL students' essays will be different from our experience of reading NS students'. Most ESL students, even those in "regular" (i.e., linguistically heterogeneous) college writing classes, have not learned to use the organizational patterns of U.S. academic prose. This does not mean they are "bad" writers or that their essays are "badly organized"; it could mean that they are very skillfully manipulating patterns of organization that we don't recognize. A reader with expectations shaped by SWE will not interact successfully (in Iser's terms) with such essays; ESL writers' essays will not trigger dialectic movements because they do not fulfill the reader's expectations.

If the "wandering viewpoint" is a way to describe the way in which the reader is present in the text, then a reader with SWE expectations continues to wander rather aimlessly in a text by an ESL writer because the reader cannot recognize the signposts left by the writer. (For instance, we have found that ESL writers tend to use a few distantly separated cohesive ties as a way of establishing coherence, something very uncommon in their NS peers' work.) Readers should allow themselves to be lost for a while, for readers who suspend judgment and thus become accustomed to recognizing a wider variety of rhetorical modes, will begin to alter their expectations, to widen them, a process which will ultimately permit them to interact with more types of texts, thereby enriching their reading processes.

In contrast, readers who rigidly insist on finding a set of distinct expectations met in every encounter with student writing squelch in themselves responses to different approaches to presenting and receiving ideas; in effect, they suppress new information. SWE, as a set of conventions, is itself a rigid and rather artificial stratum of English if, as Bakhtin (1975/1981) describes, all national languages are stratified into social dialects, characteristic group behavior, a professional jargon, generic languages, languages of generations and age groups, tendentious languages, languages of authorities, of various circles, and of passing fashions, languages that serve the specific sociopolitical purpose of the day (pp. 262–263). In this view, SWE is just a particular stratification of English, the one privileged by and identified with academia, a sublanguage which, by its nature, is sociopolitical.

In demanding that ESL students write SWE and use a deductive, linear argument, we are asking them to situate themselves within a particular sociopolitical context, and we respond to and judge their writing according to how accurately they are able to do so. If students are not natives of this culture they will be less likely to signal satisfactorily to us, the readers, their understanding of their position within the English language as a sociopolitical construct; even if their writing is in more or less error-free English, they will still be writing according to the norms of their native communities. By asking these students to use our signals according to our expectations, we are not taking language to be "a system of abstract grammatical categories"; instead, we are at least implicitly understanding "language conceived as ideologically saturated, language as world view" (Bakhtin, 1975/1981, p. 271). We require our ESL students to share and reproduce in their writing our world view, one to which they are, of course, alien. Such instruction is composition as colonization.

CHANGING THE WAY WE READ, RESPOND, AND EVALUATE

In general we would argue that all teachers should become more like the ESL readers in our study; that they acquire the ability to suspend judgment, to allow the piece of writing at hand to develop slowly, like a photographic print, shading in the details. But what does this mean in practice? It may mean that teachers with ESL students should become familiar with rhetorical traditions their students bring with them (see Reid, this volume). It certainly means that we need to consciously suppress our desire to label ESL writers' work as "out of focus" or "lacking in organization."

In our regular freshman writing classes, for example, assignments written by writing program directors are given to the teachers to be distributed. These assignments often require the ESL students in these classes, many of whom are U.S. residents who have spoken English for five or fewer years, to use conventional SWE structures such as thesis paragraphs. The ESL students comply, at least superficially, with these conventions. Eventually, however, usually in the second or third paragraph, ESL students return to the organizational conventions of their native rhetorics. This return does not go unnoticed; based on our examination of hundreds of marked essays, when ESL students stop consciously attending to the formal concerns of SWE patterns and begin focusing on what they have to say, teachers begin to note "problems" of clarity, focus, and organization. We would argue that it is here, at this point of departure from SWE expectations, that readers should suspend judgment and read on for meaning. After reading the entire text, a teacher might suggest that the introductory thesis paragraph is superfluous, instead of noting that the rest of the essay doesn't live up to the promise of the introduction. Or the teacher might suggest alternatives to seemingly disembodied topic sentences, alternatives that would meet the obligation of teaching the student how to produce passable prose that would not be dismissed, out of hand, by less open readers. In some cases, the teacher might not know how to respond to the text except by asking lots of questions about what the student was trying to say. In some situations we have known exactly where to help our ESL students; in others we have had only very vague ideas.

Perhaps the most common specific deviation from SWE expectations that we find in ESL students' papers is what seems like redundancy. Sometimes students seem to repeat themselves pointlessly or they seem to argue the same point in slightly different ways, paragraph after paragraph, each paragraph a modest addition or alteration of given information. We have chosen a similar structure for this chapter; we have argued for the same point, "that teachers should change the way they evaluate ESL writers' papers," in several ways. We hope our readers will be generous and recognize that we do so by trying to appeal separately to logic, the "facts" of research, the "authority" of theory and, finally, to our own personal experience—all of which are fairly standard "artistic" and "inartistic" proofs of Western classical rhetoric, although it might have been more traditional for us to have outlined our plan earlier in the text. More generosity is often needed when we read our students' texts.

One helpful strategy for reading seemingly redundant essays is to use a form of "topical structure" analysis like the one Connor and Farmer (1985) suggest as a revision strategy for writers. In its simple form, one circles, during the second reading, all of the grammatical subjects of all the independent clauses. Rereading the list of subjects can lead readers to revisions of their initial understanding of the essay as patterns of meaning that were not at first evident are revealed. Often the subjects seem to operate as higher-order cohesive devices. For example, one student (whose essay we used in our research) used thunder, or a variant thereof, as the subject of three very distantly removed sentences in his essay on the possibility of afterlife. Of course this bit of imagery stood out and it was fairly easy to recognize that the repetition seemed to operate as a device connecting distinct parts of his essay, but this was an essay that NS readers scored low because of its poor organization and that ESL readers scored high and found to be acceptably organized. Now, when we receive a paper like that one, we usually recognize its structure; we no longer make comments about its organization.

CONCLUSION

Research suggests that evaluative focus on sentence-level mechanics may be a waste of the teacher's time (Robb, Ross, & Shortreed, 1986) and confusing and even harmful to students (Land & Evans, 1987; Zamel, 1985). Thus, against all the forces that seem to keep our attention riveted on surface concerns, good pedagogy demands that we respond to larger features of our students' texts. As we learn to rid ourselves of surface-level tunnel vision, we will have to struggle against the forces that can lead us to rigid, oversimplified notions of how essays should be structured: rhetoric-level myopia.

Assuming that our responses to students' essays are intended to inform them in specific ways about how to make those pieces of writing (or the next ones) better, we can ask students to add to, delete from, or alter the paper; or we can let students know that they should keep up the good work. We have argued that teachers of ESL students should broaden their concept of what constitutes "good work" and that they should not automatically request additions of SWE features and deletions and modifications of everything else. In the end, because ESL texts customarily contain a lot of the "everything else," such practices should cut down on the amount of marking teachers feel they must do. At first (and even much later, especially when faced with high stacks of papers in the wee hours), reading "interactively" is hard work. It would be easy, in the midst of trying to figure out a particularly puzzling text, to dismiss the whole project as idealistic, impractical, or stupid and to return to the more comfortable, familiar mode of reading with narrow SWE rhetorical expectations.

To do so would be to ignore what is happening to our culture and our language: they are becoming more pluralistic, not coincidentally with the rise of English as the world language. If we are indeed part of a culture which admits change, this change will obviously appear at the linguistic level because one's epistemology underlies one's language. When our language changes, it is a sign that our way of thinking has changed. Unless we want to institute a structure like the Academie Française or the British Royal Academy, we have no choice but to recognize and examine the changes that are happening daily everywhere in order to see what we think now.

REFERENCES

Ahrens, C. D. (1984). *Comparing composition skills of native and non-native born students at the junior high school level.* Unpublished master's thesis, University of California at Los Angeles.
Bakhtin, M. M. (1981). *The dialogic imagination* (C. Emerson & M. Holquist, Trans.; M. Holquist, Ed.). Austin: University of Texas Press. (Original work published 1975)
Carrell, P. (1982). Cohesion is not coherence. *TESOL Quarterly, 16,* 479–488.
Connor, U. (1984). A study of cohesion and coherence in ESL students' writing. *Papers in Linguistics: International Journal of Human Communication, 17,* 301–316.
Connor, U., & Farmer, M. (1985, April). *The teaching of topical structure analysis as a revision strategy: An exploratory study.* Paper presented at the annual meeting of the American Educational Research Association, Chicago.
Fein, D. (1980). *A comparison of English and ESL compositions.* Unpublished master's thesis, University of California at Los Angeles.
Giordano, J. (1976). Community mental health in a pluralistic society. *International Journal of Mental Health, 5,* 5–15.
Halliday, M. A. K., & Hasan, R. (1976). *Cohesion in English.* London: Longman Group, Ltd.
Haugen, E. (1986). Bilinguals have more fun! *Journal of English Linguistics, 19,* 106–120.
Havighurst, R. J. (1978). Structural aspects of education and cultural pluralism. *Educational Research Quarterly, 2,* 5–19.
Hinds, J. (1983). Contrastive rhetoric: Japanese and English. *Text, 3,* 183–195.
Iser, W. (1978). *The act of reading: A theory of aesthetic response.* Baltimore: Johns Hopkins University Press. (Original work published 1976)
Kaplan, R. B. (1966). Cultural thought patterns in intercultural education. *Language Learning, 16,* 1–20.
Kaplan, R. B. (1983). Contrastive rhetoric: Some implications for the writing process. In A. Freedman, I. Pringle & J. Yalden (Eds.), *Learning to write: First language/second language* (pp. 138–161). New York: Longman.
Knoblauch, C. H., & Brannon, L. (1984). *Rhetorical traditions and the teaching of writing.* Upper Montclair, NJ: Boynton/Cook.

Kroll, B. (1983). Levels of error in ESL composition (Doctoral dissertation, University of California at Los Angeles, 1982). *Dissertation Abstracts International, 43*, 3307A–3308A. (University of Southern California Micrographics No. 2898A)

Lakoff, G., & Johnson, M. (1980). *Metaphors we live by*. Chicago: University of Chicago Press.

Land, R. E., & Evans, S. (1987). What our students taught us about paper making. *English Journal, 76*, 113–116.

Land, R. E., & Whitley, C. (1986, April). *Influences of second-language factors on the performance of freshman writers*. Papers presented at the annual meeting of the American Educational Research Association, San Francisco.

Lindsay, D. B. (1984). *Cohesion in the compositions of ESL and English students*. Unpublished master's thesis, University of California at Los Angeles.

MacCannell, D., & MacCannell, J. F. (1982). *The time of the sign: A semiotic interpretation of modern culture*. Bloomington: Indiana University Press.

McGirt, J. D. (1984). *The effect of morphological and syntactic errors on the holistic scores of native and non-native compositions*. Unpublished master's thesis, University of California at Los Angeles.

McGoldrick, M. (1982). Ethnicity and family therapy: An overview. In M. McGoldrick, J. K. Pearce, & J. Giardano (Eds.), *Ethnicity and family therapy* (pp. 3–30). New York: Guilford.

Purves, A. C. (1986). Rhetorical communities, the international student, and basic writing. *Journal of Basic Writing, 5*, 38–51.

Raimes, A. (1986). Teaching ESL writing: Fitting what we do to what we know. *The Writing Instructor, 5*, 153–166.

Robb, T., Ross, S., & Shortreed, I. (1986). Salience of feedback on error and its effect on EFL writing quality. *TESOL Quarterly, 20*, 83–93.

Scarcella, R. (1984). How writers orient their readers in expository essays: A comparative study of native and nonnative English writers. *TESOL Quarterly, 17*, 165–187.

Sommers, N. (1982). Responding to student writing. *College Composition and Communication, 33*, 148–156.

Whitley, C. (1984). *Error, content, and grading: ESL vs. NES*. Unpublished manuscript, University of California at Irvine.

Zamel, V. (1985). Responding to student writing. *TESOL Quarterly, 19*, 79–101.

Chapter 12

Reflections on Academic Discourse: How It Relates to Freshmen and Colleagues

Peter Elbow

I love what's in academic discourse: learning, intelligence, sophistication—even mere facts and naked summaries of articles and books; I love reasoning, inference, and evidence; I love theory. But I hate academic discourse. What follows is my attempt to work my way out of this dilemma. In doing so I will assume an ostensive definition of academic discourse: it is the discourse that academics use when they publish for other academics. And what characterizes that discourse? This is the question I will pursue here.

As a teacher of freshman writing courses, my problem is this. It is obvious why I should heed the common call to teach my students academic discourse. They will need it for the papers and reports and exams they'll have to write in their various courses throughout their college career. Many or even most of their teachers will expect them to write in the language of the academy. If we don't prepare them for these tasks we'll be shortchanging them—and disappointing our colleagues in other departments. It's no good just saying, "Learn to write what's comfy for you, kiddies," if that puts them behind the eight-ball in their college careers. Discourse carries power. This is especially important for weak or poorly prepared students—particularly students from poorer classes or those who are the first in their families to come to college. Not to help them with academic discourse is simply to leave a power vacuum and thereby reward privileged students who have already learned academic discourse at home or in school—or at least learned the roots or propensity for academic discourse. (Shirley Brice Heath shows how middle class urban families instinctively give home training in the skills that teachers want: labeling and defining and so forth. Children from other classes and backgrounds get plenty of language training, but their skills are mistaken by teachers for no skill.) Still, I remain troubled.

THE NEED FOR NONACADEMIC WRITING
IN FRESHMAN WRITING COURSES

I am troubled, first, by the most extreme position—the idea of giving over the freshman writing course entirely to academic discourse. Here are three brief arguments for teaching nonacademic discourse in freshman writing courses. These are not arguments against academic discourse; only for teaching something else in addition.

First, life is long and college is short. Very few of our students will ever have to write academic discourse after college. The writing that most students will need to do for most of their lives will be for their jobs—and that writing is usually very different from academic discourse. When employers complain that students can't write, they often mean that students have to *unlearn* the academic writing they were rewarded for in college. "[E]ach different 'world of work' constitutes its own discourse community with its own purposes, audiences, and genres. The FDA, for example, produces documents vastly different from those of the Air Force; lawyers write in genres different from those of accountants" (Matalene vi).

But to put the argument in terms of writing that people have to do is to give in to a deeply unwriterly and pessimistic assumption—held by many students and not a few colleagues, namely that no one would ever write except under compulsion. Why should people assume without discussion that we cannot get students to write by choice? In my view, the best test of a writing course is whether it makes students more likely to use writing in their lives: perhaps to write notes and letters to friends or loved ones; perhaps to write in a diary or to make sense of what's happening in their lives; perhaps to write in a learning journal to figure out a difficult subject they are studying; perhaps to write stories or poems for themselves or for informal circulation or even for serious publication; perhaps to write in the public realm such as letters to the newspaper or broadsides on dormitory walls. I don't rule out the writing of academic discourse by choice, but if we teach only academic discourse we will surely fail at this most important goal of helping students use writing by choice in their lives. I don't succeed with all my students at this goal, but I work at it and I make progress with many. It is not an unreasonable goal.

In a workshop with teachers not long ago I was struck with how angry many teachers got at a piece of student writing. It was not particularly good (it was about falling asleep while writing an assigned essay and waking up on a Greek island with "topless maidens"), but what infuriated these teachers was not really the mediocre quality but that the writer said in a piece of process writing that the piece was easy and fun to write and that he didn't revise it much because most people in his group liked it. I sensed resentment against the most basic impulses that are involved in being a writer: to have fun telling a story and to give pleasure to others. We need to get students to write by choice because no one can learn to write well except by writing a great deal—far more than we can assign and read.

Second, I want to argue for one *kind* of nonacademic discourse that is particularly important to teach. I mean discourse that tries to render experience rather than explain it. To render experience is to convey what I see when I look out the window, what it feels like to walk down the street or fall down—to tell what it's like to be me or to live my life. I'm particularly concerned that we help students learn to write language that conveys to others a sense of their experience—or indeed, that mirrors back to themselves a sense of their own experience from a little distance, once it's out there on paper. I'm thinking about autobiographical stories, moments, sketches—perhaps even a piece of fiction or poetry now and again.

I am really arguing that we take a larger view of human discourse. As writing teachers our job is to try to pass on the great human accomplishment of written language. Discourse that explains is part of that accomplishment, but discourse that renders is equally great—equally one of the preeminent gifts of human kind. When students leave the university unable to find words to render their experience, they are radically impoverished. We recognize the value of rendering experience when we teach reading. That is, most of the texts we teach in English courses are literary pieces that render experience. Yet we hesitate to teach students to write discourse that renders. And if we don't do it, no one else will. For virtually all of the other disciplines ask students to use language only to explain, not to render. It's important to note, by the way, that rendering is not just an "affective" matter—what something "feels" like. Discourse that renders often yields important new "cognitive" insights such as helping us see an exception or contradiction to some principle we thought we believed. (For example, a rendering of an evening's struggle with writing might well force us to adjust some dearly loved theoretical principle about the writing process.)

Third, we need nonacademic discourse even for the sake of helping students produce good academic discourse—academic language that reflects sound understanding of what they are studying in disciplinary courses. That is, many students can repeat and explain a principle in say physics or economics in the academic discourse of the textbook but cannot simply tell a story of what is going on in the room or country around them on account of that principle—or what the room or country would look like if that principle were different. The use of academic discourse often masks a lack of genuine understanding. When students write about something only in the language of the textbook or the discipline, they often distance or insulate themselves from experiencing or really internalizing the concepts they are allegedly learning. Often the best test of whether a student understands something is if she can translate it out of the discourse of the textbook and the discipline into everyday, experiential, anecdotal terms.

Thus, although we may be unsatisfied unless students can write about what they are learning in the professional discourse of the field—majors, anyway—we should be equally unsatisfied unless they can write about it *not* using the lingo of the discipline. (Vygotsky and Bakhtin make this same point: Vygotsky, when he describes the need for what he calls "scientific" or "formal" concepts to become intertwined in the child's mind with "everyday" or experienced concepts [82ff]; Bakhtin, when he explores the process by which people transform "the externally authoritative word" into the "internally persuasive word" [*Discourse and the Novel* 336ff].) I'm all for students being able to write academic discourse, but it bothers me when theorists argue that someone doesn't know a field unless she can talk about it in the discourse professionals use among themselves. There are plenty of instances of people who know a lot about engines or writing but don't know the professional discourse of engineering or composition. There's something self-serving about defining people as ignorant unless they are like us. (Besides, much of the talk about students learning academic discourse in their disciplinary courses seems to assume those students are majoring in that subject. But most students are not majors in most courses they take; for example, most students in English courses are non-majors who never take more than one or two English courses in their career. Do we really expect them to write the academic discourse of English? If so, we must mean something peculiar by "academic discourse.")

Let me repeat that I've made no negative arguments against teaching academic discourse, only positive arguments for teaching something else in addition. But the case for teaching academic discourse is usually an argument from practicality, and I insist that it's just as practical to teach other kinds of discourse—given the students' entire lives and even the needs of good academic discourse.

TRYING TO MAKE THE PROBLEM GO AWAY

The fact is that we can't teach academic discourse because there's no such thing to teach. Biologists don't write like historians. This is not news. Pat Bizzell and Joe Harris, among others, write thoughtfully about the differences among communities of discourse. Linda Flower writes: "there is no

Platonic entity called 'academic discourse' which one can define and master" (3). So although some students may need to write like historians or biologists, few of us in English can teach them to do so. To write like a historian or biologist involves not just lingo but doing history or biology—which involves knowing history and biology in ways we do not. In short, we are not qualified to teach most kinds of academic discourse.

But I want to push this further. Suppose we made an empirical study of the nature of discourse in English studies. Think of the differences we'd find—the different discourses in our field:

- The bulldozer tradition of high Germanic scholarship. Give no prominence to your own ideas. Emphasize the collecting and integrating of the ideas and conclusions of others. Or if you want to say something, avoid saying it until you have demonstrated that you have summarized and shown the shortcomings of previous works in the literature. Cite everything—sometimes even your own ideas under the guise of someone else's. (Not such an alien practice, after all: it is a commonplace among journalists that the only way to get your article to say what you want it to say is to quote someone saying it.)

- The genial slightly talky British tradition—which also connects with the rhetorical tradition (e.g., work by people like C. S. Lewis and Wayne Booth). This tradition gives us discourse that is fully scholarly and professional, but it is nevertheless likely to talk to the reader—sometimes even make anecdotal digressions or personal asides. Citations and references tend to be kept to a minimum. We can deride this as a tradition of privilege and authority ("Gentlemen don't cite everything. If you don't recognize the tacit footnotes you're not one of us"), but it is also the tradition of the amateur that welcomes the outsider. (Notice the structural implications that have gotten attached to these two traditions. Most of my teachers in college and graduate school wanted opening and closing paragraphs that provided readers a definite map of what my essay would be about and a definite summary of what it concluded: the voice of the German tradition says "Announce at the border what you have to declare." But I had other teachers who spoke for the British tradition and counted such sign-posting as a weakness in writing. I can still hear one of them: "Don't talk about what you're going to do, just do it. Just start with the point that belongs first and readers won't need an introduction." The same for transitions: "If you put your points in the right order, they won't need explanatory connections or transitions: they'll *follow*. Just think straight.")

- Poststructuralist, continental discourse: allusive, gamesome—dark and deconstructive. Again few footnotes, little help to those who haven't already read what they are alluding to.

- German Critical or Marxist discourse that is heavy on abstraction, special diction and terminology—and very consciously ideological. Practitioners would insist that anything less ideological is a cop-out.
- Psychoanalytic criticism uses its own linguistic and intellectual practices. When *College English* devoted two issues to psychoanalytic criticism in 1987, I heard colleagues complain, "These people write a completely separate language."
- The field of composition is particularly diverse. Some of its discourse is unashamedly quantitative and "social science." Imagine setting yourself the goal of publishing in *Research in the Teaching of English, College Composition and Communication,* and *PRE/TEXT*: you would need three different discourses. Steve North counts seven discourse communities in composition, involving not just different lingos but ways of knowing.
- I think of two Creoles: the Chicago Aristotelian dialect of R. S. Crane and fellows, and the New York intelligentsia dialect of Lionel Trilling and Irving Howe and fellows.
- Notice the subtle difference between the discourse of people who are established in the profession and those who are not—particularly those without tenure. Certain liberties, risks, tones, and stances are taken by established insiders that are not usually taken by the unannealed. Discourse is power.
- Notice finally the pedagogically crucial distinction between how academics write to each other and how they have come to expect students to write to them as teachers. We see here the ubiquitous authority dimension of discourse. Students must write "up" to teachers who have authority over them—often being assigned to write to experts about a subject they are just struggling to learn. In contrast, academics write "across" to fellow academics—usually explaining what they have worked out to readers who don't know it. (Sarah Freedman did an interesting piece of research in which she had teachers respond to essays by students—only some of the essays were actually written by teachers or professionals. One of her findings was that teachers were often bothered by the writing of the nonstudents—the "grown-ups" as it were—because it wasn't sufficiently deferential.)
- Suppose a student in a literature course asks me whether it's appropriate to bring in her feelings or some event from her personal life as part of the data for the interpretation of a text. There is no clear answer in English: it is appropriate in psychoanalytic and reader response criticism and certain kinds of feminist criticism—but not in many other literary discourses. What about data from the author's life and opinions? Again, for some English courses it's appropriate, for others not. Suppose a student argues against a critic's position by

bringing in that critic's class, gender, politics, or sexual affiliations—or professional training. Some English professors call this out of bounds, others do not.

Thus, I can't tell my students whether academic discourse in English means using lots of structural signposts or leaving them out, bringing in their feelings and personal reactions or leaving them out, giving evidence from the poet's life for interpretations or leaving that out, referring to the class, gender, and school of other interpreters or leaving that out—nor finally even what kind of footnotes to use. Even if I restrict myself to composition studies, I can't tell them whether academic discourse means quantitative or qualitative research or philosophical reflection. In short it's crazy to talk about academic discourse as one thing.

BUT IT WON'T GO AWAY

Not only can't I stop myself from talking about academic discourse in the singular, I can't help looking for an academic discourse I could teach in freshman writing courses. Couldn't there be some larger entity or category—academic writing in general—a generic Stop and Shop brand of academic discourse that lies beneath all those different trade names? (And I often buy generic.) A certain deep structure or freeze-dried essence of academic discourse that is larger than what we've looked for so far? A stance or a way of relating to our material that reaches across the differences between disciplines?

What would seem central to such a conception of academic discourse is the giving of reasons and evidence rather than just opinions, feelings, experiences: being clear about claims and assertions rather than just implying or insinuating; getting thinking to stand on its own two feet rather than leaning on the authority of who advances it or the fit with who hears it. In describing academic discourse in this general way, surely I am describing a major goal of literacy, broadly defined. Are we not engaged in schools and colleges in trying to teach students to produce reasons and evidence which hold up on their own rather than just in terms of the tastes or prejudices of readers or how attractively they are packaged?

Thus the conventions of academic discourse may seem difficult or ungainly, but they reflect the diligence needed to step outside one's own narrow vision—they are the conventions of a certain impersonality and detachment all working toward this large and important goal of separating feeling, personality, opinion, and fashion from what is essential: clear positions, arguments, and evidence (see Bartholomae 155; Olson 110). And so this idea of a single general intellectual goal behind the variety of different academic discourses is attractive.

But the very appeal of academic discourse as I have just described it tends to rest on the assumption that we can separate the ideas and reasons and arguments from the person who holds them; that there are such things as unheld opinions—assertions that exist uninfluenced by who says them and who hears them—positions not influenced by one's feelings, class, race, gender, sexual orientation, historical position, etc.—thinking that "stands on its own two feet." In the end, behind this conception of academic discourse in general is a bias toward objectivity or foundationalism—a bias which many of us have come to resist on the basis of work by a host of thinkers from Polanyi to Fish.

Most academics, certainly in English and composition, are more sympathetic to the contrasting rhetorical bias—a preference for seeing language in terms of speech acts: discourse is always talking to someone—trying to have an impact on someone. Grammar books and logic books may be full of disembodied propositions that we can think of in terms of disinterested truth value—messages without senders and receivers—but *discourse* as used by human beings is always interested, always located in a person speaking and an audience listening. We've learned that many of our difficulties and disputes and confusions come from falling into assuming that discourse is detached, nonrhetorical, and not a speech act—learned, as Bizzell says, that "an absolute standard for the judgment of truth can never be found, precisely because the individual mind can never transcend personal emotions, social circumstances, and historical conditions" (40).

In short, the very thing that is attractive and appealing about academic discourse is inherently problematic and perplexing. It tries to peel away from messages the evidence of how those messages are situated as the center of personal, political, or cultural interest; its conventions tend toward the sound of reasonable, disinterested, perhaps even objective (shall I say it?) men.

Am I saying that people who write academic discourse pretend to be objective or assume that there are absolute standards for truth? Of course not. (Though some do—such as this professor of physics: "Scientific communication is faceless and passionless by design. Data and conclusions stand bare and unadorned, and can be evaluated for what they are without prejudice or emotion. This kind of impersonal communication has helped science achieve the status of public knowledge, a coinage of truth with international currency. It's like Sgt. Joe Friday used to say: 'The facts, Ma'am, just the facts'" [Raymo 26].) Yet when people use academic discourse they are using a medium whose conventions tend to imply disinterested impersonality and detachment—a medium that is thus out of sync with their intellectual stance—a bias toward messages without senders and receivers. I wonder if this mismatch doesn't help explain why the discourse we see in academic journals is so often ungainly or uncomfortable and not infrequently tangled.

Let me illustrate these implications of detachment by looking at three violations of academic discourse that naive students sometimes commit. First, they overuse the first person, for example, "I'm only saying what I think and feel—this is just my opinion." Second, naive students are liable to use the second person too much and too pointedly, sometimes even speaking directly to us as particular reader ("As you stressed to us Tuesday in class, . . ."). Third, they are apt to refer to Hemingway as "Ernest." What interests me is how these violations highlight what the conventions of academic discourse usually disguise: that discourse is coming from a subject with personal interests, concerns, and uncertainties (even professional academics sometimes feel uncertain); that discourse is directed to a reader who is also situated in her subjectivity; and that discourse is about an author who is also asserted to be a person like the writer. (Notice yet another divergence among academic discourses in English: academic biographers get to call Hemingway "Ernest.")

But of course if pure objectivity is discredited, it doesn't mean we must embrace pure subjectivity and bias: "Hooray! I've read Kuhn and Fish and there's only subjectivity. Everyone has a bias, so I don't have to try to interrogate my own." Good academic discourse doesn't pretend to pure objectivity, yet it also avoids mere subjectivity. It presents clear claims, reasons, and evidence, but not in a pretense of pure, timeless, Platonic dialectic but in the context of arguments that have been or might be made in reply. Most academics reflect in their writing and teaching a belief that passionate commitment is permissible, perhaps even desirable—so long as it is balanced by awareness that it is a passionate position, what the stakes are, how others might argue otherwise. In short, as academics we don't pretend to write as God from an objective or universal spot of ground immune from history and feelings; nevertheless we feel it's possible to have a *bit* of detachment with our left eye as it were—a certain part of one's mind that flies up to the seventh sphere with Troilus and sees, "Ah yes, I'm really taking a strong position here—and I've got a big personal stake in this."

This intellectual stance transforms the dichotomy ("killer dichotomies" Ann Berthoff calls them) between subjective and objective. That is, the very act of acknowledging one's situatedness and personal stake invites, and is itself a movement toward, enlargement of view—not that it's a guarantee. Conversely, if someone pretends to be disinterested and objective, she invites smallness of view because she doesn't locate her interest in a larger picture: she tempts herself into believing that her view *is* the larger picture.

Here then, finally, is a definition of generic academic discourse that sounds right. It's essentially a rhetorical definition: giving reasons and evidence, yes, but doing so as a person speaking with acknowledged interests to others—whose interest and position one acknowledges and tries to understand. I'm for it. I try to teach it. I want my students to have it.

But there is a problem. Though this intellectual stance is characteristic of academic discourse at its best, it is also characteristic of much nonacademic discourse—such as that produced by writers like Montaigne, Woolf, Orwell, Paul Goodman, even William Gass or Joan Didion. If I get my students to achieve this admirable stance in their writing, they still might not be producing what most professors would call academic discourse or look for in assigned essays. Indeed have we not all sometimes sent and received letters that were written even in personal expressive discourse with this intellectual stance: in which we made claims, gave reasons and evidence, acknowledged our position—and just as effectively organized our discourse and set our arguments within the context of others who have written on the matter—without writing as we tend to write in our professional publications? (See *PRE/TEXT* 11.1 & 2 [1990] for a collection of personal or expressive writing engaged in the work of academic discourse.) In short, I think I've described a prominent feature of good writing—so of course it characterizes good academic writing—but it simply doesn't distinguish academic writing from nonacademic writing.

There are other attractive definitions of academic discourse which lead to the same dilemma. Flower writes: "The goals of self-directed critical inquiry, of using writing to think through genuine problems and issues, and of writing to an imagined community of peers with a personal rhetorical purpose—these distinguish academic writing . . ." (28). She further specifies two common "practices" which "stand as critical features of academic discourse which often limit entry and full participation in the academic community. . . . 1) integrating information from sources with one's own knowledge and 2) interpreting one's reading/adapting one's writing for a purpose" (3). Susan Peck MacDonald writes: "[I]t is problem-solving activity that generates all academic writing" (316). (It is interesting to see MacDonald rather than Flower focus on "problem solving," but a moment's thought explains the apparent paradox: Flower "uses up" problem solving by characterizing *all* writing as problem solving.) These too are characteristic features of good academic discourse, but they are no more useful than my earlier definition for distinguishing academic discourse from nonacademic discourse. In short, we must beware of talking as though the academy has a monopoly on a sound intellectual stance toward one's material and one's readers.

Maybe it's not, then, the intellectual stance or task that distinguishes academic discourse but certain stylistic or mechanical conventions—not the deep structure but certain surface features.

other definitions

MANNERISMS: STYLISTIC CONVENTIONS
OR SURFACE FEATURES OF ACADEMIC DISCOURSE

Just as it was interesting to dig for some common or generic intellectual practices behind the variations in different discourses, let me now try to dig for some common or generic surface features of academic discourse. An example will help: a paragraph from James Berlin's essay, "Contemporary Composition: The Major Pedagogical Theories."

> My reasons for presenting this analysis are not altogether disinterested. I am convinced that the pedagogical approach of the New Rhetoricians is the most intelligent and most practical alternative available, serving in every way the best interests of our students. I am also concerned, however, that writing teachers become more aware of the full significance of their pedagogical strategies. Not doing so can have disastrous consequences, ranging from momentarily confusing students to sending them away with faulty and even harmful information. The dismay students display about writing is, I am convinced, at least occasionally the result of teachers unconsciously offering contradictory advice about composing—guidance grounded in assumptions that simply do not square with each other. More important, as I have already indicated and as I plan to explain in detail later on, in teaching writing we are tacitly teaching a version of reality and the student's place and mode of operation in it. Yet many teachers (and I suspect most) look upon their vocations as the imparting of a largely mechanical skill, important only because it serves students in getting them through school and in advancing them in their professions. This essay will argue that writing teachers are perforce given a responsibility that far exceeds this merely instrumental task. (766)

Berlin writes a clean, direct prose. That is, I could have chosen a sentence like this one from the currently fashionable theory laden tradition:

> Now, literary hypospace may be defined as the lexical space which, having been collapsed to exclude almost all referentiality but that generated by verbal echoes alone, glows like an isotope with a half-life of meaning co-extensive with its power to turn its tropes into allotropes or "transformational" (in the Chomskyan sense) nodes, capable of liberating the "deep structures" of metaphoricity from buried layers of intertextuality. (Rother 83)

Or this sentence from R. S. Crane and the venerable Chicago Aristotelian tradition:

> [A] poet does not write poetry but individual poems. And these are inevitably, as finished wholes, instances of one or another poetic kind, differentiated not by any necessities of the linguistic instrument of poetry but primarily by the nature of the poet's conception, as finally embodied in his poem, of

a particular form to be achieved through the representation, in speech used
dramatically or otherwise, of some distinctive state of feeling, or moral choice,
or action, complete in itself and productive of a certain emotion or complex
of emotions in the reader. (96)

It's because Berlin's prose is open and clear that I look to it for some
general or common features of the academic style. Berlin has just named
what he conceives as the four "dominant theories" or approaches to composition and announced his plans to explore each in detail in his essay.
Thus in this early paragraph he is "mapping" or "signposting" for the
reader: explaining what he is going to do and laying out the structure.
Even though there is a wide range of custom as to the degree of signposting
in different academic discourses, signposting is probably the most general
or common textual convention of academic discourse. Thus the last sentence of his paragraph—introducing his thesis near the start of his essay—is
particularly conventional.

It is the convention of explicitness. That is, only nonacademic discourse
is allowed to merely imply what it is saying. A nonacademic piece can
achieve marvelous thinking and yet not really work it out explicitly; indeed
the effectiveness of such a piece may derive from having the principal
claim *lurk* rather than announce itself. Fine. But in academic writing it is
a convention always to say what you are saying. Thus there is a grain of
truth in the old perverse chestnut of advice: "First say what you're going
to say, then say it, then say what you've already said." Academic discourse
is business, not pleasure (and so business writing asks for even more explicit
signposting than most academic writing).

But there is also a convention of inexplicitness in academic discourse.
Look at the first sentence of Berlin's paragraph: "My reasons for presenting
this analysis are not altogether disinterested." He is not using this mock-
elegant double-negative to hide what he is saying, yet the conventions or
voice of academic discourse have led him to use a double negative rather
than come out and say positively what he is actually saying, namely, "I have
a stake in this analysis." And those same academic conventions have led
him to write a sentence about reasons with the verb "to be" rather than
a sentence about a person with an active verb (my reasons not being
disinterested rather than me having a stake). Perhaps some readers hear
a tone of quiet irony in his phrase, "not altogether disinterested," but I
don't hear him actually being ironic; he's just falling into a syntactic commonplace of academic discourse, the double negative combined with un-
derstatement. For after this sentence he virtually comes out and says (using
a number of "I"s), that his analysis of composition into four theories is
designed to show why his theory is best. Indeed the subtext of the whole
article is a celebration of the idea that all discourse is interested or biased—by definition—and that an "altogether disinterested" position is im-

possible. Yet in an essay that never hides its "I" and in which Berlin takes full responsibility for his interested position, discourse has led him to conclude the paragraph with a sentence about the essay arguing rather than him arguing. It seems to me, then, that in the convention or voice of his academic discourse, there are locutions left over from an intellectual stance of disinterested objectivity: the ideal of conclusions issuing "perforce" from reasons and arguments rather than from the play of interested positions. Somewhere in his new book, *Works and Lives*, Clifford Geertz makes a distinction between "author-saturated" and "author-evacuated" prose. The stylistic conventions of academic discourse are the conventions of author-evacuated prose.

Double negatives and irony are both ways of saying something without saying it. I'm not calling Berlin evasive here. Rather I'm trying to highlight the interesting fact that in an extremely non-evasive essay, his use of academic discourse led him into a locution that goes through the motions of being evasive—and a locution whose verbal conventions carry some wisps of former irony. This may sound like a paradox—conventions of both explicitness and inexplicitness—but it is not. Academic discourse tries to be direct about the "position"—the argument and reasons and claim. Yet it tends to be shy, indirect, or even evasive about the texture of feelings or attitude that lie behind that position.

Because Berlin's prose is not pretentious or obscure, it illustrates all the more clearly that academic discourse also leads to a somewhat formal language. I'm not talking about technical terms that are necessary for technical concepts; I'm talking about a tendency simply to avoid the everyday or common or popular in language. For example, academic discourse leads Berlin in just one paragraph to say "full significance of their pedagogical strategies" rather than "implications of how they teach"; "mode of operation" rather than "how they act." It leads to words and phrases like "imparting of a largely mechanical skill," "the dismay students display," "perforce," "merely instrumental task," "far exceeds." This is not difficult or convoluted language by any means; merely language that avoids the ordinary more than he probably would do if he were writing the same thoughts in a memo to the same teachers he is addressing with this article—or in *Harpers* or *Hudson Review*.

Berlin uses a special term, "epistemic," as central to this essay. One might call it a technical term that is necessary to the content (you can't talk about penicillin without the word "penicillin"). But (and colleagues argue with me about this) I don't think "epistemic" really permits him to say anything he couldn't say just as well without it—using "knowledge" and other such words. Admittedly it is the mildest of jargon these days and its use can be validly translated as follows: "A bunch of us have been reading Foucault and talking to each other and we simply want to continue to use a word that has become central in our conversation." But through my experience of teaching this essay to classroom teachers (the very audience that Berlin says he wants to reach), I have seen another valid translation: "I'm not interested in talking to people who are not already part of this conversation."

Indeed, there is what I would call a certain rubber-gloved quality to the voice and register typical of most academic discourses—not just author-evacuated but also showing a kind of reluctance to touch one's meanings with one's naked fingers. Here, by way of personal illustration, are some examples of changes made by editors of academic journals working on manuscripts of mine that were already accepted for publication. The changes are interesting for being so trivial: that is, there is no reason for them except to add a touch of distance and avoid the taint of the ordinary:

—*who has a strong sense of* changed to *who retains a deep conviction that*

—*always comes with* changed to *is always accompanied by*

—*when I dropped out of graduate school* changed to *when I interrupted my graduate education*

—*I started out just writing to aid my memory* changed to *At first I wanted only to aid my memory*

—[About a teacher I am interviewing and quoting] *he sometimes talks about students as though he doesn't give a damn about them* changed to . . . *as if they meant nothing to him*

I chose Berlin for my analysis because we can see academic discourse leading him into locutions of indirectness and detachment, even vestigal objectivity—when he is clearly taking the opposite intellectual stance. But I also chose Berlin because I want to piggy-back on his main point: "in teaching writing we are tacitly teaching a version of reality and the student's place and mode of operation in it." I agree, but I want to state an obvious corollary: in *using a discourse* we are also tacitly teaching a version of reality and the student's place and mode of operation in it. In particular we are affirming a set of social and authority relations. Here are four things that I think are taught by the surface mannerisms or stylistic conventions of academic discourse:

(1) A version of reality. The convention of explicitness and straightforward organization in academic discourse teaches that we can figure out what we really mean and get enough control over language to actually say it—directly and clearly. I confess I more or less believe this and think it's a good convention to teach. Of course I also acknowledge what has come to be called the deconstructive view of language and reality, namely that we can never get complete control over language, that there will always be eddies

of subversive meaning and wisps of contrary implication in anything we write, no matter how clear and direct we make it, so that a new critic or deconstructor can always find gaps (*aporiae*) in what looks straightforward. Indeed, as I insisted in my opening section, we should also try to teach the opposite convention of inexplicitness—teach people to relinquish control over language so that it leads where we never expected it to go, says things we didn't think we had in mind. I am talking about consciously trying to unleash the subversive forces of language (for example in freewriting) instead of trying to keep them in check. This subversive kind of writing is equally valuable and leads to an equally important view of reality. Nevertheless the convention of explicitness is something I affirm and want to teach.

(2) Academic discourse also teaches a set of social and authority relations: to talk to each other as professionals in such a way as to exclude ordinary people. That is, in the academic convention of using more formal language and longer and more complex sentences with more subordinate clauses (for example, calling that kind of language "the deployment of hypotaxis rather than parataxis"), academics are professing that they are professionals who do not invite conversation with nonprofessionals or ordinary people. Many groups act this way. Doctors don't say "thumbbone," and the medical profession went out of its way to mistranslate Freud's *ich, ueber ich* and *es* into *ego, super ego,* and *id*—rather than into the *I, over I,* and *it* that Freud clearly intended with his German (Bettelheim 49–62). It may be common for groups to try to prove that they are professional by means of this kind of exclusionary language, but I wonder if we really want to teach this discourse-stance once we notice the messages it sends: "We don't want to talk to you or hear from you unless you use our language." (Ostensibly the goal is to exclude the hoi polloi, but the bigger threat may be from intellectual non-academics who may be more learned and thoughtful.) Howard Becker is a respected sociologist who argues that there is no need for jargon and exclusionary discourse even in that field. He describes a graduate seminar engaged in revising and untangling someone's essay, where a student suddenly blurts: "Gee . . . when you say it this way, it looks like something anybody could say." Becker's comment: "You bet" (7).

(3) I often hear behind the stylistic and textual conventions of academic discourse a note of insecurity or anxiety. Students may deal with their insecurity by saying, "This is just my opinion. . . . Everyone is entitled to their own opinion" and so on. But having led many workshops for students and faculty members, I've noticed that faculty members are usually *more* anxious than students about sharing their writing with each other. Of course faculty members have greater reason for anxiety: the standards are higher, the stakes are higher, and they treat each other more badly than they treat students. But it turns out that the voice and stylistic conventions

of academic discourse serve extremely well to cover this understandable anxiety. Think about how we talk when we're nervous: our voice tends to sound more flat, gravelly, monotone, and evacuated. We tend to "cover" ourselves by speaking with more passives, more formal language, more technical vocabulary. We often discover that we sound more pompous than we intended. Bakhtin ("Discourse in Life") explores how meaning is carried by intonation and how our speech tends to lose intonation and thus meaning when we feel unsafe. Even in Berlin's fairly direct language, I hear that characteristically flat tone with little intonation. Not, probably, that he was anxious, but that he availed himself of stylistic conventions that avoid intonation and take a somewhat guarded stance.

(4) Finally, I sometimes see in the stylistic conventions of academic discourse an element of display. Despite the lack of intonation, there is often a slight effect of trying to impress or show off (though I don't see this in Berlin). That is, even though academics can write as peers and professionals to colleagues, it is helpful to notice how even grown up, full-fledged academics are sometimes so enmeshed in the rhetorical context of school discourse that they keep on writing as though they are performing for teachers with authority over them. Many academics have never written except to a teacher. We may be three thousand miles away, tenured, and middle-aged, but we are often still writing about the same field we wrote our dissertations on and writing to the very same teachers we had to impress in order to get tenure. Think about the stylistic stratagems of bright, intellectually excited, upperclass majors who grow up to be professors: how do they deal with that school situation of having to write "up" to readers with more knowledge and more authority—and needing to distinguish themselves from their peers? I believe that the conventions of academic discourse— voice, register, tone, diction, syntax, and mannerisms—often still carry vestigial traces of this authority transaction of trying to show off or impress those who have authority over us and to distinguish ourselves from our peers.

Really, of course, I'm talking about *ethos*: how do academics create authority and credibility when they write to each other? William Stafford thinks we get off easy on this score compared to poets:

> If you were a scientist, if you were an explorer who had been to the moon, if you were a knowing witness about the content being presented—you could put a draft on your hearer's or reader's belief. Whatever you said would have the force of that accumulated background of information; and any mumbles, mistakes, dithering, could be forgiven as not directly related to the authority you were offering. But a poet—whatever you are saying, and however you are saying it, the only authority you have builds from the immediate performance, or it does not build. The moon you are describing is the one you are creating. From the very beginning of your utterance you are creating your own authority. (62–63)

As academics, that is, we have various aids to authority. The most obvious one is to take a ride on the authority of others—and so (naming, finally, the most conspicuous stylistic convention in the genre) academics use footnotes and quote important figures in our writing. What we write is not just a neat idea we had that we send out to be judged on its own merits; it builds on Aristotle and echoes Foucault. And our discourse conventions teach us to be learned not only in our quotations and citations but also in the other linguistic mannerisms we use. And so—though we may be modest, open, and democratic as persons—the price we pay for a voice of authority is a style that excludes ordinary readers and often makes us sound like an insecure or guarded person showing off.

IMPLICATIONS FOR TEACHING FRESHMAN WRITING

I hope I am not too unkind in my reading of the stylistic conventions of academic discourse, but it helps me understand that I can happily devote a large proportion of my freshman writing activity to the admirable larger intellectual tasks like giving good reasons and evidence yet doing so in a rhetorical fashion which acknowledges an interested position and tries to acknowledge and understand the positions of others. (Also Flower's "self-directed critical inquiry . . . to an imagined community of peers" [28]; or MacDonald's "problem-solving.") These are the kinds of intellectual practices I want to teach—and in fact already do. But now I can continue to work on them and not feel guilty or defensive about neglecting academic discourse for merely "sensible" writing. Indeed my work on these goals should be slightly transformed by my knowledge that in pursuing them I *am* working on academic discourse—which is only one kind of discourse— and that, as Berlin implies, it involves a particular reading of the world, and as Bizzell insists, there are "personal, social, and historical interests in academic discourse." And as I see better that these admittedly sensible intellectual tasks are only some among many, I feel more secure in my commitment to spend a significant portion of the course emphasizing nonacademic discourse with other intellectual tasks—discourse that renders rather than discourse that explains.

I want to emphasize here, however, that my reason for isolating the stylistic mannerisms and giving less attention to them is not just a matter of personal distaste. Serious pedagogical consequences are at stake. The intellectual tasks of academic discourse are significantly easier for students to learn when separated from its linguistic and stylistic conventions. That is, it is not alienating for almost any students to be asked to learn to engage in the demanding intellectual tasks of clarifying claims and giving reasons and so forth (however difficult they may be), but it is definitely alienating for many students to be asked to take on the voice, register, tone, and diction of most academic discourse. If we have to learn a new intellectual stance or take on difficult intellectual goals, we'll probably have better luck if we don't at the same time have to do it in a new language and style and voice. (Teachers of English as a second language have learned that students do better on difficult school tasks if they can use the language they find comfortable.)

And as for those students who are sophisticated enough to take on the voice of academic discourse without much trouble, many of them get seduced or preoccupied with that surface dimension and learn only to mimic it while still failing to engage fully the intellectual task. Putting it crassly, students can do academic work even in street language—and indeed using the vernacular helps show whether the student is doing real intellectual work or just using academic jive.

Besides, learning new intellectual practices is not just a matter of practicing them; it is also a matter of thinking and talking about one's practice. Or, speaking academically, students need metacognition and metadiscourse to help them understand just what these new intellectual practices are that they are being asked to learn. Toward this end, many teachers make heavy use of "process writing" in which students try to describe and analyze what they have written and how they went about writing it (see Elbow and Belanoff 12 and passim).

But everybody does better at metacognition and metadiscourse if he or she can use ordinary language. Flower provides intriguing evidence for this point. She starts with her finding that "students often demonstrated the underlying cognitive abilities to analyze, synthesize, or reconceptualize that would support these high potential strategies, . . . [yet] such strategies do not appear to be live options in their repertoire. Why?" (7). She goes on to note that "metacognition could play a large role in helping students to learn and engage in new types of discourse" (8). Her essay suggests that her research process itself is probably one of the best ways to produce this meta-awareness and task awareness in students. That is, she had the students produce speak-aloud protocols of their thinking and writing, then look at those protocols, and then discuss some of them in class. Here are a couple of examples of metadiscourse or process writing that students had a chance to discuss:

> So anyway, . . . So I wrote five or six pages on nothing, but I included the words "African nationalism" in there once in a while. I thought, why this is just like high school, I can get away with doing this. I got the paper back, and it was a C minus or a C or something like that. It said "no content." And I was introduced to the world of college writing. (9)

> I started with "There are several theories as to the most efficient strategies concerning time management." Which is really bad—And I wrote like a

page of this. I just stopped and I went: This is just so bad—and I just said, like—I have to take this totally from my own point of view. (PAUSE) *But first I have to get a point of view.* (12)

Flower doesn't make this point, but it seems to me that the students probably wouldn't think so clearly and frankly about their own thinking and discourse if they weren't using ordinary language. The vernacular helps them talk turkey.

The intellectual practices of academic discourse are not only more appealing to me than its stylistic conventions, they are also more useful. That is, even though there may be differences between what counts as evidence and valid reasoning in various disciplines and even subdisciplines, the larger intellectual activities we've focused on are useful in most academic disciplines—and of course in much nonacademic writing, too. The stylistic conventions, on the other hand, seem more local and variable—and in my view carry problematic intellectual and social implications. No one seems to defend the stylistic conventions themselves—merely the pragmatic need for them. I find many academics dislike them but feel guilty and furtive about it. Richard Rorty put it bluntly in a recent interview: "I think that America has made itself a bit ridiculous in the international academic world by developing distinctive disciplinary jargon. It's the last thing we want to inculcate in the freshmen" (7). Finally, I suspect students can learn the surface features of academic style better if they have first made good progress with the underlying intellectual practices. When students are really succeeding in doing a meaty academic task, then the surface stylistic features are more likely to be integral and organic rather than merely an empty game or mimicry.

What specific teaching practices does this analysis suggest? I've tried these:

- Ask students for a midprocess draft that summarizes something (for example, a piece of reading, a difficult principle from another course, the point of view of a classmate, or a discussion): pure summary, simply trying to get it right and clear—as it were for God. Then ask them for a major revision so that the material is not just summarized but rather interpreted and transformed and used in the process of creating a sustained piece of thinking of their own—and for a real human audience. And ask also for process writing with each piece and spend some class time afterwards discussing the differences between the two intellectual tasks.

- Ask students for a piece of writing that renders something from experience. The test of success is whether it makes readers experience what they're talking about. Then ask them for a different piece of writing that is built from that writing—an essay that figures out or explains some issue or solves a conceptual (rather than personal) problem. I don't ask them to suppress their own experience for this piece, but to keep it from being the focus: the focus should be the figuring out or the solving. The test of success for this piece is whether it does the conceptual job. Again, ask for process writing with each piece of writing and then discuss in class the differences between the two intellectual tasks.

- Ask students to write a midprocess draft of an essay, and then for the next week's assignment ask them to make two revisions of the same draft: one in which they try to be completely objective and detached, the other in which they acknowledge their point of view, interest, bias—and figure out how to handle that rhetorical problem. Again, process writing with each piece and class discussion afterwards emphasizing the differences between the two intellectual tasks. This system also speaks to another concern: how to get students to do substantive rather than perfunctory revising—how to insist that revisions be genuinely different, even if not necessarily better.

As for those problematic stylistic conventions of academic discourse: my analysis helps me feel a little better about neglecting them, but I will continue to spend a bit of time on them in my course. The obvious approach would be to describe these stylistic features formally or as a genre. But Sheryl Fontaine points out that there's an uncanny similarity between teaching academic discourse formally and teaching correctness. In both cases we are back to a game of right and wrong; all authority is with the teacher (as the only representative of the academic discourse community in the room); and the student's whole task is finding right answers of which the teacher is sole arbiter.

Besides, a form or genre is always an artificial construct that represents a compromise among the actual practices of live writers. If our goal is to tell students what stylistic features are characteristic of the writing in a given discipline, no answer will fit all the particular teachers they will meet—and the answers will be even more out of whack if we are talking about the discourse teachers actually want from students on assignments, because those practices differ even more widely.

- To help students think about style and voice not as generic or formal matters but as audience matters, I use a variation on the process I just described: asking for two revisions of the same midprocess draft, perhaps one for me as teacher and the other for casual friends; or one for people who know a lot about the topic and the other for readers who don't; or one for adults and the other for children; or one for a school newspaper and the other for a teacher.

- Once in the semester I ask for a paper that explains or discusses something students are studying in another course—and again two revisions. One version is for us in this course, considered as amateurs; the other version is for students and the teacher in the other course, considered as professionals. I ask the students to try out both drafts on us and on some students in the other course—and if possible on the teacher in the other course. A rhetorical and empirical approach dictates these procedures, a way of learning by interacting with readers and seeing how they react, rather than by studying forms or genres of discourse.

- I also like to get a teacher from another discipline to visit my class and distribute copies of a couple of essays that she has assigned and graded and to talk about them. I ask her to tell what kind of assignments and tasks she gives, what she is looking for, and especially to talk in some frank detail about how she reads and reacts to student writing. I try to get this colleague to give some movies of her mind as she reads—in effect an informal speak-aloud protocol of her reading. And there are two issues I bring up if she doesn't do so: how does she react when she finds a vernacular or nonacademic voice in student writing? And does she assign any nonacademic discourse in her course (for example journal writing or stories or letters or newspaper articles about what they are studying)? I want students to hear how this teacher from another discipline reacts to these issues. I also try to get her to speculate about what her colleagues would say on all these matters.

- In effect, I'm talking about doing a bit of informal ethnography—realizing that I am the most convenient ethnographic subject. That is, in recent years I have often found myself giving my reactions to students on their papers in a more reflective way: noticing myself as a member of the profession and as an individual and trying to help students interpret my reactions in a more anthropological way. I think more about multiple audiences and find myself making comments like these: "I am bothered here—I'll bet most teachers would be—but perhaps general readers wouldn't mind." Or "I liked this passage, but I suspect a lot of teachers would take it as an inappropriately personal digression—or as too informal or slangy."

The central principle here is this: I cannot teach students the particular conventions they will need for particular disciplines (not even for particular teachers within the same discipline), but I can teach students the principle of discourse variation—between individuals and between communities. I can't teach them the forms they'll need, but I can sensitize them to the notion of differences in form so that they will be more apt to look for cues and will pick them up faster when they encounter them. Or to put it somewhat negatively, I'm trying to protect myself and keep my students from saying to my colleagues in history or psychology, "But my freshman English teacher likes this kind of writing that you failed me for!" What I want my students to go away thinking is more like this: "My freshman English teacher was good at telling us what went on in his mind as he read our papers—what he found strong and weak, what he liked and didn't like. But he set things up so we were always seeing how different members of the class and even people outside the class had different perceptions and reactions and standards and followed different conventions—how other people in other communities read differently. He tried to get us to listen better and pick up quicker on conventions and reactions." (If only we could write our students' evaluations of our teaching!) This inductive and scattered approach is messy—frustrating to students who want neat answers. But it avoids giving them universal standards that don't hold up empirically. And more than that, it is lively, interesting, and writerly because it's rhetorical rather than formal.

A FINAL NOTE: "BUT AT MY BACK . . ."

Don't forget to notice how fast academic discourse is changing—certainly in our discipline and probably in others. And these changes are really an old story. It wasn't so long ago, after all, that Latin was the only acceptable language for learned discourse. Gradually the other European dialects became acceptable—vernacular, vulgar, and of the people, more democratic, closer to the business of the everyday and to feelings. Yet it seems to me that many academics seem more nervous about changes in discourse—and especially incursions of the vernacular—than about changes in ideas or content or doctrine. Many happily proclaim that there is no truth, no right answer, no right interpretation; many say they want more voices in the academy, dialogue, heteroglossia! But they won't let themselves or their students write in language tainted with the ordinary or with the presence and feelings of the writer.

Yet despite this fear of change, change is what we are now seeing even in the deep structure or central intellectual practices of academic discourse:

- Deconstructionists make a frontal attack on straight, organized prose that purports to mean what it says. They have gotten a good hearing with their insistence that language always means something different from what it says, that seemingly plain and direct language is the most duplicitous discourse of all, and that fooling around is of the essence.
- Feminists attack the idea that good writing must follow linear or hierarchical or deductive models of structure, must persuade by trying to overpower, must be "masterful."

- Bruner and scholars of narrative attack the assumption that thinking is best when it is structured in terms of claims, reasons, warrants, and evidence. Narrative is just as good a form for thinking.
- Academic discourse has usually focused outward: on issues or data. But now the focus of academic discourse is more and more often discourse and thinking itself. In effect, much academic discourse is metadiscourse.
- In a host of ways, genres are becoming blurred. It is worth quoting Geertz:

[T]he present jumbling of varieties of discourse has grown to the point where it is becoming difficult either to label authors (What is Foucault—historian, philosopher, political theorist? What is Thomas Kuhn—historian, philosopher, sociologist of knowledge?) or to classify works. . . . It is a phenomenon general enough and distinctive enough to suggest that what we are seeing is not just another redrawing of the cultural map—the moving of a few disputed borders, the marking of some more picturesque mountain lakes—but an alteration of the principles of mapping. Something is happening to the way we think about the way we think. (19–20)

Arguments that any currently privileged set of stylistic conventions of academic discourse are inherently better—even that any currently privileged set of intellectual practices are better for scholarship or for thinking or for arguing or for rooting out self-deception—such arguments seem problematic now.

In the end, then, I conclude that I should indeed devote plenty of time in my freshman writing course to the intellectual practices of academic discourse; but also work on nonacademic practices and tasks, such as on discourse that renders rather than explains. (And our discussion about the difference between these two uses of language will help both.) Similarly, I should devote a little bit of time to the stylistic conventions or voices of academic discourse; but only as part of a larger exploration of various voices and styles—an exploration centered not on forms but on relationships with various live audiences. Let me give Joe Harris the last word: "What I am arguing against, though, is the notion that our students should necessarily be working towards the mastery of some particular, well-defined sort of discourse. It seems to me that they might better be encouraged towards a kind of polyphony—an awareness of and pleasure in the various competing discourses that make up their own" (17).[1]

---

[1]Interested readers will want to consult the growing body of empirical research on representative academic texts of different disciplines and on what happens as actual students engage in learning to use academic discourse. I am thinking of the work of people like Bazerman, Herrington, McCarthy, and Myers.

WORKS CITED

Bakhtin, Mikhail. "Discourse and the Novel." *The Dialogic Imagination: Four Essays.* Ed. Michael Holquist. Trans. Caryl Emerson and Michael Holquist. Slavic Series 1. Austin: U of Texas P, 1981. 259–422.

———. "Discourse in Life and Discourse in Art (Concerning Sociological Poetics)." *Freudianism: A Marxist Critique.* Trans. I. R. Titunik. Ed. Neal H. Bruss. New York: Academic, 1976. 93–116.

Bartholomae, David. "Inventing the University." *When A Writer Can't Write.* Ed. Mike Rose. New York: Guilford, 1985. 134–65.

Bazerman, Charles. *Shaping Written Knowledge: Genre and Activity of the Experimental Article in Science.* Madison: U of Wisconsin P, 1988.

Becker, Howard. *Writing for Social Scientists.* Chicago: U of Chicago P, 1986.

Berlin, James. "Contemporary Composition: The Major Pedagogical Theories." *College English* 44 (1982): 766–77.

Bettelheim, Bruno. *Freud and Man's Soul.* New York: Knopf, 1983.

Bizzell, Pat. "Foundationalism and Anti-Foundationalism in Composition Studies." *Pre/Text* 7.1–7.2 (1986): 37–56.

Crane, R. S. "The Critical Monism of Cleanth Brooks." *Critics and Criticism: Ancient and Modern.* Chicago: U of Chicago P, 1951. 83–107.

Elbow, Peter, and Pat Belanoff. *A Community of Writers: A Workshop Course in Writing.* New York: Random, 1989.

Flower, Linda. "Negotiating Academic Discourse." Reading-to-Write Report No. 10. Technical Report No. 29. Berkeley, CA: Center for the Study of Writing at University of California, Berkeley, and Carnegie Mellon.

Fontaine, Sheryl. "The Unfinished Story of the Interpretive Community." *Rhetoric Review* 7.1 (Fall 1988): 86–96.

Freedman, Sarah, C. Greenleaf, and M. Sperling. "Response to Student Writing." Research Report No. 23. Urbana, IL: NCTE, 1987.

Geertz, Clifford. "Blurred Genres: The Refiguration of Social Thought." *Local Knowledge: Further Essays in Interpretive Anthropology.* New York: Basic, 1983. 19–35.

———. *Works and Lives: The Anthropologist as Author.* Palo Alto: Stanford UP, 1988.

Harris, Joe. "The Idea of Community in the Study of Writing." *College Composition and Communication* 40.1 (February 1989): 11–22.

Heath, Shirley Brice. *Ways With Words: Language, Life, and Work in Communities and Classrooms.* New York: Cambridge UP, 1983.

Herrington, Anne. "Composing One's Self in a Discourse: Students' and Teachers' Negotiations." *Constructing Rhetorical Education: From the Classroom to the Community.* Ed. D. Charney and M. Secor. Carbondale: Southern Illinois UP, in press.

———. "Teaching, Writing, and Learning: A Naturalistic Study of Writing in an Undergraduate Literature Course." *Advances in Writing Research, Vol. 2: Writing in Academic Discourse.* Ed. D. Jolliffe. Norwood, NJ: ABLEX, 1988: 133–66.

Hirsch, E. D. Jr. *The Aims of Interpretation.* Chicago: U of Chicago P, 1978.

MacDonald, Susan Peck. "Problem Definition in Academic Writing." *College English* 49 (1987): 315–30.

Matalene, Carolyn B. Introduction. *Worlds of Writing: Teaching and Learning in the Discourse Communities of Work.* Ed. Carolyn B. Matalene. New York: Random, 1989. v–xi.

McCarthy, Lucille. "A Stranger in Strange Lands: A College Student Writing Across the Curriculum." *Research in the Teaching of English* 21 (1987): 233–65.

Myers, Greg. *Writing Biology.* Madison: U of Wisconsin P, 1990.

North, Stephen. *The Making of Knowledge in Composition: Portrait of an Emerging Field.* Upper Montclair, NJ: Boynton, 1987.

Olson, David R. "Writing: The Divorce of the Author from the Text." *Exploring Speaking-Writing Relationships: Connections and Contrasts.* Ed. B. M. Kroll and R. J. Vann. Urbana, IL: NCTE, 1981. 99–110.

Raymo, Chet. "Just the Facts, Ma'am." *Boston Globe* 27 February 1989: 26.

Rorty, Richard. "Social Construction and Composition Theory: A Conversation with Richard Rorty." *The Journal of Advanced Composition* 9.1 and 9.2: 1–9.

Rother, James. "Face-Values on the Cutting Floor: Some Versions of the Newer Realism." *American Literary Realism* 21.2 (Winter 1989): 67–96.

Stafford, William. "Making a Poem/Starting a Car on Ice." *Writing the Australian Crawl: Views on the Writer's Vocation.* Ann Arbor: U of Michigan P, 1978. 61–75.

Vygotsky, Lev. *Thought and Language.* Trans. Eugenia Hanfman and Gertude Vakar. Cambridge: MIT P, 1962.

Chapter 13

Arts of the Contact Zone

Mary Louise Pratt

Whenever the subject of literacy comes up, what often pops first into my mind is a conversation I overheard eight years ago between my son Sam and his best friend, Willie, aged six and seven, respectively: "Why don't you trade me Many Trails for Carl Yats . . . Yesits . . . Ya-strum-scrum." "That's not how you say it, dummy, it's Carl Yes . . . Yes . . . oh, I don't know." Sam and Willie had just discovered baseball cards. Many Trails was their decoding, with the help of first-grade English phonics, of the name Manny Trillo. The name they were quite rightly stumped on was Carl Yastrzemski. That was the first time I remembered seeing them put their incipient literacy to their own use, and I was of course thrilled.

Sam and Willie learned a lot about phonics that year by trying to decipher surnames on baseball cards, and a lot about cities, states, heights, weights, places of birth, stages of life. In the years that followed, I watched Sam apply his arithmetic skills to working out batting averages and subtracting retirement years from rookie years; I watched him develop senses of patterning and order by arranging and rearranging his cards for hours on end, and aesthetic judgment by comparing different photos, different series, layouts, and color schemes. American geography and history took shape in his mind through baseball cards. Much of his social life revolved around trading them, and he learned about exchange, fairness, trust, the importance of processes as opposed to results, what it means to get cheated,

Profession 91, 1991

taken advantage of, even robbed. Baseball cards were the medium of his economic life too. Nowhere better to learn the power and arbitrariness of money, the absolute divorce between use value and exchange value, notions of long- and short-term investment, the possibility of personal values that are independent of market values.

Baseball cards meant baseball card shows, where there was much to be learned about adult worlds as well. And baseball cards opened the door to baseball books, shelves and shelves of encyclopedias, magazines, histories, biographies, novels, books of jokes, anecdotes, cartoons, even poems. Sam learned the history of American racism and the struggle against it through baseball; he saw the depression and two world wars from behind home plate. He learned the meaning of commodified labor, what it means for one's body and talents to be owned and dispensed by another. He knows something about Japan, Taiwan, Cuba, and Central America and how men and boys do things there. Through the history and experience of baseball stadiums he thought about architecture, light, wind, topography, meteorology, the dynamics of public space. He learned the meaning of expertise, of knowing about something well enough that you can start a conversation with a stranger and feel sure of holding your own. Even with an adult—especially with an adult. Throughout his preadolescent years, baseball history was Sam's luminous point of contact with grown-ups, his lifeline to caring. And, of course, all this time he was also playing baseball, struggling his way through the stages of the local Little League system, lucky enough to be a pretty good player, loving the game and coming to know deeply his strengths and weaknesses.

Literacy began for Sam with the newly pronounceable names on the picture cards and brought him what has been easily the broadest, most varied, most enduring, and most integrated experience of his thirteen-year life. Like many parents, I was delighted to see schooling give Sam the tools with which to find and open all these doors. As the same time I found it unforgivable that schooling itself gave him nothing remotely as meaningful to do, let alone anything that would actually take him beyond the referential, masculinist ethos of baseball and its lore.

However, I was not invited here to speak as a parent, nor as an expert on literacy. I was asked to speak as an MLA member working in the elite academy. In that capacity my contribution is undoubtedly supposed to be abstract, irrelevant, and anchored outside the real world. I wouldn't dream of disappointing anyone. I propose immediately to head back several centuries to a text that has a few points in common with baseball cards and raises thoughts about what Tony Sarmiento, in his comments to the conference, called new visions of literacy. In 1908 a Peruvianist named Richard Pietschmann was exploring in the Danish Royal Archive in Copenhagen and came across a manuscript. It was dated in the city of Cuzco in

Peru, in the year 1613, some forty years after the final fall of the Inca empire to the Spanish and signed with an unmistakably Andean indigenous name: Felipe Guaman Poma de Ayala. Written in a mixture of Quechua and ungrammatical, expressive Spanish, the manuscript was a letter addressed by an unknown but apparently literate Andean to King Philip III of Spain. What stunned Pietschmann was that the letter was twelve hundred pages long. There were almost eight hundred pages of written text and four hundred of captioned line drawings. It was titled *The First New Chronicle and Good Government.* No one knew (or knows) how the manuscript got to the library in Copenhagen or how long it had been there. No one, it appeared, had ever bothered to read it or figured out how. Quechua was not thought of as a written language in 1908, nor Andean culture as a literate culture.

Pietschmann prepared a paper on his find, which he presented in London in 1912, a year after the rediscovery of Machu Picchu by Hiram Bingham. Reception, by an international congress of Americanists, was apparently confused. It took twenty-five years for a facsimile edition of the work to appear, in Paris. It was not till the late 1970s, as positivist reading habits gave way to interpretive studies and colonial elitisms to postcolonial pluralisms, that Western scholars found ways of reading Guaman Poma's *New Chronicle and Good Government* as the extraordinary intercultural tour de force that it was. The letter got there, only 350 years too late, a miracle and a terrible tragedy.

I propose to say a few more words about this erstwhile unreadable text, in order to lay out some thoughts about writing and literacy in what I like to call the *contact zones.* I use this term to refer to social spaces where cultures meet, clash, and grapple with each other, often in contexts of highly asymmetrical relations of power, such as colonialism, slavery, or their aftermaths as they are lived out in many parts of the world today. Eventually I will use the term to reconsider the models of community that many of us rely on in teaching and theorizing and that are under challenge today. But first a little more about Guaman Poma's giant letter to Philip III.

Insofar as anything is known about him at all, Guaman Poma exemplified the sociocultural complexities produced by conquest and empire. He was an indigenous Andean who claimed noble Inca descent and who had adopted (at least in some sense) Christianity. He may have worked in the Spanish colonial administration as an interpreter, scribe, or assistant to a Spanish tax collector—as a mediator, in short. He says he learned to write from his half brother, a mestizo whose Spanish father had given him access to religious education.

Guaman Poma's letter to the king is written in two languages (Spanish and Quechua) and two parts. The first is called the *Nueva corónica* 'New Chronicle.' The title is important. The chronicle of course was the main writing apparatus through which the Spanish represented their American conquests to themselves. It constituted one of the main official discourses. In writing a "new chronicle," Guaman Poma took over the official Spanish genre for his own ends. Those ends were, roughly, to construct a new picture of the world, a picture of a Christian world with Andean rather than European peoples at the center of it—Cuzco, not Jerusalem. In the *New Chronicle* Guaman Poma begins by rewriting the Christian history of the world from Adam and Eve (fig. 1), incorporating the Amerindians into it as offspring of one of the sons of Noah. He identifies five ages of Christian history that he links in parallel with the five ages of canonical Andean history—separate but equal trajectories that diverge with Noah and reintersect not with Columbus but with Saint Bartholomew, claimed to have preceded Columbus in the Americas. In a couple of hundred pages, Guaman Poma constructs a veritable encyclopedia of Inca and pre-Inca history, customs, laws, social forms, public offices, and dynastic leaders. The depictions resemble European manners and customs description, but

FIG. 1. Adam and Eve.

also reproduce the meticulous detail with which knowledge in Inca society was stored on *quipus* and in the oral memories of elders.

Guaman Poma's *New Chronicle* is an instance of what I have proposed to call an *autoethnographic* text, by which I mean a text in which people undertake to describe themselves in ways that engage with representations others have made of them. Thus if ethnographic texts are those in which European metropolitan subjects represent to themselves their others (usually their conquered others), autoethnographic texts are representations that the so-defined others construct *in response to* or in dialogue with those texts. Autoethnographic texts are not, then, what are usually thought of as autochthonous forms of expression or self-representation (as the Andean *quipus* were). Rather they involve a selective collaboration with and appropriation of idioms of the metropolis or the conqueror. These are merged or infiltrated to varying degrees with indigenous idioms to create self-representations intended to intervene in metropolitan modes of understanding. Autoethnographic works are often addressed to both metropolitan audiences and the speaker's own community. Their reception is thus highly indeterminate. Such texts often constitute a marginalized group's point of entry into the dominant circuits of print culture. It is interesting to think, for example, of American slave autobiography in its autoethnographic dimensions, which in some respects distinguish it from Euramerican autobiographical tradition. The concept might help explain why some of the earliest published writing by Chicanas took the form of folkloric manners and customs sketches written in English and published in English-language newspapers or folklore magazines (see Treviño). Autoethnographic representation often involves concrete collaborations between people, as between literate ex-slaves and abolitionist intellectuals, or between Guaman Poma and the Inca elders who were his informants. Often, as in Guaman Poma, it involves more than one language. In recent decades autoethnography, critique, and resistance have reconnected with writing in a contemporary creation of the contact zone, the *testimonio*.

Guaman Poma's *New Chronicle* ends with a revisionist account of the Spanish conquest, which, he argues, should have been a peaceful encounter of equals with the potential for benefiting both, but for the mindless greed of the Spanish. He parodies Spanish history. Following contact with the Incas, he writes, "In all Castille, there was a great commotion. All day and at night in their dreams the Spaniards were saying 'Yndias, yndias, oro, plata, oro, plata del Piru' " ("Indies, Indies, gold, silver, gold, silver from Peru") (fig. 2). The Spanish, he writes, brought nothing of value to share with the Andeans, nothing "but armor and guns con la codicia de oro, plata, oro y plata, yndias, a las Yndias, Piru" ("with the lust for gold, silver, gold and silver, Indies, the Indies, Peru") (372). I quote these words as an example of a conquered subject using the conqueror's language to

FIG. 2.   Conquista. Meeting of Spaniard and Inca. The Inca says in Quechua,
"You eat this gold?" Spaniard replies in Spanish, "We eat this gold."

construct a parodic, oppositional representation of the conqueror's own
speech. Guaman Poma mirrors back to the Spanish (in their language,
which is alien to him) an image of themselves that they often suppress
and will therefore surely recognize. Such are the dynamics of language,
writing, and representation in contact zones.

The second half of the epistle continues the critique. It is titled *Buen
gobierno y justicia* 'Good Government and Justice' and combines a description of colonial society in the Andean region with a passionate denunciation of Spanish exploitation and abuse. (These, at the time he was writing,
were decimating the population of the Andes at a genocidal rate. In fact,
the potential loss of the labor force became a main cause for reform of
the system.) Guaman Poma's most implacable hostility is invoked by the
clergy, followed by the dreaded *corregidores*, or colonial overseers (fig. 3).
He also praises good works, Christian habits, and just men where he finds
them, and offers at length his views as to what constitutes "good government
and justice." The Indies, he argues, should be administered through a

FIG. 3. Corregidor de minas. Catalog of Spanish abuses of indigenous labor force.

collaboration of Inca and Spanish elites. The epistle ends with an imaginary question-and-answer session in which, in a reversal of hierarchy, the king is depicted asking Guaman Poma questions about how to reform the empire—a dialogue imagined across the many lines that divide the Andean scribe from the imperial monarch, and in which the subordinated subject single-handedly gives himself authority in the colonizer's language and verbal repertoire. In a way, it worked—this extraordinary text did get written—but in a way it did not, for the letter never reached its addressee.

To grasp the import of Guaman Poma's project, one needs to keep in mind that the Incas had no system of writing. Their huge empire is said to be the only known instance of a full-blown bureaucratic state society built and administered without writing. Guaman Poma constructs his text by appropriating and adapting pieces of the representational repertoire of the invaders. He does not simply imitate or reproduce it; he selects and adapts it along Andean lines to express (bilingually, mind you) Andean interests and aspirations. Ethnographers have used the term *transculturation* to describe processes whereby members of subordinated or marginal groups select and invent from materials transmitted by a dominant or metropolitan culture. The term, originally coined by Cuban sociologist Fernando Ortiz in the 1940s, aimed to replace overly reductive concepts of acculturation and assimilation used to characterize culture under conquest. While subordinate peoples do not usually control what emanates from the dominant culture, they do determine to varying extents what gets absorbed into their own and what it gets used for. Transculturation, like autoethnography, is a phenomenon of the contact zone.

As scholars have realized only relatively recently, the transcultural character of Guaman Poma's text is intricately apparent in its visual as well as its written component. The genre of the four hundred line drawings is European—there seems to have been no tradition of representational drawing among the Incas—but in their execution they deploy specifically Andean systems of spatial symbolism that express Andean values and aspirations.[1]

In figure 1, for instance, Adam is depicted on the left-hand side below the sun, while Eve is on the right-hand side below the moon, and slightly lower than Adam. The two are divided by the diagonal of Adam's digging stick. In Andean spatial symbolism, the diagonal descending from the sun marks the basic line of power and authority dividing upper from lower, male from female, dominant from subordinate. In figure 2, the Inca appears in the same position as Adam, with the Spaniard opposite, and the two at the same height. In figure 3, depicting Spanish abuses of power, the symbolic pattern is reversed. The Spaniard is in a high position indicating dominance, but on the "wrong" (right-hand) side. The diagonals of his lance and that of the servant doing the flogging mark out a line of illegitimate, though real, power. The Andean figures continue to occupy the left-hand side of the picture, but clearly as victims. Guaman Poma wrote that the Spanish conquest had produced "un mundo al reves" 'a world in reverse.'

In sum, Guaman Poma's text is truly a product of the contact zone. If one thinks of cultures, or literatures, as discrete, coherently structured, monolingual edifices, Guaman Poma's text, and indeed any authoethnographic work, appears anomalous or chaotic—as it apparently did to the European scholars Pietschmann spoke to in 1912. If one does not think of cultures this way, then Guaman Poma's text is simply heterogeneous, as the Andean region was itself and remains today. Such a text is heterogeneous on the reception end as well as the production end: it will read very differently to people in different positions in the contact zone. Because it deploys European and Andean systems of meaning making, the letter necessarily means differently to bilingual Spanish–Quechua speakers and to monolingual speakers in either language; the drawings mean differently to monocultural readers, Spanish or Andean, and to bicultural readers responding to the Andean symbolic structures embodied in European genres.

In the Andes in the early 1600s there existed a literate public with considerable intercultural competence and degrees of bilingualism. Unfortunately, such a community did not exist in the Spanish court with which Guaman Poma was trying to make contact. It is interesting to note that in the same year Guaman Poma sent off his letter, a text by another Peruvian was adopted in official circles in Spain as the canonical Christian mediation between the Spanish conquest and Inca history. It was another huge encyclopedic work, titled the *Royal Commentaries of the Incas*, written, tellingly, by a mestizo, Inca Garcilaso de la Vega. Like the mestizo half brother who taught Guaman Poma to read and write, Inca Garcilaso was the son of an Inca princess and a Spanish official, and had lived in Spain since he was seventeen. Though he too spoke Quechua, his book is written in eloquent, standard Spanish, without illustrations. While Guaman Poma's life's work sat somewhere unread, the *Royal Commentaries* was edited and reedited in Spain and the New World, a mediation that coded the Andean past and present in ways thought unthreatening to colonial hierarchy.[2] The textual hierarchy persists: the *Royal Commentaries* today remains a staple item on PhD reading lists in Spanish, while the *New Chronicle and Good Government*, despite the ready availability of several fine editions, is not. However, though Guaman Poma's text did not reach its destination, the transcultural currents of expression it exemplifies continued to evolve in the Andes, as they still do, less in writing than in storytelling, ritual, song, dance-drama, painting and sculpture, dress, textile art, forms of governance, religious belief, and many other vernacular art forms. All express the effects of long-term contact and intractable, unequal conflict.

Autoethnography, transculturation, critique, collaboration, bilingualism, mediation, parody, denunciation, imaginary dialogue, vernacular expression—these are some of the literate arts of the contact zone. Miscomprehension, incomprehension, dead letters, unread masterpieces, absolute heterogeneity of meaning—these are some of the perils of writing in the contact zone. They all live among us today in the transnationalized metropolis of the United States and are becoming more widely visible, more pressing, and, like Guaman Poma's text, more decipherable to those who once would have ignored them in defense of a stable, centered sense of knowledge and reality.

CONTACT AND COMMUNITY

The idea of the contact zone is intended in part to contrast with ideas of community that underlie much of the thinking about language, communication, and culture that gets done in the academy. A couple of years ago, thinking about the linguistic theories I knew, I tried to make sense of a utopian quality that often seemed to characterize social analyses of language by the academy. Languages were seen as living in "speech communities," and these tended to be theorized as discrete, self-defined, coherent entities, held together by a homogeneous competence or grammar shared identically and equally among all the members. This abstract idea of the speech community seemed to reflect, among other things, the utopian way modern nations conceive of themselves as what Benedict Anderson calls "imagined communities."[3] In a book of that title, Anderson observes that with the possible exception of what he calls "primordial villages," human communities exist as *imagined* entities in which people "will never know most of their fellow-members, meet them or even hear of them, yet in the minds of each lives the image of their communion." "Communities are distinguished," he goes on to say, "not by their falsity/genuineness, but by *the style in which they are imagined*" (15; emphasis mine). Anderson proposes three features that characterize the style in which the modern nation is imagined. First, it is imagined as *limited*, by "finite, if elastic, boundaries"; second, it is imagined as *sovereign*; and, third, it is imagined as *fraternal*, "a deep, horizontal comradeship" for which millions of people are prepared "not so much to kill as willingly to die" (15). As the image suggests, the nation-community is embodied metonymically in the finite, sovereign, fraternal figure of the citizen-soldier.

Anderson argues that European bourgeoisies were distinguished by their ability to "achieve solidarity on an essentially imagined basis" (74) on a scale far greater than that of elites of other times and places. Writing and literacy play a central role in this argument. Anderson maintains, as have others, that the main instrument that made bourgeois nation-building projects possible was print capitalism. The commercial circulation of books in the various European vernaculars, he argues, was what first created the invisible networks that would eventually constitute the literate elites and those they ruled as nations. (Estimates are that 180 million books were put into circulation in Europe between the years 1500 and 1600 alone.)

Now obviously this style of imagining of modern nations, as Anderson describes it, is strongly utopian, embodying values like equality, fraternity, liberty, which the societies often profess but systematically fail to realize. The prototype of the modern nation as imagined community was, it seemed to me, mirrored in ways people thought about language and the speech community. Many commentators have pointed out how modern views of language as code and competence assume a unified and homogeneous social world in which language exists as a shared patrimony—as a device, precisely, for imagining community. An image of a universally shared literacy is also part of the picture. The prototypical manifestation of language is generally taken to be the speech of individual adult native speakers face-to-face (as in Saussure's famous diagram) in monolingual, even mono-dialectical situations—in short, the most homogeneous case linguistically and socially. The same goes for written communication. Now one could certainly imagine a theory that assumed different things—that argued, for instance, that the most revealing speech situation for understanding language was one involving a gathering of people each of whom spoke two languages and understood a third and held only one language in common with any of the others. It depends on what workings of language you want to see or want to see first, on what you choose to define as normative.

In keeping with autonomous, fraternal models of community, analyses of language use commonly assume that principles of cooperation and shared understanding are normally in effect. Descriptions of interactions between people in conversation, classrooms, medical and bureaucratic settings, readily take it for granted that the situation is governed by a single set of rules or norms shared by all participants. The analysis focuses then on how those rules produce or fail to produce an orderly, coherent exchange. Models involving games and moves are often used to describe interactions. Despite whatever conflicts or systematic social differences might be in play, it is assumed that all participants are engaged in the same game and that the game is the same for all players. Often it is. But of course it often is not, as, for example, when speakers are from different classes or cultures, or one party is exercising authority and another is submitting to it or questioning it. Last year one of my children moved to a new elementary school that had more open classrooms and more flexible curricula than the conventional school he started out in. A few days into the term, we asked him what it was like at the new school. "Well," he said, "they're a lot nicer, and they have a lot less rules. But know *why* they're nicer?" "Why?" I asked. "So you'll obey all the rules they don't have," he replied. This is a very coherent analysis with considerable elegance and explanatory power, but probably not the one his teacher would have given.

When linguistic (or literate) interaction is described in terms of orderliness, games, moves, or scripts, usually only legitimate moves are actually named as part of the system, where legitimacy is defined from the point of view of the party in authority—regardless of what other parties might see themselves as doing. Teacher–pupil language, for example, tends to be described almost entirely from the point of view of the teacher and teaching, not from the point of view of pupils and pupiling (the word doesn't even exist, though the thing certainly does). If a classroom is analyzed as a social world unified and homogenized with respect to the teacher, whatever students do other than what the teacher specifies is invisible or anomalous to the analysis. This can be true in practice as well. On several occasions my fourth grader, the one busy obeying all the rules they didn't have, was given writing assignments that took the form of answering a series of questions to build up a paragraph. These questions often asked him to identify with the interests of those in power over him—parents, teachers, doctors, public authorities. He invariably sought ways to resist or subvert these assignments. One assignment, for instance, called for imagining "a helpful invention." The students were asked to write single-sentence responses to the following questions:

> What kind of invention would help you?
> How would it help you?
> Why would you need it?
> What would it look like?
> Would other people be able to use it also?
> What would be an invention to help your teacher?
> What would be an invention to help your parents?

Manuel's reply read as follows:

A grate adventchin

Some inventchins are GRATE!!!!!!!!!!! My inventchin would be a shot that would put every thing you learn at school in your brain. It would help me by letting me graduate right now!! I would need it because it would let me play with my friends, go on vacachin and, do fun a lot more. It would look like a regular shot. Ather peaple would use to. This inventchin would help my teacher parents get away from a lot of work. I think a shot like this would be GRATE!

Despite the spelling, the assignment received the usual star to indicate the task had been fulfilled in an acceptable way. No recognition was available, however, of the humor, the attempt to be critical or contestatory, to parody the structures of authority. On that score, Manuel's luck was only slightly better than Guaman Poma's. What is the place of unsolicited oppositional discourse, parody, resistance, critique in the imagined classroom community? Are teachers supposed to feel that their teaching has been most successful when they have eliminated such things and unified the social world, probably in their own image? Who wins when we do that? Who loses?

Such questions may be hypothetical, because in the United States in the 1990s, many teachers find themselves less and less able to do that even if they want to. The composition of the national collectivity is changing and so are the styles, as Anderson put it, in which it is being imagined. In the 1980s in many nation-states, imagined national syntheses that had retained hegemonic force began to dissolve. Internal social groups with histories and lifeways different from the official ones began insisting on those histories and lifeways *as part of their citizenship,* as the very mode of their membership in the national collectivity. In their dialogues with dominant institutions, many groups began asserting a rhetoric of belonging that made demands beyond those of representation and basic rights granted from above. In universities we started to hear, "I don't just want you to let me be here, I want to belong here; this institution should belong to me as much as it does to anyone else." Institutions have responded with, among other things, rhetorics of diversity and multiculturalism whose import at this moment is up for grabs across the ideological spectrum.

These shifts are being lived out by everyone working in education today, and everyone is challenged by them in one way or another. Those of us committed to educational democracy are particularly challenged as that notion finds itself besieged on the public agenda. Many of those who govern us display, openly, their interest in a quiescent, ignorant, manipulable electorate. Even as an ideal, the concept of an enlightened citizenry seems to have disappeared from the national imagination. A couple of years ago the university where I work went through an intense and wrenching debate over a narrowly defined Western-culture requirement that had been instituted there in 1980. It kept boiling down to a debate over the ideas of national patrimony, cultural citizenship, and imagined community. In the end, the requirement was transformed into a much more broadly defined course called Cultures, Ideas, Values.[4] In the context of the change, a new course was designed that centered on the Americas and the multiple cultural histories (including European ones) that have intersected here. As you can imagine, the course attracted a very diverse student body. The classroom functioned not like a homogeneous community or a horizontal alliance but like a contact zone. Every single text we read stood in specific historical relationships to the students in the class, but the range and variety of historical relationships in play were enormous. Everybody had a stake in nearly everything we read, but the range and kind of stakes varied widely.

It was the most exciting teaching we had ever done, and also the hardest. We were struck, for example, at how anomalous the formal lecture became in a contact zone (who can forget Atahuallpa throwing down the Bible because it would not speak to him?). The lecturer's traditional (imagined) task—unifying the world in the class's eyes by means of a monologue that rings equally coherent, revealing, and true for all, forging an ad hoc community, homogeneous with respect to one's own words—this task became not only impossible but anomalous and unimaginable. Instead, one had to work in the knowledge that whatever one said was going to be systematically received in radically heterogeneous ways that we were neither able nor entitled to prescribe.

The very nature of the course put ideas and identities on the line. All the students in the class had the experience, for example, of hearing their culture discussed and objectified in ways that horrified them; all the students saw their roots traced back to legacies of both glory and shame; all the students experienced face-to-face the ignorance and incomprehension, and occasionally the hostility, of others. In the absence of community values and the hope of synthesis, it was easy to forget the positives; the fact, for instance, that kinds of marginalization once taken for granted were gone. Virtually every student was having the experience of seeing the world described with him or her in it. Along with rage, incomprehension, and pain, there were exhilarating moments of wonder and revelation, mutual understanding, and new wisdom—the joys of the contact zone. The sufferings and revelations were, at different moments to be sure, experienced by every student. No one was excluded, and no one was safe.

The fact that no one was safe made all of us involved in the course appreciate the importance of what we came to call "safe houses." We used the term to refer to social and intellectual spaces where groups can constitute themselves as horizontal, homogeneous, sovereign communities with high degrees of trust, shared understandings, temporary protection from legacies of oppression. This is why, as we realized, multicultural curricula should not seek to replace ethnic or women's studies, for example. Where there are legacies of subordination, groups need places for healing and mutual recognition, safe houses in which to construct shared understandings, knowledges, claims on the world that they can then bring into the contact zone.

Meanwhile, our job in the Americas course remains to figure out how to make that crossroads the best site for learning that it can be. We are looking for the pedagogical arts of the contact zone. These will include, we are sure, exercises in storytelling and in identifying with the ideas, interests, histories, and attitudes of others; experiments in transculturation and collaborative work and in the arts of critique, parody, and comparison (including unseemly comparisons between elite and vernacular cultural forms); the redemption of the oral; ways for people to engage with suppressed aspects of history (including their own histories), ways to move *into and out of* rhetorics of authenticity; ground rules for communication across lines of difference and hierarchy that go beyond politeness but maintain mutual respect; a systematic approach to the all-important concept of *cultural mediation*. These arts were to play in every room at the extraordinary Pittsburgh conference on literacy. I learned a lot about them there, and I am thankful.

NOTES

[1]For an introduction in English to these and other aspects of Guaman Poma's work, see Rolena Adorno. Adorno and Mercedes Lopez-Baralt pioneered the study of Andean symbolic systems in Guaman Poma.

[2]It is far from clear that the *Royal Commentaries* was as benign as the Spanish seemed to assume. The book certainly played a role in maintaining the identity and aspirations of indigenous elites in the Andes. In the mid-eighteenth century, a new edition of the *Royal Commentaries* was suppressed by Spanish authorities because its preface included a prophecy by Sir Walter Raleigh that the English would invade Peru and restore the Inca monarchy.

[3]The discussion of community here is summarized from my essay "Linguistic Utopias."

[4]For information about this program and the contents of courses taught in it, write Program in Cultures, Ideas, Values (CIV), Stanford Univ., Stanford, CA 94305.

WORKS CITED

Adorno, Rolena. *Guaman Poma de Ayala: Writing and Resistance in Colonial Peru.* Austin: U of Texas P, 1986.

Anderson, Benedict. *Imagined Communities: Reflections on the Origins and Spread of Nationalism.* London: Verso, 1984.

Garcilaso de la Vega, El Inca. *Royal Commentaries of the Incas.* 1613. Austin: U of Texas P, 1966.

Guaman Poma de Ayala, Felipe. *El primer nueva corónica y buen gobierno.* Manuscript. Ed. John Murra and Rolena Adorno. Mexico: Siglo XXI, 1980.

Pratt, Mary Louise. "Linguistic Utopias." *The Linguistics of Writing.* Ed. Nigel Fabb et al. Manchester: Manchester UP, 1987. 48–66.

Treviño, Gloria. "Cultural Ambivalence in Early Chicano Prose Fiction." Diss. Stanford U, 1985.

Chapter 14

Questioning Academic Discourse

Vivian Zamel

Much discussion surrounds how to determine and define what academic discourse is (see, for example, Bartholomae, 1986; Bizzell, 1988; Coles and Wall, 1987; Elbow, 1991; Harris, 1989; Rose, 1985). At the most general level academic discourse is understood to be a specialized form of reading, writing, and thinking done in the "academy" or other schooling situations. It has been referred to as the "peculiar ways of knowing, selecting, evaluating, reporting, concluding and arguing that define the discourse of our community" (Bartholomae, 1986, p. 4). Because it appears to require a kind of language with its own vocabulary, norms, sets of conventions, and modes of inquiry, academic discourse has come to characterize a separate culture, one within which each discipline may represent a separate cultural community. It is from this notion of a separate culture that we get the terms discourse or interpretive "community." Bartholomae (1986) has captured this notion of acquiring the language of the new community in his oft-quoted article, "Inventing the University." As he puts it,

> The students have to appropriate (or be appropriated by) a specialized discourse, and they have to do this as though they were members of the academy, or historians or anthropologists or economists; they have to invent the university by assembling and mimicking its language. . . . They must learn to speak our language. (pp. 4–5)

Students entering a new community must take on its ways of knowing and its "ways with words." The idea of a culture suggests the kind of immersion, engagement, contextualization, fullness of experience, that is necessary for someone to be initiated into and to be conversant in that culture, for someone to understand the ways in which that culture works. Returning to Bartholomae's quote, students need to act as if they were "members of the academy, or historians or anthropologists or economists." Elbow (1991), too, stresses this notion and points out that writing well within the disciplines requires not just using the "lingo" of the discipline but *doing* the discipline (p. 138). Doing academic discourse, in other words, involves far more than an academic exercise.

Unfortunately, the description of a discourse or interpretive community has too often been reduced to identifying the language, conventions, and generic forms that supposedly represent the various disciplines and teaching toward these, so that, for example, students are given practice writing the kind of essays that they might be expected to do in sociology or economics. Bartholomae (1986) notes what happens when students struggle to appropriate academic discourse in this way and indicates that the consequence of learning can become more a matter of "imitation or parody than a matter of invention and discovery" (p. 11). Elbow (1991) makes a similar argument about the limitations of teaching academic language and notes the ways in which it "masks a lack of genuine understanding" (p. 137). Bizzell (1988), despite her earlier conceptualization of the academic conventions students needed to learn when they entered college, comes to acknowledge that to think of academic literacy in this way is "misleading and politically oppressive" (p. 14). Land and Whitley (1989), referring specifically to the writing of ESL college students, point to the problematic nature of asking students to reproduce mechanically the conventions of academic writing, an approach that is not only unlikely to be successful, but also disenfranchises our students. Sommers (1992), recollecting her own experiences as an academic, speaks of the influence that the tendency to appropriate a way of using language and a way of seeing and interpreting had on her own work:

> I, like so many of my students, was reproducing acceptable truths, imitating the gestures and rituals of the academy, not having confidence enough in my own ideas, not trusting the native language I had learned. I had surrendered my own authority to someone else, to those other authorial voices. (p. 28)

As she observes the struggles of her students as they "defer to the voice of the academy," she notes the ways in which they "disguise themselves in the weighty, imponderable voice of acquired authority," losing themselves in the process (p. 29). It is clear that becoming acculturated into a new academic community does not simply involve practicing the discipline-specific language, norms, and conventions that many textbooks on academic reading and writing seem to imply.

Related to the issue of reductionist and formulaic approaches to academic writing is the question of whether academic discourse communities are such monolithic, unchanging, and easily identifiable entities. Harris (1989), for example, argues that academic disciplines are not as coherent and well-defined as some of us think and suggests that these disciplines ought to be viewed as "polyglot," as a system whereby "competing beliefs and practices" overlap and intersect (p. 20). Elbow (1991), too, questions whether academic discourse and the discourses of particular communities can be delineated so readily. To push his argument, he surveys the range of discourses that fall within the discipline of English, from the tradition of high Germanic scholarship, to critical or Marxist discourse, to the diversity of approaches to composition studies. As he looks at the multiple discourses in his field, he concludes:

> I can't tell my students whether academic discourse means using lots of structural signposts or leaving them out, bringing in their feelings and personal reactions or leaving them out, giving evidence from the poet's life for interpretations or leaving them out, referring to the class, gender, and school of other interpreters or leaving them out. . . . In short, it's crazy to talk about academic discourse as one thing. (pp. 139–140)

The tendency to categorize academic discourse and the discourses of particular communities can lead to theoretical frameworks and instructional models that oversimplify our understanding of academic work and reduce it to a fixed idea that does not reflect reality. One illustration of that reality is Walvoord and McCarthy's (1990) rich and detailed naturalistic study in which the authors collaborated with faculty across four disciplines, collecting observational notes, examining assignments and drafts of student writing, conducting interviews with teachers and students, and studying logs kept by teachers and students. Underlying this study is the assumption that "language processes must be understood in terms of the contexts in which they occur" (p. 21), which is why these contexts were examined in such rigorous detail and from a number of different perspectives. This study reveals the complex array of factors, such as individual teachers' methods, intentions, and expectations and individual students' approaches to and interpretations of assignments, which shape the work of these classrooms and often give rise to the difficulties students experience as they struggle to meet their teachers' expectations. Importantly, by examining these factors within each classroom, these teachers come to understand the importance of careful reflection about teaching, the need to consider what students are expected to do and how they might be guided in the process, and the critical role that writing plays in helping students learn about the work of academic disciplines.

Yet another exploration of academic work was undertaken by Wendy Schoener (1992) at the University of Massachusetts at Boston because she was dissatisfied by the underconceptualized ways in which academic discourse had been treated in textbooks and in some of the literature on teaching English for academic purposes. She began to investigate the expectations and norms of other academic course work by following ESL students into these courses, observing and taping classes, transcribing and analyzing classroom exchanges, interviewing professors and students, collecting writing assignments and students' texts, and examining professors' responses to these texts. Schoener discovered that only by having access to and understanding the full context and complexity of these classrooms could one begin to anticipate what was expected of students, so embedded was the work in the particulars of the course content, so influenced was the work by the ongoing contributions of the participants, so marked was the work by the particular pedagogical assumptions of the individual teachers.

I have begun some exploratory research of my own, interviewing ESL students who attended my composition course about their experiences in other courses, examining the writing these students have been assigned as well as the professors' comments about and evaluation of these papers. This line of inquiry suggests that academic discourse is not unitary, that the disciplines themselves are not fixed, but, like all cultures, are subject to continual reshaping as others enter the discourse community and change its terms. This research helps us understand why teaching academic discourse as if it consisted of a uniform set of norms and conventions not only does not represent the reality that students will encounter but may make it even more difficult for them to deal with this reality because such a model of instruction removes them from the kinds of experiences that demonstrate how knowledge is genuinely made in a community:

> To present 'academic discourse' to basic readers and writers as if it were a unified body of literacy conventions and procedures to be mastered is to mystify what our students most need to have demystified: how work gets done in the university. For while we speak broadly of the university as a 'discourse community', particular interpretive communities come into existence only when particular students and teachers are gathered there. When this happens, neither students nor teachers leave their histories behind; they bring them to class, to every academic discussion, and to every reading and writing assignment. (Coles and Wall, 1987, p. 313)

Other questions have been raised by composition theorists about the tendency to separate the personal from the academic, to exclude and undervalue one discourse and privilege the other (Coles and Wall, 1987; Elbow, 1985; Elbow, 1991; Fox, 1990; Harris, 1989; Ritchie, 1989; Robinson, 1985; Spellmeyer, 1989). Spellmeyer (1989), for example, challenges discourse community theorists who have mistaken the pose of objectivity for an absence of personal commitment. He argues compellingly that understanding can never be objective, that the only way for students to become insiders in the world of academic culture is to bring their own personal values, experiences, knowledge, and questions to bear on this culture. It is in this way, Spellmeyer (1989) contends, that students can discover an "enlarging horizon that every discourse can open to [their] view," that students can "gradually enter the community of 'knowers' while retaining [their] own voice in the process" (p. 274). Elbow (1991), too, points to the problematic language of academic prose with its tendency to exclude the personal voice, to remove the author from the text, and argues that a detached and impersonal stance is a pretense, for we cannot separate the "ideas and reasons and arguments from the person who holds them" (p. 140).

Fishman and McCarthy (1992), drawing on their understanding of the facilitative power of the native language in the acquisition of a foreign language, make a similar case for the essential role that "expressivism" plays as people learn the languages and conventions of unfamiliar communities. They speak to the importance of integrating private life and public expression, blending personal and academic languages, and maintain that it is precisely when we deny students their personal attempts at expression that we limit their capacity for making sense and clarifying meaning as they engage with those in a new community, thus lessening their ability to understand and identify with them:

> Unless our expressions testify to our inner lives, we are unable to see ourselves mirrored or clarified by them. And unless we are so mirrored, our opportunities for finding common cause or identifying with others are greatly reduced. (p. 651)

It can be argued further that the most engaging kind of writing is familiar, exploratory, tentative (Popkin, 1992; Zeiger, 1985), that the best expository writing is marked by subjective experience, by voice, by the unconventional stance that shifts back and forth between the personal and the outside world being examined (Elbow, 1985). The February 1992 issue of *College Composition and Communication,* one of the preeminent academic journals in composition, is a case in point. This issue convincingly illustrates that the personal voice, the well-crafted story, exploratory and introspective pieces, not only can but do play a critical role in how knowledge is made in a discipline. Sommers' (1992) own piece in this issue refers to her earlier tendency, as an academic, to treat her research as an "academic subject, not a personal one," of keeping herself "clean and distant from any kind of scrutiny," of "never asking myself how I was being displaced from my own work," of speaking in an "inherited academic voice," one that was not her own (pp. 26–27). She now is able to acknowledge how this "fictionalized self" kept her from her most "passionate convictions" (p. 27), how personal stories and experiences give us our authority to speak. And in order to demonstrate this very notion, she weaves together recollections of her childhood, day-to-day experiences with her daughters, conversations with colleagues, the influence of her mentors. The richness and complexity of this prose draws attention to the limitations of writing determined by a uniform set of criteria and argues for a re-vision of what we have come to define as academic work.

Finally, there is the problem of describing academic discourse so that those teaching ESL and composition can prepare students for the "real" work of the university. This hierarchical model implies a unidirectional movement whereby our courses serve some greater end, without ever raising questions about that end. One danger is that teaching toward what is viewed as the "real stuff" of academia forces conformity and submission and limits and undermines both our own expertise and that of our students. It is assumed, both by faculty across the curriculum and, all too often, by ESL and writing faculty, that since the content and academic practices students are expected to study and know reside in other discipline-specific courses, language/reading/writing courses ought to focus on those "skills" or approaches students will need later on. Spack (1988) underlines the problematic nature of such an approach, arguing that ESL teachers not only should not but cannot teach the work of other disciplines. Fox (1990) maintains that when writing courses are viewed as serving the institution, they have the "enormous potential to work oppressively" (p. 68). Land and Whitley (1989), who understand the political implications of this situation, warn against enacting "composition as colonization" (p. 289). Using the same metaphor, Wilson (1992) indicates that when we teach our students in this way, our relationship to them is that of "colonizer to the colonized" (p. 679). This metaphor extends to us as well when we allow our work to be determined by those who are viewed as having greater authority and power.

But to what extent should other disciplines dictate what we do in our own courses? To what extent are the approaches to learning and evaluation adopted in these disciplines ones that we should embrace and emulate? To what extent is the writing students are assigned in these courses the kind of work that we believe leads to genuine understanding and an enlargement of perspective? Do the experiences students have in these courses suggest that we have much to learn from the professors who teach them? Schoener's (1992) research and my beginning inquiry into ESL students' experiences in these courses reveal the generally unimaginative and formulaic coursework students are asked to do. And Chiseri-Strater's (1991) ethnographic study of students' experiences in university classrooms reveals the authoritarian ways that subject matter is approached, with the result that students are discouraged, silenced, and kept from engaging with the material and work they are assigned.

It seems then that we ought to be raising questions about the hierarchical divisions we contribute to when we fail to acknowledge our own expertise and instead make curricular and pedagogical choices that are determined from without. Naturally, the ways in which our own role is diminished when we fulfill a "service" function in our institutions is inextricably tied to the work in which we involve our students. Preparing students for what is deemed as more authentic or important work may not only limit what we ask them to do, but blind us to the expertise they bring with them. As Coles and Wall (1987) point out,

> the tendency of 'outer-directed' pedagogies so far has been to over-emphasize what it is that students must learn in order to become members of our community. The focus . . . is on what must change in our students, how they must become other than they are in order to accommodate our discourse. We feel the need to focus also on those motives and abilities that grow from our students' histories that may be sustained and extended. (p. 299)

Yet another danger that stems from a hierarchical model is that it sets up the unrealistic and unwarranted expectations that ESL and writing courses will complete the process of "initiation" and that in the case of students who are found "underprepared" or "deficient," these courses will serve a gatekeeping function in the institution. Such expectations, based on a deficit model of language and learning, exclude students from the very work they are trying to take part in; these students are labeled as "outsiders" who do not have the "requisite values, knowledge, and skills to belong," who "lack these necessary qualifications" (Cooper and Holtzman, 1989, p. 204). Furthermore, assumptions such as these prevent faculty from recognizing their students' resources, their students' rich and full histories, give rise to the frustration and resentment that faculty report when students struggle in their courses, and perpetuate the myth that the problems these faculty encounter are not essentially ones that they can or need to deal with (Rose, 1985). We need to recognize that writing-across-the-curriculum means that the entire academic community assumes the responsibility of teaching reading, writing, critical approaches. Doing otherwise, taking on the responsibility, as if this were possible, of teaching someone else's curriculum serves to marginalize us as well as our students.

Given these problems, what can we do in our writing courses? I am arguing that we resist reductionist, narrowly conceptualized, and exclusionary notions of academic discourse. Rather than focusing on the presumable differences among discourses (both across content areas and between personal and academic prose), work which can keep us from seeing what is "universal to all discourses" (Spellmeyer, 1989, p. 270), we ought to look for and teach toward those "points of commonality" that allow beginning writers to discover "in their own commitments the areas of concern they already share with us" (p. 266). Rather than concluding that beginning student writers lack literacy, we need to see in their writing those " 'fundamentals' [that] characterize academic literacy at its best: a focused exploration of a complex topic" (Fox, 1990, p. 80). Rather than acting as though the "academy has a monopoly on a sound intellectual stance," we need to turn our attention to those features of writing that transcend boundaries, features that characterize all "good writing" (Elbow, 1991, pp. 142–143). Rather than stressing the surface features of academic writing, we ought to focus our instruction on the deep structure of challenging intellectual activity, with the understanding that surface features will be more readily learned in the context of meaningful and purposeful work.

I propose that we involve students in authentic work by immersing them in reading, writing, and language, by engaging them in rich course material, by providing them with multiple and extensive opportunities to inquire into, raise questions about, critically examine this material, by inviting them to see connections between their own perspectives and course content, by helping them develop new frameworks of understanding, by allowing them to actively construct knowledge by locating meaning in their observations and interpretations. This is exactly the sort of work I think students need to be involved in across the curriculum as they are introduced to unfamiliar subject matter, new concepts, differing methods of approaching content. From the collaborative work I have been doing with faculty representing a range of disciplines, it is clear that these teachers recognize the limitations of their traditional methods of covering and assigning course material, and some are beginning to revise their pedagogy by engaging students in the ways I have mentioned.

In my own writing courses, I have experimented with a number of charged themes such as work and language. Most recently, students explored the myth and the reality of the American Dream and analyzed those situations and conditions that enable or constrain the "dream" so many of them have embraced. They examined key documents such as the *Declaration of Independence* and the *Gettysburg Address* and important court decisions such as *Brown v. Board of Education*. They read newspaper accounts and analyzed reports in the media related to immigration experiences and issues. They read revealing interviews in Studs Terkel's *American Dreams:*

Lost and Found and carried out interviews of their own. They read poetry by Langston Hughes, speeches by Martin Luther King, Jr., autobiographical pieces by Ann Moody and Audre Lorde, and considered the civil rights movement in light of the promises of the American Dream. They read selections by authors such as Amy Tan, Maxine Hong Kingston, Richard Rodriquez, and Ronald Takaki, pieces which illustrate the complicated relationship between language, cultural identity, and power. They read about research that corroborated the first-hand experiences of these authors and demonstrated that these authors' experiences as well as their own were interwoven within a far more complex set of societal factors. Through all of this work, I invited students' reactions, their analyses and interpretations, their attempts to use new concepts and language, and urged them to make connections between this work and their own experiences and assumptions. Intrinsic to this work was a sequence of reading and writing that built on itself, so that as the semester progressed, students could refer back to previous work, both published texts and their own, to demonstrate their growing expertise.

What this kind of work produced was not neat and predictable essays that could be plotted along some standardized continuum. Rather, it generated rich, compelling and memorable pieces that reflected the questions and issues students were grappling with, their active engagement with the material, their use of the material to think about the world around them, to think about the ways in which this material and their world intersect, to think about their thinking. They became authors alongside the authors they read, thus reclaiming authority for themselves, even quoting one another in the process. In short, their work represented a dialectical interplay between themselves and the course content, indicating not only the way the material affected them, but the ways in which they were contributing to the material. One illustration of the kinds of texts students wrote was a paper in which a student not only used the refrain from one of Langston Hughes's poems to repeatedly punctuate her paper, thereby raising questions about the "American Dream," but also quoted an original verse that another student had composed. This remarkable paper incorporated as well references to the *Declaration of Independence,* a critical look at civil rights in this country, and concluded with a retelling of a Vietnamese folktale. As this student writer shifted among and responded to the different texts she had read and (re)considered, she created new relationships among them and influenced other readers with her own re-vision of these texts. She had entered a rich and complex conversation with other authors, bringing her own voice and authority to bear on their voices. This student had clearly "invented" rather than merely "imitated."

This work illustrates what can happen when students not only learn and write about content but also reshape it in some fundamental way. It illustrates the difference between the consumption of knowledge and the construction of knowledge. I would like to think that this kind of work points as well to the critical role that we can play in our institutions. We need to argue that academic discourse is not fixed, prescribed and imposed from without, that "teaching academic literacy" ought to be a "process of constructing academic literacy, creating it anew in each class through the interaction of the professor's and students' cultural resources" (Bizzell, 1988, p. 150). And just as this discourse is created anew as teachers and students engage one another, it is (re)conceptualized as teachers across disciplines share with one another their cultural resources. Walvoord and McCarthy's (1990) collaborative work demonstrates what can happen when faculty from different disciplines take on this responsibility and re-search the ways they can help students learn.

We need to raise questions about the nature, value, and use of academic discourse, about its assumptions about what it includes and what it doesn't, about who belongs and who doesn't. These are the sorts of questions underlying the nationwide debates on reforming the canon, on acknowledging diversity, on the role of multiple languages, literacies, interpretations, on participatory models of pedagogy and evaluation, debates which are slowly redefining the landscape and borders of the academic community. Sommers (1992) urges us to encourage and empower students "not to serve the academy and accommodate it, . . . but rather to write essays that will change the academy" (p. 30). Clearly, we need to join with our students in this endeavor: Rather than serving the academy, accommodating it, and being appropriated by it, we ought to work with others to engage in an enterprise that is far more dynamic, complex, collaborative and intellectually engaging, an enterprise whereby we and our students contribute to, complicate, and transform the academy. This is, after all, the way all cultures, including academic ones, come to be, continually re-created by those who enter and the languages they bring with them.

REFERENCES

Bartholomae, D. (1986). Inventing the university. *Journal of Basic Writing, 5*, 4–23.

Bizzell, P. (1988). Arguing about literacy. *College English, 50*, 141–153.

Chiseri-Strater, E. (1991). *Academic literacies: The public and private discourse of university students.* Portsmouth, NH: Boynton/Cook.

Coles, N., & Wall, S. V. (1987). Conflict and power in the reader—responses of adult basic writers. *College English, 49*, 298–314.

Cooper, M., & Holtzman, M. (1989). *Writing as social action.* Portsmouth, NH: Boynton/Cook.

Elbow, P. (1985). The shifting relationships between speech and writing. *College Composition and Communication, 36*, 283–303.

Elbow, P. (1991). Reflections on academic discourse: How it relates to freshmen and colleagues. *College English, 53,* 135–155.

Fishman, S. & McCarthy, L. P. (1992). Is expressivism dead? *College English, 54,* 647–661.

Fox, T. (1990). Basic writing as cultural conflict. *Journal of Education, 172,* 65–83.

Geertz, C. (1983). *Local knowledge: Further essays in interpretive anthropology.* New York: Basic Books.

Harris, J. (1989). The idea of community in the study of writing. *College Composition and Communication, 40,* 11–22.

Land, R. E. & Whitley, C. (1989). Evaluating second language essays in regular composition classes: Toward a pluralistic U.S. rhetoric. In D. M. Johnson & D. H. Roen (Eds.), *Richness in writing* (pp. 284–293). New York: Longman.

Popkin, C. (1992). A plea to the wielders of academic dis(of)course. *College English, 54,* 173–181.

Ritchie, J. S. (1989). Beginning writers: Diverse voices and individual identity. *College Composition and Communication, 40,* 152–174.

Robinson, J. L. (1985). Literacy in the department of English. *College English, 47,* 482–498.

Rose, M. (1985). The language of exclusion: Writing instruction at the university. *College English, 47,* 341–359.

Schoener, W. (1992). Were they prepared?: College ESL students in mainstream classes. MATSOL Conference, Boston, MA.

Sommers, N. (1992). Between the drafts. *College Composition and Communication, 43,* 23–31.

Spack, R. (1988). Initiating ESL students into the academic discourse community: How far should we go? *TESOL Quarterly, 22,* 29–51.

Spellmeyer, K. (1989). A common ground: The essay in the academy. *College English, 51,* 262–276.

Walvoord, B. E., & McCarthy, L. P. (1990). *Thinking and writing in college: A naturalistic study of students in four disciplines.* Urbana, IL: NCTE.

Wilson, M. (1992). Writing History: Textbooks, heuristics, and the Eastern European Revolutions of '89. *College English, 54,* 662–680.

Zeiger, W. (1985). The exploratory essay: Enfranchising the spirit of inquiry in college composition. *College English, 47,* 454–466.

Chapter 15

Dancing With Professors: The Trouble With Academic Prose

Patricia Nelson Limerick

In ordinary life, when a listener cannot understand what someone has said, this is the usual exchange:

Listener: I cannot understand what you are saying.

Speaker: Let me try to say it more clearly.

But in scholarly writing in the late 20th century, other rules apply. This is the implicit exchange:

Reader: I cannot understand what you are saying.

Academic Writer: Too bad. The problem is that you are an unsophisticated and untrained reader. If you were smarter, you would understand me.

The exchange remains implicit, because no one wants to say, "This doesn't make any sense," for fear that the response, "It would, if you were smarter," might actually be true.

While we waste our time fighting over ideological conformity in the scholarly world, horrible writing remains a far more important problem. For all their differences, most right-wing scholars and most left-wing scholars share a common allegiance to a cult of obscurity. Left, right and center all hide behind the idea that unintelligible prose indicates a sophisticated mind. The politically correct and the politically incorrect come together in the violence they commit against the English language.

University presses have certainly filled their quota every year, in dreary monographs, tangled paragraphs and impenetrable sentences. But trade

The New York Times, 1993

199

publishers have also violated the trust of innocent and hopeful readers. As a prime example of unprovoked assaults on innocent words, consider the verbal behavior of Allan Bloom in "The Closing of the American Mind," published by a large mainstream press. Here is a sample:

> If openness means to "go with the flow," it is necessarily an accommodation to the present. That present is so closed to doubt about so many things impeding the progress of its principles that unqualified openness to it would mean forgetting the despised alternatives to it, knowledge of which makes us aware of what is doubtful in it.

Is there a reader so full of blind courage as to claim to know what this sentence means? Remember, the book in which this remark appeared was a lamentation over the failings of today's *students*, a call to arms to return to tradition and standards in education. And yet, in 20 years of paper grading, I do not recall many sentences that asked, so pathetically, to be put out of their misery.

Jump to the opposite side of the political spectrum from Allan Bloom, and literary grace makes no noticeable gains. Contemplate this breathless, indefatigable sentence from the geographer Allan Pred, and Mr. Pred and Bloom seem, if only in literary style, to be soul mates:

> If what is at stake is an understanding of geographical and historical variations in the sexual division of productive and reproductive labor, of contemporary local and regional variations in female wage labor and women's work outside the formal economy, of on-the-ground variations in the everyday content of women's lives, inside and outside of their families, then it must be recognized that, at some nontrivial level, none of the corporal practices associated with these variations can be severed from spatially and temporally specific linguistic practices, from languages that not only enable the conveyance of instructions, commands, role depictions and operating rules, but that also regulate and control, that normalize and spell out the limits of the permissible through the conveyance of disapproval, ridicule and reproach.

In this example, 124 words, along with many ideas, find themselves crammed into one sentence. In their company, one starts to get panicky. "Throw open the windows; bring in the oxygen tanks!" one wants to shout. "These words and ideas are nearly suffocated. Get them air!" And yet the condition of this desperately packed and crowded sentence is a perfectly familiar one to readers of academic writing, readers who have simply learned to suppress the panic.

Everyone knows that today's college students cannot write, but few seem willing to admit that the professors who denounce them are not doing much better. The problem is so blatant there are signs that students are catching on. In my American history survey course last semester, I presented a few writing rules that I intended to enforce inflexibly. The students looked more and more peevish; they looked as if they were about to run down the hall, find a telephone, place an urgent call and demand that someone from the A.C.L.U. rush up to campus to sue me for interfering with their First Amendment rights to compose unintelligible, misshapen sentences.

Finally one aggrieved student raised her hand and said, "You are telling *us* not to write long, dull sentences, but most of our assigned reading is *full* of long, dull sentences."

As this student was beginning to recognize, when professors undertake to appraise and improve student writing, the blind are leading the blind. It is, in truth, difficult to persuade students to write well when they find so few good examples in their assigned reading.

The current social and political context for higher education makes this whole issue pressing. In Colorado, as in most states, the legislators are convinced that the university is neglecting students and wasting state resources on pointless research. Under those circumstances, the miserable writing habits of professors pose a direct and concrete danger to higher education. Rather than going to the state legislature, proudly presenting stacks of the faculty's compelling and engaging publications, you end up hoping that the lawmakers stay out of the library and stay away, especially, from the periodical room, with its piles of academic journals. The habits of academic writers lend powerful support to the impression that research is a waste of the writers' time and of the public's money.

Why do so many professors write bad prose?

Ten years ago, I heard a classics professor say the single most important thing—in my opinion—that anyone has said about professors: "We must remember," he declared, "that professors are the ones nobody wanted to dance with in high school."

This is an insight that lights up the universe—or at least the university. It is a proposition that every entering freshman should be told, and it is certainly a proposition that helps to explain the problem of academic writing. What one sees in professors, repeatedly, is exactly the manner that anyone would adopt after a couple of sad evenings sidelined under the crepe-paper streamers in the gym, sitting on a folding chair while everyone else danced. Dignity, for professors, perches precariously on how well they can convey this message: "I am immersed in some very important thoughts, which unsophisticated people could not even begin to understand. Thus, I would not *want* to dance, even if one of you unsophisticated people were to ask me."

Think of this, then, the next time you look at an unintelligible academic text. "I would not *want* the attention of a wide reading audience, even if a wide audience were to *ask* for me." Isn't that exactly what the pompous and pedantic tone of the classically academic writer conveys?

Professors are often shy, timid and even fearful people, and under those circumstances, dull, difficult prose can function as a kind of protective camouflage. When you write typical academic prose, it is nearly impossible to make a strong, clear statement. The benefit here is that no one can attack your position, say you are wrong or even raise questions about the accuracy of what you have said, if they cannot *tell* what you have said. In those terms, awful, indecipherable prose is its own form of armor, protecting the fragile, sensitive thoughts of timid souls.

The best texts for helping us understand the academic world are, of course, Lewis Carroll's "Alice's Adventures in Wonderland" and "Through the Looking Glass." Just as devotees of Carroll would expect, he has provided us with the best analogy for understanding the origin and function of bad academic writing. Tweedledee and Tweedledum have quite a heated argument over a rattle. They become so angry that they decide to fight. But before they fight, they go off to gather various devices of padding and protection: "bolsters, blankets, hearthrugs, tablecloths, dish covers and coal scuttles." Then, with Alice's help in tying and fastening, they transform these household items into armor. Alice is not impressed: " 'Really, they'll be more like bundles of old clothes than anything else, by the time they're ready!' she said to herself, as she arranged a bolster round the neck of Tweedledee, 'to keep his head from being cut off,' as he said." Why this precaution? Because, Tweedledee explains, "it's one of the most serious things that can possibly happen to one in a battle—to get one's head cut off."

Here, in the brothers' anxieties and fears, we have an exact analogy for the problems of academic writing. The next time you look at a classically professorial sentence—long, tangled, obscure, jargonized, polysyllabic— think of Tweedledum and Tweedledee dressed for battle, and see if those timid little thoughts, concealed under layers of clauses and phrases, do not remind you of those agitated but cautious brothers, arrayed in their bolsters, blankets, dish covers and coal scuttles. The motive, too, is similar. Tweedledum and Tweedledee were in terror of being hurt, and so they padded themselves so thoroughly that they could not be hurt; nor, for that matter, could they move. A properly dreary, inert sentence has exactly the same benefit; it protects its writer from sharp disagreement, while it also protects him from movement.

Why choose camouflage and insulation over clarity and directness? Tweedledee, of course, spoke for everyone, academic or not, when he confessed his fear: It is indeed, as he said, "one of the most serious things that can possibly happen to one in a battle—to get one's head cut off." Under those circumstances, logic says: tie the bolster around the neck, and add a protective hearthrug or two. Pack in another qualifying clause or two. Hide behind the passive-voice verb. Preface any assertion with a phrase like "it could be argued" or "a case could be made." Protecting one's neck does seem to be the way to keep one's head from being cut off.

Graduate school implants in many people the belief that there are terrible penalties to be paid for writing clearly, especially writing clearly in ways that challenge established thinking in the field. And yet, in academic warfare (and I speak as a veteran), your head and your neck are rarely in serious danger. You can remove the bolster and the hearthrug. Your opponents will try to whack at you, but they seldom, if ever, land a blow—in large part because they are themselves so wrapped in protective camouflage and insulation that they lose both mobility and accuracy.

So we have a widespread pattern of professors protecting themselves from injury by wrapping their ideas in dull prose, and yet the danger they try to fend off is not a genuine danger. Express yourself clearly, and it is unlikely that either your head—or, more important, your tenure—will be cut off.

How, then, do we save professors from themselves? Fearful people are not made courageous by scolding; they need to be coaxed and encouraged. But how do we do that, especially when this particular form of fearfulness masks itself as pomposity, aloofness and an assumed air of superiority?

Fortunately, we have available the world's most important and illuminating story on the difficulty of persuading people to break out of habits of timidity, caution and unnecessary fear. I borrow this story from Larry McMurtry, one of my rivals in the interpreting of the American West, though I am putting this story to a use that Mr. McMurtry did not intend.

In a collection of his essays, "In a Narrow Grave," Mr. McMurtry wrote about the weird process of watching his book "Horseman, Pass By" being turned into the movie "Hud." He arrived in the Texas Panhandle a week or two after filming had started, and he was particularly anxious to learn how the buzzard scene had gone. In that scene, Paul Newman was supposed to ride up and discover a dead cow, look up at a tree branch lined with buzzards and, in his distress over the loss of the cow, fire his gun at one of the buzzards. At that moment, all of the other buzzards were supposed to fly away into the blue Panhandle sky.

But when Mr. McMurtry asked people how the buzzard scene had gone, all he got, he said, were "stricken looks."

The first problem, it turned out, had to do with the quality of the available local buzzards—who proved to be an excessively scruffy group. So more appealing, more photogenic buzzards had to be flown in from some distance and at considerable expense.

But then came the second problem: how to keep the buzzards sitting on the tree branch until it was time for their cue to fly.

That seemed easy. Wire their feet to the branch, and then, after Paul Newman fires his shot, pull the wire, releasing their feet, thus allowing them to take off.

But, as Mr. McMurtry said in an important and memorable phrase, the film makers had not reckoned with the "mentality of buzzards." With their feet wired, the buzzards did not have enough mobility to fly. But they did have enough mobility to pitch forward.

So that's what they did: with their feet wired, they tried to fly, pitched forward and hung upside down from the dead branch, with their wings flapping.

I had the good fortune a couple of years ago to meet a woman who had been an extra for this movie, and she added a detail that Mr. McMurtry left out of his essay: namely, the buzzard circulatory system does not work upside down, and so, after a moment or two of flapping, the buzzards passed out.

Twelve buzzards hanging upside down from a tree branch: this was not what Hollywood wanted from the West, but that's what Hollywood had produced.

And then we get to the second stage of buzzard psychology. After six or seven episodes of pitching forward, passing out, being revived, being replaced on the branch and pitching forward again, the buzzards gave up. Now, when you pulled the wire and released their feet, they sat there, saying in clear, nonverbal terms: "We *tried* that before. It did not work. We are not going to try it again." Now the film makers had to fly in a high-powered animal trainer to restore buzzard self-esteem. It was all a big mess; Larry McMurtry got a wonderful story out of it; and we, in turn, get the best possible parable of the workings of habit and timidity.

How does the parable apply? In any and all disciplines, you go to graduate school to have your feet wired to the branch. There is nothing inherently wrong with that: scholars should have some common ground, share some background assumptions, hold some similar habits of mind. This gives you, quite literally, your footing. And yet, in the process of getting your feet wired, you have some awkward moments, and the intellectual equivalent of pitching forward and hanging upside down. That experience—especially if you do it in a public place like a graduate seminar—provides no pleasure. One or two rounds of that humiliation, and the world begins to seem like a very treacherous place. Under those circumstances, it does indeed seem to be the choice of wisdom *to sit quietly on the branch*, to sit without even the *thought* of flying, since even the thought might be enough to tilt the balance and set off another round of flapping, fainting and embarrassment.

Yet when scholars get out of graduate school and get Ph.D.'s, and, even more important, when scholars get tenure, the wire is truly pulled. Their feet are free. They can fly wherever and whenever they like. Yet by then the second stage of buzzard psychology has taken hold, and they refuse to fly. The wire is pulled, and yet the buzzards sit there, hunched and grumpy. If they teach in a university with a graduate program, they actively instruct young buzzards in the necessity of keeping their youthful feet on the branch.

This is a very well-established pattern, and it is the ruination of scholarly activity in the modern world. Many professors who teach graduate students think that one of their principal duties is to train the students in the conventions of academic writing.

I do not believe that professors enforce a standard of dull writing on graduate students in order to be cruel. They demand dreariness because they think that dreariness is in the students' best interests. Professors believe that a dull writing style is an academic survival skill because they think that is what editors want, both editors of academic journals *and* editors of university presses. What we have here is a chain of misinformation and misunderstanding, where everyone thinks that the other guy is the one who demands dull, impersonal prose.

Let me say again what is at stake here: universities and colleges are currently embattled, distrusted by the public and state funding institutions. As distressing as this situation is, it provides the perfect setting and the perfect timing for declaring an end to scholarly publication as a series of guarded conversations between professors.

The redemption of the university, especially in terms of the public's appraisal of the value of research and publication, requires all the writers who have something they want to publish to ask themselves the question: Does this have to be a closed communication, shutting out all but specialists willing to fight their way through thickets of jargon? Or can this be an open communication, engaging specialists with new information and new thinking, but also offering an invitation to nonspecialists to learn from this study, to grasp its importance and, by extension, to find concrete reasons to see value in the work of the university?

This is a country desperately in need of wisdom, and of clearly reasoned conviction and vision. And that, at the bedrock, is the reason behind this campaign to save professors from themselves and to detoxify academic prose. The context is a bit different, but the statement that Willy Loman made to his sons in "Death of a Salesman" keeps coming to mind: "The woods are burning, boys, the woods are burning." In a society confronted by a faltering economy, racial and ethnic conflicts, and environmental disasters, "the woods are burning," and since we so urgently need everyone's contribution in putting some of those fires out, there is no reason to indulge professorial vanity or timidity.

Ego is, of course, the key obstacle here. As badly as most of them write, professors are nonetheless proud and sensitive writers, resistant to criticism. But even the most desperate cases can be redeemed and persuaded to think of writing as a challenging craft, not as existential trauma. A few years ago, I began to look at carpenters and other artisans as the emotional model for writers. A carpenter, let us say, makes a door for a cabinet. If the door does not hang straight, the carpenter does not say, "I will *not* change that door; it is an expression of my individuality; who cares if it will not close?" Instead, the carpenter removes the door and works on it until it fits. That attitude, applied to writing, could be our salvation. If we thought more like carpenters, academic writers could find a route out of the trap of ego and vanity. Escaped from that trap, we could simply work on successive drafts until what we have to say is clear.

Colleges and universities are filled with knowledgeable, thoughtful people who have been effectively silenced by an awful writing style, a style with its flaws concealed behind a smokescreen of sophistication and professionalism. A coalition of academic writers, graduate advisers, journal editors, university press editors and trade publishers can seize this moment—*and pull the wire*. The buzzards *can* be set free—free to leave that dead tree branch, free to regain their confidence, free to soar.

Chapter 16

The Politics of Teaching
Literate Discourse

Lisa D. Delpit

I have encountered a certain sense of powerlessness and paralysis among many sensitive and well-meaning literacy educators who appear to be caught in the throes of a dilemma. Although their job is to teach literate discourse styles to all of their students, they question whether that is a task they can actually accomplish for poor students and students of color. Furthermore, they question whether they are acting as agents of oppression by insisting that students who are not already a part of the "mainstream" learn that discourse. Does it not smack of racism or classism to demand that these students put aside the language of their homes and communities and adopt a discourse that is not only alien, but that has often been instrumental in furthering their oppression? I hope here to speak to and help dispel that sense of paralysis and powerlessness and suggest a path of commitment and action that not only frees teachers to teach what they know, but to do so in a way that can transform and subsequently liberate their students.

DISCOURSE, LITERACY, AND GEE

The chapter got its start as I pondered the dilemmas expressed by educators. It continued to evolve when a colleague sent a set of papers to me for comment. The papers, authored by literacy specialist James Paul Gee ("Literacy, Discourse, and Linguistics: Introduction" and "What Is Liter-

---

Freedom's Plow: Teaching in the Multicultural Classroom, 1993

acy?"), are the lead articles of a special issue of the *Journal of Education*[1] devoted solely to Gee's work. The papers brought to mind many of the perspectives of the educators I describe. My colleague, an academic with an interest in literacy issues in communities of color, was disturbed by much of what she read in the articles and wanted a second opinion.

As I first read the far-reaching, politically sensitive articles, I found that I agreed with much that Gee wrote, as I have with much of his previous work. He argues that literacy is much more than reading and writing, but rather, that it is part of a larger political entity. This larger entity he calls a Discourse, construed as something of an "identity kit," that is, ways of "saying–writing–doing–being–valuing–believing," examples of which might be the Discourse of lawyers, the Discourse of academics, or the Discourse of men. He adds that one never learns simply to read or write, but to read and write within some larger Discourse, and therefore within some larger set of values and beliefs.

Gee maintains that there are primary Discourses, those learned in the home, and secondary Discourses, which are attached to institutions or groups one might later encounter. He also argues that all Discourses are not equal in status, that some are socially dominant—carry with them social power and access to economic success—and some nondominant. The status of individuals born into a particular Discourse tends to be maintained because primary Discourses are related to secondary Discourses of similar status in our society (for example, the middle-class home Discourse to school Discourse, or the working class African American home Discourse to the black church Discourse). Status is also maintained because dominant groups in a society apply frequent "tests" of fluency in the dominant Discourses, often focused on its most superficial aspects—grammar, style, mechanics—so as to exclude from full participation those who are not born to positions of power.

These arguments resonate in many ways with what I also believe to be true. However, as I reread and pondered the articles, I began to get a sense of my colleague's discomfort. I also began to understand how that discomfort related to some concerns I have about the perspectives of educators who sincerely hope to help educate poor children and children of color to become successful and literate, but who find themselves paralyzed by their own conception of the task.

There are two aspects of Gee's arguments which I find problematic. First is Gee's notion that people who have not been born into dominant Discourses will find it exceedingly difficult, if not impossible, to acquire such a Discourse. He argues strongly that Discourses cannot be "overtly" taught, particularly in a classroom, but can only be acquired by enculturation in the home or by "apprenticeship" into social practices. Those who wish to gain access to the goods and status connected to a dominant

Discourse must have access to the social practices related to that Discourse. That is, to learn the "rules" required for admission into a particular dominant Discourse, individuals must already have access to the social institutions connected to that Discourse—if you're not already in, don't expect to get in.

This argument is one of the issues that concerned my colleague. As she put it, Gee's argument suggests a dangerous kind of determinism as flagrant as that espoused by the geneticists: Instead of being locked into "your place" by your genes, you are now locked hopelessly into a lower-class status by your Discourse. Clearly, such a stance can leave a teacher feeling powerless to effect change, and a student feeling hopeless that change can occur.

The second aspect of Gee's work that I find troubling suggests that an individual who is born into one Discourse with one set of values may experience major conflicts when attempting to acquire another Discourse with another set of values. Gee defines this as especially pertinent to "women and minorities," who, when they seek to acquire status Discourses, may be faced with adopting values which deny their primary identities. When teachers believe that this acceptance of self-deprecatory values is *inevitable* in order for people of color to acquire status Discourses, then their sense of justice and fair play might hinder their teaching these Discourses.

If teachers were to adopt both of these premises suggested by Gee's work, not only would they view the acquisition of a new Discourse in a classroom impossible to achieve, but they might also view the goal of acquiring such a Discourse questionable at best. The sensitive teacher might well conclude that even to try to teach a dominant Discourse to students who are members of a nondominant oppressed group would be to oppress them further. And it is this potential conclusion which concerns me. While I do agree that Discourses may embody conflicting values, I also believe there are many individuals, who have faced and overcome the problems that such a conflict might cause. I hope to provide another perspective on both of these premises.

OVERCOMING OBSTACLES TO ACQUISITION

One remedy to the paralysis suffered by many teachers is to bring to the fore stories of the real people whose histories directly challenge unproductive beliefs. Mike Rose[2] has done a poignantly convincing job detailing the role of committed teachers in his own journey toward accessing literate Discourse, and his own role as a teacher of disenfranchised veterans who desperately needed the kind of explicit and focused instruction Rose was able to provide in order to "make it" in an alien academic setting. But there are many stories not yet documented which exemplify similar journeys, supported by similar teaching.

A friend and colleague who teaches in a college of education at a major mid-Western university told me of one of her graduate students whom we'll call Marge. Marge received a special fellowship funded by a private foundation designed to increase the numbers of faculty holding doctorates at black colleges. She applied to the doctoral program at my friend's university and traveled to the institution to take a few classes while awaiting the decision. Apparently, the admissions committee did not quite know what to do with her, for here was someone who was already on campus with a fellowship, but who, based on GRE scores and writing samples, they determined was not capable of doing doctoral level work. Finally, the committee agreed to admit Marge into the master's program, even though she already held a master's degree. Marge accepted the offer. My friend— we'll call her Susan—got to know Marge when the department head asked her to "work with" the new student who was considered "at risk" of not successfully completing the degree.

Susan began a program to help Marge learn how to cope with the academic setting. Susan recognized early on that Marge was very talented, but that she did not understand how to maneuver her way through academic writing, reading, and talking. In their first encounters, Susan and Marge discussed the comments instructors had written on Marge's papers, and how the next paper might incorporate the professor's concerns. The next summer Susan had Marge write weekly synopses of articles related to educational issues. When they met, Marge talked through her ideas while Susan took notes. Together they translated the ideas into the "discourse of teacher education." Marge then rewrote the papers referring to their conversations and Susan's extensive written comments.

Susan continued to work with Marge, both in and out of the classroom, during the following year. By the end of that year, Marge's instructors began telling Susan that Marge was a real star, that she had written the best papers in their classes. When faculty got funding for various projects, she became one of the most sought after research assistants in the college. And when she applied for entry into the doctoral program the next fall, even though her GRE scores were still low, she was accepted with no hesitation. Her work now includes research and writing that challenge predominant attitudes about the potential of poor children to achieve.

The stories of two successful African American men also challenge the belief that literate Discourses cannot be acquired in classroom settings, and highlight the significance of teachers in transforming students' futures. Clarence Cunningham, now a Vice Chancellor at the largest historically black institution in the United States, grew up in a painfully poor community in rural Illinois. He attended an all-African-American elementary school in the 1930s in a community where the parents of most of the children never even considered attending high school. There is a school picture of a ragtag group of about 35 children hanging in his den. As he shows me that picture, he talks about the one boy who grew up to be a principal in Philadelphia, one who is now a vice president of a major computer company, one who was recently elected Attorney General of Chicago, another who is a vice president of Harris Bank in Chicago, another who was the first black pilot hired by a major airline. He points to a little girl who is now an administrator, another who is a union leader. Almost all of the children in the photo eventually left their home community, and almost all achieved impressive goals in life.

Another colleague and friend, Bill Trent, who is a professor and researcher at a major research university, has told me of growing up in inner-city Richmond, Virginia, "the capitol of the Confederacy" in the 1940s and 1950s (personal communication, April, 1991). His father, a cook, earned an eighth-grade education by going to night school. His mother, a domestic, had a third-grade education. Neither he nor his classmates had aspirations beyond their immediate environment. Yet, many of these students completed college, and almost all were successful, many notable. There are teachers, ministers, an electronics wizard, state officials, career Army officers, tennis ace Arthur Ashe, and the brothers Max and Randall Robinson, the national newscaster and the director of Trans-Africa, respectively.

How do these men explain the transformations that occurred in them and their classmates' lives? Both attribute their ability to transcend the circumstances into which they were born directly to their teachers. First, their teachers successfully taught what Gee calls the "superficial features" of middle-class Discourse—grammar, style, mechanics—features that Gee claims are particularly resistant to classroom instruction. And the students successfully learned them.

These teachers also successfully taught the more subtle aspects of dominant Discourse. According to both Trent and Cunningham, their teachers insisted that students be able to speak and write eloquently, maintain neatness, think carefully, exude character, and conduct themselves with decorum. They even found ways to mediate class differences by attending themselves to the hygiene of students who needed such attention—washing faces, cutting fingernails, and handing out deodorant.

Perhaps more significant than what they taught is what they believed. As Trent says, "They held visions of us that we could not imagine for ourselves. And they held those visions even when they themselves were denied entry into the larger white world. They were determined that, despite all odds, we would achieve." In an era of overt racism when much was denied African Americans, the message drilled into students was "The one thing people can't take away from you is what's between your ears." The teachers of both men insisted that they must achieve because "You must do twice as well as white people to be considered half as good."

As Cunningham says, "Those teachers pushed us, they wouldn't let us fail. They'd say, 'The world is tough out there, and you have to be tougher'" (personal communication, April, 1991). Trent recalls that growing up in the "inner-city," he had no conception of life beyond high school, but his high school teachers helped him to envision one. While he happily maintained a C average, putting all of his energy into playing football, he experienced a turning point one day when his coach called him inside in the middle of practice. There, while he was still suited up for football, all of his teachers gathered to explain to him that if he thought he could continue making C's and stay on the team he had another thought coming. They were there to tell him that if he did not get his act together and make the grades they knew he was capable of, then his football career would be over.

Like similar teachers chronicled elsewhere (for example, Ladson-Billings,[3] and Walker[4]), these teachers put in overtime to ensure that the students were able to live up to their expectations. They set high standards and then carefully and explicitly instructed students in how to meet them. "You can and will do well," they insisted, as they taught at break times, after school, and on weekends to ensure that their students met their expectations. All of these teachers were able to teach in classrooms the rules for dominant Discourses, allowing students to succeed in mainstream America who were not only born outside of the realms of power and status, but who had no access to status institutions. These teachers were not themselves a part of the power elite, not members of dominant Discourses. Yet they were able to provide the keys for their students' entry into the larger world, never knowing if the doors would ever swing open to allow them in.

The renowned African American sociologist E. Franklin Frazier also successfully acquired a Discourse into which he was not born. Born in poverty to unschooled parents, Frazier learned to want to learn from his teachers and from his self-taught father. He learned his lessons so well that his achievements provided what must be the ultimate proof of the ability to acquire a secondary dominant Discourse, no matter what one's beginnings. After Frazier completed his master's degree at Clark University, he went on to challenge many aspects of the white-dominated oppressive system of segregation. Ironically, at the time Frazier graduated from Clark, he received a reference from its president, G. Stanley Hall, who gave Frazier what he must have thought was the highest praise possible in a predominantly white university in 1920. "Mr. Frazier . . . seems to me to be quite gentlemanly and *mentally white*" (emphasis added, quoted in Platt,[5] p. 15). What better evidence of Frazier's having successfully acquired the dominant Discourse of academe?

These stories are of commitment and transformation. They show how people, given the proper support, can "make it" in culturally alien environments. They make clear that standardized test scores have little to say about one's actual ability. And they demonstrate that supporting students' transformation demands an extraordinary amount of time and commitment, but that teachers *can* make a difference if they are willing to make that commitment.

Despite the difficulty entailed in the process, almost any African American or other disenfranchised individual who has become "successful" has done so by acquiring a Discourse other than the one into which he or she was born. And almost all can attribute that acquisition to what happened as a result of the work of one or more committed teachers.

ACQUISITION AND TRANSFORMATION

But the issue is not only whether students can learn a dominant secondary Discourse in the classroom. Perhaps the more significant issue is, should they attempt to do so? Gee contends that for those who have been barred from the mainstream, "acquisition of many mainstream Discourses . . . involves active complicity with the values that conflict with one's home and community-based Discourses." There can be no doubt that in many classrooms students of color do reject literacy, for they feel that literate Discourses reject them. Keith Gilyard, in his jolting autobiographical study of language competence,[6] graphically details his attempt to achieve in schools that denied the very existence of his community reality:

> I was torn between institutions, between value systems. At times the tug of school was greater, therefore the 90.2 average. On other occasions the streets were a more powerful lure, thus the heroin and the 40 in English and a brief visit to the Adolescent Remand Shelter |. I . . . saw no middle ground or more accurately, no total ground on which anomalies like me could gather. I tried to be a hip schoolboy, but it was impossible to achieve that persona. In the group I most loved, to be fully hip meant to repudiate a school system in which African-American consciousness was undervalued or ignored; in which, in spite of the many nightmares around us, I was urged to keep my mind on the Dream, to play the fortunate token, to keep my head straight down and "make it." And I pumped more and more dope into my arms. It was a nearly fatal response, but an almost inevitable one. (p. 160)

Herb Kohl[7] writes powerfully about individuals, young and old, who choose to "not-learn" what is expected of them rather than to learn that which denies them their sense of who they are:

> Not-learning tends to take place when someone has to deal with unavoidable challenges to her or his personal and family loyalties, integrity, and identity.

In such situations there are forced choices and no apparent middle ground. To agree to learn from a stranger who does not respect your integrity causes a major loss of self. The only alternative is to not-learn and reject the stranger's world. (pp. 15–16)

I have met many radical or progressive teachers of literacy who attempt to resolve the problem of students who choose to "not learn" by essentially deciding to "not teach." They appear to believe that to remain true to their ideology, their role must be to empower and politicize their most disenfranchised students by refusing to teach what Gee calls the superficial features (grammar, form, style, and so forth) of dominant Discourses.[8] Believing themselves to be contributing to their students' liberation by deemphasizing dominant Discourses, they instead seek to develop literacy *solely* within the language and style of the students' home Discourse.

Feminist writer bell hooks writes of one of the consequences of this teaching methodology.[9] During much of her post-secondary school career she was the only black student in her writing courses. Whenever she would write a poem in black Southern dialect, the teachers and fellow students would praise her for using her "true authentic voice" and encourage her to write more in this voice (p. 11). Hooks writes of her frustration with these teachers who, like the teachers I describe, did not recognize the need for African American students to have access to many voices and who maintained their stance even when adult students or the parents of younger students demanded that they do otherwise.

I am reminded of one educator of adult African American veterans who insisted that her students needed to develop their "own voices" by developing "fluency" in their home language. Her students vociferously objected, demanding that they be taught grammar, punctuation, and "standard English." The teacher insisted that such a mode of study was "oppressive." The students continued venting their objections in loud and certain tones. When asked why she thought her students had not developed "voice" when they were using their voices to loudly express their displeasure, she responded that it was "because of who they are," that is, apparently because they were working class, black, and disagreed with her. Another educator of adults told me that she based her teaching on liberating principles. She voiced her anger with her mostly poor, working-class students because they rejected her pedagogy and "refused to be liberated." There are many such stories to recount (see, also, Yorio[10]).

There are several reasons why students- and parents-of-color take a position that differs from the well-intentioned position of the teachers I have described. First, they know that members of society need access to dominant Discourses to (legally) have access to economic power. Second, they know that such Discourses can be and have been acquired in classrooms because they know individuals who have done so. And third, and most significant to the point I wish to make now, they know that individuals have the ability to transform dominant Discourses for liberatory purposes—to engage in what Henry Louis Gates calls, "changing the joke and slipping the yoke" (quoted in Martin[11] p. 204), that is, using European philosophical and critical standards to challenge the tenets of European belief systems.

bell hooks[12] speaks of her black women teachers in the segregated South as being the model from which she acquired both access to dominant Discourses and a sense of the validity of the primary Discourse of working-class African American people. From their instruction, she learned that black poets were capable of speaking in many voices, that the Dunbar who wrote in dialect was as valid as the Dunbar who wrote sonnets. She also learned from these women that she was capable of not only participating in the mainstream, but redirecting its currents: "Their work was truly education for critical consciousness. . . . They were the teachers who conceptualized oppositional world views, who taught us young black women to exult and glory in the power and beauty of our intellect. They offered to us a legacy of liberatory pedagogy that demanded active resistance and rebellion against sexism and racism" (p. 50).

Carter G. Woodson called for similar pedagogy almost 70 years ago. He extolled teachers in his 1933 *Mis-Education of the Negro* to teach African-American students not only the language and canon of the European "mainstream," but to teach as well the life, history, language, philosophy, and literature of their own people. Only this kind of education, he argued, would prepare an educated class which would serve the needs of the African-American community.

Acquiring the ability to function in a dominant Discourse need not mean that one must reject one's home identity and values, for Discourses are not static, but are shaped—however reluctantly—by those who participate within them and by the form of their participation. Many who have played significant roles in fighting for the liberation of people of color have done so through the language of dominant Discourses, from Frederick Douglass to Ida B. Wells, to Mary McCloud Bethune, to Martin Luther King, to Malcolm X. As did bell hooks' teachers, today's teachers can help economically disenfranchised students and students-of-color both to master the dominant Discourses and to transform them. How is the teacher to accomplish this? I suggest several possibilities.

WHAT CAN TEACHERS DO?

First, teachers must acknowledge and validate students' home language without using it to limit students' potential. Students' home Discourses are vital to their perception of self and sense of community connectedness. One

Native American college student I know says he cannot write in standard
English when he writes about his village "because that's about me!" Then he
must use his own "village English" or his voice rings hollow even to himself.
June Jordan[13] has written a powerful essay about teaching a course in black
English and the class's decision to write a letter of protest in that language
when the brother of one of the students was killed by police. The point must
not be to eliminate students' home languages, but rather to add other voices
and Discourses to their repertoires. As bell hooks[14] and Henry Gates[15] have
poignantly reminded us, racism and oppression must be fought on as many
fronts and in as many voices as we can muster.

Second, teachers must recognize the conflict Gee details between students' home Discourses and the Discourse of school. They must understand
that students who appear to be unable to learn are in many instances
choosing to "not learn" as Kohl puts it, choosing to maintain their sense
of identity in the face of what they perceive as a painful choice between
allegiance to "them" or "us." The teacher, however, can reduce this sense
of choice by transforming the new Discourse so that it contains within it
a place for the students' selves. To do so, they must saturate the dominant
Discourse with new meanings, must wrest from it a place for the glorifica-
tion of their students and their forbears.

An interesting historical example is documented by James Anderson.[16]
Anderson writes of Richard Wright, an African American educator in the
post-Reconstruction era, who found a way through the study of the "classical" curriculum to claim a place of intellectual respect for himself and
his people. When examined by the U.S. Senate Committee on Education
and Labor, one senator questioned Wright about the comparative inferiority and superiority of the races. Wright replied:

> It is generally admitted that religion has been a great means of human
> development and progress, and I think that about all the great religions
> which have blest this world have come from the colored races—all . . . I
> believe, too, that our methods of alphabetic writing all came from the colored
> race, and I think the majority of the sciences in their origin have come from
> the colored races. . . . Now I take the testimony of those people who know,
> and who, I feel are capable of instructing me on this point, and I find them
> saying that the Egyptians were actually wooly-haired negroes. In Humboldt's
> Cosmos (Vol. 2, p. 531) you will find that testimony, and Humboldt, I
> presume, is pretty good authority. The same thing is stated in Herodotus,
> and in a number of other authors with whom you gentlemen are doubtless
> familiar. Now if that is true, the idea that the negro race is inherently inferior,
> seems to me to be at least a little limping. (p. 30)

Noted educator Jaime Escalante prepared poor Latino students to pass
the tests for advanced calculus when everyone else thought they would do

well to master fractions. To do so, he also transformed a new Discourse by placing his students and their ancestors firmly within its boundaries. In a line from the movie chronicling his success, *"Stand and Deliver,"* he entreated his students, "You *have* to learn math. The Mayans discovered zero. Math is in your blood!"

And this is also what those who create what has been called "Afrocentric" curricula do. They too seek to illuminate for students (and their teachers) a world in which people with brown and black skin have achieved greatness and have developed a large part of what is considered the great classical tradition. They also seek to teach students about those who have taken the language born in Europe and transformed it into an emancipatory tool for those facing oppression in the "new world." In the mouths and pens of Bill Trent, Clarence Cunningham, bell hooks, Henry Louis Gates, Paul Lawrence Dunbar, and countless others, the "language of the master" has been used for liberatory ends. Students can learn of that rich legacy, and they can also learn that they are its inheritors and rightful heirs.

A final role that teachers can take is to acknowledge the unfair "Discourse-stacking" that our society engages in. They can discuss openly the injustices of allowing certain people to succeed, based not upon merit, but upon which family they were born into, upon which Discourse they had access to as children. The students, of course, already know this, but the open acknowledgment of it in the very institution which facilitates the sorting process is liberating in itself. In short, teachers must allow discussions of oppression to become a part of language and literature instruction. Only after acknowledging the inequity of the system, can the teacher's stance then be "Let me show you how to cheat!" And of course, to cheat is to learn the Discourse which would otherwise be used to exclude them from participating in and transforming the mainstream. This is what many black teachers of the segregated South intended when they, like the teachers of Bill Trent and Clarence Cunningham, told their students that they *had* to "do better than those white kids." We can again let our students know that they can resist a system that seeks to limit them to the bottom rung of the social and economic ladder.

Gee may not agree with my analysis of his work, for, in truth, his writings are so multifaceted as not to be easily reduced to simplistic positions. But that is not the issue. The point is that some aspects of his work can be disturbing for the African American reader, and reinforcing for those who choose—wrongly, but for "right" reasons—not to educate black and poor children.

Individuals *can* learn the "superficial features" of dominant Discourses, as well as their more subtle aspects. Such acquisition can provide a way both to turn the sorting system on its head and to make available one more voice for resisting and reshaping an oppressive system. This is the alternative perspective I want to give to teachers of poor children and children of color, and this is the perspective I hope will end the paralysis and set teachers free to teach, and thereby to liberate. When teachers are committed to teaching all students, and when they understand that through their teaching change *can* occur, then the chance for transformation is great.

NOTES

1. James P. Gee, *Journal of Education: Literacy, Discourse and Linguistics, Essays by James Paul Gee*, Vol. 171, No. 1, 1989.
2. Mike Rose. *Lives on the Boundary* (New York: The Free Press, 1989).
3. Gloria Ladson-Billings and Annette Henry. "Blurring the Borders: Voices of African Liberatory Pedagogy in the United States and Canada," *Journal of Education*, Vol. 172, No. 2, pp. 72–88, 1990.
4. Emilie V. Siddle Walker, "Caswell County Training School, 1933–1969: Relationships Between Community and School," *Harvard Educational Review*, in press.
5. Anthony M. Platt, *E. Franklin Frazier Reconsidered* (New Brunswick, NJ: Rutgers University Press, 1991).
6. Keith Gilyard, *Voices of the Self* (Detroit: Wayne State University Press, 1991).
7. Herb Kohl, *I Won't Learn From You! The Role of Assent in Education* (Minneapolis, MN: Milkweed Editions, 1991).
8. Gee's position here is somewhat different. He argues that grammar and form should be taught in classrooms, but that students will never acquire them with sufficient fluency as to gain entry into dominant Discourses. Rather, he states, such teaching is important because it allows students to gain "meta-knowledge" of how language works, which in turn, "leads to the ability to manipulate, to analyze, to resist while advancing" (p. 13).
9. bell hooks. *Talking Back* (Boston, MA: South End Press, 1989).
10. Carlos Yorio, "The Other Side of the Looking Glass," *Journal of Basic Writing*, Vol. 8, No. 1, 1989.
11. Reginald Martin, "Black Writer as Black Critic: Recent Afro-American Writing," *College English*, Vol. 52, No. 2, Feb. 1990.
12. hooks, op. cit.
13. June Jordan, "Nobody Mean More to Me Than You and the Future Life of Willie Jordan," *Harvard Educational Review*, Vol. 58, No. 3, 1988.
14. hooks, op. cit.
15. Henry L. Gates, *Race, Writing and Difference* (Chicago: University of Chicago Press, 1986).
16. James D. Anderson, *The Education of Blacks in the South, 1860–1935* (Chapel Hill, NC: University of North Carolina Press, 1988).

Chapter 17

Discourse, Artifacts, and the Ozarks: Understanding Academic Literacy

Linda Lonon Blanton

We ESL teachers live in interesting times. Once, not so long ago, few people, even in our own institutions, understood what we did or paid much attention to it. Now, more than likely, the sheer numbers of non-native English speakers enrolling in our schools, particularly in community colleges and public universities, force English as a Second Language (ESL) concerns and programs to the fore.

Unfortunately, this prominence comes at a time of dwindling financial resources; in many institutions the practice of staffing newly-added-on sections of courses with less costly part-time and/or adjunct faculty continues apace. As a result, program coordination and cohesion break down as faculty come and go—without opportunities to exchange ideas and experiences, to plan courses and curricula, or to even make each other's acquaintance.

Our professional fragmentation in the workplace comes, even more unfortunately, at a point in our theoretical evolution when we need to generate new and different conversations about preparing second language (L2) students for the academic mainstream. We have reached the point where we now know that it is not enough for our students to become fluent speakers of English; we know that it is not enough for them to be literate in English; and we also know that higher education places demands on their literacy that are different from those placed by most workaday contexts.

Despite the times—and, in some ways, because of them—we need to intensify our conversations about the demands placed on students' lan-

Journal of Second Language Writing, 1994

guage and literacy capabilities by higher education and figure out what it all means for our ESL programs. Some of the dialog among teachers of L2 students may end up sounding similar to the dialog among those teaching first language (L1) students, as it should: While entering higher education along different avenues, both L2 and L1 students ultimately have placed on them the same language and literacy demands. Yet, inevitably, some dialog will be uniquely ours.

The following is written to add to the current conversations. Because our conversations about academic literacy are so new, I begin with basic notions that provide us a foundation for building new approaches to preparing L2 students for the academic mainstream.

ACADEMIC DISCOURSE COMMUNITY: FACT OR FICTION?

I agree with Cooper (1989) that we cannot be altogether certain if *academic discourse community* is a metaphor for a complex linguistic and social phenomenon that otherwise eludes our grasp; or if, in fact, such a collection of people really exists, the collective formed by shared values, interests, underlying assumptions, and language use.

Like Cooper (1989), I prefer to assume the latter. For me, the notion of a discourse community is predicated on the same assumptions about language as the sociolinguistic notion of *speech community*. Heath (1983), in a powerful study of two very different social communities in the Piedmont of the Carolinas, establishes anew the viability and reality of speech community. In her study, Heath documents the influence of social communities, linguistically cohesive and homogeneous enough to function as speech communities, to shape children's language development, literacy, language behaviors, and even their relationship to school and learning.

I also prefer to assume the latter for personal reasons. Having grown up in the Ozark Mountains, not too distant or dissimilar from the Piedmont, I know firsthand the power of community to mold language, language behavior, and operational assumptions about reading, writing, books, and schooling. So, for me, speech community has an experiential reality. I conclude, though, that the notion of speech community seems more based in reality when the actual community is somewhat isolated by physical boundaries, such as a river, mountains, or a highway. For those who grew up in diffuse urban and suburban areas, the concept may seem more elusive.

It takes only a slight conceptual shift to move from speech community to *discourse community*—that is, a social group that shares certain behaviors and assumptions about language and its use, one of them being the valuing of written language over oral language. And I doubt if anyone—certainly not an academic—would dispute that people who consider themselves part of the academy place greater store in writing than in speaking, in what is written over what is spoken. Brodkey (1987) argues:

> To the extent that the academic community is a community, it is a literate community, manifested not so much at conferences as in bibliographies and libraries, a community whose members know one another better as writers than speakers. (p. 12)

Observing the everyday behavior and language of academics also gives clues to their values. Academics "publish or perish"; they don't "talk or perish." They give "papers" at conferences; they don't just "speak."

I assume then that there is an entity called an academic discourse community. It is a collective of individuals (teachers, researchers, scholars, students) dispersed in time and space but connected to the academy in some way, individuals who value written language over spoken language. Although experience tells us that not all students enter the academy valuing written language over spoken language, they don't leave without understanding its value within a system that treats it as currency.

Written language in the academy is often packaged as reports, abstracts, analyses, proposals, briefs, articles, essays, monographs, books, reviews, and bibliographies. These may well exhibit certain common rhetorical forms and features, but what they share, or even if such an accounting is possible, we do not fully know.

ACADEMIC DISCOURSE COMMUNITY: STATIC OR FLUID?

Just as members of a speech community may come and go, opt in or out, discourse communities are in constant flux. Just as people may belong to more than one speech community, they can surely belong to more than one discourse community (Harris, 1989). I know people who do. Some students achieve success in the academic discourse community, join, and even stay; some do not. The same applies to faculty, scholars, and researchers.

To think of a speech or discourse community as other than constantly in the making is to distort what we know to be the nature of language and language use. History tells us that we must accept language change as a given. Even in our own speech or in the speech of others, we may be well aware of vocabulary coming and going. For me, *FAX, rap music,* and *hard drive* are fairly new terms. And because of a computer disaster that befell me in writing this paper, I now attach new meaning to the term *back-up.*

Syntactic and morphological changes are much harder than lexical change to hold in awareness. Yet, we accept that the grammar of Chaucer's English had changed by Shakespeare's day; any earlier than Chaucer, at least as much as we can reconstruct it from writing, English strikes us as a foreign language.

We surely know that English will continue changing, as will any language. As English strives for symmetry and regularity in its morphology, in particular, forms such as the third person singular/present tense marker will disappear, as they have in English dialects not so closely tied to literacy. And these remnant forms will not disappear any too soon, some of our students might say.

If a discourse community is not thought to be constantly in the making, then it must be thought of as a fixed social structure that exists apart from its members. According to Cooper (1989):

> Thought of in this [latter] way, a discourse community is a way of labeling individuals as insiders or outsiders, as people who either have the requisite values, knowledge, and skills to belong, or lack these necessary qualifications. Everyone inside is all alike and significantly different from those who are outside. In this sense a discourse community is a way of regulating who has access to resources, power, even to discourse itself, and it creates gatekeepers to make sure that the right people get in and all others are excluded. (p. 205)

Cooper's depiction of a discourse community as static brings to mind a venerable and entrenched social club of wealthy, old, white men, who could not conceive of admitting women or minorities into their realm.

As unappealing as it is, the image is useful in helping me hold firm to a pedagogical stance of conscious resistance to the gatekeeper role—and resistance to a static notion of academic discourse. Even though I am obligated to give grades and serve in other administrative ways that control students' access to higher education, at the same time I can work toward a pedagogy that keeps the gate open for more students—and questions what it takes to get through it. Nobody served to exclude me; I will try my best not to exclude others.

If, however, we treat academic discourse itself as static form rather than the fluid expression of individuals—their thoughts, experiences, and discoveries—we guarantee that many of our students will not stay long in our institutions, nor even feel included enough to want to stay; we preclude their participating in the process of academic discourse in the making. We could do likewise in our professional dialog with each other, unless we maintain an inclusive stance.

In short, academic discourse **will** change, just as language changes. It will change as those participating in its making change it and themselves. Change will not necessarily make it better or worse, but, inevitably, different. There are some, however, including myself, who think that as it changes, it has plenty of room for improvement. Marius (1990) recalls reading somewhere that 80% of the articles published in academic journals are never cited, presumably because they are not of interest to anyone.

For me, academic discourse often lacks the stories that we all have to tell from our own experience, stories that allow us to connect to others and them to us. What we need, I think, is a discourse that reflects our diverse experiences and heritages—our plurality (Geisler, 1992)—while retaining our sense of shared purpose. For me individually, then, it needs to reflect my Ozark upbringing, a significant portion of my language and literacy experience; others must fit together their own pieces as they construct their own understandings of academic literacy. Each one's understanding—and even each one's discourse—while the same, is different, continually reinvented but bearing the tension of connection to a network of others of like purpose.

I discuss these opinions without conceit, having tried to write in the detached, impersonal style that is often held up as exemplary of academic discourse and finding myself incapable of doing so. So, I write with my own voice, trying as best I can to meet the expectations of my audience of fellow ESL teachers, and hope that my ideas and experience relate to theirs.

The point is that many of us, including our students, have stories to tell and ideas to share that can illuminate us all. The more diverse the backgrounds and experience of those participating in the community of writers connected to the academy, the faster academic discourse will change, and it's likely to become far more interesting than it is now.

Before leaving the discussion on the nature of an academic discourse community, I want to admit some concern about the word *community*. Even though I accept the notion of speech community—and I have said that it has an experiential reality for me—and by extension, I accept the notion of discourse community, *community* as a term carries with it a sense of warmth and cohesion that may not exist in any social–linguistic groupings that I know. Not in the community I grew up in and not in the academy where I work. Maybe another word is better. As Harris (1989) says:

> As teachers and theorists of writing, we need a vocabulary that will allow us to talk about certain forces as social rather than communal, as involving power but not always consent. Such talk could give us a fuller picture of the lived experience of teaching, learning, and writing in a university today. (p. 21)

Our vocabulary may improve as our discourse evolves.

OUR ANSWERS DEPEND ON THE QUESTIONS WE ASK

ESL teachers at the college level know that it is simply not enough for students to become fluent in English—that we have to help students prepare to read and write in their mainstream academic courses—but we have not been altogether sure about how to do that. In part, we have perceived the problem as our not knowing exactly what academic discourse is (Spack, 1988).

Without knowing exactly what academic discourse is, we have taught academic content, presuming—I suppose—that if we ask students to read in subject areas taught in the academy, how these subjects are written about will surely rub off on our students. Judging by the exercises in some of the textbook readers claiming to prepare students for mainstream courses, the vocabulary, sentence structures, and verb forms are part of what make the readings "academic."

Our efforts to teach L2 students to write pieces of discourse modeled after those we ask them to read should be abandoned, as should even our efforts to teach students to write in the various academic disciplines, Spack (1988) argues (p. 30); the latter should be left to the teachers of those disciplines. (For further discussion that calls into question a modeling approach to composition, see also Connors, 1981; Raimes, 1983, 1991; Zamel, 1982, among others.) In other words, engineering faculty should teach students of engineering to write like engineers, and so on. This makes imminently good sense, and I hope we will heed Spack's advice.

Like Spack (1988), I faithfully followed the lessons in textbooks purporting to teach students academic reading and writing and felt dissatisfied with the results. I, too, thought the solution to preparing L2 students for academic success as readers and writers lay in determining what academic discourse was and what L2 students needed to know in order to produce it.

Despite Spack's (1988) wisdom in directing us away from teaching in disciplines in which we have no background and experience, I think that she, along with most of the rest of us, have simply been asking the wrong questions. We've asked *what academic discourse is,* and we've asked *what students need to know in order to produce it.* These questions presuppose answers framed as definition and declarative knowledge.

In order to define academic discourse, we would need to know what academic texts had in common. Presumably, we would need to analyze enough of them until we had an exhaustive list of their recurring linguistic characteristics and forms. These forms and how to use them would, I suppose, then comprise the knowledge that students needed in order to write academic texts, presuming they had access to the subject matter.

Instead, I think we should be asking *what academic readers and writers do.* In fact, Spack's (1988) valuable suggestions (pp. 40–46) are more in response to this question than those she, herself, asks, suggestions she expands and extends in a more recent article (Spack, 1993, pp. 188–192). If we accept the view that language is a social activity, that language is a medium and a means by which we conduct our business and our lives, then it follows that discourse, as written language, is a social activity: It is something we do with each other.

All people, unless they are severely damaged in some physiological or psychological way, *language* (verb); some people—academics more than most—*discourse* (verb). If we ask what academic readers and writers do, the nature of the question frames the kind of answer we look for; it directs us to examine actions/behaviors, not knowledge and linguistic form.

DISCOURSE AS SOCIAL ACTIVITY

We human beings language in order to conduct the affairs of our daily lives—to console a friend, get the car repaired, buy a toothbrush, interview for a job, argue with the plumber, and so on. We academics may discourse for different reasons, but still to conduct our professional affairs—to keep our jobs, get tenure or a promotion, impress our colleagues or simply share with them, help ourselves clarify our own thoughts and experience.

Rarely do human beings language for its own sake. In my childhood experience in the Ozarks, being perceived of as languaging for its own sake left speakers open to the charge of being vacuous, and what they said, meaningless. ("Oh, they jus' like to hear theirsef talk; don't pay 'em any mind; they's jus' a bag a wind," my grandmother used to say.)

What remains after people language or discourse, for example, a transcript of a conversation, a recorded message on an answering machine, an essay or article to send off to a professional journal, is an artifact of the activity itself. It is what's left after the activity is done. By extension, responding to the form of the message will likely effect no change in the message maker or the behavior of the message maker during the production of the next message.

It's easy to see where my line of thinking is going: For teachers to respond to students' writing after the writing is done is to respond to the artifact of the writing, not to the writing itself. What we put on a student's paper—a correction, a grade, a question, or suggestion—will likely make no difference in the student's behavior during the generation of the next piece of writing. The teacher focusing on the artifact is like the coach coming onto the playing field after the game is over.

If we view academic discourse as activity, we need to guide L2 students into engaging in the activity in the same ways that academic readers and writers do. Our students are then acquiring the behaviors of academic readers and writers; as they read and write, they are becoming academic readers and writers. If we answer the question of what academic readers and writers do, we will know what to ask of our students and what to set as our classroom priorities. By focusing on behaviors, language takes its rightful place as a medium and a means of executing certain tasks, formed and shaped by the need to complete the task at hand. This is real language.

THE BEHAVIORS OF ACADEMIC READERS AND WRITERS

Researchers in literacy and language acquisition put **interactions with texts** at the heart of literacy, formal learning, and academic success (Bartholomae & Petrosky, 1986; Bissex, 1980; Carson, 1993; Cummins, 1984; Goodman & Goodman, 1977; Graves, 1983; Heath & Branscombe, 1985; Heath & Mangiola, 1991; Hudelson, 1984; Krashen, 1985; Leki, 1993; Rigg & Allen, 1989; Rigg & Enright, 1986; Salvatori, 1986; Spack, 1988, 1993; Urzua, 1987; Wall, 1986; Zamel, 1992, among others). Yet, interacting with texts is in itself a complex of behaviors that needs to be teased out to give us more guidance for the classroom.

As I analyze my own trial and error attempts to become an academic reader and writer, observe the writing activities of colleagues, and examine my own and colleagues' reactions to the writing of L1 and L2 students, I "see" the following literate behaviors, all of which involve interacting with texts (Heath & Mangiola, 1991, p. 7).

Academic readers and writers:

1. Interpret texts in light of their own experience and their own experience in light of texts;
2. Agree or disagree with texts in light of that experience;
3. Link texts to each other;
4. Synthesize texts, and use their synthesis to build new assertions;
5. Extrapolate from texts;
6. Create their own texts, doing any or all of the above;
7. Talk and write about doing any or all of the above;
8. Do Numbers 6 and 7 in such a way as to meet the expectations of their audience.

According to Heath and Mangiola (1991), academic behaviors can be independent of any particular academic subject, but underlie success in all academic areas. This accords with Spack's (1988) contention that L2 students should not work with us in the various disciplines they are either already in or plan to pursue; rather, they need from us the kind of work that can transfer to other disciplines (p. 41).

It is important to distinguish here between **literate behaviors**, which underlie L2 students'—or any students'—becoming proficient academic readers and writers, and **literacy skills**, which lie outside of a text as a whole. Literacy skills are "mechanistic abilities that focus on separating out and manipulating discrete elements of a text—such as spelling, vocabulary, grammar, topic sentences, and outlines" (Heath & Mangiola, 1991, p. 40). Further, academic literacy is "not the same thing as learning to read and write; it is learning to talk reading and writing" (Heath, 1985, p. 15). While a student's literacy skills undoubtedly transfer to other disciplines, we will surely discover that it is behaviors and not skills that make the critical difference for students' academic success.

In the discussion that follows, I explore various aspects of what "interacting with texts" means and also examine the role of personal experience in academic reading and writing. Then, I end with some implications of the overall discussion for the ESL classroom.

INTERACTING WITH TEXTS

I came into an awareness of what it means for readers to treat a text as "dead on the page" while working with immigrant L2 students whose prior schooling had been so disrupted and disjointed that they were most likely not proficient readers and writers of any language. (See Blanton, 1992a, 1992b, 1992c, 1993, for discussions related to this experience.) In my work with these students, I gained a clear understanding of the chasm lying between functional and academic literacy.

Briefly, functionally-but-not-academically literate students decode the words of texts, but seem unaware that they can and should bring their own thoughts and experience to bear in order to create a reading of their own. When the last word on the last page is decoded, they seem to be finished with their reading; for them, failure as a reader is failing to remember what the words of the text say. In Heath's (1985) terms, they can read—and write—but they can't "talk reading and writing" (p. 15).

A while back, I began to gradually realize that I, too, had once been that kind of reader, the result of years of schooling where all the answers to someone else's questions were either "right" or "wrong." And I am aware that I still have to stop myself at times from attempting to commit to memory the language of a text, as if I cannot trust my mind to assign significance for myself. In other words, I recognize myself in my students.

Students who have no experience in "talking reading and writing" claim no individualized perspective on reading and writing as activities or on the subject matter of the activity. They seem to factor themselves as individuals out of the picture, and they seem to reduce textual and perceptual complexity to a reductive simplicity.

To illustrate, I recently asked an advanced ESL reading and writing class—as one of the first activities of the semester—to read a book review in which the reviewer (Susan Larson, a New Orleans writer) told a little about the contents of the book (*A Good Scent from a Strange Mountain*) and a lot about the author (Robert Olen Butler) (see Butler, 1992; Larson, 1992). In their initial responses to my questions, they showed no awareness of the "layers" involved: that (1) they, the readers, were reading something written by (2) a reviewer about (3) an author who had written (4) a book. Their sole concentration was on (4) the book, which they took to be the only matter at hand.

To remedy the situation, I asked students to decide if Larson liked the book and to pull from the review five or six phrases she used to make them think so. With my directions cluing them into a different realm of the text, they decided that she really liked the book; and they came up with phrases such as "graceful style," "beautiful stories," "respect for his characters" to support their contention. Then, I asked them to assume the identity of Butler, the author, and to write in their journals about Larson's review of "their" book.

I was pleased that between that class meeting and the next, one of the students went to the library on her own initiative and checked out Butler's book; during the break, she showed it to her classmates, who then passed it around, some seemingly checking on its tangible reality. I also told the class that that very weekend I had run into Susan Larson; after hearing about their work on her review, she sent them her regards and the message that she had "really, really liked the book" and "had meant every word she wrote." Some of their jaws dropped with disbelief, as I conveyed Larson's message to them, as if something printed on paper could have little to do with "real" people; others beamed with self-importance.

Whatever else we do with L2 students to prepare them for the academic mainstream, we must foster the behaviors of "talking" to texts, talking and writing about them, linking them to other texts, connecting them to their readers' own lives and experience, and then using their experience to illuminate the text and the text to illuminate their experience. Along the way, L2 students also acquire English.

THE ROLE OF PERSONAL EXPERIENCE IN LANGUAGE ACQUISITION AND LEARNING

For some time, teachers of both L1 and L2 writing at the college level have tended to regard experiential/expressive writing in one of several ways: It is the kind of writing students do until they are proficient enough to tackle academic writing; it is the best and only kind of writing for students to do as they write to discover themselves and their own thought processes; or, it is inappropriate at the college level where students are in training to become academic readers and writers.

Yet, parallel to this either–or thinking, discussion continues on the value of experiential/expressive writing in academic discourse, as well as in learning itself (Bartholomae & Petrosky, 1986; Britton, 1988; Bruffee, 1984; Cummins, 1989; Elbow, 1991; Emig, 1982; Mlynarczyk, 1991; Salvatori, 1986; Spack, 1988; Wall, 1986; Zamel, 1992, among others).

To place writing at the heart of learning, as a mode of learning—formal or otherwise—is to concede a powerful role to the experiential/expressive. As explained by Britton (1988), the only way for any of us to access new concepts and ideas is to refine and extend what we already know. This means that we have to process that which is new, and outside of ourselves, through our own individual experience by talking and writing about it in our own individual voices. Otherwise, we rely on memory, and mouth or copy others' words; what we "know"—if memorized, mouthed, or copied—we know by rote.

I doubt if anyone would call this learning. Yet, sadly, the prevalent transmission models of pedagogy do just that: "Students play their assigned role of receiving knowledge while teachers play their assigned role of transmitting it" (Cummins, 1989, p. 35). Using a banking metaphor to depict the same pedagogical practices, Freire (1970) laments that "education . . . becomes an act of depositing, in which students are depositories and the teacher is the depositor. Instead of communicating, the teacher . . . makes deposits which the students patiently receive, memorize, and repeat" (p. 58).

Viewed either way—pedagogy as banking or transmission—the results are the same: Students' experience is excluded and "the most basic functions of language, namely meaningful communication in both oral and written modes" about that experience, are "suppressed" (Cummins, 1989, p. 35). As a result, all students are handicapped, since they are cut off from the ways in which they, as human beings, can best learn.

L2 students are particularly disadvantaged in learning what a school curriculum offers and even more so in acquiring English, since they don't have opportunities to engage in the acts of meaningful communication through which language is acquired (Cummins, 1989; Krashen, 1985; Mohan, 1986). (For related discussions on the language and literacy development of children, see Bissex, 1980; Freeman & Freeman, 1989; Goodman & Goodman, 1977; Graves, 1983; Heath & Mangiola, 1991; Hudelson, 1984, 1989; Lindfors, 1980; Peyton & Mackinson-Smyth, 1989; Rigg & Allen, 1989; Rigg & Enright, 1986; Smith, 1978; Urzua, 1987; Wells, 1986, among others.)

Instead, if we view writing and talking as modes of learning, it follows then that we all (our students, ourselves) have to write and talk our way to claiming and understanding not only our own experience by bringing others' ideas and experience to bear on it, but by connecting it to the world outside as well—a veritable two-way street. The experiential—which students bring to school and, if lucky enough to be in schools that value interaction, they gain at school—is not, then, simply a bridge to the mainstream; it is its very source.

For basically the same reasons, Elbow (1991) argues:

> In order to promote genuine understanding of the academic discourse of assigned texts, students need to use informal, nonacademic writing to "render" rather than explain experience, to translate the "discourse of the textbook and the discipline into everyday, experiential, anecdotal terms"; to do otherwise is to keep students from "experiencing or really internalizing the concepts they are allegedly learning." (p. 137)

Concepts not internalized cannot be applied; from them, no ideas or applications can be generated; and they do no more than remain as discrete bits for as long as the memory holds out.

In our classrooms, response journals, dialog journals, working journals, and double-entry notebooks can all provide direct means for L2 students to write their way to comprehension through the dialectical process—the dialog with the self and between the self and others—that lies "at the heart of learning to read and write critically" (Berthoff, 1981, p. 45). (See Peyton & Reed, 1990, for a discussion of dialog writing; Spack & Sadow, 1983, for an explanation of teacher–student working journals; Berthoff, 1981, and Zamel, 1992, on double-entry notebooks; and Spack, 1985, on response journals.)

THE ROLE OF PERSONAL EXPERIENCE
IN ACADEMIC READING AND WRITING

In addition to its crucial role in language acquisition and learning, personal/life experience provides a critical element in students' development as academic readers and writers—in relating to texts as academic readers and writers do. The following discussion attempts to argue that, even in ESL classes that prepare students for academic study, there is no way around the personal and experiential.

We probably all agree that individuals whom we consider academically proficient speak and write with something we call *authority*; that is one characteristic—perhaps the major characteristic—of the voice of an academic reader and writer. The absence of authority is viewed as powerlessness, and much has been written recently about the issue of powerlessness among basic L1 readers and writers and L2 students who often share the same fate (Bartholomae & Petrosky, 1986; Blanton, 1992b; Cummins, 1989; Elbow, 1991; Freire, 1970, 1983; Johnson, 1989; Salvatori, 1986; Wall, 1986, among others).

Powerlessness results from being cut off from oneself and one's own ideas and life experience, from being in classes where students' answers to others' questions are either "right" or "wrong" (Bartholomae & Petrosky, 1986). If we take the broad view, powerlessness comes from being in classes and with teachers where transmission/banking pedagogies prevail (as discussed in the preceding section). Viewed from the perspective of reading and writing, powerlessness results from students never having opportunities to bring their own views and experience to bear on texts (Bartholomae & Petrosky, 1986; Salvatori, 1986; Wall, 1986). They develop no awareness that reading is supposed to be such a transaction—that, without it, comprehension is impossible. In my experience, nonacademic readers and writers think they are comprehending when they are actually doing no more than decoding. For them, reading **is** decoding, and they are powerless before texts, particularly before printed texts.

Conversely, empowerment—or achieving certainty—comes about through acts of speaking and writing about texts, through developing individual responses to texts (Bartholomae & Petrosky, 1986). A student who develops an individual response to a text—who can "talk" to it and talk about it, who can agree or disagree with its author, who can relate that individual response to the text and write about it—is behaving as an academic reader and writer (Heath & Mangiola, 1991). That student's voice is individual because his or her response is individual; it is also a voice expressing certainty in speaking about something "owned" by the speaker.

A voice of certainty assumes a posture of authority as the reader/writer's individual response is balanced with audience expectations. In fact, Wall (1986) argues that when we consider a piece of academic discourse "mature" and "authoritative," what we are admiring, in fact, is the writer's success in achieving balance between the personal/individual and the expectations of an audience (p. 106). Given this point of view, "mature" academic discourse is not even possible without the reader/writer's individual and personal involvement or, conversely, without the reader/writer's involvement of the individual and personal.

IMPLICATIONS FOR THE ESL CLASSROOM

To conclude this discussion, I will briefly state what I believe to be the most basic implications of these ideas and issues for the classroom. ESL classes that foster academic literacy are classes where:

1. Reading and writing are integrated;
2. Language is not the subject of the class; rather, it is the medium in which students and teachers and students and texts interact;

3. Class work is activity-oriented and collaborative;
4. Language use is necessitated by the need to complete the tasks at hand;
5. Tasks call for interacting with texts—reading them, talking about them, extrapolating from them, linking them to each other, relating one's own experience to them, calling on them to shed new light on one's experience and one's experience on them, synthesizing them, and writing one's own texts that do any or all of the above;
6. Texts do not constitute the sole authority on any subject;
7. Students' experience is called for and valued in text interaction;
8. Tasks provide opportunities for students to claim authority as they balance their individual responses with a growing awareness of audience;
9. Language use occurs in the context of meaningful communication;
10. The teacher facilitates and fosters the acquisition of literate behaviors; she or he does not serve in the role of "transmitter" of knowledge.

Although I believe each one of these implications to be valid, I do not claim them to be easy to implement. Some involve changing entrenched thinking and procedures—our own as well as those of our institutions. Others involve changing who we see ourselves to be and who our students are in relationship to us.

In my own efforts to practice what I preach, daily I meet with tensions that come from the feeling of working without a net and from not meeting students' expectations, expectations formed from classes where external linguistic and rhetorical forms constituted the curriculum with lessons subsequently designed to teach discrete bits of language. In other words, one of the greatest difficulties in implementing these recommendations is that students expect us to continue teaching them as we have taught them.

Just last week, a student asked why I wasn't teaching topic sentences; others have asked why I don't correct the grammar in all the writing in their portfolios. They don't like the labor and uncertainty of it—wrestling with their own ideas to figure out what they really think, being asked questions that have no right or wrong answers, drafting and redrafting until they finally get their thoughts focused and supported, throwing out some parts of their writing and "revisioning" others. They'd rather learn by rote, be told what they need to know, and have their teachers shoulder the responsibility for their learning.

In changing our approach, we have to work at helping our students understand better what it means to read and write like college students. As our students read and write, and inevitably flounder about, they will gradually perceive that who they are and what they know comes into sharper focus as they interact with substance that they make meaningful. I think my grandmother would have approved.

REFERENCES

Bartholomae, D., & Petrosky, A. (1986). Facts, artifacts and counterfacts: A basic reading and writing course for the college curriculum. In D. Bartholomae & A. Petrosky (Eds.), *Facts, artifacts and counterfacts: Theory and method for a reading and writing course* (pp. 3–43). Upper Montclair, NJ: Boynton/Cook.

Berthoff, A. E. (1981). *The making of meaning: Metaphors, models, and maxims for writing teachers.* Montclair, NJ: Boynton/Cook.

Bissex, G. (1980). *GYNS AT WK: A child learns to read and write.* Cambridge, MA: Harvard University Press.

Blanton, L. L. (1992a). Talking students into writing: Using oral fluency to develop academic literacy. *TESOL Journal, 1*(4), 23–26.

Blanton, L. L. (1992b). Reading, writing, and authority: Issues in developmental ESL. *College ESL, 2,* 11–19.

Blanton, L. L. (1992c). A holistic approach to college ESL: Integrating language and content. *ELT Journal, 46,* 285–293.

Blanton, L. L. (1993). Reading as performance: Reframing the function of reading. In J. G. Carson & I. Leki (Eds.), *Reading in the composition classroom: Second language perspectives* (pp. 234–246). Boston: Heinle & Heinle.

Britton, J. (1988). Writing, learning and teacher education. In J. S. Davis & J. D. Marshall (Eds.), *Ways of knowing: Research and practice in the teaching of writing* (pp. 15–44). Iowa City, IA: Iowa Council of Teachers of English.

Brodkey, L. (1987). *Academic writing as social practice.* Philadelphia: Temple University Press.

Bruffee, K. A. (1984). Collaborative learning and the "conversation of mankind." *College English, 46,* 635–652.

Butler, R. O. (1992). *A good scent from a strange mountain.* New York: Henry Holt.

Carson, J. G. (1993). Reading for writing: Cognitive perspectives. In J. G. Carson & I. Leki (Eds.), *Reading in the composition classroom: Second language perspectives* (pp. 85–104). Boston: Heinle & Heinle.

Connors, R. J. (1981). The rise and fall of the modes of discourse. *College Composition and Communication, 32,* 444–455.

Cooper, M. M. (1989). Why are we talking about discourse communities? Or, foundationalism rears its ugly head once more. In M. M. Cooper & M. Holzman (Eds.), *Writing as social action* (pp. 202–243). Portsmouth, NH: Heinemann.

Cummins, J. (1984). *Bilingualism and special education: Issues in assessment and pedagogy.* Clevedon, England: Multilingual Matters.

Cummins, J. (1989). The sanitized curriculum: Educational disempowerment in a nation at risk. In D. M. Johnson & D. H. Roen (Eds.), *Richness in writing: Empowering ESL students* (pp. 19–38). New York: Longman.

Elbow, P. (1991). Reflections on academic discourse: How it relates to freshmen and colleagues. *College English, 53,* 135–155.

Emig, J. (1982). Inquiry paradigms and writing. *College Composition and Communication, 33,* 64–85.

Freeman, Y. S., & Freeman, D. E. (1989). Whole language approaches to writing with secondary students of English as a second language. In D. M. Johnson & D. H. Roen (Eds.), *Richness in writing: Empowering ESL students* (pp. 177–192). New York: Longman.

Freire, P. (1970). *Pedagogy of the oppressed.* New York: Continuum.

Freire, P. (1983). Banking education. In H. Giroux & D. Purpel (Eds.), *The hidden curriculum and moral education: Deception or discovery?* Berkeley, CA: McCutcheon.

Geisler, C. (1992). Exploring academic literacy: An experiment in composing. *College Composition and Communication, 45,* 39–54.

Goodman, K. S., & Goodman, Y. M. (1977). Learning about psycholinguistic processes by analyzing oral reading. *Harvard Educational Review, 47,* 317–333.

Graves, D. (1983). *Writing: Children and teachers at work.* Portsmouth, NH: Heinemann.

Harris, J. (1989). The idea of community in the study of writing. *College Composition and Communication, 40,* 11–22.

Heath, S. B. (1983). *Ways with words: Language, life and work in communities and classrooms.* Cambridge: Cambridge University Press.

Heath, S. B. (1985). Literacy or literate skills?: Considerations for ESL/EFL learners. In P. Larson, E. Judd, & D. Messerschmidt (Eds.), *On TESOL '84* (pp. 15–28). Washington, DC: TESOL.

Heath, S. B., & Branscombe, A. (1985). "Intelligent writing" in an audience community: Teacher, students, and researcher. In S. W. Freedman (Ed.), *The acquisition of written language: Response and revision* (pp. 3–32). Norwood, NJ: Ablex.

Heath, S. B., & Mangiola, L. (1991). *Children of promise: Literate activity in linguistically and culturally diverse classrooms.* Washington, DC: National Education Association.

Hudelson, S. (1984). Kan yu ret and rayt en ingles: Children become literate in English as a second language. *TESOL Quarterly, 18,* 221–238.

Hudelson, S. (1989). A tale of two children. In D. M. Johnson & D. H. Roen (Eds.), *Richness in writing: Empowering ESL students* (pp. 84–99). New York: Longman.

Johnson, D. M. (1989). Enriching task contexts for second language writing: Power through interpersonal roles. In D. M. Johnson & D. H. Roen (Eds.), *Richness in writing: Empowering ESL students* (pp. 39–54). New York: Longman.

Krashen, S. D. (1985). *Insights and inquiries.* Hayward, CA: Alemany Press.

Larson, S. (1992, March 15). East is east [Book review]. *Times-Picayune,* pp. E7, E8.

Leki, I. (1993). Reciprocal themes in ESL reading and writing. In J. G. Carson & I. Leki (Eds.), *Reading in the composition classroom: Second language perspectives* (pp. 9–32). Boston: Heinle & Heinle.

Lindfors, J. W. (1980). *Children's language and learning.* Englewood Cliffs, NJ: Prentice-Hall.

Marius, R. (1990). On academic discourse. *ADE Bulletin, 96,* 4–7.

Mlynarczyk, R. (1991). Is there a difference between personal and academic writing? *TESOL Journal, 1*(1), 17–20.

Mohan, B. A. (1986). *Language and content.* Reading, MA: Addison-Wesley.

Peyton, J. K., & Mackinson-Smyth, J. (1989). Writing and talking about writing: Computer networking with elementary students. In D. M. Johnson & D. H. Roen (Eds.), *Richness in writing: Empowering ESL students* (pp. 100–119). New York: Longman.

Peyton, J. K., & Reed, L. (1990). *Dialogue journal writing with nonnative English speakers: A handbook for teachers.* Alexandria, VA: TESOL.

Raimes, A. (1983). Tradition and revolution in ESL teaching. *TESOL Quarterly, 17,* 535–552.

Raimes, A. (1991). Out of the woods: Emerging traditions in the teaching of writing. *TESOL Quarterly, 25,* 407–430.

Rigg, P., & Allen, V. G. (Eds.). (1989). *When they don't all speak English: Integrating the ESL students into the regular classroom.* Urbana, IL: National Council of Teachers of English.

Rigg, P., & Enright, D. S. (Eds.). (1986). *Children and ESL: Integrating perspectives.* Washington, DC: TESOL.

Salvatori, M. (1986). The dialogical nature of basic reading and writing. In D. Bartholomae & A. Petrosky (Eds.), *Facts, artifacts and counterfacts: Theory and method for a reading and writing course* (pp. 137–166). Upper Montclair, NJ: Boynton/Cook.

Smith, F. (1978). *Understanding reading* (2nd ed.). New York: Holt, Rinehart & Winston.

Spack, R. (1985). Literature, reading, writing, and ESL: Bridging the gaps. *TESOL Quarterly, 19*, 703–725.

Spack, R. (1988). Initiating ESL students into the academic discourse community: How far should we go? *TESOL Quarterly, 22*, 29–51.

Spack, R. (1993). Student meets text, text meets student: Finding a way into academic discourse. In J. G. Carson & I. Leki (Eds.), *Reading in the composition classroom: Second language perspectives* (pp. 183–196). Boston: Heinle & Heinle.

Spack, R., & Sadow, C. (1983). Student–teacher working journals in ESL composition. *TESOL Quarterly, 17*, 575–593.

Urzua, C. (1987). "You stopped too soon": Second language children composing and revising. *TESOL Quarterly, 21*, 279–304.

Wall, S. V. (1986). Writing, reading and authority: A case study. In D. Bartholomae & A. Petrosky (Eds.), *Facts, artifacts and counterfacts: Theory and method for a reading and writing course* (pp. 105–136). Upper Montclair, NJ: Boynton/Cook.

Wells, G. (1986). *The meaning makers.* Portsmouth, NH: Heinemann.

Zamel, V. (1982). Writing: The process of discovering meaning. *TESOL Quarterly, 16*, 195–209.

Zamel, V. (1992). Writing one's way into reading. *TESOL Quarterly, 26*, 463–485.

Chapter 18

The Ownership of English

H. G. Widdowson

The following is the text of a plenary address delivered in April, 1993, in Atlanta at the 27th Annual TESOL (Teachers of English to Speakers of Other Languages) Convention. The oral character of the presentation has been preserved.

* * *

Given the theme of this convention, Designing Our World, and at a time when territorial disputes and matters of ownership and identity are so prominent in the affairs of the world in general, this is perhaps an appropriate occasion to raise the question of how we stake out our own territory as English teachers in delimiting and designing our world. And to ask who does the designing and on what authority.

To start with, who determines the demarcation of the subject itself? We are teaching English and the general assumption is that our purpose is to develop in students a proficiency which approximates as closely as possible to that of native speakers. But who are these native speakers?

One answer might be: the English. And why not? A modest proposal surely. England is where the language originated and this is where the English (for the most part) live. The language and the people are bound together by both morphology and history. So they can legitimately lay claim to this linguistic territory. It belongs to them. And they are the custodians.

If you want real or proper English, this is where it is to be found, preserved, and listed like a property of the National Trust.

Of course English, of a kind, is found elsewhere as well, still spreading, a luxuriant growth from imperial seed. Seeded among other people but not ceded to them. At least not completely. For the English still cling tenaciously to their property and try to protect it from abuse. Let us acknowledge (let us concede) that there are other kinds of English, offshoots and outgrowths, but they are not real or proper English, not the genuine article.

As an analogy, consider a certain kind of beverage. There are all kinds of cola, but only one which is the real thing. Or, further afield, an analogy, from the French. They have, until just recently, successfully denied others the right to use the appellation *Champagne* for any wine that does not come from the region of that name where Dom Perignon first invented it. There may be all kinds of derivative versions elsewhere, excellent no doubt in their way, but they are not real or proper Champagne, even though loose talk may refer to them as such. Similarly, there is real English, Anglais real, Royal English, Queen's English, or (for those unsympathetic to the monarchy) Oxford English. The vintage language.

I do not imagine that such a view would gain much support in present company. The response is more likely to be outrage. You cannot be serious. Well, not entirely, it is true. As I have expressed it, in somewhat extravagant terms, this position is one which very few people would associate themselves with. It is reactionary, arrogant, totally unacceptable. And the argument is patently absurd. Perhaps as I have expressed it. But then why is it absurd? The particular associations of England, Queen and country, and Colonel Blimp which I have invoked to demonstrate the argument also in some respects disguise it. If we now remove the position from these associations and strip the argument down to its essential tenets, is it so readily dismissed? Is it indeed so uncommon after all? I want to suggest that the ideas and attitudes which I have just presented in burlesque are still very much with us in a different and less obvious guise.

To return briefly to Champagne. One argument frequently advanced for being protective of its good name has to do with quality assurance. The label is a guarantee of quality. If any Tom, Jane, or Harry producing fizzy wine is free to use it, there can be no quality control. Recently an English firm won a court case enabling it to put the name Champagne on bottles containing a nonalcoholic beverage made from elderflowers. Elderflowers! The Champagne lobby was outraged. Here, they said, was the thin end of the wedge. Before long the label would be appearing on bottles all over the place containing concoctions of all kinds calling themselves Champagne, and so laying claim to its quality. The appellation would not be *controllée*. Standards were at stake. The same point can be made, is made, about the local Georgian beverage. There can only be one. This is it. Be wary of variant products of lower quality.

And the same point is frequently made about English. In this case, you cannot, of course, preserve exclusive use of the name and indeed it would work against your interests to do so, but you can seek to preserve standards by implying that there is an exclusive quality in your own brand of English, aptly called standard English. What is this quality, then? What are these standards?

The usual answer is: quality of clear communication and standards of intelligibility. With standard English, it is argued, these are assured. If the language disperses into different forms, a myriad of Englishes, then it ceases to serve as a means of international communication; in which case the point of learning it largely disappears. As the language spreads, there are bound to be changes out on the periphery; so much can be conceded. But these changes must be seen not only as peripheral but as radial also and traceable back to the stable centre of the standard. If this centre does not hold, things fall apart, mere anarchy is loosed upon the world. Back to Babel.

In itself, this argument sounds plausible and it is difficult to refute. But for all that, there is something about it which is suspect. Let us replay it again. Standard English promotes the cause of international communication, so we must maintain the central stability of the standard as the common linguistic frame of reference.

To begin with, who are we? Obviously the promoters of standard English must themselves have standard English at their disposal. But to maintain it is another matter. This presupposes authority. And this authority is claimed by those who possess the language by primogeniture and due of birth, as Shakespeare puts it. In other words, the native speakers. They do not have to be English, of course, that would be too restrictive a condition, and one it would (to say the least) be tactless to propose especially in present company, but they have to be to the language born. Not all native speakers, you understand. In fact, come to think of it, not most native speakers, for the majority of those who are to the language born speak nonstandard English and have themselves to be instructed in the standard at school. We cannot have any Tom, Jane, and Harry claiming authority, for Tom, Jane, and Harry are likely to be speakers of some dialect or other. So the authority to maintain the standard language is not consequent on a natural native-speaker endowment. It is claimed by a minority of people who have the power to impose it. The custodians of standard English are self-elected members of a rather exclusive club.

Now it is important to be clear that in saying this I am not arguing against standard English. You can accept the argument for language maintenance, as indeed I do, without accepting the authority that claims the right to maintain it. It is, I think, very generally assumed that a particular subset of educated native speakers in England, or New England, or wherever, have the natural entitlement to custody of the language, that the preservation of its integrity is in their hands: their right and their responsibility. It is this which

I wish to question. Not in any spirit of radical rebellion against authority as such but because I think such questioning raises a number of crucial issues about the learning and teaching of the language.

Consideration of who the custodians are leads logically on to a consideration of what it is exactly that is in their custody. What is standard English? The usual way of defining it is in reference to its grammar and lexis: It is a variety, a kind of superposed dialect which is socially sanctioned for institutional use and therefore particularly well suited to written communication. In its spoken form it can be manifested by any accent. So it is generally conceded that standard English has no distinctive phonology. The same concession is not, however, extended to its graphology. On the contrary, it is deviant spelling which, in Britain at least, is most frequently singled out for condemnation. There is something of a contradiction here. If standard English is defined as a distinctive grammatical and lexical system which can be substantially realized in different ways, then what does spelling have to do with it? It is true that some spelling has a grammatical function (like the 's which distinguishes the possessive from the plural) but most of it does not. If you are going to ignore phonological variation, then, to be consistent, you should surely ignore graphological variation as well and overlook variations in spelling as a kind of written accent.

The reason it is not overlooked, I think, is that standard English, unlike other dialects, is essentially a written variety and mainly designed for institutional purposes (education, administration, business, etc.). Its spoken version is secondary, and typically used by those who control these institutions. This means that although it may not matter how it is spoken, it emphatically does matter how it is written. Furthermore, because writing, as a more durable medium, is used to express and establish institutional values, deviations from orthographic conventions undermine in some degree the institutions which they serve. They can be seen as evidence of social instability: a sign of things beginning to fall apart. So it is not surprising that those who have a vested interest in maintaining these institutions should be so vexed by bad spelling. It is not that it greatly interferes with communication: It is usually not difficult to identify words through their unorthodox appearance. What seems to be more crucial is that good spelling represents conformity to convention and so serves to maintain institutional stability.

Similar points can be made about grammatical features. Because language has built-in redundancy, grammatical conformity is actually not particularly crucial for many kinds of communicative transaction. What we generally do in the interpretative process is actually to edit grammar out of the text, referring lexis directly to context, using lexical items as indexical clues to meaning. We edit grammar back in when we need it for fine tuning. If the reason for insisting on standard English is because it guarantees effective communication, then the emphasis should logically be on vocabulary rather than grammar. But the champions of standard English do not see it in this way: On the contrary, they focus attention on grammatical abuse. Why should this be so? There are, I think, two reasons.

Firstly, it is precisely because grammar is so often redundant in communicative transactions that it takes on another significance, namely that of expressing social identity. The mastery of a particular grammatical system, especially perhaps those features which are redundant, marks you as a member of the community which has developed that system for its own social purposes. Conversely, of course, those who are unable to master the system are excluded from the community. They do not belong. In short, grammar is a sort of shibboleth.

So when the custodians of standard English complain about the ungrammatical language of the populace, they are in effect indicating that the perpetrators are outsiders, nonmembers of the community. The only way they can become members, and so benefit from the privileges of membership, is to learn standard English, and these privileges include, of course, access to the institutions which the community controls. Standard English is an entry condition and the custodians of it the gatekeepers. You can, of course, persist in your nonstandard ways if you choose, but then do not be surprised to find yourself marginalized, perpetually kept out on the periphery. What you say will be less readily attended to, assigned less importance, if it is not expressed in the grammatically approved manner. And if you express yourself in writing which is both ungrammatical and badly spelled, you are not likely to be taken very seriously.

Standard English, then, is not simply a means of communication but the symbolic possession of a particular community, expressive of its identity, its conventions, and values. As such it needs to be carefully preserved, for to undermine standard English is to undermine what it stands for: the security of this community and its institutions. Thus, it tends to be the communal rather than the communicative features of standard English that are most jealously protected: its grammar and spelling.

I do not wish to imply that this communal function is to be deplored. Languages of every variety have this dual character: They provide the means for communication and at the same time express a sense of community, represent the stability of its conventions and values, in short its culture. All communities possess and protect their languages. The question is which community, and which culture, have a rightful claim to ownership of standard English? For standard English is no longer the preserve of a group of people living in an offshore European island, or even of larger groups living in continents elsewhere. It is an international language. As such it serves a whole range of different communities and their institutional purposes and these transcend traditional communal and cultural boundaries. I am referring to the business community, for example, and the community of researchers and scholars in science and technology and other disciplines. Standard English, especially in its written form, is their language. It provides for effective communication, but at the same time it establishes the status and stability of the institutional conventions which define these international activities. These activities develop their own conventions of thought and procedure, customs and codes of practice; in short, they in effect create their own cultures, their own standards. And obviously for the maintenance of standards it is helpful, to say the least, to have a standard language at your disposal. But you do not need native speakers to tell you what it is.

And indeed in one crucial respect, the native speaker is irrelevant. What I have in mind here is vocabulary. I said earlier that the custodians of standard English tend to emphasize its grammatical rather than its lexical features. I have suggested that one reason for this is that grammar is symbolic of communal solidarity. "Ungrammatical" expressions mark people as nonmembers. What you then do is to coax or coerce them somehow into conformity if you want to make them members (generally through education) or make them powerless on the periphery if you don't. So much for grammar. What then of lexis.

It is said that standard English is a variety, a kind of dialect, in that it is defined by its lexis and grammar. In fact, when you come to look for it, standard lexis is very elusive. It is my belief that it does not actually exist. And on reflection it is hard to see how it could exist. To begin with, the notion of standard implies stability, a relatively fixed point of reference. So if I invent a word, for example, it is not, by definition, standard. But people are inventing words all the time to express new ideas and attitudes, to adjust to their changing world. It is this indeed which demonstrates the essential dynamism of the language without which it would wither away. So it is that different groups of users will develop specialist vocabularies, suited to their needs but incomprehensible to others. When I look at my daily newspaper, I find innumerable words from the terminology of technology, law, financial affairs, and so on which I simply do not understand. They may claim to be English, but they are Greek to me. Are they standard English? One way of deciding might be to consult a standard reference work, namely a learners' dictionary. But most of these words of restricted technical use do not appear. This is because, reasonably enough, the dictionary only contains words of wide range and common occurrence. If this is the way standard is to be defined, then these words of restricted use do not count by definition. Yet they are real enough, and indeed can be said to represent the reality of English as an international language. For the reason why English is international is because its vocabulary has diversified to serve a range of institutional uses.

As I indicated earlier, the custodians of standard English express the fear that if there is diversity, things will fall apart and the language will divide up into mutually unintelligible varieties. But things in a sense have already fallen apart. The varieties of English used for international communication in science, finance, commerce, and so on are mutually unintelligible. As far as lexis is concerned, their communicative viability depends on the development of separate standards, and this means that their communication is largely closed off from the world outside.

The point then is that if English is to retain its vitality and its capability for continual adjustment, it cannot be confined within a standard lexis. And this seems to be implicitly accepted as far as particular domains of use are concerned. Nobody, I think, says that the abstruse terms used by physicists or stockbrokers are nonstandard English. It is generally accepted that communities or secondary cultures which are defined by shared professional concerns should be granted rights of ownership and allowed to fashion the language to meet their needs, their specific purposes indeed. And these purposes, we should note again, are twofold: They are communicative in that they meet the needs of in-group transactions, and they are communal in that they define the identity of the group itself.

The same tolerance is not extended so readily to primary cultures and communities, where the language is used in the conduct of everyday social life. Lexical innovation here, equally motivated by communicative and communal requirement, is generally dismissed as deviant or dialectal. Take, for example, the two words *depone* and *prepone*. The first is a technical legal term and therefore highly respectable. The second *prepone* is not. It is an Indian English word of very general currency, coined to contrast with *postpone*. To postpone an event means to put it back, to prepone an event is to bring it forward. The coinage exploits the morphology of English in an entirely regular way. It is apt. But it is also quaint. An odd Indian excrescence: obviously nonstandard. And yet there is clearly nothing deviant in the derivational process itself, and indeed we can see it at work in the formation of the related words *predate* and *postdate*. But these are sanctioned as entirely ordinary, proper, standard English words. What, then, is the difference? The difference lies in the origin of the word. *Prepone* is coined by a nonnative-speaking community, so it is not really a proper English word. It is not pukka. And of course the word *pukka* is itself only pukka because the British adopted it.

Where are we then? When we consider the question of standard English what we find, in effect, is double standards. The very idea of a standard implies stability, and this can only be fixed in reference to the past. But language is of its nature unstable. It is essentially protean in nature, adapting its shape to suit changing circumstances. It would otherwise lose its vitality and its communicative and communal value. This is generally acknowledged in the case of specialist domains of use but is not acknowledged in the case of everyday social uses of the language. So it is that a word like *depone* is approved and a word like *prepone* is not.

But the basic principle of dynamic adaptation is the same in both cases. And in both cases the users of the language exploit its protean potential and fashion it to their need, thereby demonstrating a high degree of linguistic capability. In both cases the innovation indicates that the language has been learned, not just as a set of fixed conventions to conform to, but as an adaptable resource for making meaning. And making meaning which you can call your own. This, surely, is a crucial condition. You are proficient in a language to the extent that you possess it, make it your own, bend it to your will, assert yourself through it rather than simply submit to the dictates of its form. It is a familiar experience to find oneself saying things in a foreign language because you can say them rather than because they express what you want to say. You feel you are going through the motions, and somebody else's motions at that. You are speaking the language but not speaking your mind. Real proficiency is when you are able to take possession of the language, turn it to your advantage, and make it real for you. This is what mastery means. So in a way, proficiency only comes with nonconformity, when you can take the initiative and strike out on your own. Consider these remarks of the Nigerian writer, Chinua Achebe (1975):

> I feel that the English language will be able to carry the weight of my African experience. . . . But it will have to be a new English, still in communion with its ancestral home but altered to suit its new African surroundings. (p. 62)

Achebe is a novelist, and he is talking here about creative writing. But what he says clearly has wider relevance and applies to varieties of English in this country and elsewhere. The point is that all uses of language are creative in the sense that they draw on linguistic resources to express different perceptions of reality. English is called upon to carry the weight of all kinds of experience, much of it very remote indeed from its ancestral home. The new English which Achebe refers to is locally developed, and although it must necessarily be related to, and so in communion with, its ancestral origins in the past, it owes no allegiance to any descendants of this ancestry in the present.

And this point applies to all other new Englishes which have been created to carry the weight of different experience in different surroundings, whether they are related to specialist domains of use or to the contexts of everyday life. They are all examples of the entirely normal and necessary process of adaptation, a process which obviously depends on nonconformity to existing conventions or standards. For these have been established elsewhere by other people as appropriate to quite different circumstances. The fact that these people can claim direct descent from the founding fathers has nothing to do with it. How English develops in the world is no business whatever of native speakers in England, the United States, or anywhere else. They have no say in the matter, no right to intervene or pass judgement. They are irrelevant. The very fact that English is an international language means that no nation can have custody over it. To grant such custody of the language, is necessarily to arrest its development and so undermine its international status. It is a matter of considerable pride and satisfaction for native speakers of English that their language is an international means of communication. But the point is that it is only international to the extent that it is not their language. It is not a possession which they lease out to others, while still retaining the freehold. Other people actually own it.

As soon as you accept that English serves the communicative and communal needs of different communities, it follows logically that it must be diverse. An international language has to be an independent language. It does not follow logically, however, that the language will disperse into mutually unintelligible varieties. For it will naturally stabilize into standard form to the extent required to meet the needs of the communities concerned. Thus it is clearly vital to the interests of the international community of, for example, scientists or business people, whatever their primary language, that they should preserve a common standard of English in order to keep up standards of communicative effectiveness. English could not otherwise serve their purposes. It needs no native speaker to tell them that. Furthermore, this natural tendency towards standardization will be reinforced by the extending of networks of interaction through developments in telecommunications and information technology. For there is little point in opening up such amazing new transmission systems if what you transmit makes no sense at the other end. The availability of these new channels calls for the maintenance of a common code. And these are therefore likely to have greater influence on stabilizing the language than the pronouncements of native speakers.

The essential point is that a standard English, like other varieties of language, develops endo-normatively, by a continuing process of self-regulation, as appropriate to different conditions of use. It is not fixed by exo-normative fiat from outside: not fixed, therefore, by native speakers. They have no special say in the matter, in spite of their claims to ownership of real English as associated with their own particular cultural contexts of use.

And yet there is no doubt that native speakers of English are deferred to in our profession. What they say is invested with both authenticity and authority. The two are closely related, and a consideration of their relationship brings us to certain central issues in language pedagogy. An example follows.

Over recent years, we have heard persuasive voices insisting that the English presented in the classroom should be authentic, naturally occurring language, not produced for instructional purposes. Generally, what this means, of course, is language naturally occurring as communication in native-speaker contexts of use, or rather those selected contexts where standard English is the norm: real newspaper reports, for example, real magazine articles, real advertisements, cooking recipes, horoscopes, and what have you. Now the obvious point about this naturally occurring language is that, inevitably, it is recipient designed and so culturally loaded. It follows that access to its meaning is limited to those insiders who share its cultural presuppositions and a sense of its idiomatic nuance. Those who do not, the outsiders, cannot ratify its authenticity. In other words, the language is only authentic in the original conditions of its use, it cannot be in the classroom. The authenticity is nontransferable. And to the extent that students cannot therefore engage with the language, they cannot make it their own. It may be real language, but it is not real to them. It does not relate to their world but to a remote one they have to find out about by consulting a dictionary of culture. It may be that eventually students will wish to acquire the cultural knowledge and the idiomatic fluency which enable them to engage authentically with the language use of a particular native-speaking community by adopting their identity in some degree, but there seems no sensible reason for insisting on them trying to do this in the process of language learning. On the contrary, it would seem that language for learning does need to be specially designed for pedagogic purposes so that it can be made real in the context of the students' own world.

The importance of getting students engaged with the language, cognitively, affectively, personally, is widely accepted as established wisdom. Let the learners be autonomous (at least up to a point), allow them to make the language their own, let them identify with it, let not the teacher impose authority upon them in the form of an alien pattern of behaviour. Very well. But this injunction is totally at variance with the insistence on authentic language, which is an imposition of another authority, namely that of native-speaker patterns of cultural behaviour. If natural language learning depends on asserting some ownership over the language, this cannot be promoted by means of language which is authentic only because it belongs to somebody else and expresses somebody else's identity. A pedagogy which combines authenticity of use with autonomy of learning is a contradiction. You cannot have it both ways.

The notion of authenticity, then, privileges native-speaker use (inappropriately, I have argued) as the proper language for learning. But it also, of course, privileges the native-speaker teachers of the language. For they, of course, have acquired the language and culture as an integrated experience and have a feel for its nuances and idiomatic identity which the nonnative speaker cannot claim to have. Indeed, native speakers alone can be the arbiters of what is authentic since authenticity can only be determined by insiders. So if you give authenticity primacy as a pedagogic principle, you inevitably grant privileged status to native-speaker teachers, and you defer to them not only in respect to competence in the language but also in respect to competence in language teaching. They become the custodians and arbiters not only of proper English but of proper pedagogy as well.

But what if you shift the emphasis away from contexts of use to contexts of learning, and consider how the language is to be specially designed to engage the student's reality and activate the learning process? The special advantage of native-speaker teachers disappears. Now, on the contrary, it is nonnative-speaker teachers who come into their own. For the context of learning, contrived within the classroom setting, has to be informed in some degree by the attitudes, beliefs, values and so on of the students' cultural world. And in respect to this world, of course, it is the native-speaker teacher who is the outsider. To the extent that the design of instruction depends on a familiarity with the student reality which English is to engage with, or on the particular sociocultural situations in which teaching and learning take place, then nonnative teachers have a clear and, indeed, decisive advantage.

In short, the native-speaker teacher is in a better position to know what is appropriate in contexts of language use, and so to define possible target objectives. Granted. But it is the nonnative-speaker teacher who is in a better position to know what is appropriate in the contexts of language learning which need to be set up to achieve such objectives. And that, generally speaking, is not granted. Instead what we find is that native-speaker expertise is assumed to extend to the teaching of the language. They not only have a patent on proper English, but on proper ways of teaching it as well.

So it is that the approaches to pedagogy which are generally promoted as proper are those which are appropriate to contexts of instruction in which native-speaker teachers operate. And their prestige, of course, exerts a powerful influence so that teachers in other contexts are persuaded to conform and to believe that if the approaches do not fit, it is their fault.

So it is that native speakers write textbooks and teachers' books, make pronouncements and recommendations, and bring to remote and hitherto benighted places the good news about real English and good teaching to lighten their darkness. Real English: their English. Good teaching: their teaching. But both are contextually limited by cultural factors. Their English is that which is associated with the communicative and communal needs of their community, and these may have little relevance for those learning English as an international language.

And their teaching is suited to particular contexts of instruction which in many respects are quite different from those which obtain in the world at large. Consider, for example, a language school in England, with English as the ambient language outside the classroom, the students well off and well motivated, but quite different in linguistic and cultural background both from each other, and from the teacher. In such a context it is, of course, necessary to focus on what can be established as a common denominator. Everybody is here in England, for example, and everybody is human. And so you devise an approach to teaching which combines authenticity with an appeal to universal natural learning and humanistic response. This is an example of appropriate pedagogy. Such an approach is necessary and of course it works in these local conditions. Highly commendable. But it is exclusive in that it excludes possibilities which might be particularly appropriate elsewhere—translation, for example. The problem is when an absolute virtue is made of local necessity by claims of global validity, when it is assumed that if the approach works here it ought to work, or made to work, everywhere else. This is a denial of diversity.

For of course there is no reason why it should work elsewhere where quite different conditions obtain. It is difficult to resist the conclusion that such an approach, which makes a virtue of necessity, is only privileged because of the authority vested in the teachers by virtue of their native-speaker status. This is not to say that it may not offer ideas worth pondering, but then these ideas have to be analysed out of the approach and their relevance evaluated in reference to other contexts. You should not assume, with bland arrogance, that your way of teaching English, or your way of using English, carries a general guarantee of quality. To put the point briefly: English and English teaching are proper to the extent that they are appropriate, not to the extent that they are appropriated.

TESOL has recently made public its opposition to discrimination against the nonnative teacher, as a matter of sociopolitical principle. This is obviously to be welcomed. But if it is to be more than a token gesture, such a move needs to be supported by an enquiry into the nature of the subject we are teaching, what constitutes an appropriate approach, what kinds of competence is required of teachers—in other words an enquiry into matters of pedagogic principle which bring sociopolitical concerns and professional standards into alignment. In this convention we are concerned with designing our world. Our world. Possessive. Who are we then? What is this world we own? TESOL has designs upon us. Us. I think we need to be cautious about the designs we have on other people's worlds when we are busy designing our own.

REFERENCE

Achebe, C. (1975). The African writer and the English language. In *Morning yet on creation day*. London: Heinemann.

Chapter 19

Strangers in Academia:
The Experiences of Faculty and
ESL Students Across the Curriculum

Vivian Zamel

> *When I go into a classroom these days, I look around and feel like I'm in a
> different country.*
>
> —Professor of Management

> *A few weeks ago a professor came by the reading, writing and study skills center
> where I tutor. He was with a young Asian woman, obviously one of his students.
> He "deposited" her in the center, claiming that she desperately needed help with
> her English. The woman stared into the distance with a frightened, nervous
> look on her face and tried to force a smile. She handed me a paper she had
> written on the labor union and asked if I could help her make corrections.
> After a short introductory discussion, we looked at the paper that we were about
> to revise—it was filled with red marks indicating spelling, punctuation, and
> grammar errors; the only written response was something along the lines of
> "You need serious help with your English. Please see a tutor."*
>
> —From a tutor's journal

> *Students in the lab speak to one another in their own language so that they
> make sure they know what they are doing. So they may look like they are not
> listening to the lab teacher. He feels so isolated from them. He feels he has no
> control, no power. So he may get angry.*
>
> —An ESL student

These comments show evidence of tensions and conflicts that are becoming
prevalent in institutions of higher education as student populations become

more diverse. One clear indication that faculty across the disciplines are concerned about the extent to which diverse student populations, particularly students whose native language is not English, constrain their work is the number of workshops and seminars that have been organized, and at which I have participated, in order to address what these faculty view as the "ESL Problem."[1] In the course of preparing to work with faculty, and in order to get a sense of their issues and concerns, I surveyed instructors about their experiences working with non-native speakers of English. As Patricia Laurence has pointed out, though we acknowledge and discuss the diversity of students, "we neglect the 'polyphony'" that represents faculty voices (24). While I did not receive many responses to my request for feedback, those responses that were returned did indeed reflect this polyphony.

Some faculty saw this invitation to provide feedback as an opportunity to discuss the strengths and resources these students brought with them, indicated that ESL students, because of their experience and motivation, were a positive presence in their classes, and noted the contributions ESL students made in discussions that invited cross-cultural perspectives. One professor took issue with the very idea of making generalizations about ESL students. But this pattern of response did not represent the attitudes and perspectives revealed by other faculty responses. One professor, for example, referred to both silent students, on the one hand, and "vocal but incomprehensible students" on the other. But, by far, the greatest concern had to do with students' writing and language, which faculty saw as deficient and inadequate for undertaking the work in their courses. I got the clear sense from these responses that language use was confounded with intellectual ability—that, as Victor Villanueva, recounting his own schooling experiences, puts it, "bad language" and "insufficient cognitive development" were being conflated (11).

In order to demonstrate the range of faculty commentary, I've selected two faculty responses, not because they are necessarily representative, but because they reveal such divergent views on language, language development, and the role that faculty see themselves as playing in this development. I've also chosen these responses because they may serve as mirrors for our own perspectives and belief systems, and thus help us examine more critically what we ourselves think and do, both within our own classrooms and with respect to the larger institutional contexts in which we teach. In other words, although these responses came from two different disciplines, it is critical for each of us to examine the extent to which we catch glimpses of our own practices and assumptions in these texts. The first response was written by an English Department instructor:

> One of my graduate school professors once told me that he knew within the first two weeks of the semester what his students' final grades would be. Recently I had a Burmese-born Chinese student who proved my professor

wrong. After the first two essays, there was certainly no reason to be optimistic about this student's performance. The essays were very short, filled with second language errors, thesaurus words, and sweeping generalizations. In the first essay, it was obvious he had been taught to make outlines because that's all the paper was, really—a list. In the second essay, instead of dealing directly with the assigned text, the student directed most of his energy to form and structure. He had an introduction even though he had nothing to introduce. In his conclusion, he was making wild assertions (even though he had nothing to base them on) because he knew conclusions were supposed to make a point. By the fourth essay, he started to catch on to the fact that my comments were directed toward the content of his essays, not the form. Once he stopped worrying about thesis sentences, vocabulary, and the like, he became a different writer. His papers were long, thoughtful, and engaging. He was able to interpret and respond to texts and to make connections that I term "double face" as a way to comment on the ways in which different cultures define such terms as "respect." Instead of 1 1/4 pages, this essay was seven pages, and it made several references to the text while synthesizing it with his experience as someone who is a product of three cultures. This change not only affected the content of his writing, but also his mechanics. Though there were still errors, there were far fewer of them, and he was writing well enough where I felt it was safe to raise questions about structure and correctness.

This response begins with the recognition that we need to be wary of self-fulfilling prophecies about the potential of students, and indeed this instructor's narrative demonstrates compellingly the dangers of such prophecies. This instructor goes on to cite problems with the student's performance, but he speculates that these problems may have to do with previous instruction, thus reflecting a stance that counteracts the tendency to blame students. Despite the student's ongoing difficulties, the instructor does not despair over the presence of second language errors, over the short essays, the "sweeping generalizations," the empty introduction, the "wild assertions." Instead, this instructor seems to persist in his attempts to focus the student on content issues, to respond to the student seriously, to push him to consider the connections between what he was saying and the assigned reading, to take greater risks, which he succeeds in doing "by the fourth essay." In this, I believe, we see the instructor's understanding that it takes multiple opportunities for students to trust that he is inviting them into serious engagement with the course material, that it takes time to acquire new approaches to written work. What seems to be revealed in this response is the instructor's belief in the student's potential, his appreciation for how language and learning are promoted, his refusal to draw conclusions about intellectual ability on the basis of surface features of language—all of which, in turn, helped the student become a "different writer," a change that affected the content of his writing, that had an impact on the very errors that filled his first papers, that even illuminated the instructor's reading of the assigned texts. This response suggests a rich and complicated notion of language, one that recognizes that language evolves in and responds to the context of saying something meaningful, that language and meaning are reciprocal and give rise to one another.

This response, especially the final section about surface level errors, foreshadows the other faculty response, which was written by an art history instructor and which reveals a very different set of assumptions and expectations:

> My experience with teaching ESL students is that they have often not received adequate English instruction to complete the required essay texts and papers in my classes. I have been particularly dismayed when I find that they have already completed 2 ESL courses and have no knowledge of the parts of speech or the terminology that is used in correcting English grammar on papers. I am certainly not in a position to teach English in my classes. (The problem has been particularly acute with Chinese/S. E. Asian students.) These students may have adequate intelligence to do well in the courses, but their language skills result in low grades. (I cannot give a good grade to a student who can only generate one or two broken sentences during a ten-minute slide comparison.)

The first assumption I see in this response is the belief that language and knowledge are separate entities, that language must be in place and fixed in order to do the work in the course. This static notion of language is further revealed by the instructor's assumption that language use is determined by a knowledge of parts of speech or grammatical terminology. Given this belief, it is understandable why she is dismayed by what she characterizes as students' lack of knowledge of grammar, a conclusion she has seemingly reached because her corrective feedback, presumably making use of grammatical terms, has not proven successful. This practice itself is not questioned, however; students or their inadequate English language instruction are held accountable instead. If students had been prepared appropriately, if the gatekeeping efforts had kept students out of her course until they were more like their native language counterparts, her commentary suggests, students would be able to do the required work. There is little sense of how the unfamiliar terms, concepts, and ways of seeing that are particular to this course can be acquired. Nor is there an appreciation for how this very unfamiliarity with the course content may be constraining students' linguistic processes. She does not see, focusing as she does on difference, how she can contribute to students' language and written development, how she can build on what they know. Despite indicating that students may have "adequate intelligence to do well in the course," she doesn't seem to be able to get past their language problems when it comes to evaluating their work, thus missing the irony of grading on the basis of that which she acknowledges she is not "in a position to teach." The final parenthetical statement reveals further expectations about student work, raising questions about the extent to which her very expectations, rather than linguistic difficulties alone, contribute to the "broken sentences" to which she refers.

What we see at work here is in marked contrast to the model of possibility revealed in the first response. What seems to inform this second response is a deficit model of language and learning whereby students' deficiencies are foregrounded. This response is shaped by an essentialist view of language in which language is understood to be a decontextualized skill that can be taught in isolation from the production of meaning and that must be in place in order to undertake intellectual work. What we see here is an illustration of "the myth of transience," a belief that permeates institutions of higher education and perpetuates the notion that these students' problems are temporary and can be remediated—so long as some isolated set of courses or program of instruction, but not the real courses in the academy, takes on the responsibility of doing so (see Rose, "Language"). Such a belief supports the illusion that permanent solutions are possible, which releases faculty from the ongoing struggle and questioning that the teaching-learning process inevitably involves.

In these two faculty responses, we see the ways in which different sets of expectations and attitudes get played out. In the one classroom, we get some sense of what can happen when opportunities for learning are created, when students are invited into a thoughtful process of engaging texts, when students' writing is read and responded to in meaningful and supportive ways. In the other classroom, although we have little information about the conditions for learning, we are told that one way that learning is measured is by technically correct writing done during a 10-minute slide presentation, and this, I believe, is telling. For students who are not adequately prepared to do this work, there is little, the instructor tells us, she can do. Given this deterministic stance, students are closed off from participating in intellectual work.

At the same time that I was soliciting faculty responses to get a sense of their perceptions and assumptions, I began to survey ESL students about what they wanted faculty to know about their experiences and needs in classrooms across the curriculum. I wanted, in other words, to capture the polyphony of students' voices as well. I felt that the work I was engaging in with faculty could not take place without an exploration of students' views, especially since, although faculty have little reservation discussing what they want and expect from students, informing us about their frustrations and disappointments, the students' perspective is one that faculty often hear little about. And since I have become convinced that our role in our institutions ought not to be defined solely by the service we perform for other faculty (either by making our students' English native-like or keeping the gates closed until this is accomplished) but in helping faculty understand the role they need to begin to play in working with all students, the students' perspective was critical.

Within the last two years, I have collected more than 325 responses from first and second year ESL students enrolled in courses across a range of disciplines.[2] I discovered from looking at these responses a number of predominant and recurring themes. Students spoke of patience, tolerance, and encouragement as key factors that affected their learning:

> Teachers need to be more sensitive to ESL students needs of education. Since ESL students are face with the demands of culture adjustment, especially in the classroom, teaches must be patients and give flexible consideration. . . . For example—if a teacher get a paper that isn't clear or didn't follow the assignment correctly, teacher must talk and communicate with the students.

Students articulated the kinds of assistance they needed, pointing, for example, to clearer and more explicitly detailed assignments and more accessible classroom talk:

> In the classes, most teachers go over material without explaining any words that seems hard to understand for us. . . . I want college teachers should describe more clearly on questions in the exams, so we can understand clearly. Also, I think the teachers should write any important information or announcement on the board rather than just speaking in front of class, because sometimes we understand in different way when we hear it than when we read it.

Students spoke with pride about how much they knew and how much they had accomplished through working, they felt, harder than their native English-speaking counterparts did, and they wanted faculty to credit and acknowledge them for this.

> I would like them to know that we are very responsible and we know why we come to college: to learn. We are learning English as well as the major of our choice. It is very hard sometimes and we don't need professors who claimed that they don't understand us. The effort is double. We are very intelligent people. We deserve better consideration . . . ESL students are very competent and deserve to be in college. We made the step to college. Please make the other step to meet us.

At the same time, an overwhelming number of students wanted faculty to know that they were well aware they were having language difficulties and appreciated responses that would help them. But they also expressed their wish that their work not be discounted and viewed as limited. They seemed to have a very strong sense that because of difficulties that were reflected in their attempts at classroom participation and in their written work, their struggles with learning were misperceived and underestimated:

> The academic skills of students who are not native speakers of English are not worse than academic skills of American students, in some areas it can be much better. Just because we have problems with language . . . that some professors hate because they don't want to spend a minute to listen a student, doesn't mean that we don't understand at all.

Students referred to professors who showed concern and seemed to appreciate students' contributions. But the majority of students' responses described classrooms that silenced them, that made them feel fearful and inadequate, that limited possibilities for engagement, involvement, inclusion.

While these students acknowledged that they continue to experience difficulties, they also voiced their concern that these struggles not be viewed as deficiencies, that their efforts be understood as serious attempts to grapple with these difficulties. While faculty may feel overwhelmed by and even resentful of working with such students, these students indicated that they expect and need their instructors to assist them in this undertaking, even making suggestions as to how this can be done. Indeed, the very kind of clarity, accessible language, careful explanation, and effort that faculty want students to demonstrate are the kinds of assistance students were asking of faculty. Without dismissing the concerns of the art instructor, these students nevertheless believed, as does the English instructor, that teaching ought to be responsive to their concerns.

Yet another source of information about students' classroom experiences comes from my ongoing case-study of two students who attended a composition course I taught two years ago and who have met with me regularly since that time to discuss the work they are assigned, their teachers' responses to and evaluation of their work, the classroom dynamics of their courses, the roles they and their teachers play, and the kinds of learning that are expected in their classes.

One of the students who has been participating in this longitudinal investigation is Motoko, a student from Japan who has taken a range of courses and is majoring in sociology. She described courses in which lively interaction was generated, in which students were expected to participate, to write frequent reaction papers and to undertake projects based on first-hand research, to challenge textbook material and to connect this material to their own lived experiences. But in most of her courses the picture was quite different. Lectures were pervasive, classes were so large that attendance wasn't even taken, and short answer tests were often the predominant means of evaluating student work. With respect to one class, for example, Motoko discussed the problematic nature of multiple-choice exams which, she believes, distort the information being tested and deliberately mislead students. In regard to another course, she described what she viewed as boring, even confusing lectures, but she persevered: "Because I don't like the professor, I work even harder. I don't want him to laugh at me. I don't want to be dehumanized. I came here to learn something, to gain something." In yet another course in which only the professor talked, she indicated that she was "drowning in his words." Even a class which assigned frequent written work, which Motoko completed successfully, disappointed her because she had such difficulty understanding the assignments and because her writing was not responded to in what she perceived as a thoughtful, respectful way. Motoko confided that despite her success in this course, she had lost interest in working on her papers.

The other student whose classroom experiences I've been following is Martha, a student from Colombia who, like Motoko, has taken a range of courses, and whose major is biology. Unlike Motoko, who had managed to negotiate "drowning words" and problematic assignments, Martha's sense of discouragement about the purposelessness of much of her work is far more pervasive. With respect to many of her courses, she complained about the absence of writing (which she views as essential for learning), the passive nature of class discussions, contrived assignments that "don't help her think about anything," and the lifeless comments she received. It was in her science courses, however, that she felt the greatest dissatisfaction and frustration. About one chemistry course, she spoke of "just trying to follow the lectures and get a grade in a huge class" that she characterized as a "disaster." She talked of the sense of superiority her professors project, of her inability to learn anything meaningful from assignments which require everyone "to come up with the same information." Her experiences have provoked her to write numerous pieces which reflect her growing sense of despair and which provide a rich commentary on her perspective and experiences. In one of these pieces she has labeled the way professors behave as "academic harassment." In yet another, she questions the purpose of schooling, assignments, and written work: "Each teacher should ask her or himself the next question: Why do I assign a writing paper on this class? Do you want to see creativity and reflection of students or do or want a reproduction of the same book concept?" She is frustrated by the "lack of connections with the material we listen on lectures," the "monotony of the teaching method," the "limited style of questions," the "stressful process of learning." She concludes:

> I have no new words in my lexicon. And how do I know that? From my writing. No fluency. Why? I don't write. I was moving forward and now I'm

stagnant. . . . Frustration and lack of interest are the present feelings with my classes because there is not any planned "agenda" to encourage the students to improve ourselves by writing. There is no rich opportunity to break barriers and answer questions to others and also to myself. There is no REACTION and INTERACTION . . . It does not really matter how many courses the students take in order to improve skills of writing because what it counts is the responsibility encouraged by the teacher's method! the kind of responsibility developed around us is first with *ourselves!* It is an incentive for us to be listened and respected by our writing work! You get into it. Reading provides you grammar. Reading and writing are not separate in the process. It is a combined one. Doble team. Reacting and interacting.

This account, like others Martha has written, reveals her commitment to learning, her insightful understanding of how learning is both promoted and undermined, how writing in particular plays an essential role in this learning, how critical it is for teachers to contribute to and encourage learning. She, like Motoko and the other students surveyed, has much to tell us about the barriers that prevent learning and how these barriers can be broken. And lest we conclude that what these students perceive about their experiences is specific to ESL learners, recent studies of teaching and learning in higher education indicate that this is not the case. For example, Chiseri-Strater's ethnography of university classrooms reveals the authoritarian and limited ways that subject matter is often approached, the ways in which students, even those who are successful, are left silent and empty by the contrived and inconsequential work of many classrooms.

This ongoing exploration of the expectations, perceptions and experiences of both faculty and students has clarified much for me about the academic life of ESL students and what we ought to be doing both within our classrooms and beyond. Given the hierarchical arrangement of coursework within post-secondary schools, given the primacy accorded to traditional discipline-specific courses, it is not surprising that ESL and other writing-based courses have a marginalized position, that these courses are thought to have no authentic content, that the work that goes on in these courses is not considered to be the "real" work of the academy.

This view typically gets played out through coursework that is determined by what students are assumed to need in courses across the curriculum, coursework whose function it is to "guard the tower," to use Shaughnessy's term, and keep the gates closed in the case of students who are not deemed ready to enter ("Diving"). This often implies instruction that focuses on grammar, decontextualized language skills, and surface features of language. And we know from what faculty continue to say about these issues that this is precisely what is expected of English and ESL instruction—and, unfortunately, many of us have been all too ready to comply. Mike Rose speaks to the profoundly exclusionary nature of such a pedagogy and argues that a focus on mechanical skills and grammatical features reduces the complexity of language to simple and discrete problems, keeps teachers from exploring students' knowledge and potential, and contributes to the "second-class intellectual status" to which the teaching of writing has been assigned ("Language" 348). Furthermore, the problematic assumption that writing or ESL programs are in place to serve the academy, that their function is to benefit other academic studies, prevents us from questioning our situation within the larger institution. "Service course ideology," Tom Fox points out, "often leaves the curricular decisions in the hands of those who are not especially knowledgeable about writing instruction," which ultimately means that "political questions—in fact, *any* questions that challenge existing definitions of basic writing—become irrelevant to the bureaucratic task of reproducing the program" ("Basic" 67).

While skills-based and deficit models of instruction bring these kinds of pressures to bear on our work with students, our teaching has further been constrained by composition specialists who make claims about the need for students to adopt the language and discourse conventions of the academy if they are to succeed. David Bartholomae's article, "Inventing the University," is often cited and called upon to argue that students need to approximate and adopt the "specialized discourse of the university" (17). In the ESL literature, a reductive version of this position has been embraced by professionals who maintain that the role that ESL coursework ought to play is one of preparing students for the expectations and demands of discipline-specific communities across the curriculum. Such an approach, however, misrepresents and oversimplifies academic discourse and reduces it to some stable and autonomous phenomenon that does not reflect reality. Such instruction, like coursework shaped by limited conceptualizations of language, undermines *our* expertise and position. And because such instruction privileges and perpetuates the status quo, because it exaggerates the "distinctiveness of academic discourse [and] its separation from student literacy" (Fox, "Basic" 70), such a pedagogy has been characterized in terms of assimilation, colonization, domination, and deracination (Clark; Fox; Gay; Horner; Trimbur).

While there is growing debate about this instructional approach in the field of composition, there have been fewer attempts to problematize this model of teaching in ESL composition, where the norms and conventions of the English language and its discourses have particularly powerful political implications.[3] Hence the need to raise questions about such an instructional focus when it is applied to our work with non-native speakers of English. As I have argued elsewhere, we need to critique approaches that are reductive and formulaic, examine the notion that the language of the academy is a monolithic discourse that can be packaged and transmitted to students, and argue that this attempt to serve the institution in these ways contributes to our marginal status and that of our students.

Those of us who have tried to accommodate institutional demands have, no doubt, found this to be a troubling and tension-filled undertaking, since even when we focus on standards of language use or conventions of academic discourse, students, especially those who are still acquiring English, are not necessarily more successful in meeting the expectations of other faculty. There seems to be little carry-over from such instructional efforts to subsequent work since it is the very nature of such narrowly conceptualized instruction that undercuts genuine learning. As Fox argues, writing teachers who uphold a mythical and fixed set of institutional standards and skills are enacting a pedagogy that, however well-intentioned, is an "unqualifiable failure" ("Standards" 42). Those of us who have resisted and questioned such a pedagogy, embracing a richer and more complicated understanding of how language, discourse, and context are intertwined, may be able to trace the strides students make and to appreciate the intelligence their language and writing reveal, and yet find that this is not extended by other faculty who cannot imagine taking on this kind of responsibility.

We need to recognize that in the same way that faculty establish what Martha calls "barriers" between themselves and students, in the same way that faculty "exoticize" ESL students, we too, especially if our primary work is with ESL students, are perceived as "outsiders."[4] And as long as these boundaries continue to delineate and separate what we and other faculty do, as long as we are expected to "fix" students' problems, then misunderstandings, unfulfilled expectations, frustration, and even resentment will continue to mark our experiences. But this need not be the case. We are beginning to see changes in institutions in response to the growing recognition that faculty across the disciplines must take responsibility for working with all students. Studies, such as the ethnography undertaken by Walvoord and McCarthy, have documented the transformation of faculty from a range of disciplines who became more responsive to the needs of their students as they undertook their own classroom research and examined their own assumptions and expectations.

In my own work with faculty at a number of different institutions, including my own, what first begins as a concern about "underprepared" or "deficient" ESL students often leads to a consideration of the same kinds of pedagogical issues that are at the heart of writing across the curriculum initiatives. But these issues are reconsidered with specific reference to working with ESL students. Together, we have explored our instructional goals, the purposes for assigned work, the means for reading and evaluating this work, the roles that engagement, context, and classroom dynamics play in promoting learning. Through this collaboration faculty have begun to understand that it is unrealistic and ultimately counterproductive to expect writing and ESL programs to be responsible for providing students with the language, discourse, and multiple ways of seeing required across courses. They are recognizing that the process of acquisition is slow-paced and continues to evolve with exposure, immersion, and involvement, that learning is responsive to situations in which students are invited to participate in the construction of meaning and knowledge. They have come to realize that every discipline, indeed every classroom, may represent a distinct culture and thus needs to make it possible for those new to the context to practice and approximate its "ways with words." Along with acknowledging the implications of an essentialist view of language and of the myth of transience, we have considered the myth of coverage, the belief that covering course content necessarily means that it has been learned. Hull and Rose, in their study of the logic underlying a student's unconventional reading of a text, critique "the desire of efficiency and coverage" for the ways it "limit[s] rather than enhance[s] [students'] participation in intellectual work" (296), for the ways it undermines students' entry into the academy. With this in mind, we have raised questions about what we do in order to cover material, why we do what we do, what we expect from students, and how coverage is evaluated. And if the "cover-the-material" model doesn't seem to be working in the ways we expected, we ask, what alternatives are there?

We have also examined the ways in which deficit thinking, a focus on difference, blinds us to the logic, intelligence and richness of students' processes and knowledge. In *Lives on the Boundary*, Mike Rose cites numerous cases of learners (including himself) whose success was undercut because of the tendency to emphasize difference. Studies undertaken by Glynda Hull and her colleagues further attest to how such belief systems about students can lead to inaccurate judgments about learners' abilities, and how practices based on such beliefs perpetuate and "virtually assure failure" (325). The excerpt from the tutor's journal quoted at the beginning of this article, along with many of the faculty and student responses that I have elicited, are yet other indications of what happens when our reading of student work is derailed by a focus on what is presumed to be students' deficiencies. Thus we try to read students' texts to see what is there rather than what isn't, resisting generalizations about literacy and intelligence that are made on the basis of judgments about standards of correctness and form, and suspending our judgments about the alternative rhetorical approaches our students adopt.

In addition to working with faculty to shape the curriculum so that it is responsive to students' needs and to generate instructional approaches that build on students' competence, we address other institutional practices that affect our students. At the University of Massachusetts, for example, the Writing Proficiency Exam, which all students must pass by the time they are juniors, continues to evolve as faculty across the curriculum work together, implementing and modifying it over time. While the exam is impressive, immersing students in rich, thematically-integrated material to read, think about, and respond to, it nevertheless continues to be reconsidered and questioned as we study the ways in which the exam impinges on students' academic lives. And so, for instance, in order to address the finding that ESL students were failing the exam at higher rates than native speakers of English—a situation that is occurring at other institutions as well (see Ray)—we have tried to ensure that faculty understand how to look below the surface of student texts for evidence of proficiency, promoting a kind of reading that benefits not just ESL students but all students. The portfolio option, which requires students to submit papers written in courses as well as to write an essay in response to a set of readings, has proven a better alternative for ESL students to demonstrate writing proficiency. This is not surprising, given that the portfolio allows students to demonstrate what they are capable of when writing is imbedded within and an outgrowth of their courses.

Throughout this work, one of the most critical notions that I try to bring home is the idea that what faculty ought to be doing to enhance the learning of ESL students is *not* a concession, a capitulation, a giving up of standards— since the unrevised approaches that some faculty want to retain may never have been beneficial for *any* students. As John Mayher has pointed out, teaching and learning across college courses are by and large dysfunctional for all students, even those that succeed. What ESL students need—multiple opportunities to use language and write-to-learn, course work which draws on and values what students already know, classroom exchanges and assignments that promote the acquisition of unfamiliar language, concepts, and approaches to inquiry, evaluation that allows students to demonstrate genuine understanding—is good pedagogy for everyone. Learning how to better address the needs of ESL students, because it involves becoming more reflective about teaching, because it involves carefully thinking through the expectations, values, and assumptions underlying the work we assign, helps faculty teach everyone better. In other words, rather than seeing the implications of inclusion and diversity in opposition to excellence and academic standards (as they often are at meetings convened to discuss these issues), learning to teach ESL students, because this challenges us to reconceptualize teaching, contributes to and enhances learning, and for all students. As Gerald Graff has argued in response to those who voice their concerns about the presence of new student populations in their institutions and the negative consequences that this change brings,

> Conservatives who accuse affirmative action programs of lowering academic standards never mention the notorious standard for ignorance that was set by white male college students before women and minorities were permitted in large numbers on campus. It has been the steady pressure for reform from below that has raised academic standards. (88)

Needless to say, given the complexity of this enterprise, these efforts have not transformed classrooms on an institution-wide basis. As is obvious from the surveys and case studies I have undertaken, change is slow, much like the process of learning itself. Shaughnessy referred to the students who entered the CUNY system through open admissions as "strangers in academia" to give us a sense of the cultural and linguistic alienation they were experiencing (*Errors*). In listening to the comments of faculty (note, for example, the comment of the professor of management), it occurs to me that they too are feeling like strangers in academia, that they no longer understand the world in which they work. Janice Neulieb similarly points out that although it is common to view students as "other," as alienated from the academic community, our differing cultural perspectives result in our own confusion and alienation as well.

As we grapple with the kinds of issues and concerns raised by the clash of cultures in academia, we continue to make adjustments which, in turn, generate new questions about our practices. This ongoing dialogue is both necessary and beneficial. Like other prominent debates in higher education on reforming the canon and the implications of diversity, this attempt to explore and interrogate what we do is slowly reconfiguring the landscape and blurring the borders within what was once a fairly well-defined and stable academic community. According to Graff, this is all to the good because this kind of transformation can revitalize higher education and its isolated departments and fragmentary curricula. Within composition, the conflicts and struggles that inevitably mark the teaching of writing are viewed as instructive because they allow students and teachers to "reposition" themselves, raising questions about conventional thinking about instruction and challenging us to imagine alternative pedagogies (Lu; Horner). What Pratt calls the "contact zone," because it represents a site of contestation, is embraced because it enables us to redraw disciplinary boundaries, to reexamine composition instruction, and to revise our assumptions about language and difference.

When faculty see this kind of redefinition as a crisis, I invite them to reconsider their work in light of the way the word "crisis" is translated into Chinese. In Chinese, the word is symbolized by two ideographs—one meaning danger, the other meaning opportunity. Because the challenges that students bring with them may make us feel confused, uncertain, like strangers in our own community, there will be dissonance, jarring questions, ongoing dilemmas, unfulfilled expectations. We can see this reflected in the second faculty response, a response which insists that there are students who don't belong in the academy, that its doors be kept closed. But, as we saw in the first response, perplexities and tensions can also be generative, creating possibilities for new insights, alternative interpretations, and an appreciation for the ways in which these enrich our understanding.

Seen from the fresh perspective that another language can provide, the Chinese translation of crisis captures the very nature of learning, a process involving both risk and opportunity, the very process that ideally students ought to engage in, but which we ourselves may resist when it comes to looking at our own practices. But as Giroux urges, teachers must "cross over borders that are culturally strange and alien to them" so that they can "analyze their own values and voices as viewed from different ideological and cultural spaces" (254–55). It is when we take risks of this sort, when we take this step into the unknown, by looking for evidence of students' intelligence, by rereading their attempts as coherent efforts, by valuing, not just evaluating, their work, and by reflecting on the critical relationship between our work and theirs, that opportunities are created not only for students but for teachers to learn in new ways.

NOTES

1. The acronym ESL (English as a Second Language) is used here because it is the commonly used term to refer to students whose native language is not English. Given the inherently political nature of working with ESL learners, it is important to note that at urban institutions, such as the University of Massachusetts at Boston, most of these students are residents of the United States. Furthermore, in the case of a number of these students, English may be a third or fourth language.
2. This investigation of student responses was first initiated by Spack, whose findings were published in *Blair Resources for Teaching Writing: English as a Second Language*. My ongoing survey builds on her work.
3. See, however, the work of Benesch, McKay, Raimes, and Zamel—all of whom have raised questions about the ideological assumptions underlying much ESL writing instruction.
4. I am indebted here to Patricia Bizzell, whom I first heard use the term *exoticize* to characterize how faculty often react towards ESL students.

WORKS CITED

Bartholomae, David. "Inventing the University." *Journal of Basic Writing* 5 (Spring 1986): 4–23.
Benesch, Sarah. "ESL, Ideology, and the Politics of Pragmatism." *TESOL Quarterly* 27 (1993): 705–17.
Chiseri-Strater, Elizabeth. *Academic Literacies: The Public and Private Discourse of University Students*. Portsmouth: Boynton, 1991.
Clark, Gregory. "Rescuing the Discourse of Community." *CCC* 45 (1994): 61–74.
Fox, Tom. "Basic Writing as Cultural Conflict." *Journal of Education* 172 (1990): 65–83.
———. "Standards and Access." *Journal of Basic Writing* 12 (Spring 1993): 37–45.
Gay, Pamela. "Rereading Shaughnessy from a Postcolonial Perspective." *Journal of Basic Writing* 12 (Fall 1993): 29–40.
Giroux, Henry. "Postmodernism as Border Pedagogy: Redefining the Boundaries of Race and Ethnicity." *Postmodernism, Feminism, and Cultural Politics: Redrawing Educational Boundaries*. Ed. Henry Giroux. Albany: State U of New York P, 1991. 217–56.

Graff, Gerald. *Beyond the Culture Wars*. New York: Norton, 1992.

Horner, Bruce. "Mapping Errors and Expectations for Basic Writing: From 'Frontier Field' to 'Border Country.'" *English Education* 26 (1994): 29–51.

Hull, Glynda, and Mike Rose. "'This Wooden Shack Place': The Logic of an Unconventional Reading." *CCC* 41 (1990): 287–98.

Hull, Glynda, Mike Rose, Kay Losey Fraser, and Marisa Castellano. "Remediation as Social Construct: Perspectives from an Analysis of Classroom Discourse." *CCC* 42 (1991): 299–329.

Laurence, Patricia. "The Vanishing Site of Mina Shaughnessy's *Errors and Expectations*." *Journal of Basic Writing* 12 (Fall 1993): 18–28.

Lu, Min-Zhan. "Conflict and Struggle in Basic Writing." *College English* 54 (1992): 887–913.

Mayher, John S. "Uncommon Sense in the Writing Center." *Journal of Basic Writing* 11 (Spring 1992): 47–57.

McKay, Sandra Lee. "Examining L2 Composition Ideology: A Look at Literacy Education." *Journal of Second Language Writing* 2 (1993): 65–81.

Neuleib, Janice. "The Friendly Stranger: Twenty-Five Years as 'Other.'" *CCC* 43 (1992): 231–43.

Pratt, Mary Louise. "Arts of the Contact Zone." *Profession 91* (1991): 33–40.

Raimes, Ann. "Out of the Woods: Emerging Traditions in the Teaching of Writing." *TESOL Quarterly* 25 (1991): 407–30.

Ray, Ruth. "Language and Literacy from the Student Perspective: What We Can Learn from the Long-term Case Study." *The Writing Teacher as Researcher*. Ed. Donald A. Daiker and Max Morenberg. Portsmouth: Boynton, 1990. 321–35.

Rose, Mike. *Lives on the Boundary: The Struggles and Achievements of America's Underprepared*. New York: Free P, 1989.

———. "The Language of Exclusion: Writing Instruction at the University." *College English* 47 (1985): 341–59.

Shaughnessy, Mina. "Diving In: An Introduction to Basic Writing." *CCC* 27 (1976): 234–39.

———. *Errors and Expectations*. New York: Oxford UP, 1977.

Spack, Ruth. *Blair Resources for Teaching Writing: English as a Second Language*. New York: Prentice, 1994.

Trimbur, John. "'Really Useful Knowledge' in the Writing Classroom." *Journal of Education* 172 (1990): 21–23.

Villanueva, Victor. *Bootstraps: From an American Academic of Color*. Urbana: NCTE, 1993.

Walvoord, Barbara E., and Lucille B. McCarthy. *Thinking and Writing in College: A Naturalistic Study of Students in Four Disciplines*. Urbana: NCTE, 1990.

Zamel, Vivian. "Questioning Academic Discourse." *College ESL* 3 (1993): 28–39.

Borrowing Others' Words:
Text, Ownership, Memory,
and Plagiarism

Alastair Pennycook

A number of years ago, when I was teaching at Xiangtan University in China, I asked my first-year undergraduate English majors to write a brief biography of a well-known person (such exciting tasks do we set our students). When I was grading these, I came across one toward the bottom of the pile that had a strange quality to it. It was a short piece on Abraham Lincoln (Why Abraham Lincoln? I wondered), written in rather simple but perfectly "correct" prose: "Abraham Lincoln was born in a log cabin in 1809 . . ." (or words to that effect). It had the ring of a text from elsewhere, of language borrowed and repeated. Because I was at the time supervising my fourth-year students' teaching practice in Yiyang, a small town in the north of Hunan, I asked one of them what he thought about this text. He looked at the first two lines and smiled. The text, he explained, was from one of the high school textbooks. So did that mean, I asked, that it had been copied? Well, not necessarily, the student replied, and then demonstrated that he too knew the text by heart: "Abraham Lincoln was born in a log cabin . . ." When I got back to Xiangtan University, I sought out the first-year student and asked him about his text. He explained that although he felt that he had not really done the task I had set, because I had asked them to do some research prior to writing, he had felt rather fortunate that I had asked them to write something which he already knew. Sitting in his head was a brief biography of Abraham Lincoln, and he was quite happy to produce it on demand: "Abraham Lincoln was born in a log cabin . . ."

Whereas I might have responded to this with moral outrage or delivered a lecture on plagiarism, or "academic norms," I found instead that I was rather fascinated by the issues it raised: questions about ownership of texts, practices of memory, and writing. Because all language learning is, to some extent, a practice of memorization of the words of others, on what grounds do we see certain acts of textual borrowing as acceptable and others as unacceptable? How have the boundaries been drawn between the acceptable memorizing and use of word lists, phrases, sentences (remember *English 900* with its 900 sentences to be memorized?), paragraphs, poems, quotations, and so on and the unacceptable reuse of others' words? How is it that notions of ownership of text have developed? When does one come to own a language sufficiently that to say something "in one's own words" makes sense? And how can we come to deal with different relationships to text and memorization in different cultural contexts? I recall some time after this incident talking to some of my Chinese colleagues about memorization and language learning. I was arguing that although memorization of texts might be a useful learning technique, it could never lead to productive, original language use (this, we have been taught to believe, is one of those "facts" of second language acquisition). I gave as an example one of our colleagues who was acknowledged as one of the most eloquent and fluent speakers in the department, suggesting that he could never have become so if he had been a mere memorizer. The others smiled, for this other colleague was known not only as an excellent user of English but also as someone with a fine talent for memorizing texts. Again, pause for thought. I knew that when we sat and drank beer and talked philosophy, he wasn't speaking texts to me. How had he come to own the language as he did, when that had apparently been done by borrowing others' language?

When I worked in Hong Kong more recently, parallel puzzles about ownership of text emerged in "moderation meetings," in which a number of us teaching on the same course compare grades for the same essays. Although such meetings often produce, in any case, quite extraordinarily divergent views on what is and what is not a good piece of writing, there is nothing like the hint of something borrowed to radically split the meeting down the middle: Some teachers will heap praise on an essay while others are pouring scorn on it. The issue, almost invariably, is whether it is the student's "own work." And the trigger for both the praise and the scorn can sometimes be as little as a two- or three-word phrase. For some, it is a felicitous phrase, appropriately used, suggesting someone with a good feel for language; for others, it is a phrase that could not be part of this student's "competence" (such is the tyranny of our knowledge of students' interlanguages and competency levels), thus casting doubt not only over the origins of this phrase but also the origins of the rest of the text. The lines are drawn and the arguments rage over whether the essay warrants a D (or worse) or an A. Ironically, once the spectre of doubtful ownership is raised, teachers start to look for grammatical errors as a sign of good writing and to become suspicious when such errors are crucially absent. Our criteria are turned on their head: Suddenly we are looking either for language that is "too good" in order to incriminate the student, or we are looking for evidence of errors in order to exonerate the student. Thus, we end up in the "paradoxical state of affairs that the worse an essay is linguistically, the better mark it is perceived to merit" (Hutton, 1990). From being teachers constantly in search of sophisticated and standard language use, we become detectives in search of evidence that some chunk of language has been illegitimately used.

Indeed, once we start to explore the whole question of textual borrowing, the notion of ownership of text and learning becomes very complex. It is important to understand the cultural and historical specificity of notions of ownership and authorship and to explore the implications of these concepts' being increasingly promoted as international norms. Plagiarism also needs to be particularized in other ways: In terms of the particular cultural and educational context in which it is being discussed—what are the relationships to text, knowledge, and learning in a particular cultural context? And in terms of the nature of the institution and the particular language in which it is seen to be occurring: Is an educational institute promoting or thwarting creative thoughts, and in what language is it asking students to function academically? And in terms of what is understood as shared language or knowledge and particular language or knowledge: At what point does a phrase or an idea become owned? And at what point does it become public? Other interesting complexities arise: How do we understand the relationship between language and knowledge? What are we to make of the academic emphasis on repeating the ideas of others while doing so in our own words? Why is it that many teachers seem to react to supposed acts of plagiarism with such moral outrage? How important is the notion of intentionality: Is the issue that certain words are not the students' own, or is it more important to understand the intention behind the apparent borrowing? And is it perhaps useful to distinguish between notions of good and bad plagiarism?

THE ORIGINALITY MYTH:
FROM DIVINE TO DISCURSIVE VENTRILOQUY

Constructing the Author

In order to understand how Western views on textual ownership have developed, we need to examine in greater detail what it means to be original, an author, and how it is that author, authenticity, and authority are so closely intertwined in Western thought. What, then, does it mean to be original, to say something new? In his genealogy of Western imagination, Kearney (1988) identifies three dominant paradigms, the *mimetic* (premodern), the *productive* (modern), and the *parodic* (postmodern). In the premodern, mimetic era (biblical, classical, and medieval), the image stood as a representation of reality, as a means through which nature, and especially God, could be worshiped. For both Aristotle and Plato, imagination remained "largely a *reproductive* rather than a *productive* activity, a servant rather than a master of meaning, imitation rather than origin" (p. 113, emphasis in original). The great monotheistic religions are still tied to a position that it is divine, not human, inspiration that produced their texts (a view notoriously transgressed by Salman Rushdie). It was not until the great shift of thinking in Europe that became known as the Enlightenment that this view of imagination shifted and was replaced by the productive paradigm of the modern. In this view, the imagination was no longer viewed as a mimetic capacity but as a productive force: "As a consequence of this momentous reversal of roles, meaning is no longer primarily considered as a transcendent property of divine being; it is now hailed as a transcendental product of the human mind" (p. 155). Shifting from the earlier onto-theological view of meaning, the humanist subject now became the center of creativity. It is this view of meaning as held in place by the humanist subject which, once coupled with the notion of property rights, produced an understanding of individual ownership of ideas and language.

This understanding of imagination is clearly closely tied to the development of the notion of the author. The medieval concept of the author put great store on the authority and authenticity bestowed on a text by the *auctor*. In this view, texts were given truth and authority by dint of having been written long ago by famous men: As Minnis (1984) suggests, the only good author was a dead author. But it was the development of print, Ong (1982) argues, that "created a new sense of the private ownership of words" (p. 131). Tracing back the history of the development of the notion of the author, Foucault (1984) suggests that there was, in the 17th or 18th centuries, a reversal of the need for authorial attribution. Prior to this, he suggests, literary work was generally accepted without a notion of an author, an observation that accords with Kearney's (1988) that the premodern imaginative work was generally unauthored because it was the representation of reality or the creation of a religious icon through which God could be worshiped that was of importance, not the image-making itself. Scientific work (texts on medicine, cosmology, and natural science), by contrast, were accepted as true by dint of their authorship. This, Foucault suggests, was reversed in the 17th and 18th centuries, when the authorship of individual works of literature as individual acts of creativity became crucial, whereas the scientific domain evolved into a more general unauthored agreement on scientific truths. Kearney (1988) suggests that "the coming into being of the notion of 'author' constitutes the privileged moment of individualization in the history of ideas, knowledge, literature, philosophy, and the sciences" (p. 101).

What is of significance in the description of these shifts of creativity and authorship is the need to see a stress on "new" meaning, on originality, on individual creativity, as very much an aspect of Western modernity, and thus both a very particular cultural and a very particular historical emphasis, albeit one with a great deal of salience in the world today. It is with the rise of such individualization that the history of literary plagiarism started to emerge (the notion of copyright and thus "intellectual property" was encoded in British law in 1710; see Willinsky, 1990). Thus, as Willinsky (1990) puts it, "this contest of creative imitation, invention, and authority, which has been at the heart of the force of the book as an intellectual property, is secured by the concept of an originating author, an actual body that gave life to words" (p. 77). In this development, then, we can see the conjunction between the development of the notion of the author and the development of individual property rights, which, allied to other developments such as printing, produced a very particular vision of ownership of language and ideas.

Modernist Tensions

Despite the strength of this vision, backed up as it was not only by philosophical underpinnings but also by legal sanctions, it also seems to have been a view with many tensions and ambiguities. One thing that is immediately striking when reading about textual borrowing is how remarkably common it has been and still is, and thus how textual borrowing has always been with us to an extent that the purer humanists and modernists would be unwilling to admit. As Mallon (1989) puts it, "the Romans rewrote the Greeks. Virgil is, in a broadly imitative way, Homer, and for that matter, typologists can find most of the Old Testament in the New" (p. 4). White's (1965) study of plagiarism in the English Renaissance raises similar interesting concerns. As he points out, the classical heritage on which the Renaissance drew was itself a period full of imitation: A great deal of the flourishing of Roman arts was based on free imitation of Greek works. When the writers of the European Renaissance turned back to their classical heritage, they not only revived art that had based itself on free imitation, but they also based their own work on the free imitation of this period. But this has always been the case for a great deal of artistic creation: As T. S. Eliot (1975) put it, the "most individual parts" of an artist's work may be precisely those "in which the dead poets, his ancestors, assert their immortality most vigorously" (p. 38).

What emerges from studies of literary plagiarism such as Mallon (1989) or Shaw (1982) is a very confused and complex picture.[1] First of all, the list of accused plagiarists is long and prestigious, including Laurence Sterne, Samuel Coleridge, Thomas De Quincey, Edgar Allan Poe, Norman Mailer, Alex Hailey (*Roots*), Dee Brown (*Bury My Heart at Wounded Knee*), Martin Luther King, Gail Sheehy (*Passages*), Jacob Epstein (*Wild Oats*), Helen Keller, and many more. Second, part of the difficulty here lies in the relationship between the demand for originality and the reverence of other writers, a tension that occurs when "the demand for novelty meets the sensitive writer's normal worship of the great literary past" (Mallon, 1989, p. 24). There is, therefore, a constant interplay between creativity and previous writing, a relationship which, as we shall see, is particularly significant in the context in which we teach. Third, the writers themselves or their supporters will often go to extreme lengths to exonerate the writer from accusations of unoriginality. Anything from poor note-taking to psychological disturbances, from unconscious errors to clever parodying are suggested once it is shown that a great author's originality is brought into question. The debates around Laurence Sterne's *Tristram Shandy*, for example, are intriguing because his work is seen both as highly original, a precursor to much later 20th-century literary experimentation, and also as heavily reliant on a number of other sources. The common explanation among Sterne scholars is that there was a kind of mockery going on here, a parodying of others' work, and that those who accuse him of plagiarism misunderstand his work, his humor, and his originality.

The Individualist-Romanticist view of originality that emerged in the modern era, then, also carried with it many of the seeds of its own destruction, rife as it was contradictions, borrowings, and pretended originalities. An understanding of the whole Orientalist-Romanticist trait in

---

[1]Indeed, as Mallon (1989) and Shaw (1982) show, there seem to be some strange psychological aspects to plagiarism, including a tendency to "give the game away" (Shaw, 1982, p. 330). It was De Quincey, for example, who leveled the accusations of plagiarism against Coleridge soon after the latter's death in 1834, an accusation which, as Mallon suggests, was ironic because De Quincey had previously stated a great aversion to such accusations and because he himself was yet another in the great line of literary plagiarists. According to Mallon (1989), "Coleridge's case suggests that he may have been addicted not just to opium but to plagiarism itself, flirting with the equivalent of an overdose in the risks of exposure he ran" (pp. 34–35). Plagiarists, it seems, like Dostoevski's Raskolnikov, arsonists who return to the scene of the crime, and serial killers who write ever more revealing notes to the police and newspapers, draw attention to themselves, whether as a result of guilt, a desire to be found out, or the thrill of flirting with the threat of exposure. "Giving the game away," suggests Shaw, "proves to be the rule rather than the exception among plagiarists" (p. 330).

European writing (the search for the "exotic" in distant places to revive the flagging powers of European creativity) reveals how the great claims to European exploration and discovery were another powerful set of myths. The actual physical invasions and colonizations of this period were of course very real, but the discoveries of difference were in many ways little more than repetitions of European tropes. As Tatlow's (1993) discussion of Gauguin shows, for example, what was really discovered in these voyages of European discovery was nothing but another part of the European imaginary: monsters, cannibals, and primitive natives. Furthermore, as Tatlow suggests, Gauguin was, like most artists, part of a larger tradition of massive borrowing: "Like Brecht, Gauguin borrowed from everywhere. His disdain for originality was his mark of it and, as Delacroix observed of Raphael: 'Nowhere did he reveal his originality so forcefully as in the ideas he borrowed' " (p. 5).

Once one starts to take a closer look at the context of textual borrowing, then, it is hard not to feel that language use is marked far more by the circulation and recirculation of words and ideas than by a constant process of creativity. One thing that emerges from a recent book on spurious quotations and misquotations (Keyes, 1992), for example, is the vast amount of constant borrowing that goes on in the field of quotations. In one chapter, Keyes reports research by Robert Newcomb that reveals that many aphorisms generally attributed to Benjamin Franklin were in fact lifted from other sources, virtually word for word. Although Franklin pointed to this practice when he asked, "Why should I give my Readers bad lines of my own when good ones of other People's are so plenty?" (quoted in Keyes, p. 31), he never acknowledged that his great collection of aphorisms were indeed the good lines of others. As Keyes shows, in fact, many of the famous lines attributed to various American presidents also have much older origins. These include Kennedy's "Ask not what your country can do for you; ask what you can do for your country," which is remarkably similar to various other sayings such as Oliver Wendell Holmes Jr.'s 1884 request to an audience to "recall what our country has done for each of us, and to ask ourselves what we can do for our country in return" (Keyes, 1992, p. 91). Other famous examples include Franklin Roosevelt's "The only thing we have to fear is fear itself," which had already been said in more or less the same words by Montaigne in 1580, Francis Bacon in 1623, the Duke of Wellington in 1832, and Thoreau in 1851. By the time we get to Ronald Reagan, whose fallible memory and inability to distinguish between fact and fiction are legendary, examples abound. It is worth noting here that because these examples are known to us today because they exist in the writings or sayings of well-known writers, so they must surely be but the tip of a vast iceberg of such repetitions.

Now it is tempting to chuckle at these famous sayings echoing through the years, and perhaps to cluck one's tongue at the thought that some of this must have been done wittingly. Yet I believe that these simple examples point to a far more significant series of questions. First, is it perhaps the case that there really is nothing, or at least very little, new to be said? As Goethe (1963/1829) once said "Alles Gescheite ist schon gedacht worden, man muß nur versuchen, es noch einmal zu denken" (Everything clever has already been thought; one must only try to think it again; *Maximen und Reflexionen*, p. 52). Rather than the generativist-grammarian view of language as an infinite production of sentences—a view that suggests that such linguists have rarely been in a conversation, read a newspaper, or indeed encountered any form of language use—is it not far more significant to focus on the social production and the circulation of meanings? A view of language that relates its use to social, cultural, and ideological domains suggests that we need to go beyond a view of language as an infinite series of decontextualized sentences or as the idiosyncratic production of a completely free-willed subject. Second, if it is in fact so hard to pin down the real originator of a quotation, are we perhaps engaged here in a false teleology, an impossible search for the first speaking or writing of certain words? Indeed, is it not possible that in some ways our endless books of apparently dubiously attributed quotations (or indeed all of our cherished canon of "authored" works) are a product of a search both to attribute authorship to certain words and to elevate writers to their canonical status by attributing pithy sayings to them? Is it the case that the insistence on the authorship of quotations, poems, books, and so on has less to do with authorial (author-real?) creation of texts and far more to do with textual creation of authors?

Postmodern Uncertainty: The Death of the Author

The notion of the individual as creative guarantor of meaning and originality, this particular vision of self and authenticity, has, of course, taken a fair battering since Marx, Freud, and others have questioned the notion of the unmediated and authentic expression of self. Dominant though this modernist paradigm of the author has been, it is now being questioned by the parodic paradigm of the postmodern. In the wake of both the "death of God" and the "death of the subject," imagination and creativity become nothing but a play of images themselves, images that neither reference a reality nor are the products of a human subject. According to Kearney (1988), "one of the greatest paradoxes of contemporary culture is that at a time when the image reigns supreme the very notion of a creative human imagination seems under mounting threat" (p. 3). The postmodern and poststructuralist positions on language, discourse, and subjectivity, therefore, raise serious questions for any notion of individual creativity or authorship. If, instead of a Self or an Identity, we consider the notion of subjectivity, or indeed subjectivities (we are, in a sense, the fragmented products of different discourses), then we arrive at more or less a reversal of the speaking subject creating meaning: We are not speaking subjects but spoken subjects, we do not create language but are created by it. As I suggested earlier, the question then becomes not so much one of who authored a text but how we are authored by texts.[2] Thus, the development of a notion of creativity can be seen to move from an external position, in which the origin of meanings has some determinate source, especially in the word of God (the divine ventriloquist);[3] through an internal version of meaning, in which the individual was seen as the originator and guarantor of meaning (the speaking subject); and back to an external model, where meanings play off each other without any stable referent (discursive ventriloquy).

As Kearney (1988) suggests, "Postmodernism casts a suspecting glance on the modernist cult of creative originality" (p. 21). This skepticism about creative originality is linked not only to the "death of the subject," but also more specifically to the announcement of the "death of the author," signaled most emphatically by Roland Barthes (1977). Arguing, like Foucault (1984), that the notion of the author was very much a construction of modernity, Barthes (1977) states that "a text is not a line of words releasing a single 'theological' meaning (the 'message' of the Author-God) but a multi-dimensional space in which a variety of writings, none of them original, blend and clash. The text is a tissue of quotations drawn from the innumerable centres of culture" (p. 146). "[T]o give writing its future," Barthes argues, "it is necessary to overthrow the myth: the birth of the reader must be at the cost of the death of the Author" (p. 148). Barthes suggests that by doing away with the notion of the author, writing can no longer be seen as an act of representation, and meaning can no longer be attached to some authorial intent. Linking this idea to speech act theory, he suggests that all writing is nothing but "a performative," having "no other content . . . than the act by which it is uttered" (p. 146).[4]

---

[2]Of course, there are dangers with this position. Although it helps to move away from the foundational concept of a core self or rationality, it may leave us little more than discursive ventriloquists. We need, therefore, to theorize a notion of agency or voice in order that we do not reduce subjectivity to nothing but a product of the discursive. There is not space here, however, to elaborate on this.

[3]I have borrowed this phrase from Coleridge, who, in defense of the accusations leveled against him declared "I regard truth as a divine ventriloquist" (quoted in Mallon, 1989, p. 31).

[4]Jacques Derrida, also taking issue with the idea that meaning in speech act theory is guaranteed by the author's intentions, speculates about the possibility of understanding "performatives" as scripted performances rather than individual acts. Perhaps, he suggests, language is not so much made up of infinite individual acts but rather is subject to what he calls a generalized citationality (see Norris, 1983). See also Derrida (1988) for an interesting debate with Searle.

If this line of thinking raises many questions about authorship, Swan's (1994) discussion of Helen Keller's supposed plagiarism starts to raise different postmodernist issues concerning the body and its boundaries. For Helen Keller, deaf and blind since the age of 2, perception was almost entirely tactile, and thus texts for her took on a different context in relationship to memory. As Helen Keller explained, her "friends often read 'interesting fragments' to her 'in a promiscuous manner,' and . . . if she then uses them in her writing, it is difficult to trace the 'fugitive sentences and paragraphs' which have been spelled into her hand" (Swan, 1994, pp. 57–58). But Swan is pointing to far deeper concerns here than the fact that Helen Keller must have developed very particular memory practices. Working through the psychoanalytic theories of Lacan, he points to fundamentally different understandings of language and boundaries: Because "touch *is* perception," it was an immense battle to construct for Keller an understanding that "the boundaries between self and other that her blind groping continually transgresses" have parallels in the "boundaries between her words and the words of others" (p. 97). This discussion starts to open up a range of issues to do with modes of perception, memory, texts, and the understanding of personal and social boundaries. If we look at Helen Keller's case not as one limited to the particular perceptual constraints with which she had to work but rather as opening up concerns about bodies, texts, and ownership, we can also admit the possibility that different cultures and different psyches may operate with fundamentally different understandings of self and other and therefore of boundaries and ownership.

Finally, drawing this discussion back to issues more closely related to language learning, it is worth noting the ideas of Bakhtin (1986/1936), who insists on the dialogic nature of language: "the real unit of language that is implemented in speech . . . is not the individual, isolated monologic utterance, but the interaction of at least two utterances—in a word, dialogue" (Voloinov, 1973, p. 117). By this he means not so much that language is used in communication but rather that all language use carries histories of its former uses with it. "Our speech, that is, all our utterances," are therefore "filled with others' words" (Bakhtin, 1986, p. 89). Commenting on the importance of this idea of "appropriating others' words" for language learning, Lensmire and Beals (1994) suggest that "We are born and develop, learn to speak, read and write, awash in the words of others. . . . Our words are always someone else's words first; and these words sound with the intonations and evaluations of others who have used them before, and from whom we have learned them" (p. 411). Put together, these challenges to the notion of the author and individual creativity, and this argument that meanings are in a sense in circulation, that language is constantly cycled and recycled, raise profound questions about how we consider the notion of textual borrowing or plagiarism.

TEACHERS AND CHANGING TEXTUAL PRACTICES

What I have been trying to show here is that looking more carefully at traditions of ascribing meaning and creativity to God, the individual, or discourse raises a number of concerns about how meaning, texts, and textual borrowing are understood and thus challenges any easy ascription of a notion of plagiarism. An understanding of the notion of authorship and originality as a very particular cultural and historical orientation to meaning raises profound questions about plagiarism. We need to take seriously the "postmodern conviction that the very concept of a creative imagination is a passing illusion of Western humanist culture" (Kearney, 1988, p. 28). I have been trying to question the premises on which a simple version of plagiarism is based, by showing that this particular version of meaning, originality, and authorship is located within a Western cultural and historical tradition that stresses creative and possessive individualism. Furthermore, Western claims to originality have always been made along-side a tradition of wholesale borrowing of language and ideas. Questions and research following from Foucault's (1977/1984) key question, What is an author? therefore suggest that "the author in this modern sense is a relatively recent invention, but . . . it does not closely reflect contemporary writing practices" (Woodmansee, 1994, p. 15).

Hunting Down Those Borrowed Words

As teachers, therefore, we are presented by something of a dilemma. For those of us brought up in this Western tradition, we often find ourselves vehement defenders of "correct" textual practices, desperately trying to promote our version of language and ownership. This position, however, is filled with tensions. As I shall discuss in the next section, it faces very real challenges if we start to take seriously different textual and learning practices in other cultures. But, as I want to show here, it also faces challenges from its own inconsistencies. These are of two main kinds: On the one hand, as I suggested in the last section, the Western cult of originality has existed alongside wholescale borrowing, and thus whether we see Coleridge and others as devious plagiarists or as careless scholars, this history of plagiarism suggests a certain ingenuousness to the accusations made by teachers. Indeed, in light of the vehemence with which many teachers pursue apparent plagiarizers (see below), it is worth considering the vehemence with which many literary scholars defend their adored writers: "Scholars will tie themselves up in knots exonerating Coleridge" (Mallon, 1989, pp. 32–33). At the very least, there is a degree of hypocrisy here as teachers on the one hand accuse their students of lacking originality, while on the other they defend their cherished creative geniuses against suggestions that they were simply resaying what had been said before. On the other hand, it would seem in any case that textual practices are changing: Even if there once were clearly defined lines between the borrowed and the original, they are starting to fade in a new era of electronic intertextuality.

Perhaps the best example of plagiaristic hypocrisy can be found in the following report from the *New York Times* (June 6, 1980; quoted in Mallon, 1989, p. 100):

> Stanford University said today it had learned that its teaching assistants' handbook section on plagiarism had been plagiarized by the University of Oregon. Stanford issued a release saying Oregon officials conceded that the plagiarism section and other parts of its handbook were identical with the Stanford guidebook. Oregon officials apologized and said they would revise their guidebook.

On one level, this is merely laughable. Yet I am left wondering how this could actually have happened. What was going on here when guidelines to avoid plagiarism were being copied? This case certainly suggests that the same double-standards that seem to obtain in literary circles may also be the case in the academic domain, with one set of standards for the guardians of truth and knowledge and another for those seeking entry. Beyond the obvious observation that plagiarism exists on a large scale in the academic world (see, e.g., Mallon, 1989), there are two other domains that produce a degree of skepticism. First, in the same way that Western literary practices center around the notion of the individual creator and yet constantly echo the lines of others, academic work also stresses the individual, creative thinker, and writer and yet constantly emphasizes a fixed canon of disciplinary knowledge. This problem is most obvious for undergraduate students (and especially if they are writing in a second language) who, while constantly being told to be original and critical, and to write things in their "own words," are nevertheless only too aware that they are at the same time required to acquire a fixed canon of knowledge and a fixed canon of terminology to go with it.

The second problem concerns the power relations between different academics and between academics and their students or research assistants. One aspect of this is the common practice of senior academics (particularly in the sciences but also in other areas) putting their names at the head of papers in the writing and researching of which they have had little or no role.[5] More generally, however, this issue touches on far broader ques-

---

[5]A controversial case of plagiarism of a questionnaire at Hong Kong University, which was eventually settled in the Hong Kong Court of Appeal in 1993, had its origins in just such a practice. According to Linda Koo Chih-ling, who brought the case of plagiarism against a colleague, the origins of the dispute go back to 1983, when she refused to put the name of a senior colleague on a paper she had written (interview in the *South China Morning Post*,

tions of the origins of academic ideas and who gets credit for them. Just as questions have been raised about Wordsworth's solitary male creative genius, because it seems he borrowed heavily from his sister, Dorothy, so it is evident that much of what gets claimed as the result of original academic work actually draws heavily on the work of silent others—women, graduate students, research assistants, and so on.

The extent of moral rectitude and vehemence with which teachers sometimes pursue student plagiarizers can be extreme. Given the emphasis on the creative individual as producer and owner of his or her thoughts, it seems that the borrowing of words is often discussed in terms of "stealing," of committing a crime against the author of a text. This particular connection presumably has its origins in the peculiarly Western conjunction between the growth of the notion of human rights and the stress on individual property (see, e.g., Pollis & Schwab, 1979), thus making the reuse of language already used by others a crime against the inalienable property rights of the individual. It is worth noting here in passing that whereas other student "misdeeds," such as grammatical errors, failure to understand a text and so on, may incur frustration, censure, and perhaps wrath, I cannot think of anything else that is viewed as a crime in this way. Although some language purists may rail against the ways language gets bent and twisted in both our and our students' hands and mouths, rarely is this taken up in such moralistic terms. Plagiarism, Kolich (1983) suggests, "is a highly emotional subject, and the issue of how to deal with it seems muddled by moral confusion, apprehension, and general loathing" (p. 141). It seems that there is a very clear idea here that texts are "owned" by their "original" creators and that to use those words and ideas without acknowledging their ownership is indeed to transgress a moral (and legal) boundary. In Deckert's (1993) study of attitudes toward plagiarism, for example, he asked the students to identify instances where "the writer *committed* plagiarism" (p. 145; emphasis added).

And yet even this notion of possessive individualism does not seem to account sufficiently for the moral outrage that is expressed and the zeal with which transgressors are pursued. As Kolich (1983) points out, "The mere hint that a student may have cribbed an essay transforms us from caring, sympathetic teachers into single-minded guardians of honor and truth" (p. 142). Accounts of plagiarism abound with stories of the "hunt," the attempt to catch the offender and bring him or her to trial. "I was thrilled by the chase," recalls Murphy (1990, p. 900), a chase which finally

---

August 28, 1993). From then on, she claims, she has been ostracized and discriminated against. And, like literary scholars tying themselves in knots to exonerate their cherished literary heroes, an internal inquiry (labeled a "kangaroo court" by Linda Koo) has since been working to downplay the implications of the decision by the Court of Appeal.

led to the student's confession of having copied some sections from a book. "Within the week," reports Murphy, "he was suspended from the university" (p. 900).[6] Perhaps another way of explaining the outrage expressed at plagiarism is to look not so much at a notion of ownership but rather at authorship and authority. Plagiarism, in a number of ways, undermines the authority of both teacher and text. Furthermore, if I am right that this tradition is under challenge from a number of quarters, the ferocity of this hunting down of borrowed words may be seen as part of a desperate rearguard action against changing textualities.

Changing Textual Practices

The postmodern and poststructuralist critiques of the notion of originality that I discussed in the last section tend to operate at a certain level of philosophical abstraction. There is another side to postmodernism, however, which tends to deal in more material changes. From this point of view, we might also ask how communication is changing in post-Fordist industrial contexts, how our writing practices themselves are undergoing rapid changes through e-mail, word-processing, collaborative writing, electronic words, and so on. Thus, if the view of textuality discussed in the previous section is postmodern to the extent that it follows the epistemological shifts brought about by postmodern philosophical changes, there is also a postmodern approach grounded in the notion that postmodernism is a real condition of late capitalist society. That is to say, whereas on the one hand we may point to the death of the author brought about by deconstructionist approaches to texts, on the other we may see the death or the demise of the author as a product of changes in communication in societies dominated by electronic media. Following more this second line of thinking, Scollon (1994) argues that "we are currently seeing a shift away from the long dominant Utilitarian ideology with its emphasis on the presentation of a unique, individual author who is the 'owner' of the text toward a much more diffused form of referencing which has much in common with the forms of authorship and responsibility of oral traditions" (p. 33). Scollon goes on to argue that referencing the writing of others is only partly about establishing ownership of language; it is also about establishing the authorial self of the writer. Thus, teaching attribution in academic writing may run into a number of difficulties since "the authorial self may well constitute an unacceptable ideological position" (p. 35)

As Scollon (1994) suggests, writing practices are changing, and it is now common to find multiple layering effects in academic texts, where the

---

[6]Murphy (1990) also discusses the problems with such witch hunts, including a traumatic account of accusations made against an anorexic woman.

supposed origin of a quote becomes ever murkier. To give one instance of this, while researching the ideas for this article, I came across the following example of layered quotation: In an unpublished manuscript, Morgan (1995) says this about an article by Ann Raimes (1991): "Giroux is then quoted as saying that academic discourse communities are 'often more concerned with excluding new members than with ways of admitting them'" (p. 14). So Morgan claims Raimes is quoting Giroux. I was interested to see what Giroux had actually said, so I had a look at Raimes (1991), where the relevant passage reads thus: "Another thorny problem is whether we view the academic discourse community as benign, open, and beneficial to our students or whether we see discourse communities as powerful and controlling, and, as Giroux (cited in Faigley, 1986) puts it, 'often more concerned with ways of excluding new members than with ways of admitting them' (p. 537)" (p. 416). So Raimes is claiming that Faigley is quoting Giroux. Still in search of the Giroux quote, I went in search of Faigley, which reads: "Giroux finds discourse communities are often more concerned with ways of excluding new members than with ways of admitting them. He attacks non-Marxist ethnographies for sacrificing 'theoretical depth for methodological refinement' (p. 98)" (Faigley, 1986, p. 537). So Faigley appears to be paraphrasing the supposed Giroux quote but quoting another piece of Giroux. And at this point the trail seems to go rather cold: Giroux's words, which the other two articles suggest are quoted, turn out, it seems, to be Faigley's. The reference seems to be to Giroux's *Theory and Resistance in Education: A Pedagogy for the Opposition* in Faigley's bibliography, but the phrase "theoretical depth and methodological refinement" does not appear on page 98 of the book (or at least the copy I looked at). And so, as these words and ideas circulate around the academic community, it becomes unclear quite what their origins are. And does it matter? The ideas attributed to Giroux are interesting, but do we need to know who really said them originally? Within contemporary academic writing practices, with layers of citations, e-mail, cutting and pasting, and so on, the adherence to supposed norms of authoriality are becoming increasingly hazy.

Another interesting way in which our textual practices seem to be changing is happening alongside the greater use of the pronoun *I* in academic writing. Formerly, writers would often refer to their own published work as texts "out there," as objective entities to be referred to or quoted. Thus, Nunan (1988), for example, frequently refers to his own work in these terms: "The course design model developed by Nunan (1985a) is similar in many respects to that devised by Richards" (p. 19); or "For example, Nunan (1986c) studied a number of 'communicative' classrooms. . . . In the Nunan data, a study of the lesson plans . . ." (p. 139); or "This is made clear in the following quote: 'While objective needs . . .' (Nunan 1989a, p. 5)" (p. 45). In this tradition, even if one is the author of the text, it is treated like any other in terms of quoting and referencing. This practice fixes text, ownership, and authorship in a clear and objective system.

By 1992, however, Nunan (1992) appears to be using a mixed style: on the one hand employing the old style: "This is exemplified in the action research programs described by Nunan (1989) . . ." (p. 103), but on the other hand shifting to greater use of *I*: "In the second investigation, I looked at a number of different aspects of language teaching pedagogy, including teachers' decision-making (Nunan, 1991a)" (p. 95); or "In fact, in a recent survey I found that it was the most frequently employed data collection method, being used in half of the studies analysed (Nunan, 1991b)" (p. 136). Once this shift occurs, as it seems to be doing in a great deal of academic writing, the relationship to one's own texts clearly changes, enabling a shift from direct quotation to easier incorporation. The reference may still be there, but there is a slipperiness over the reusability of one's own words (self-plagiarism?), a process greatly enhanced by the ease of cutting and pasting between documents on a computer.[7]

It would seem, then, that both the postmodern skepticism about the myth of originality and the more material considerations about changing writing practices point toward the need to reevaluate beliefs in originality and textual ownership. There is therefore a degree of hypocrisy in the defense of the culture of originality because postmodern understandings of language and meaning, by contrast, point to the possibility of little more than a circulation of meanings. One of the central issues that emerges from this discussion, however, is that there is a discourse available to teachers educated in the Western tradition which stresses the centrality of originality and creativity. This is of particular significance when cultural traditions regarding text, ownership, and memorization collide with each other, as is the case in many writing programs and ESL classes. Scollon (1995) argues that "the traditional view of plagiarism constitutes, in fact, an ideological position which privileges a concept of the person established within the European Enlightenment, and . . . as such it obscures our understanding of the construction of identity in intercultural discourse" (p. 3). It is to this relationship between the Western understanding of textual ownership and other cultural practices that I now wish to turn.

TEXTUAL CULTURES IN CONFLICT

Before returning to the Chinese contexts with which I started this article, it is important to clarify my understanding of culture. What I wish to avoid

---

[7]This example seems to be more a case of the rebirth of the academic author rather than the death of the author. My point, however, is that it shows how textual practices are changing in terms of the relationship between text, authority, and ownership.

here is the construction of a crude East/West dichotomy or to assume some essentialist version of Chinese culture. First, in discussing what I described as a "Western" view of text, I was attempting to sketch and critique a dominant tradition that has emerged from European and American contexts. Within the so-called West, there are of course, as Heath (1983) and others have shown, a diversity of literacy practices. Some of these may coincide to a certain extent with literacy practices from other cultural contexts, whereas others may not. My chief interest was to describe what has increasingly been promoted as a global academic norm and to contextualize it as a particular cultural and historical practice. Second, by turning to look at China and Hong Kong, I am not attempting to construct some "exotic Other" but rather to return to the teaching contexts with which I am most familiar (most of my life as a teacher has been spent in Japan, China, and Hong Kong) and the contexts in which my own doubts about notions of textual ownership were formed. Furthermore, by looking at how students in Hong Kong dealt with the everyday difficulties of studying, I hope to be able to discuss these contexts in terms of the everyday practicalities faced by students.

Third, in talking of cultural difference, I want to avoid simplistic arguments such as "it's OK to plagiarize in Chinese." This both begs the question (it does nothing to question the notion of plagiarism) and fails to engage with a sense of difference. Rather, what I am trying to get at is the ways in which relationships to text, memory, and learning may differ. To deal equitably with our students, we need to appreciate such differences. Finally, it is important to understand the notion of cross-cultural communication not as some idealized cultural exchange, but rather as a place of struggle and contestation, because alongside the tradition of emphasizing the creativity of the West, there has also been a tradition of deriding other cultures for their supposedly stagnant or imitative cultural practices (see Blaut, 1993). Thus, I want to suggest along with Scollon (1994) that because plagiarism is a complex notion related to "the cultural construction of human identity, accusations of plagiarism may all too easily mask ideological arrogance" (p. 45). The important point here is that whereas we can see how the notion of plagiarism needs to be understood within the particular cultural and historical context of its development, it also needs to be understood relative to alternative cultural practices. It is to an exploration of ways of understanding learning in a Chinese context that I shall now turn.

Deriding Chinese Learners

It is not uncommon in discussions of plagiarism to hear those cultural Others—our students—derided as rote learners. Different educational approaches are seen as deficient and backward. Masemann (1986) points to "the implicit evolutionary thinking about pedagogy in which teaching is conceived as progressing from 'rote' to 'structured' to 'open' " (p. 18). In this view, memorization is a traditional and outmoded pedagogical practice. Derisory views on Chinese education have a long history, dating back in Hong Kong well into the 19th century. Thus, the otherwise fairly liberal Frederick Stewart, headmaster of the Central School in Hong Kong and a strong advocate of bilingual education, nevertheless showed little respect for Chinese educational practices: In his education report for 1865,[8] he wrote, "The Chinese have no *education* in the real sense of the word. No attempt is made at a simultaneous development of the mental powers. These are all sacrificed to the cultivation of memory." (p. 138). Such views were commonly held by many colonizers who worked in Hong Kong or China. The Rev. S. R. Brown, Headmaster of the Morrison Education Society School, wrote in a report in 1844 that Chinese children are usually pervaded by "a universal expression of passive inanity: . . . The black but staring, glassy eye, and open mouth, bespeak little more than stupid wonder gazing out of emptiness." This view is linked to Brown's view of Chinese schools, where a boy may learn "the names of written characters, that in all probability never conveyed to him one new idea from first to last." Despite this lack of education, the Chinese boy also comes "with a mind to be emptied of a vast accumulation of false and superstitious notions that can never tenant an enlightened mind, for they cannot coexist with truth" (cited in Sweeting, 1990, p. 21). The principal characteristics of Chinese boys are "an utter disregard of truth, obscenity, and cowardliness" (p. 22).

Such views reemerged in the 1882 Education Commission's interview with the Bishop of Victoria:[9] "You know the way they learn; they memorate [sic], they hear the Chinese explanation, and this goes on from morning to night for years, and they get the classics into them" (1882, p. 6). And later, "When a Chinaman goes to school he is given a little book, and he just simply sits and pores over it, not understanding the meaning of a character, and he goes on growing and getting other books which he does not understand at all, and at the end, when he is in his teens, he begins to have some explanation given to him" (p. 11). This view can be found again in an article by Addis (1889) on education in China: "In truth Chinese education is—*pace* the sinologues—no education at all. It is no 'leading out of' but a leading back to. Instead of expanding the intelligence, it contracts it; instead of broadening sympathies, it narrows them; instead of making a man honest, intelligent and brave, it has produced

---

[8]The Annual Report on the State of the Government Schools for the Year 1865, published in the *Hong Kong Blue Book*, 1865.

[9]*Report of the Education Commission Appointed by His Excellency Sir John Pope Hennessy . . . to Consider Certain Questions Connected With Education in Hong Kong*, 1882.

few who are not cunning, narrow-minded and pusillanimous" (p. 206). He then goes on to discuss the sinologues' excuses for Chinese education: "It is natural that those, who have devoted much time and labour to the study of a language and literature like Chinese, should be disposed to overrate the value of that which has cost them so much industry and effort to acquire, and occasional encomiums of the Chinese methods of instruction are only what we might expect. We are told, for instance, that it is eminently suited to the present system of government" (p. 206). He goes on: "The truth is that if the comparative test be applied, almost the only merit which can be claimed for Chinese education is that it strengthens the memory" (p. 206). The poor state of Chinese education he compares with Hong Kong where "half a century ago the island was peopled by a few half savage settlers steeped in ignorance and superstition" but where "a foreign Government, by the impartial administration of wise and just laws, has made this dot on the ocean so attractive" (pp. 206–207).

Such views, with Chinese learners cast as passive, imitative memorizers, to be enlightened by the advent of the creative West, echo down to the present (see Deckert, 1992, 1993; Jochnowitz, 1986). Sampson (1984) points to how Western teachers in China "respond to memorization by Chinese students with such derision and scorn" (p. 162), and Biggs (1991) discusses similar stereotypes perpetuated by external examiners at Hong Kong University and discussions of Asian students studying in Australia. From within such discursive constructs of our memorizing students, it is easy to see alternative learning practices and relationships to text as little more than backward, outmoded learning strategies. Once the students' authorial creativity is questioned and once they are positioned within these discourses of cultural derogation, students are treated as potential or actual criminals, with large warning signs posted around their assignments to make clear what the law is. "If you copy other writers' words," teaching materials for first-year Arts Faculty students at Hong Kong University warn, "pretending they are your own, you are engaging in what is known as plagiarism. *If you plagiarise in this way, you are guilty of intellectual dishonesty. You will be penalised heavily for this. Take care to avoid it, therefore*" (emphasis in original).

Cultures of Memory and Text

In comparing cultures of memorization, it is tempting to make a comparison between former Western practices of memorization and more recent Chinese (and other) practices, thus perhaps suggesting that the West has simply developed a more modern attitude to the text. Thus one might see in the following advice on English teaching by Herbert Palmer (1930) an earlier evolutionary stage in the West: "*Memorizing* or *Repetition* is especially good, because, by aid of it, the form and flame of expression adhere to the mind, and little by little Taste is acquired, good literature becoming a sort of

personal property of the recipient, to act as an antagonism to the mediocre"
(p. 32). While acknowledging the importance of understanding these
historical antecedents, I wish to avoid any argument that suggests some
evolutionary path to cultural change, and I want to suggest that cultural
difference may be more profound than such surface similarities might
suggest.

It is important first of all to consider different ways in which language
is understood. Harris (1980) argues that "the European is the inheritor
of an intellectual tradition which is strongly biased in favour of regarding
languages as superficially different but fundamentally equivalent systems
of expression" (p. 21). This view is in part a result of a belief that language
represents a more or less similar "real world." This surrogationist (or rep-
resentationist) orientation of Western thinking on language (whereby languages are seen as "surrogational systems" [p. 33], as representations of
reality or of thoughts) is a very particular cultural and historical tradition.
By contrast, the Confucian doctrine of *cheng ming* works with the opposite
assumption, namely that "things are conceived of as conforming to the
natural order not in themselves, but in virtue of corresponding to their
names" (Harris, 1980, p. 48). In this quite different understanding of
language, in which primacy is accorded to language and not to the "real"
world, notions such as metaphor, which suggests that some word "stands
for" something else, become quite different because reality is in the language and not in the world.

This kind of reversal may be seen, I think, in the contemporary significance in Chinese society[10] of performing acts according to homophonic
reference: for example, students breaking beer bottles (*xiǎo píng(zi):* small
bottle) in a reference to Deng Xiao Ping, or people eating crabs after the
fall of the Gang of Four in a reference to the phrase *héngxíng bàdào*. This
four-character phrase is made up of "walking sideways" (= running amok)
and "feudal rule" and together suggests how rule without order (walking
sideways = tyranny) rides roughshod over the people. In the same way that
smashing bottles challenges Deng Xiao Ping, eating crabs (standing metaphorically for "walking sideways") can signal the end of tyrannical rule. What
I think is interesting here is the way in which reality appears to reflect
language rather than the other way round: Objects in the world are changed
in order to effect change through language. This kind of reversal of language
and reality, in which "doing language" can stand in for doing reality, also
seems to occur in other cultures: Christie's (1995) discussion of literacy
among the Yolngu people of Northern Australia suggests a similar relation-

---

[10]I am not suggesting that Chinese society is still determined by Confucian doctrines such
as *Cheng ming*. Rather, I want to suggest that such doctrines reflect a long tradition of a
particular understanding of the relationship between language and the world that reverses
the polarity of much Western thinking.

ship whereby it is language that shapes reality and not reality that shapes language. Indeed, there is a provocatively intriguing parallel here between this reversal and a poststructuralist view of language in which, as I suggested earlier, the issue is not so much how authors produce texts but how texts produce authors.

What I am trying to suggest, therefore, is the possibility that the memorization of texts is not a pointless practice from this point of view, because the issue is not one of understanding the world and then mapping language onto it but rather of acquiring language as texts as a precursor to mapping out textual realities. This view of texts and language, which is derided from a Western point of view because the learning of texts is seen as meaningless unless coupled to "prior understanding," also ties in with (perhaps produces) a respect for textual authority. This veneration of old textual authority—akin in some ways to the medieval European view of the text—is often seen as an inherently conservative construction of authority. I want to suggest, however, that it is not necessarily so; rather, it can also be understood as according primary importance to the text rather than to the world. To assume a material reality that is described by language may well be an equally conservative position. In any case, I think these speculations at least point to some profoundly different possibilities in how language, texts, and memorization may be understood.

This view is supported by explorations of what Chinese learners actually do when they memorize. Biggs (1991) has pointed out that there is a major contradiction in common perceptions of Asian students: On the one hand, they are held up as paragons of educational excellence, while on the other hand they are derided as rote learners. In an attempt to resolve this paradox, Marton, Dall'Alba, and Tse Lai Kun (in press) have shown that there are important distinctions to be drawn *within* forms of memorization rather than *between* memorization and understanding: "The traditional Asian practice of repetition or memorization can have different purposes. On the one hand, repetition can be associated with mechanical rote learning. On the other hand, memorization through repetition can be used to deepen and develop understanding. If memorization is understood in this latter way, the paradox of the Chinese learner is solved" (p. 16). The point here, then, is that research into Chinese learning practices shows that there are different types or levels of memorization. And thus, a student's "ownership" over a text may have different causes and different effects.

The Everyday Contexts of Borrowing

Importantly, too, we need to try to understand the ways in which our students develop particular relationships to texts and learning within the everyday contexts of their lives as students. To this end I conducted informal interviews with Hong Kong Chinese students at the University of Hong Kong who had been "caught" plagiarizing. A number of different concerns emerge here. In most cases, it seemed that there was a complex mixture of things going on: It could not simply be said that students had just copied a passage and hoped to get away with it. Some were aware that the essay had not been very good and complained of heavy workloads—four assignments due in one week, for example. In these cases, students seemed to be aware that they had not done a particularly good job (the "plagiarism" was more a symptom of careless work than a deliberate strategy). Other students showed less awareness that they had done much wrong but revealed similar careless study habits in which highlighted parts of texts were reused in the essay. This was sometimes also linked to a broader dissatisfaction with the first year at the university—students complaining of little incentive to work hard (the first year only requires a pass) and disappointment with the quality of the lectures and tutorials. From this point of view, these study habits became more a case of resistance than of ignorance, ineptitude, or dishonesty. Indeed, the notion of plagiarism as resistance is one worth exploring further.

One interesting issue that was raised concerned the distinction between plagiarizing ideas and plagiarizing language. The problem, as one student put it, was that the ideas he was discussing were clearly not his own, so if he took the ideas but rephrased the language, he would be plagiarizing ideas but not words. To him, it seemed almost more honest to simply keep the language the same and leave the ideas. As another student explained, she had understood the author and felt that to rewrite in her own words would be less effective than using the author's own words. She knew that rewriting would bring about more mistakes and probably a less powerful message. Another student explained that if you understand the material but use language from the text, that may be the best means to achieve such clarity. According to another student, "It's my usual practice. . . . When I find something that seems to be meaningful, I will try to take it from the article." Referring specifically to the passage for which he had been criticized, he explained: "I think the language of the passage is quite good, so I don't take time to change the words."

Interestingly, many of these comments echo those reported by Sherman (1992) from her Italian students:

> They were virtually unanimous that it was a good idea to reproduce large tracts from source material when dealing with an academic subject. They found my requirements for "own wording" rather quaint. . . . They pointed out that the opinion or the facts could not be better expressed than they were by the source writer, and that they themselves could hardly presume to improve on a publicly acknowledged expert. Taking over his words was thus necessary in order to cover the subject, and also a mark of respect for the originator. (p. 191)

Another student who was unsure what she was supposed to have done wrong (indeed, it wasn't very clear to me either) argued that secondary school had never prepared them for such issues, either practically or theoretically. In school there were few chances to write essays: Most of the time they were required to take tests, for which of course books could not be used and memorization was a key strategy. Essays were generally only for English classes and required interpretation of texts, not citation of facts. Other students made similar comments, one explaining that he didn't see much wrong with what he had done because "In secondary school no teacher forbids us to do something like that." It was a question of which subject was being studied: If it was English, which was the only class designed to "improve my English," they were expected to write in their own words and be original; but in other classes there was no problem in borrowing from other sources—they were supposed to answer the question; how they wrote the answers didn't matter. Another issue raised was the status of translated words: One major piece of work a student had done in Form 7 (Grade 13) involved using Chinese sources, which she had translated, using the translated pieces as they were. Her teacher had been more concerned with the content and correct referencing than with the origins of chunks of language. In fact, the question of textual ownership in relation to translation opens up a whole new domain for investigation (see Duranti, 1993).

A number of quite challenging issues were raised by several students, showing that many of them, while sometimes unsure about the rules of textual borrowing, were nevertheless aware of issues to do with texts and learning.[11] One argued that both of the writing processes he used (either trying to write original texts or using much more language from the readings) could be useful. There was a satisfaction in being able to write in one's own words but useful things to be learned from reusing the structures and words from others' texts. This process of memorization of such texts, he pointed out, had been a crucial part of how he had learned English at high school. Some students pointed to what they saw as the hypocrisy and unfairness of the system in which they were required to do little more than regurgitate ideas but always required to do so in a foreign language. It was also suggested that there was a degree of hypocrisy in lectures where it was evident that a lecturer was doing little more than reproducing chunks of the course text (with their good textual memories, students were very good at spotting this) and yet never acknowledged the source. If they took close notes, memorized them, and rewrote them in an exam, they could be accused of plagiarism. Another student directly confronted the strict

---

[11]Indeed, I have elsewhere (Pennycook, 1994) argued that these students may be more aware of issues around textual borrowing than their teachers.

attitudes to borrowing from other texts since it failed to take into account what students learned. Perhaps, she suggested, this was a teacher's problem not a student's. The important point here is that she was questioning the idea that antiplagiarism attitudes were linked to better learning. From a student point of view they may not necessarily be so: "Whether I copy or not, I know the material. I don't think we should be forced to say it in our own words. . . . I don't think if one plagiarises, that means he doesn't learn anything. . . . Perhaps plagiarism is a way of learning."

A final issue that emerged from these interviews (and also other work I have been doing with students at Hong Kong University) concerns the extent to which these students feel the English language remains a language of colonialism, a language which, although important to them for social, academic, and economic advancement, remains a colonial imposition. Thus in a number of students I found an interesting ambivalence, on the one hand an acknowledgment of the importance of English and sometimes a fondness for English (these are the students that have made it to university through their knowledge of English), on the other hand an anger at the imposition of English in their lives. As one student put it, "the teaching of English is a kind of cultural intrusion in Hong Kong and may be regarded as a political weapon" (Ma Wai Yin, 1993, p. 2). The important issue here is that there is often a deep split between the English/academic domain and the Cantonese/daily life domain in these students' lives. Many seem to feel that they have no ownership over English—it remains an alien language—and thus to write "in their own words" is not something that can be done in English. They are obliged to study in a foreign language and they return the chunks of language in the form in which they receive them.

What I think this brief summary of the interviews points to is the complexity of things going on behind the surface phenomenon of apparent plagiarism. Students come to our classes with different cultural and educational backgrounds, with different understandings of texts and language, with different approaches to learning. They are also confronted by a range of more local concerns such as particular assignments which may require little more than the regurgitation of a set curriculum. Some students were led into trouble through a mixture of heavy workloads and inappropriate study skills: good reading habits but overuse of highlighted sections in their writing. It certainly seemed important to distinguish here between good and bad plagiarism, that is, between those who reused parts of texts very well and those who seemed to randomly borrow. Other students seemed to take a more active view in all this and to see their borrowing strategies either as an unappreciated approach to learning or as an act of resistance to the university and the English language context they are obliged to work in.

CONCLUSIONS AND EDUCATIONAL IMPLICATIONS

I have been trying in this article to complexify and situate different understandings of texts, memory, and learning, to show how relations between texts and learning are far more complex than a simple accusation of plagiarism will allow. The issue of textual borrowing goes to the heart of a number of key issues in second language education: the role of memory, the nature of language learning, the ownership of texts, the concepts of the author, authority, and authenticity, and the cross-cultural relations that emerge in educational contexts. For some, the position I have been trying to establish here may seem too relativistic, allowing no grounds for asserting that someone's writing practices are unacceptable. My point, however, is that although of course we still need to leave a space open to criticize unacceptable borrowing practices, unilateral accusations of plagiarism are inadequate and arrogant. Part of the problem here lies with the use of the term *plagiarism* as if it described some clearly definable practice. What I have been trying to show here, by contrast, is that behind this clumsy term may lurk any number of different concerns, and so, despite the demands on our time that such reflexivity may make, I believe it is incumbent on us as teachers to develop an understanding of the complexity of issues involved in language learning and textual borrowing.

Another argument might suggest that whatever complexities there may be in textual relationships and memorization, there are nevertheless a very clear set of standards in academic practice to which we need to get our students to adhere. I also want to suggest, however, that this argument is inadequate. It articulates nothing but a normative view on so-called standards, does nothing to challenge the ways in which academic systems operate, and fails to take into account any of the complexities that our students may bring in terms of their own relationship to texts and memory. I am suggesting, therefore, that many of the ways we approach supposed plagiarism are pedagogically unsound and intellectually arrogant. It is not adequate to observe simply on the one hand that students "copy" or that on the other hand they need to learn academic writing practices. Both observations are trivially true but insufficient in terms of an awareness of cultural difference and a self-reflexivity about the practices to which we adhere. Part of any discussion of citation, paraphrase, textual borrowing, and so forth needs, as Willinsky (1990) observes, to include discussion of how and why these notions have been constructed, how authorship, authenticity, and authority have been linked together, and how these practices may be in a process of flux. It is not enough, however, to focus only on Western writing practices as a "cultural syllabus" (Sherman, 1992, p. 197). Also needed is an attempt to understand the other side of the coin—our students' textual and language learning worlds as well as the constraints on their lives and their perceptions of how academic norms operate and may be flouted.

Given the difficulties in establishing any clear sense of authoriality, it is important to understand authorship, authority, and plagiarism as located not within some objectively describable system of textual relations but rather in "an historically established system for the distribution of social power and privilege" (Scollon, 1995, p. 25). Thus I hope to encourage others to pause and consider what is going on, to try to consider self-reflexively how a particular notion of authorship and ownership has grown up, how it is a very particular cultural and historical tradition and may now be undergoing transformation, how our students may be operating from fundamentally different positions about texts and memory. All language learning is to some extent a process of borrowing others' words and we need to be flexible, not dogmatic, about where we draw boundaries between acceptable or unacceptable textual borrowings.

REFERENCES

Addis, C. S. (1889). Education in China. *The China Review, 18*, 205–212.
Bakhtin, M. (1986/1936). *Speech genres and other late essays.* Austin: University of Texas Press.
Barthes, R. (1977). The death of the author. In *Image, music, text* (pp. 142–148). (Translated by S. Heath). Glasgow, Scotland: Fontana/Collins.
Biggs, J. (1991). Approaches to learning in secondary and tertiary students in Hong Kong: Some comparative studies. *Educational Research Journal, 6*, 27–39.
Blaut, J. M. (1993). *The colonizer's model of the world: Geographical diffusionism and eurocentric history.* New York: The Guilford Press.
Christie, M. (1995, Winter). The Yolngu regain their literacy. *Fine Print*, pp. 14–17.
Deckert, G. (1992, November). A pedagogical response to learned plagiarism among tertiary-level ESL students. *Occasional Papers in Applied Language Studies*, Hong Kong Baptist College, pp. 49–56.
Deckert, G. (1993). Perspectives on plagiarism from ESL students in Hong Kong. *Journal of Second Language Writing, 2*, 131–148.
Derrida, J. (1988). *Limited Inc.* (Trans. S. Weber). Evanston, IL: Northwestern University Press.
Duranti, A. (1993). Beyond Bakhtin, or the dialogic imagination in academia. *Pragmatics, 3*, 333–340.
Eliot, T. S. (1975). Tradition and individual talent. In F. Kermode (Ed.), *Selected prose of T. S. Eliot* (pp. 37–44). London: Faber & Faber.
Faigley, L. (1986). Competing theories of process: A critique and a proposal. *College English, 48*, 527–542.
Foucault, M. (1977/1984). What is an author? In D. F. Bouchard (Ed.), *Language, counter-memory, practise: Selected essays and interviews* (pp. 113–138). Ithaca, NY: Cornell University Press. (Reprinted in *The Foucault Reader* (Paul Rabinow, Ed.), 1994, pp. 101–120)
Goethe, J. W. (1963/1829). *Maximen und Reflexionen.* München, Germany: Deutscher Taschenbuch Verlag.
Harris, R. (1980). *The language makers.* London: Duckworth.
Heath, S. B. (1983). *Ways with words: Language, life and work in communities and classrooms.* London: Cambridge University Press.

Hutton, C. (1990, June). *Originality as an academic requirement*. Paper presented at the Conference on the Teaching of English Language/Literature in the Hong Kong Context, Chinese University of Hong Kong.

Jochnowitz, G. (1986). Teaching at a provincial Chinese university. *American Scholar, 55,* 521–527.

Kearney, R. (1988). *The wake of imagination*. Minneapolis: University of Minnesota Press.

Keyes, R. (1992). *"Nice guys finish seventh": False phrases, spurious sayings, and familiar misquotations*. New York: HarperCollins.

Kolich, A. M. (1983). Plagiarism: The worm of reason. *College English, 45,* 141–148.

Lensmire, T. J., & Beals, D. E. (1994). Appropriating others' words: Traces of literature and peer culture in a third-grader's writing. *Language in Society, 23,* 411–426.

Mallon, T. (1989). *Stolen words: Forays into the origins and ravages of plagiarism*. New York: Tricknor & Fields.

Marton, F., Dall'Alba, G., & Kun, T. L. (in press). The paradox of the Chinese learner. In D. A. Watkins & J. A. Biggs (Eds.), *The Asian learner: Research and practice*. Hong Kong: Hong Kong University Press.

Masemann, V. L. (1986). Critical ethnography in the study of comparative education. In P. G. Altbach & G. P. Kelly (Eds.), *New approaches to comparative education* (pp. 11–25). Chicago: University of Chicago Press.

Minnis, A. J. (1984). *The medieval theory of authorship*. London: Scholar Press.

Morgan, B. (1995). *Language, power and publishing: A micro-perspective*. Unpublished paper, Ontario Institute for Studies in Education.

Murphy, R. (1990). Anorexia: The cheating disorder. *College English, 52,* 898–903.

Ma Wai Yin, E. (1993). *My relationship to English*. Course assignment for English for Arts students, Hong Kong University.

Norris, C. (1983). *The deconstructive turn: Essays in the rhetoric of philosophy*. London: Methuen.

Nunan, D. (1988). *The learner-centred curriculum*. Cambridge: Cambridge University Press.

Nunan, D. (1992). *Research methods in language teaching*. Cambridge: Cambridge University Press.

Ong, W. (1982). *Orality and literacy: The technologizing of the word*. London: Methuen.

Palmer, H. E. (1930). *The teaching of English*. London: John Murray.

Pennycook, A. (1994). The complex contexts of plagiarism: A reply to Deckert. *Journal of Second Language Writing, 3,* 277–284.

Pollis, A., & Schwab, P. (1979). Human rights: A western construct with limited applicability. In A. Pollis & P. Schwab (Eds.), *Human rights: Cultural and ideological perspectives* (pp. 1–18). New York: Praeger.

Raimes, A. (1991). Out of the woods: Emerging traditions in the teaching of writing. *TESOL Quarterly, 25,* 407–427.

Sampson, G. P. (1984). Exporting language teaching methods from Canada to China. *TESL Canada Journal, 1,* 19–31.

Scollon, R. (1994). As a matter of fact: The changing ideology of authorship and responsibility in discourse. *World Englishes, 13,* 33–46.

Scollon, R. (1995). Plagiarism and ideology: Identity in intercultural discourse. *Language in Society, 24,* 1–28.

Shaw, P. (1982, Summer). Plagiary. *American Scholar,* pp. 325–327.

Sherman, J. (1992). Your own thoughts in your own words. *ELT Journal, 46,* 190–198.

Swan, J. (1994). Touching words: Helen Keller, plagiarism, authorship. In M. Woodmansee & P. Jaszi (Eds.), *The construction of authorship: Textual appropriation in law and literature* (pp. 57–100). Durham, NC: Duke University Press.

Sweeting, A. E. (1990). *Education in Hong Kong, pre-1841 to 1941: Fact & opinion*. Hong Kong: Hong Kong University Press.

Tatlow, A. (1993). *"Those savages—that's us": Textual anthropology.* Inaugural lecture from the Chair of Comparative Literature, University of Hong Kong, October 22, 1992. Published in *Supplement to the Gazette* (Hong Kong University), Vol. 40, 1.

Vološinov, V. N. (1973/1929). *Marxism and the philosophy of language.* (Trans. by Ladislav Matejka & I. R. Titunik). Cambridge, MA: Harvard University Press.

White, H. O. (1965). *Plagiarism and imitation during the English Renaissance: A study in critical distinctions.* New York: Octagon Books.

Willinsky, J. (1990). Intellectual property rights and responsibilities: The state of the text. *The Journal of Educational Thought, 24,* 68–82.

Woodmansee, M. (1994). On the author effect: Recovering collectivity. In M. Woodmansee & P. Jaszi (Eds.), *The construction of authorship: Textual appropriation in law and literature* (pp. 15–28). Durham, NC: Duke University Press.

Chapter 21

The (In)Visibility of the Person(al) in Academe

Ruth Spack

> *For three hundred years black Americans insisted that "race" was no usefully*
> *distinguishing factor in human relationships. During those same three centuries*
> *every academic discipline, including theology, history, and natural science,*
> *insisted "race" was the determining factor in human development. When blacks*
> *discovered they had shaped or become a culturally formed race, and that it had*
> *specific and revered difference, suddenly they were told there is no such thing*
> *as "race," biological or cultural, that matters and that genuinely intellectual*
> *exchange cannot accommodate it.*
> —Toni Morrison, "Unspeakable Things Unspoken" (3)

Writing from a self-identified white perspective, Pamela Caughie suggests
that the traditional reluctance to discuss race in the classroom is related
to politeness, the fear of being "impertinent" or "indiscreet" (778). Writing
from a self-identified black perspective, Toni Morrison does not let white
people off the hook so easily, as the epigraph demonstrates. Morrison and
other scholars have given voice to formerly "unspeakable things" such as
"race," "class," "gender," "culture," "religion," "(native) language," and "sexual orientation"—all terms whose meanings are contested—and these concepts have entered pedagogical discussions in ways that challenge even
revolutionary theories and practices. The teacher-student relationship has
become more complex now that we live in an age when multiculturalism

---

has been acknowledged. Many of us have a sense of having moved into and become part of a new era. And thus uncertainty exists as to what should be taught, how it should be taught, and who should teach it. Depending on the teacher, the text, and the students—on who's teaching what to whom—the classroom may become a place of intellectual growth or of unproductive conflict.

In discussions of multicultural education, the emphasis is often on the texts—the canonical debate—and the students, whose experience, Richard Miller claims, is "the most important site upon which the culture wars are being waged" (281). While I do not deny the significant role that texts and students play, my aim in this article is to focus on the person teaching in and writing about the multicultural English classroom. As teachers and researchers, we have been reading our classrooms—including actual texts and students as texts—but, for the most part, we have not turned our gaze on ourselves. Yet given the cultural work that many of us are doing, we need to understand who we are as historical, political, social, and cultural beings in order to gain a fuller sense of the complexity of the relationship between teacher, student, and text.

This awareness first came to me as I began to teach world literature to students who actually live in or have lived in that larger world. And it has intensified more recently as I have done scholarly work on a Sioux writer. As a Jewish woman born in the United States, I have had to ask myself, what gives me the authority to teach or write about these texts, given that they do not reflect my own experience? To find an answer to this question (lest I be consigned to teaching and writing only about Jewish female US writers), I undertook to study the testimonies of other teachers and scholars on their own struggles to define their authority in the world of academic multiculturalism. In particular, I was interested in learning how and by whom a teacher/scholar's authority is defined. Through this investigation, I came face to face with the dilemmas that arise out of teachers' own embodied existences as I discovered how those teachers make visible—or keep invisible—their racial/class/cultural/religious/language/sexual identities. I became aware of some ways in which pedagogy and scholarship demand or allow for this (in)visibility through concealment or disclosure of the personal lives of teachers and scholars. Inevitably, to find the answer I was searching for, I was compelled to undergo the wrenching process of examining my own identity.

THE QUESTION OF SUBJECTIVITY

The focus on the person teaching in the classroom and on the personal in scholarly writing has evolved out of feminist challenges to the Western academy's traditional privileging of objectivity. Claiming that the dominance of abstract, rational rhetoric allows "white, Western, elite males" to remain in power (Maher 91), many feminist researchers validate personal experience as a base of knowledge and argue that there is virtue, not deficiency, in women's culturally constructed nurturing role, the moral imperative to "care" and to be connected to others (Gilligan 19). Educator Kathleen Weiler points out that the feminist pedagogy that emerged from this research has adopted liberatory pedagogy's notion of transforming the teacher from lecturer to participant in the learning process. The leading proponent of liberatory pedagogy, Brazilian educator Paulo Freire, calls for critical reflection on individual experience and collective action for social change. The goal is for oppressed peoples to see how they contribute to their own oppression and to release themselves from it; and so, as in feminist pedagogy, the teacher's role is to empower those who have been silenced by the dominant ideology.

However, when theories such as these are applied to actual practice, their limitations and contradictions are revealed (Weiler). The teacher's position in society as a whole, and within the academic institution in particular, matters in ways that these theories have not taken into account. Self-identified feminist women "of color" (a term I will continue to use to avoid the identity-erasing label "nonwhite") and lesbians have recently pointed out that most feminists use the term "woman" to reflect a universal, shared experience when they really mean only "White, heterosexual, middle-class woman" (Weiler 459). Their argument parallels that of African American educator Lisa Delpit, who argues that educational theorists whom she identifies as white devise what they perceive to be universal teaching approaches, in the process silencing teachers of color in pedagogical debates about appropriate classroom practices for students of color (280–82). This perception, shared by many (as evidenced in the numerous responses to Delpit's work), points to the cruel irony of liberatory feminist educators' call for personal knowledge to empower those who have been silenced.

Delpit's demand that the academy embrace "alternative world views" is mirrored in the conclusions Carolyn Matalene draws from her experience teaching English in China. Matalene discovered that the "rhetoric" of the North American academy—feminist or otherwise—is really only "Western rhetoric": a structuring of thought that values "originality and individuality" in ways that are not shared universally (790). The emphasis on the person(al) may be difficult for teachers educated outside of the United States because discourse practices are "integrally connected with the identity or sense of self of the people who practice them," and thus a change of discourse practices can mean a change of identity (Gee 270). Fan Shen, raised in China and now teaching English in the US, for example, describes overcoming a resistance to using the words "I" and "self," words which in China would have signaled selfishness, disrespect, and boastfulness, and eventually following a perceived "American" principle of "protecting and promoting individuality" (460). Other bicultural teachers are less willing or able to conform. Min-Zhan Lu prefers to struggle with conflicting world views and advocates "transforming as well as preserving the discourse" (447).

While the subject positions of students—their different histories, especially as they relate to privilege and power—have been the focus of liberatory pedagogies, postmodern educators such as Weiler now emphasize the need to make conscious the subject positions of teachers as well:

> [T]eachers are not abstract; they are women or men of particular races, classes, ages, abilities, and so on. The teacher will be seen and heard by students not as an abstraction, but as a particular person with a certain defined history and relationship to the world. (Weiler 454)

I recognize that an overemphasis on subjectivity can be problematic. As self-described "black male feminist" Michael Awkward notes, so many scholars have been "getting personal" that they are more likely to ask of one another, "How does your work reflect the politics of your (racial/gendered/sexual) positionality?" than to ask, "What is your theoretical approach?" (4). Nevertheless, the results of my research suggest that this is an area we cannot afford to ignore. To say that the identity of the teacher/scholar is not significant is to deny the reality of the classroom and the academy.

THE SUBJECT POSITION OF THE TEACHER

The differing positions of power or privilege of teachers vis-à-vis students inform the classroom experience. According to Hull and Rose, when composition specialists integrate reading and writing in a classroom that is characterized by "a rich mix of class and culture" (287), they are compelled to explore issues related to their own background and expectations. In their study, a "lower-middle-class" student's interpretation of a poem is found to be "unusual, a little off, not on the mark" (287, 285). Analyzing tapes of Rose's conference with the student, the researchers detect the teacher's unacknowledged tendency to measure a student's interpretation against that of the teacher, whose ideas reflect those of a "conventional/middle class reader" (294).

Understanding the significance of the subjectivity of the teacher, David Bleich begins "Reading as Membership" with autobiography, revealing his membership in the " 'community' of Jews, particularly Jewish men, in the 'community' of working-class people" (6). He goes on to describe an "urban" ninth-grade classroom that became the site of conflicting values, making a point of identifying the two teachers (one of whom was Bleich) as white while describing the class as composed primarily of African American students. Bleich discusses what happened when the teachers presented to this class works by Zora Neale Hurston, which they assumed would be received as readily as they had been in a "suburban white" classroom. However, one student's written response to reading "Sweat" and "Story in Harlem Slang" shows how wrong they were and provides a rare glimpse into an attitude that is often silenced in the classroom:

> . . . The stories themselves not only offended me but it offended my entire race.
>
> I don't appreciate reading or writing about the low class of my people. The main part of our race we look at is our doctors, lawyers, famous speakers, inventors, etc.
>
> Far as pimps, hoes [whores], drug dealers, street-hangers, and gangs, we don't look down on them because they come in all different colors including the Caucasians. If you want to discuss my race let's talk about people like Martin Luther King, Jr., Malcolm X, Nelson Mandela, Louis Farrakhan, Frederick Douglass, and many, many more. (7–8; Bleich's bracketed interpolation)

Bleich's analysis of this occasion reveals the importance of the racial identity not only of the student but also of the teacher:

> We teachers did not consider that Ms. G.'s feelings might take this form. We forgot that we are seen at every moment (by some, perhaps many, black students) as representatives of the white majority rather than of the unspecified entity "society." . . .
>
> . . . Other black students in class wondered what it meant that white teachers assigned these works. (8)

Experiences such as Rose's and Bleich's suggest the need for teachers to interrogate our own identity and conditioning in order to become freer from bias or at least open enough to acknowledge the multiple perspectives that students bring to the intellectual enterprise.

Pamela Caughie immerses readers in a classroom drama in which she examines her cultural, language, and racial identity when she describes teaching Mahasweta Devi's Bengali short story "Breast-Giver" for the first time. Caughie was shaken by that fact that students rejected her "casually" stated interpretation of a scene, yet accepted the identical interpretation when it was "innocently" offered the next day by a graduate student born in India whom Caughie had previously invited to the class to discuss the story (775). Caughie suggests that the main reason the students accepted the visitor's interpretation was "her authority as a native speaker"; she adds that "Glory wore a sari that day" (776). Understanding now that a teacher's position is neither casual nor innocent, Caughie raises a critical question, "who can speak, and with what kind of authority, in the multicultural classroom?" (776). From her acknowledged feminist perspective, authority is established through experience; however, a white feminist who teaches the works of Indian, African American, or other writers of color may be denied that authority of experience.

As poignant as Caughie's analysis of her situation is, it becomes problematic when examined closely. For Caughie does not acknowledge her own role in promoting the guest lecturer as the authority. Nor does she note the irony of allowing a person of privilege to present herself as an authority on the less privileged in her country. (Nor, for that matter, does she question the notion of teacher authority itself.) Nevertheless, Caughie's recognition of the dilemma of the teacher's subject position helps us to analyze other narratives of teaching in which teachers interact with students whose racial identity does not match their own. In her university classes in South Africa, for example, Moyra Evans finds that the black African students she teaches do not necessarily respond well to the politically charged novels of contemporary black African writers. In fact, arguing that the attack on the traditional canon might be a disservice to these students, she says:

> Black African students often relate more easily to Shakespeare (for example Macbeth and the witches), and to nineteenth-century literature (which manifests similarities in the rural way of life and thought), than do many urban, English-speaking students. (8)

However, having heard this paper delivered at a conference and having met the speaker, I know that Evans identifies as white. So I must wonder if the students would have responded differently to the politically charged novels of black African writers if their teacher had been a black African. It is hard to believe that the answer is anything but yes. Given the political history of the country in which Evans teaches, there can be little doubt that students would view William Shakespeare as a safer choice than Chinua Achebe in the presence of an identifiably white teacher. In the multicultural classroom, as Caughie points out, "reticences, misperceptions, deceptions, and distrust may structure the pedagogical exchange" (787).

Self-identified teachers of color are emerging from silence to raise significant issues in print about racial, cultural, and language identity. Borrowing a term from Daphne Patai, Indira Karamcheti identifies herself as one of those "academics who are blessed with the 'surplus visibility' of race or ethnicity" (13) and then reveals the problem of the "person" in "personal" approaches to knowledge:

[T]he minority teacher does not necessarily have the choice of deliberately engaging the machinery of the personal in order to question authority. Authority has already been problematized by the fact of visible difference. (13)

Cheryl Johnson's concern about the effect of her appearance on classroom dynamics reflects the view that the body is "directly involved in a political field; power relations . . . invest it . . . force it to carry out tasks . . . to emit signs" (Foucault 25):

As a black woman who teaches courses on the literature of black women writers . . . I have wondered how much my students' reading of my racial/gendered body informs their reading of the literary texts. (Johnson 410)

Johnson wonders if students see her as an "absolute authority" on what she calls the literature of black women because they think her "*experience*" gives her insight into the truth of the text (410). Her question echoes the dilemma of the authority of experience posed by Caughie, but now the teacher identifies herself as black, not white, and the question of the personal takes on new meaning. Johnson tells how, in a one-on-one conference, a student she identifies as "non-black" had " 'crossed the line' and become personal" with her in their discussion of literary works by African American writers, thus undermining her "professionalism" (413). She speculates that stereotypical views of black women as " 'inherently' nurturing and caring" may distort students' appreciation of a black female teacher's intellectual talents, causing them to view her instead as their "mammy" (413). Johnson's dilemma reveals that feminist pedagogy's promotion of an ethic of care can have unforeseen and undesirable consequences.

Johnson's definition of professionalism appears not to invoke the personal, a view that would be challenged by many other professionals. And her sense that she is "caught, trapped, inside a concept of nurturance" (Kirsch 725) is a phenomenon shared by other female teachers, regardless of color, as the literature on feminist pedagogy reveals. But her experience shows that personal issues and gender issues cannot be conveniently divorced from racial issues, and none of these issues can be separated from teaching. The perceptions of many other teachers mirror what she says.

Karamcheti shows how in her case the issue of race—"as a category of the personal" (15)—is connected to professional credibility. As a freshman composition teacher, her authority is challenged implicitly when students speak slowly and loudly to her or compliment her on her ability to speak English well. As a teacher of postcolonial literature, her authority is granted by virtue of her "authenticity": "my bloodlines, my physical and visible affinity with my subject matter" (16). Similarly, Frances Aparicio, a self-identified Latina scholar from Puerto Rico, finds that her authority is continually defined by others. On the one hand, in spite of the fact that she has a privileged background, she is sometimes seen as a beneficiary of affirmative action (585). On the other, her multicultural scholarship has increased her value in an academic marketplace where "cultural diversity [has] become commodified" and "ethnicity has become marketable" (578). These identities are created according to who needs what at any given moment.

Another " 'minority' teacher," Lavina Shankar, claims that the " 'dominant' 'majority' " assign her to membership in a culture club with "the colored, the foreigners, the immigrants, the Easterners, the colonized (especially female) subjects, the Third World citizens, the 'subalterns.' " Yet this assignment ignores the complexity of her experience, which includes a highly traditional academic background: she was nurtured in British schools on a diet of canonical literature written by European males identified as white. Ironically, she says, some students assume she chooses to teach texts by writers of color because of who she is (visibly) and where she was raised (India); however, those choices are based on her exposure to these texts only as a graduate student in the United States.

Shankar's experience reveals that it is not really possible to know a teacher's identity by reading the body. Skin color may provide clues to but does not reveal "race" and certainly does not reveal educational background. By the same token, professional status may provide clues to but does not always reveal "class." From the perspective of students, for example, all faculty may appear to be middle or upper class by virtue of their being "intellectuals," no matter what their background may be (Nisonoff, Tracy, and Warner 16).

Scholars have proposed numerous solutions to these dilemmas arising out of the teacher's subject position. One solution is to match students' and teachers' identities. Elsa Auerbach, for example, argues for the place of bilingual or multilingual teachers in the English as a Second Language classroom:

> [W]ho is better qualified to draw out, understand, and utilize learners' experiences than those who themselves have had similar experiences? There is something about actually having lived these realities which enables immigrant teachers to make connections that are otherwise not possible. (26)

This approach makes sense up to a point but ignores the reality that few of us in the US academy are pure representatives of any one experience; we have multiple identities that cross language, cultural, racial, religious, and other boundaries, as do the students we teach. Furthermore, socially constructed readings of the teacher are not limited to students whose

identity does not match their teacher's, as Johnson points out, because of
the diversity even within particular communities:

> [B]lack students may inscribe one or more various, sometimes conflicting,
> codes onto the body of the black professor such as Afrocentrism, black
> nationalism, womanism, feminism, assimilation, or other perspectives arising
> from each student's subjectivity. Black professors are often expected to in-
> terpret or fashion these codes into academic masks or costumes which would
> signify their commitment to a particular ideology about race and gender.
> (416)

We might be similar to students in one realm yet not in another; similar
backgrounds are not so similar after all and do not necessarily lead to
"harmonious" relationships (Johnson 416).

Another solution proposed is to hide one's identity, when there is a
choice, as a way to avoid having to deal with limiting codes or stereotypes.
Unfortunately, that decision may force a choice between self-protection
and authenticity, as Bonnie Zimmerman shows:

> While a lesbian teacher might be very wise to withhold information about
> her sexuality in other classes, there is no justification for doing so in a course
> about lesbianism taught to predominantly lesbian students. (25)

Deciding whether and how to reveal an invisible identity is extraordinarily
difficult. In my own case, my "whiteness" is visible and I have no choice
but to be viewed accordingly. My religion, on the other hand, is not as
easy to read; I must decide if and when to disclose it—and circumstances
sometimes necessitate the disclosure. At any rate, hiding identity does not
necessarily lead to stable teacher-student relationships. This is true not
only of racial, cultural, religious, and sexual identities but also of identities
related to class. In their study of class differences in a small liberal arts
college, Laurie Nisonoff, Susan Tracy, and Stanley Warner report that
faculty members who come from poor or working-class backgrounds usually
identify with students from similar backgrounds but may "resent being
treated as 'hired help' by economically elite students" (16).

Teachers whose identities cannot easily be hidden—however they might
be misread—suggest another way to circumvent the personal: using approaches that require reverting to traditional texts and detached pedagogical stances:

> Maybe there was some safety in teaching the "old" curriculum because we
> could place some distance between us and the text; our participation was
> not personal. (Johnson 417)

The minority teacher can cast himself or herself as the traditional . . .
no-nonsense professional for whom the personal has nothing to do with
anything. . . . To refuse to engage the personal—to silence it—is one way
of resisting the commodification of the multicultural body. (Karamcheti 16,
17)

But there is a fallacy in the assumption that certain texts are safe or that
teaching approaches can disengage the personal. Such an assumption may
be based on evidence that students in the "old" days did not speak out against
curricula and pedagogy that they found objectionable. That once-silent
students (many of whom are now faculty members) eventually *did* demand
change is one reason that I am even writing about these issues today. And,
in fact, neither Johnson nor Karamcheti in the end advocates this safe,
impersonal approach, nor do they find it feasible. From Karamcheti's
perspective as a person born outside the United States, "the personal in this
country is irrepressible" (17), an attitude that contrasts ironically with the
Western feminist notion that the self is repressed in the academy. Understanding that she cannot suppress the personal, Karamcheti calls for a
"performance" of "guerrilla theatre" that "keeps the audience off balance":

Performance of race means to make race visible, and thereby to undermine
its authority in the classroom; simultaneously to question its meaningfulness
and to insist on its importance in shaping our understanding of the world.
(17)

Johnson ultimately agrees that racially charged issues must be confronted
in the classroom, but an internal voice warns her not to let African
American experiences silence those of other cultural backgrounds. Yet she
still feels a pull toward providing an opportunity for African American
students to "own" a subject matter that they strongly identify with (417).
This push-and-pull dilemma informs scholarship as well as pedagogy.

THE SUBJECT POSITION OF THE SCHOLARLY
WRITER

In "Unspeakable Things Unspoken: The Afro-American Presence in American Literature," Toni Morrison, noting that " 'race' is still a virtually unspeakable thing" (3), calls for a re-examination of the American canon
for what she calls "the ghost in the machine": the ways in which the
"invisible" has shaped much of American literature (11). Morrison is interested in the "intellectual feats" an author must perform to erase "other"
cultures from a society "seething with [their] presence" (12). While Morrison focuses on fiction, I believe the unspoken can be uncovered in

nonfiction as well and, more specifically, in articles published in scholarly journals. Morrison likens the development of the United States as a country to a "performance" and contends that the "audience" has managed somehow to "reconstruct the play, its director, its plot and its cast in such a manner that its very point never surfaces" (12). If the development of English Studies, too, is a performance, then its critics can attempt to reconstruct the play, its director, its plot, and its cast by looking beneath the surface of its scholarship to discover, as Morrison says, that invisible things are "not necessarily 'not-there' " (11).

That scholar-writers rarely explore the implications of what self-identified white scholar Peggy McIntosh calls "white privilege" may be a function of not being able to see " 'whiteness' as a racial identity" (15). Reflecting on her own experience, McIntosh acknowledges that "whites are taught to think of their lives as . . . neutral, normative" (4). Karamcheti contends that when writers who are not identified as "minority" insert details about themselves into their scholarship, they are making a choice to "reveal the illusory nature of impartiality, objectivity, and authority itself" (13). But new accounts of teaching, such as Karamcheti's own, challenge that privileged position because it does not recognize that the choice does not exist for everyone and therefore holds to the very notion of universality that it may set out to reject. Jane Tompkins's landmark essay, "Pedagogy of the Distressed," in which she discusses her recently liberated classroom, is worth revisiting to make this point. Using her own experience as a source of knowledge, Tompkins likens teaching to sex, something that was not open to discussion in the old days (655). Consciously or unconsciously, she extends the sex metaphor to her changed classroom. The newly legitimate model is improved: her classes are "better" (657); the "intensity and quality" of the experience are "higher"; she can "concentrate better on . . . how things feel"; and she is able to "forge a connection" with her students, those "fleshly, desiring selves"; but she "feels guilty . . . that [it] is pleasurable" (658, 657).

Tompkins writes with the authority of someone who is not seriously challenged by unexpected or unwanted readings of her body by her students. A rereading of Tompkins's textual self shows that, under the guise of self-revelation, she conceals much by choosing here not to articulate her own subject position, her power and privilege. We are told, in the biodata at the bottom of the page, that she "teaches English at Duke University," which hints at prestige, and that she is the author of a book on American fiction published by Oxford University Press, which gives her cachet. Yet she does not acknowledge that her (unmentioned) tenure gives her the security to write the way she wants to about herself. Her (unspecified) professorial status and her national reputation allow her the freedom not to have to defend her scholarly honor before she launches into personal reflection. Her (unidentified, white) racial identity allows her not to have to acknowledge that "[b]eing of the main culture, [she] could also criticize it fairly freely" (McIntosh 11). Her whiteness—combined with her (unannounced) marital status—may also free her to use sexually charged language, a more difficult choice, for example, for women of color, gays, and lesbians, who have been sexualized in the dominant rhetoric and who might therefore think twice before describing the students they teach as "fleshly" and "desiring." Thus does Tompkins benefit from the invisible privilege of the tenured, oft-cited, white, heterosexual scholar.

Such invisibility is no longer always the norm. Tompkins's article opened the way for other scholars, and in *College English*'s Comment & Response section the following year she did deal with her subjectivity as she addressed criticism of "Pedagogy of the Distressed." Since these pieces appeared, the occasional self-identified white academic writer with trappings of power (for example, a university associate professor who indicates this status in the biodata) has made the self visible in terms of race and class when discussing teaching experiences:

> The practices I describe have evolved out of my own experiences as *a white, middle-class woman* teaching first-year composition and graduate courses in rhetoric and social theory. . . . (Jarratt 36; emphasis added)

However, Gesa Kirsch and Joy Ritchie argue that such identifications are "facile" if the writers do not investigate what has shaped their own perspectives (9). And, at any rate, even such identifications are rare. Speaking of a character in Ernest Hemingway's *To Have and Have Not*, Morrison notes that "Eddie is white, and we know he is because nobody says so" (*Playing* 72). More often than not, we know similarly when writers of scholarly articles are white—because nobody says so. I am not advocating that we all identify ourselves racially in order to have credibility. Identity is too complex a construction to be captured in a word or two. And AnnLouise Keating has already argued persuasively against the dangerous tendency to perpetuate a black/white dichotomy that has allowed people in positions of power to use racialized categories to maintain that power. Nevertheless, as even Keating acknowledges, it is important to unwrap what McIntosh calls "an invisible package of unearned assets" (1). We need to examine the ways in which we may unwittingly preserve a system that situates people in dominant and subordinate positions.

Morrison claims that the assumption of whiteness that informs writers' work can exist outside the written text as well, for readers of American fiction conventionally have been positioned as white by authors of every color (*Playing* xii). Similarly, in the field of anthropology, Renato Rosaldo shows that readers of ethnographies about the "other" are typically assumed to be members of the (unidentified) white middle-class community of the scholar-writer, who signifies that membership by employing terms such as "we," as opposed to "they" (202). Rosaldo refers to this phenomenon as the "cultural invisibility within which the North American upper middle class hides itself from itself" (203). In scholarship on teaching English, this positioning of the audience is apparent, ironically even in situations where race and class are central to the discussion of the classroom. In an article that reveals sensitivity to diverse world views, Hull and Rose's opening sentences nonetheless suggest that the authors assume that readers of *College Composition and Communication* hold the same world view as they:

> This is a paper about student interpretations of literature that strike the teacher as unusual, a little off, not on the mark. When we teachers enter classrooms with particular poems or stories in hand, we also enter with expectations about the kind of student response that would be most fruitful, and these expectations have been shaped, for the most part, in literature departments in American universities. (287)

GETTING PUBLISHED—AND BEING HEARD

Whether the Western academy has been constructed in such a way as to demand that scholars "leave our emotional, subjective, and private natures behind" (Maher 96) is open to debate, given the cross-cultural perspectives I have discussed. Yet it is hard to deny that many disciplines—embodied in editors and editorial boards—have resisted the self, often identified by the term "the personal," in scholarly writing. And there is evidence of journal editors' complicity in this self concealment, for example, in two articles about publishing decisions in mainstream journals. James Raymond, editor of *College English* from 1985 to 1992, says he accepted only a few articles that unveiled the "author as a person" (479), basing his judgments about who had "earned" authority on purely "rhetorical principles" (482, 481). (Ironically, one of the articles he did accept, Min-zhan Lu's "From Silence to Words," challenges the very notion of universal rhetorical principles.) Richard Gebhardt, editor of *College Composition and Communication* during many of the same years (1987 to 1993), emphasizes his willingness to embrace subjectivity; but he creates a hierarchy of the personal: only authors who are "leaders" have their articles featured in the "Personal Perspective Essay" section (7).

Given the monitoring of the personal, and by extension the person, in scholarly publications, it has been extremely difficult for scholars of color to break into print, and the dilemmas of writing are similar to those faced in the classroom. How does one (re)present the self? What language and theoretical perspective does one adopt? Who can speak, and with what kind of authority?

Shankar discusses how difficult it is for a bicultural scholar born in Asia to position the self in Western scholarship. She points out that academic writers who were raised in an Eastern culture and who now teach in the United States must struggle even with the choice of pronoun: the use of "we" to claim common experience with other US academics can disassociate them from their past. Karamcheti suggests that denial of self is possible when the teacher of color becomes a scholar-writer, but she mocks that stance even as she explains it:

> Denying the visual evidence of race or ethnicity, this role insists on the authenticity of guild membership—card-carrying status in the union of academic professionals, usually demonstrated, at least in humanistic fields at the current time, by the use of complex post-structuralist concepts, language, and theory to analyze postcolonial, minority subjects. (16–17)

Johnson, like Karamcheti, apparently plays a dual role: personalizing the issue of race while simultaneously using poststructuralist language to discuss it, appropriating terms such as "signifiers," "essentialized," "positioned," and "socially constructed" (410). Johnson may also be using language in more subversive ways. Morrison advocates mining the works of African American writers to examine the language they use to address "the question of difference": the ways the language may be "unpoliced, seditious, confrontational, manipulative, inventive, disruptive, masked and unmasking" ("Unspeakable Things Unspoken" 11). Such a reading might identify Johnson's calling a student "non-black" as a rhetorical ploy that challenges the notion that the term "white" is normative. However, the question of who should or must do this type of study is controversial. On the one hand, scholars of color may be pressured to do this cultural work. Karamcheti claims that "minority" scholars are made to feel that it is their scholarly duty to show how resistance to authority is manifest through subversion (17). Conversely, identifiable white critics of texts written by authors of color may be viewed as inadequate to the task because they have neither experienced racial oppression nor been immersed in the culture. In "Black Writing, White Reading," self-identified white scholar Elizabeth Abel wrestles with this dilemma as she investigates what she calls white feminist readings of black women's texts.

These "white readings," even when they are recognized as insightful, have created controversy. A disturbing perception holds that the academic world embraces multiculturalism only when it is promoted by scholars who are identified as white and whose own power and privilege are thus consolidated (Aparicio). Self-identified black scholar Ann duCille, for example, points out that although African American writers and scholars for years have emphasized the important contribution of African American culture to the American literary tradition, it was not until white scholar Shelley Fisher Fishkin published *Was Huck Black? Mark Twain and African-American*

Voices (1993) that "the academy, the publishing industry, and the media sat up and took notice" (599).

When scholars of color do reach print, their work may be viewed as "too conflictive, too divisive, or perhaps too ethnocentric" by "Anglo" academics, according to Aparicio (580). Only a very few scholars of color are elevated to positions of prominence, the work of the majority being left on the margins, often treated with condescension or ignored altogether (Aparicio 580; Awkward 11).

MY JEWISH IDENTITY AND MULTICULTURAL LITERATURE

My research into teacher identity inevitably led me to examine my own identity in order to address the question of who has the authority to teach in the multicultural classroom. As I reflected on who I am in relation to what and whom I teach, one aspect of my identity emerged as a source of insight.

As a Jew born in the United States whose extended family was directly affected by the Nazi Holocaust and by Soviet terrorism, I was raised to believe that Jews are victims. From early childhood, I was taught to appreciate the freedom that "America" represents and to identify with other peoples who have been enslaved, oppressed, or discriminated against. But in the current climate of academic multiculturalism, it is difficult to view myself as a member of a persecuted community. From a certain multicultural perspective, in spite of the fact that for centuries, as Sander Gilman has compellingly documented, Jews have been constructed and represented as racialized Others, Jews are seen as part of a white power structure that serves a gatekeeping role to prevent people of color from entering and gaining ascendancy in the academy. One part of me understands this position. But another part is uncomfortable with it, for this very argument can be viewed as a variation on an age-old theme of anti-Semitism.

In fact, it has been used as an excuse not to include Jewish literature in ethnic studies courses. A case in point is Edward Alexander's description of a meeting of the Task Force on Ethnicity on his university's campus. Writing from a self-identified Jewish perspective, Alexander reports in disgust that many members of the task force argued that Jews should not be included as a minority group about which the American majority needed to be sensitized. According to Alexander, "multiculturalists do not recognize antisemitism as a form of racism" (65). He expresses shock and dismay that "devotees of diversity" are silent in the face of overt expressions of anti-Semitism on the same college campuses where verbal attacks against any other ethnic group are not countenanced (64).

Unlike Alexander, I do not lump all "multiculturalists" together, nor do I ignore the ongoing debate concerning the differences between racism and anti-Semitism (see Bourne). As a Jew living in the United States today, I do not face systematic exploitation. As a person identified as white, I recognize the automatic advantages I have had. Nevertheless, I share Alexander's concern that those who are not Jewish may not understand how disabling anti-Semitism can be. I begin with two incidents in my own classroom that I will label anti-Semitic, although I am willing to entertain other interpretations of what happened.

Several years ago, students in a composition course were discussing an article about quotas for Asian American students in US universities. Suddenly, a student from Greece, whom I will call Alexis, said that he could explain why such quotas exist: because Jews control the universities in America and want to keep the Asians out. I am not proud to admit that at that moment I was stunned into silence. I heard the students talking for a while (I have no idea what they were saying), and could only think about myself: *"Does this student know I am Jewish? Maybe not. If he does know, does it make any difference to him?"* When I finally did speak, nothing I said could deter Alexis from sticking to his position.

The second anti-Semitic incident occurred later in the same semester, in the same classroom, with the same student. Alexis referred to the Jews imprisoned in Auschwitz as "convicts." At first, I thought he misunderstood the meaning of the word *convict*, and I explained it. Alexis said he knew what it meant. I then explained that the victims at Auschwitz were not convicts, they were innocent people who had been forcibly removed from their homes and sent to the concentration camp. Alexis, who by then knew my Jewish identity, looked me in the eye and said, "Whatever."

I don't think anyone can be surprised that at these moments I was having trouble with the multicultural argument that the Jewish people are not a minority group about which other people need to be sensitized. But that is not the only reason I am retelling these incidents. The other important factor is that they deeply affected my teaching, including my choice of reading assignments.

One of the first things that happened was that I became hypersensitive to references to Jews in literary works by writers who are not Jewish. Even texts that I loved reading and sharing with students became problematic if I felt the least discomfort at the way a Jew was represented. For example, I had often assigned Richard Wright's *Black Boy*. In the thirteenth chapter, Wright explains how at age eighteen he gained access to library books and educated himself through reading. His belief that he had learned more language from reading novels than from studying grammar was a message I wanted students to hear. But after the anti-Semitic incidents with Alexis, my eye was directed to a passage in this chapter that I had heretofore not focused on; and it made me decide not to assign this particular book again. Here is the passage, in which Wright begins to consider which white men might help him get books from a library:

> I weighed the personalities of the men on the job. There was Don, a Jew; but I distrusted him. His position was not much better than mine and I knew that he was uneasy and insecure; he had always treated me in an offhand, bantering way that barely concealed his contempt. I was afraid to ask him to help me to get books; his frantic desire to demonstrate a racial solidarity with the whites against Negroes might make him betray me. (268)

I do not intend here to defend my decision not to assign this book (which is a form of censorship that I deplore), only to share the mental process of making that decision. Right or wrong, I did not want to give anti-Semitic ammunition to any more Alexises who might show up in my classroom.

My paranoia soon extended beyond my own classroom. As I was compiling an anthology of international stories, I had little difficulty selecting stories written by authors from China, Japan, Russia, Iran, Sudan, India, Nigeria, France, and so on. But when it came to choosing a work written by a Jewish author about Jewish characters, I was almost paralyzed by the task. No matter what I read, I found too many references to Judaism or Jewish history that would be difficult to explain, or too many Jewish characters who might be viewed negatively. I even rejected a favorite story, Grace Paley's "The Loudest Voice," which is about a Jewish girl who participates in a Christmas nativity play. The problem was with the following line, spoken by the Jewish husband to his Jewish wife:

> "You're in America! Clara, you wanted to come here. In Palestine the Arabs would be eating you alive. . . ." (58)

I simply couldn't consider including this anti-Arab sentiment in a class in which I was likely to have Arab students, and, more particularly, Palestinian or pro-Palestinian students. I feared that students like Alexis would use this as evidence of the Jews' bigotry and hatred.

As the deadline for publication of my anthology neared, I finally decided on a relatively innocuous story by a turn-of-the-century US writer whose pen name was Bruno Lessing. "The Americanization of Shadrach Cohen" tells the story of the conflict between an immigrant father and his sons and can be especially meaningful to students. Still, I almost didn't include it because the fictional Cohen family came from Russia with money and set up a lucrative business in New York City, unlike most Eastern European immigrants at that time (including my own family) who escaped persecution and arrived in poverty. I was afraid that the story might confirm students' stereotype of male Jews as rich businessmen. I finally, defensively, settled on adding the following headnote to the story: "In the latter part of the nineteenth century, many Jewish immigrants fled their countries primarily to escape religious persecution. Most came to America with little money and had to struggle to survive."

For my teaching, I sought works of literature that presented another side of Jewish life. The first time I taught "The German Refugee" by Bernard Malamud, I chose it primarily because I wanted to include a story in which Jews could be viewed as victims. "The German Refugee" tells of Oskar Gassner, who escapes Nazi Germany in 1939, leaving his Christian wife behind, and who suffers terribly in the United States. But even this story fueled my paranoia because of the way in which one student reacted to it. At the end of the story, Oskar commits suicide. In the following passage, the last paragraph of the story, the narrator (Oskar's English tutor) finds a recent letter from Oskar's anti-Semitic mother-in-law, who

> writes in a tight script it takes me hours to decipher, that her daughter, after Oskar abandons her, against her own mother's fervent pleas and an-guish, is converted to Judaism by a vengeful rabbi. One night the Brown shirts appear, and though the mother wildly waves her bronze crucifix in their faces, they drag Frau Gassner, together with the other Jews, out of the apartment house, and transport them in lorries to a small border town in conquered Poland. There, it is rumored, she is shot in the head and topples into an open tank ditch, with the naked Jewish men, their wives and children, some Polish soldiers, and a handful of gypsies. (212)

This passage always moved me to tears until a student wrote a journal entry that focused on the "vengeful rabbi":

> . . . [Oskar] finds that the very Church he believed in . . . forcefully converted his wife to Judaism which indirectly yet so obviously led her to death. He was betrayed by his religion, something his soul depended on through the tough times. . . .

I was stunned. As I saw it, in a story that revealed the terrible persecution of the Jewish people, this student focused on a negative aspect of Judaism. In her mind, apparently, Judaism was parallel to Nazism in terms of its destruction of Oskar's life. I was so shaken by this journal entry that I decided not to teach this story again.

Fortunately, I later came to my senses. When I was writing another textbook and wanted to include a story about the Jewish American experi-ence, I took another look at "The German Refugee." This time I ap-proached it with my literary training, not my Jewish identity, at the fore-front. What I saw was that the line about the "vengeful rabbi" was seen through the perspective of the *anti-Semitic mother-in-law.* Anything she says is suspect. Had I initially approached the literature in this way, I could have treated it as I did all other literature and not taken every comment I didn't like as a personal affront or as an attack on my people.

While I cannot yet come to any closure on this issue, I can share what I have learned through this reflection on my Jewish identity and the teaching of literature. First, I need to be sensitive to the fact that any story can appear to be representative of an entire culture, even if neither the author nor I intend it to be. So, just as every Jewish story seemed to me to be saying something about all Jews (and about me in particular), so might a story from India appear to a student from India or a story from China appear to a student from China (and I have had experience in my own classroom with this phenomenon). Furthermore, just as Jewish stories have numerous obscure cultural and historical references, so do most stories, even if I don't recognize them. The problem for me was that I knew too much about my own culture.

And second, I now challenge the notion that the best person to teach a work of literature is the person whose own experience is reflected in the text. My experience shows that I am not necessarily the right person to teach Jewish literature, even though I am Jewish. Someone with more distance from (I do not mean less engagement with) the Jewish experience actually may be better than I. And so, at this moment, the answer to the question of "who can speak, and with what kind of authority, in the multicultural classroom?" seems to be that it is not the teacher who can speak with the authority of experience, but one who speaks with the authority that comes from being an open-minded reader—one who can allow for multiple (if not all) interpretations of a text, and one who remembers that a work of literature is first and foremost a work of art and not a cultural artifact.

CONCLUDING THOUGHTS

I believe that academics can and should find a way to open up a conversation about "unspeakable things" and to make our classrooms safe places to continue the conversation. We need to help one another avoid the mines that are scattered throughout the multicultural terrain, rather than to allow our unspoken thoughts to explode in "anger and rage" (Karamcheti 17) and "bitterness and resentment" (Delpit 282). Having said that, I am less certain about how this process should play out. Once we agree to speak, what should the forum be? Faculty development programs as currently conceived appear not to be the answer. For example, in "race awareness" workshops, often there is little opportunity for the kind of listening that allows a speaker to think things through and thus to transform understanding. In some cases, the facilitators are to blame: sessions are poorly conceived and poorly run. But Christine Sleeter's research suggests that such staff development workshops do not work primarily because most white participants are resistant to viewpoints that challenge their longheld power and privilege (168). Sleeter argues that, since racism is institutionalized, the only way to effect change is to change the teaching population to include people whose diverse world views impel them to "expose, challenge, and deconstruct racism" rather than accept it as inevitable (168). This argument makes sense, and we should turn theory into action to accomplish that goal. But it is not enough just to integrate the academic neighborhood, to use Trudy Palmer's analogy. Old-timers cannot expect the new neighbors to do all the work and then, as Ann duCille claims happens too often, watch as their energy becomes so depleted that they do not have the chance to benefit from the results of their efforts (605). Reconstruction of the institution needs to be a communal project.

My own evolving understanding of unspeakable things has come through listening to the students and teaching assistants I work with, whose insights into their own multiple identities have helped me recognize my own. Also edifying have been the numerous articles and books I have read, many of which are listed in the bibliography, about which I have had fruitful discussions with colleagues. But reading about and discussing these things will not make a difference unless transformed views are applied to the classroom. Learning how these issues are tied to—are inseparable from—the very subject we teach is essential. We may be able to move toward the achievement of that goal by pooling our multicultural knowledge to reconceptualize the texts we teach, reconsider texts we don't now teach, and reevaluate our own positions vis-à-vis whom and what we teach.

Yet, even if we can find ways to move toward more enlightened teaching, the question of who has the authority to do the scholarly work in this area remains. Should only people of color analyze the works of authors of colors? Does one need to have experienced racial oppression or to have been raised in a particular culture in order to write about it? To answer these questions with "yes" is to suggest that scholars should be limited in the range of scholarship they can pursue, an idea that flies in the face of academic freedom. I agree with Michael Awkward that we need to distinguish between "a desire to see representatives of the borders gain access to mainstream power" and "an impulse to suggest that only those markedly affiliated with 'minority' space can persuasively read the expressivity which derives from that space" (6). The idea that authority resides in experience is an alluring but potentially debilitating notion. It deprives us of the opportunity to engage imaginatively with texts outside our immediate experience. And, ironically, it may lead to exclusivity even when inclusivity is the goal. The position that certain groups have proprietorship of certain texts paradoxically reinforces the very situation it is trying to subvert. Taken to its logical conclusion—given the male/female and white person/person of color ratio of the faculty in institutions of higher education—the result of faculty's teaching and studying only texts that reflect their own subjectivities would be that the majority of texts taught and studied would be those written by European American males identified as white. Even as that ratio changes, it does not make sense to have departments in which only African Americans have expertise in African American literature, only Asian Americans have expertise in Asian American literature, and so on. Surely such divisions cannot be what we mean by diversity.

Perhaps the question is not so much who should do the scholarship but how the scholarship should be done. African American scholars have complained, for example, that too many scholars have demeaned African American literature, especially literature by women writers, either by not treating it with disciplinary rigor or by essentializing the black female subject (Carby; duCille). Although these complaints are directed toward white scholars, the tendency to essentialize—to treat social groups as stable or homogeneous entities—exists not only across but also within cultures, as Lisa Lowe points out in her discussion of Asian American discourses on ethnicity. The antidote to this tendency may lie in the recognition of the diversity and complexity—or, to borrow Lowe's phrase, the "heterogeneity, hybridity, multiplicity"—of all literary works.

However we struggle to define it, the reality of diversity has forever changed the classroom. Even though powerful political forces are working against cultural pluralism in the academy, the truth is that the days of white (middle-class European American native English-speaking male) teachers "innocently" and "casually" teaching white texts to white students are long gone. Yet, as I have tried to show, just adding "multicultural" to the curriculum and to the student body is inadequate. We need to confront the unspeakable ourselves, as teachers and as scholars, and not assume or expect that the students we teach and the texts we analyze will do all of the work of multiculturalism for us.

EPILOGUE

While I was writing this article, I ran into a neighbor at a linen store where we were making purchases for our college-age sons, who have been friends since childhood. After we exchanged information about our families, our conversation turned to our professional lives. As head of a diversity program at another university, she was interested in what I am doing, and so I told her about my work. I learned that she is conducting research on the experience of Hispanics in higher education administration because, as a self-described "dark-skinned Puerto Rican who speaks English with a Spanish accent," she herself has felt silenced by white faculty and other administrators for whom English is the first language. I fell silent as I reflected on the difference between the relatively safe space I inhabit in the world of academic multiculturalism and the unprotected space she inhabits in the world at large. When I found my voice again, I told her that I didn't think I could finish this article because, as a white person, I felt I should not comment on these issues. She insisted that I had a right to air my views but suggested that I emphasize that the voices of teachers of color must be heard and respected. At that moment, we were simultaneously called to side-by-side cash registers. We wrote checks for our respective purchases and added the appropriate driver's license numbers for verification. Her cashier looked at her and asked for more proof of her identity. My cashier smiled at me and told me to have a nice day.

WORKS CITED

Abel, Elizabeth. "Black Writing, White Reading: Race and the Politics of Feminist Interpretation." *Critical Inquiry* 19 (1993): 470–98.

Alexander, Edward. "Multiculturalism's Jewish Problem." *Academic Questions* 5 (1992): 63–68.

Aparicio, Frances R. "On Multiculturalism and Privilege: A Latina Perspective." *American Quarterly* 46 (1994): 575–88.

Auerbach, Elsa Roberts. "Reexamining English Only in the ESL Classroom." *TESOL Quarterly* 27 (1993): 9–32.

Awkward, Michael. *Negotiating Difference: Race, Gender, and the Politics of Positionality.* Chicago: U of Chicago P, 1995.

Bleich, David. "Reading as Membership." *ADE Bulletin* 102 (1992): 6–10.

Bourne, Jenny. "Homelands of the Mind: Jewish Feminism and Identity Politics." *Race & Class* 29 (1987): 1–24.

Carby, Hazel. "The Multicultural Wars." *Radical History Review* 54 (1992): 7–18.

Caughie, Pamela L. " 'Not Entirely Strange, . . . Not Entirely Friendly': *Passing* and Pedagogy." *College English* 54 (1992): 775–93.

Delpit, Lisa D. "The Silenced Dialogue: Power and Pedagogy in Educating Other People's Children." *Harvard Educational Review* 58 (1988): 280–97.

duCille, Ann. "The Occult of True Black Womanhood: Critical Demeanor and Black Feminist Studies." *Signs* 19 (1994): 591–629.

Evans, Moyra. "Teaching Literature to ESL Undergraduates: A South African Perspective." Convention of Teachers of English to Speakers of Other Languages. Atlanta, April 1993.

Foucault, Michel. *Discipline and Punish: The Birth of the Prison.* 1975. Trans. Alan Sheridan. New York: Vintage, 1979.

Freire, Paulo. *Pedagogy of the Oppressed.* 1970. Trans. Myra Bergman Ramos. New York: Continuum, 1992.

Gebhardt, Richard C. "Diversity in a Mainline Journal." *College Composition and Communication* 43 (1992): 7–10.

Gee, James Paul. "Orality and Literacy: From *The Savage Mind* to *Ways with Words*." *TESOL Quarterly* 20 (1986): 719–46.

Gilligan, Carol. *In a Different Voice: Psychological Theory and Women's Development.* Cambridge: Harvard UP, 1982.

Gilman, Sander. *The Jew's Body.* New York: Routledge, 1991.

Hull, Glynda, and Mike Rose. " 'This Wooden Shack Place': The Logic of an Unconventional Reading." *College Composition and Communication* 41 (1990): 287–98.

Jarratt, Susan C. "Rhetorical Power: What Really Happens in Politicized Classrooms." *ADE Bulletin* 102 (1992): 34–39.

Johnson, Cheryl L. "Participatory Rhetoric and the Teacher as Racial/Gendered Subject." *College English* 56 (1994): 409–33.

Karamcheti, Indira. "Caliban in the Classroom." *Radical Teacher* 44 (1993): 13–17.

Keating, AnnLouise. "Interrogating 'Whiteness.' (De)Constructing 'Race.' *College English* 57 (1995): 901–18.

Kirsch, Gesa E. "Feminist Critical Pedagogy and Composition." *College English* 57 (1995): 723–29.

Kirsch, Gesa E., and Joy S. Ritchie. "Beyond the Personal: Theorizing a Politics of Location in Composition Research." *College Composition and Communication* 46 (1995): 7–29.

Lowe, Lisa. "Heterogeneity, Hybridity, Multiplicity: Marking Asian American Differences." *Diaspora* 1 (1991): 24–44.

Lu, Min-zhan. "From Silence to Words: Writing as Struggle." *College English* 49 (1987): 437–48.

Maher, Frances A. "Toward a Richer Theory of Feminist Pedagogy: A Comparison of 'Liberation' and 'Gender' Models for Teaching and Learning." *Journal of Education* 169 (1987): 91–100.

Malamud, Bernard. "The German Refugee." *Idiots First.* New York: Farrar, 1963. 195–212.

Matalene, Carolyn. "Contrastive Rhetoric: An American Writing Teacher in China." *College English* 47 (1985): 789–808.

McIntosh, Peggy. *White Privilege and Male Privilege: A Personal Account of Coming to See Correspondences through Work in Women's Studies.* Working Papers Series. No. 189. Wellesley, MA: Center for Research on Women, 1988. Quoted with permission of the author. Available from the Wellesley College Center for Research on Women, Wellesley, MA 02181.

Miller, Richard E. "Ships in the Night Revisited." *College Composition and Communication* 46 (1995): 279–82.

Morrison, Toni. *Playing in the Dark.* New York: Vintage, 1992.

———. "Unspeakable Things Unspoken: The Afro-American Presence in American Literature." *Michigan Quarterly Review* 28 (1989): 1–34.

Nisonoff, Laurie, Susan J. Tracy, and Stanley Warner. "Stories Out of School: Poor and Working-Class Students at a Small Liberal Arts College." *Radical Teacher* 41 (1992): 15–19.

Paley, Grace. "The Loudest Voice." 1956. *The Little Disturbances of Man.* New York: Penguin, 1985. 53–63.

Palmer, Trudy Christine. "Changes in the Neighborhood: Integrating the Academy and Diversifying the Curriculum." *Women's Studies* 20 (1992): 217–24.

Raymond, James C. "I-Dropping and Androgyny: The Authorial *I* in Scholarly Writing." *College Composition and Communication* 44 (1993): 478–83.

Rosaldo, Renato. *Culture and Truth: The Remaking of Social Analysis.* 2d ed. Boston: Beacon, 1993.

Shankar, Lavina Dhingra. "Pro/(Con)fessing Otherness: Trans(cending)national Identities in the English Classroom." *Teaching What You're (Not): Identities, Knowledge, and Politics.* Ed. Katherine J. Mayberry. New York: New York UP (in press).

Shen, Fan. "The Classroom and the Wider Culture: Identity as a Key to Learning English Composition." *College Composition and Communication* 40 (1989): 459–66.

Sleeter, Christine E. "How White Teachers Construct Race." *Race, Identity, and Representation in Education.* Ed. Cameron McCarthy and Warren Crichlow. New York: Routledge, 1993. 151–71.

Tompkins, Jane. "Pedagogy of the Distressed." *College English* 52 (1990): 653–60.

———. "Comment & Response: Jane Tompkins Responds." *College English* 53 (1991): 601–5.

Weiler, Kathleen. "Freire and a Feminist Pedagogy of Difference." *Harvard Educational Review* 61 (1991): 449–73.

Wright, Richard. *Black Boy: A Record of Childhood and Youth.* 1937. New York: Perennial, 1989.

Zimmerman, Bonnie. "Lesbianism 101." *Politics of Education: Essays from* Radical Teacher. Ed. Susan Gushee O'Malley, Robert C. Rosen, and Leonard Vogt. Albany: State U of New York P, 1990. 22–34.

Chapter 22

Blurred Voices:
Who Speaks for the Subaltern?

Norma González

I was not taught about language. It was simply there. "Nothing worth learning can be taught," Oscar Wilde is said to have once observed. My own lack of consciousness about language in my childhood is illustrated by an offhand remark I overheard referring to the fact that my great-grandmother, Yaya, could not speak English. "Well, of course she speaks English," I had insisted. "I understand her and she talks to me, and I understand English." I was convinced that what was intelligible to me was intelligible to her because somehow we understood and communicated. Languages had blurred and it was difficult to disentangle where one left off and another began. There was no boundedness to language, no readily identifiable edges that could be marked off. There was only communication, however and whenever it took place. How often have I heard of Latino adults who as children were admonished to speak only English in the schoolgrounds, and their unspoken dread that somehow they would not be able to tell the difference. As languages blur, the contexts that they evoke intermingle and blend.

Although I was aware that language use with Yaya was fraught with the seductive pull of her *cuentos* and the sublime narratives of her childhood, I could not fathom that she did not speak English. Even in my immature state, I could discern that a person who did not speak English was invisible. He or she did not exist. English was the currency of exchange for securing personhood.

On Becoming a Language Educator, 1997

Yet my Yaya existed, and the world that she created for me through her crafting of language often bore little resemblance to the world that I then inhabited. I became aware of the legacy of bilingual children everywhere: the arbitrariness of the sign. When she drank *cafecito*, it was more milk than coffee, sugary and served in a glass. It was not the same as coffee, which was dark and bitter and always in a cup. A *vaso de leche* was milk warmed to just before boiling and was drunk with *pan de huevo*. A glass of milk, on the other hand, was cold and drunk with cookies.

I learned that the world was not carved into discrete and knowable chunks that were simply labeled differently in different languages. When she spoke of the *sierra*, of the smoky campsites of Mexican miners on their treks to mining camps, the images that she conjured could not be mapped onto any English equivalents. Ineffably, I knew that the dimensions of Spanish were far different from the dimensions of English. They did not feel the same, taste the same, nor sound the same. Spanish was the language of family, of food, of music, of ritual; in short, of identity. It was the language of endearments to children. It was the language of dressing in white in long processions in dark churches. It was the language of tinkling music on Saturday morning. English was for arithmetic, for the doctor's office, for the teacher. English was the newspaper and television. Even though we mixed languages effortlessly, the underlying symbolism was correspondingly parallel: Home and hearth were woven with Spanish; out there was constructed with English.

In the course of my schooling, I initially and unquestioningly accepted the division between English as productive currency and Spanish as the discourse of connection. This demarcation further extended to English as objective and scientific, and Spanish as subjective and evocative. As a fledgling academic, it became easy to hide behind the cloak of objectivity because it rendered messy topics distant and impersonal. Once shrouded in academese, racism, poverty and other facile constructs became sanitized and anaesthetized. By objectifying the researched, by assuming an impersonal stance toward the data, I could validate my academic credentials as a social scientist. And so, it became possible to talk about language patterns without reference to the relations of symbolic domination that surround those patterns. Language contact could be bandied about with no reference to the devaluation and denigration of one language to another. The intersection of social class and language could be confined to a discrete variable subject to quantification. In short, the use of the phenomenally multiplex medium of language could be stripped to its phonetic, morphemic, and syntactic carcass.

Of course, it is only now in retrospect, having been fitted with academic lenses, that I can label the then-familiar world with theoretical constructs. But it has been a treacherous journey, replete with detours, often ricocheting from one side of the academic fence to the other, while pushing forth to forge an identity, both personal and academic. It is only now in retracing and reflecting on this experience that I can label the dilemmas with which I struggled. Because academic language use and its attendant ideology had distanced me in some ways from my own community, I struggled with voicing that which was experiential.

As an aftermath of grappling with these issues, the validity of reflection on one's personal experiences as a source of social theory took on for me an intensely revelatory dimension. As discourses seek to redefine theoretical perspectives that can be constructed only from the insider's point of view, as natives begin to talk back, the voices that are heard may be neither unified nor cohesive. There are levels and intersections of shared subjectivities. Mexican-origin adolescents, born and reared in the United States, often find little in common with newly immigrated youth, and minority discourse is inherently imbued with multiple perspectives. Contradiction and ambiguity are not to be thrust away as confounding variables, but as the essence of analysis. As I have continued as a researcher within my own community, I have found that the integrated and cohesive pictures of culture, which did not always mesh with my own experience, were not always forthcoming. Further, I have found that in studying language with predigested structures, we can often defeat the creative forces that it unleashes.

I had been drawn to the study of language in context partly because of the magnetic sway of the assemblages linguists had fashioned for phenomena that I had implicitly accepted as everyday occurrences. To learn that there was a term like *code-switching* for what was a commonplace household discourse pattern was to somehow validate and elevate the practice to the realm of That Which Is Worthy Of Study. Yet, these same constructs did not always resonate with my own experience. The conclusion I drew was that my own experience was somehow nonstandard, that my subjectivity clouded the clearer interpretations of others who were more adept than I at fashioning theory. But because knowledge and power are intimately bound up with each other, I could not have the knowledge of my experience without the power to assert that knowledge. Like my great-grandmother, I too was invisible because I did not control the discourse.

When I began anthropological fieldwork investigating language socialization practices in my home community, it became impossible to disassociate the interminglings of language with the larger contexts in which people played out their lives. During the course of my fieldwork, the sting of race and class distinctions, unemployment and underemployment, lack of health care, divorce, death, alcoholism and drug abuse; all were touched on in one form or another in the interviews on language use that I conducted. But if all of these elements coincided in their barbs, so did the soothing balsam of warm and supportive networks of kinship and friendship, and multiple strands of complementary and mutual affiliations and relationships. The study of language use in the community became, in a sense, a study of oppositions: the opposition of being both insider and outsider, of objectivity and subjectivity, of language solidarity and language schism, of language as private, personal domain, and language as publicly constituted discourse.

As an anthropologist, I was not the detached and disinterested social scientist. I became a participant/observer, not in an exotic or unknown land, as anthropologists usually do, learning the language for the first time, but within my own intimate circles, where the nuances were well-known, and hence, less salient to the insider. I recalled a graduate school conversation with the only other two Latinos in my department at the time. One had been advised that doing fieldwork in one's own community was not as valid as working in a foreign setting. The anthropological cliché of fish being the last to discover water was tossed about. Could I truly make the familiar strange? Was my linguistic subjectivity an entree into the inner realms of the insider's point of view, or was it a filter that obscured the emergence of patterns visible only to the outsider?

Because the neighborhoods where I worked were nonexotic to me, the angst of dealing with the anthropological rite of passage of immersion in an alien population was absent. I couldn't help but wonder how non-Mexicans, driving through these streets, would picture the lifestyles of the people within these homes. I had observed women from other areas of the city discreetly lock their car doors as they entered into the South-side quadrant, and police presence was never far away. What of everyday life, though, as it hummed along in these neighborhoods? What happens within the walls of these homes that is not reported in the mass media, and is the genesis for the transmission of intergenerational knowledge? Is the concept of otherness really that marked within the emic conceptualization of the community? Or was it a construct from without, an etic formulation to explain away discontinuities?

Yet another dilemma remained: Somewhere out there, there had to be households that fit the traditional markers of U.S. Mexican ethnicity, that combined the essence of what it is to be Mexican. Academic discourse had constructed a picture of a normative culture out there somewhere. If I could only objectify the data, its rationality would emerge as it had in the academic literature. Even though I implicitly knew that the households within my own circles of kinship and friendship were nonstandard in some way, somewhere it must be possible to study households that would truly represent the population. Because my experience with the community was subjective, I felt it could not be accurate, and that even though I knew that all Spanish, or *barrios*, or levels of poverty, or degrees of Catholicism, are not created equal, I searched for canons of cultural practices. I knew that the straddling of two cultural systems impelled a surge toward identification, definition, and redefinition. I knew that music (romantic, nostalgic, gripping, seductive, throbbing, Mexican music) was a formative force in molding identity. I knew that joking and teasing and verbal play were integral parts of linguistic context: that the best teasers were never alone. I knew how subtle shifts in discourse marked qualitatively significant shifts in cueing speech events: that people slipped in and out of speaking styles effortlessly and glibly, crafting intricate verbal art that would drive sociolinguists berserk. I knew that the children of the members of my age cohort had felt the linguistic homogenization of Sesame Street and other such shows. Who better than an insider could grasp the complexities of language use?

THE DISCARDING OF PARADIGM

One anecdote in my early fieldwork experience illustrates how I came to discard notions of quantification and objectivity and rely more heavily on the shared subjectivity of self-reflection.

I began my first study on language use with a particular notion of how anthropological research should be done in general, and language socialization research in particular. I first started out with ideas of coding linguistic exchanges with categories focusing on participant structures, child's turns at talk, types of interactions sanctioned, turn-taking, child-initiated speech, and so on. I tinkered endlessly with methodological models, trying to interject a quantifiable (and hence more valid) dimension. I labored under the assumption that identifiable patterns would emerge under these pre-packaged constructs that would readily explicate the sources and content of variation in language use in households. I soon came to a halt in the research process because language practices I encountered were not content to be boxed into the prefabricated niches that had been molded. For a while, I insisted that I simply had to search harder, to tinker longer with the scenarios I was presented, and that somehow the refined, orderly, and cohesive picture that other language socialization studies described would emerge. This did not happen. Instead, I was jolted out of the frames that I had complacently embraced. I came uncomfortably face to face with contradiction, ambiguity, and the blurring of boundaries between categories.

On my first ethnographic interview, Marina Escobedo sat at her small dining room table as she spoke rapidly. Her voice belied her impassioned hope that her children never get involved in drugs:

> . . . I mean, I've seen families where people will go into the home, and a father and a mother, or an aunt or an uncle, will come, will walk in, and will roll up a joint and smoke it, like it's a cigarette, with the kids around. Then the first time they have difficulty with their child, if they catch the

teenage kids with it, and they say, 'Why are you doing this?' And the kid retaliates by saying, 'Look, you do it.' . . . There was a situation recently . . . there was a family where there were two teen-age boys, OK? Aunts and uncles, everybody in the family smoked it. Their parents are both in jail because of it, OK? These kids have grown up with marijuana and drugs as a normal thing in the family life, OK? Normal, completely. I mean they have never passed a day when it was not in their normal everyday activities, where somebody wasn't rolling it, somebody wasn't selling it, somebody wasn't doing something, it was normal. OK, and they all went out on a picnic. Unfortunately, the kids stole the stuff from a couple of their aunts, and went off to the corner . . . and got caught doing it. And the aunts ANGRILY, I mean really indignant confronted them and asked them, well WHY did you do this. You know, 'why are you doing this?' And the kids say, well YOU do it. 'But you have to have some respect.' And the kids go, 'well, you don't'. And they get all upset. They came and they were talking to their brother, and [ ] said, well, what do you expect from these children? You do it in front of them, you're their role model to them, they look up to you.

I cringe inwardly as she detailed the picnic scene, as I always feel a pang of distress whenever the subject of Hispanic kids and drugs surfaces. My intent was to provide an ethnographic description of the processes of language socialization within Tucson U.S. Mexican households. It was not to feed stereotypes of drugs, gangs, and violence. It was a contradiction that is played out in the many images of "Mexican-ness." The community I know is a nurturing web of familial alliances and friendship, of an inter-weaving of connections from a shared and inherited Mexican Tucson where the past slips effortlessly into the present, as omnipresent as the Santa Cruz River, and as omniferous as the Sonoran desert from whose soils it has flourished and blossomed.

It is a community in the true sense of a fellowship of shared commonalities in an arid and parched ecosystem into which its early Mexican settlers sowed the seeds of *compadrazgo* and *confianza* from which their descendants now reap the fruits. The unwelcome intrusion of drugs onto my panglossian best of all possible worlds is both disturbing and irritating. Yet, the contradiction surfaces surreptitiously on my first interview in the field.

I mull over the word respect, so often bandied about by social scientists in discussing Mexican children. An ironic permutation of the word inspires drug users to accuse their young nephews of not having respect because they use marijuana. The concept seemed somehow anachronistic. Respect, *respeto*, conjured up presences of Spanish dons and doñas, of devoted mothers and stalwart fathers, of priests and peons, all entwined by the consolidating laces of mutual respect. It was not a hallmark of drug use.

I gratefully mused on what a stroke of luck it was that I had encountered such an articulate and open informant on my first foray into the field. Who could have predicted that I would stumble onto a veritable torrent of mores, strategies, and ideology within her tiny, easily overlooked house. Her home conveyed the struggle of a family aching to make ends meet. The furnishings were sparse, even spartan. It was difficult to imagine a family of six crowded into the confined quarters. The interior was unremarkable except for one thing—books. As one entered the small frame house, the eye rested on an antiquated set of encyclopedias within a modest bookcase. Her conversation was punctuated by sporadic bursts to the bookcase, from which she would retrieve some book or other and which she would eagerly display for my perusal.

Marina was unabashedly outspoken. She chatted candidly about her distress in dealing with her oldest child, born with a birth defect. She spoke of her tireless efforts to shield her children from profanity, from alcohol abuse, and her undeviating involvement in her sons' classrooms and school work. She intrigued me. As I scrupulously tried to record the outpouring of discourse she directed toward me, a small red warning flag of social science methodology went off in my head. Granted, this woman was extraordinarily astute and articulate. She was an outstanding informant. But, I wondered, how typical is she of the neighborhood I was attempting to personify?

I was unsettled by what I perceived to be the unrepresentativeness of Marina. Marina did not fit the demographic profile of the neighborhood. She lived smack in the middle of it, her income level was consistent with it, but somehow, she didn't fit. She had been raised on the far east side of Tucson. She had attended a local Community College for a year, and she had been in the military and in law enforcement. How many other mothers in the neighborhood liked martial arts and guns?

I soon discovered that every other household I encountered had characteristics that complicated a comparative sample. I had ostensibly set out to do a microethnography of language practices within the home, using traditional sociolinguistic methods, and focusing on such publishable constructs as participant structures, turn-taking, and the allocation of communicative resources. Instead, I was being furnished with a methodologically discomforting reality: the nonuniformity of the field. The categories that I had tried to identify were in a constant state of flux. I had tried to capture the heterogeneity of the population by dividing the sample according to some notion of naturally occurring divisions within the community. I had opted for a residential variable, that is, comparing families from *barrio* settings with families from non-*barrio* settings. This had proved problematic. Marina, originally tied to her *barrio* street, during the course of my fieldwork, moved to the eastside non-*barrio* home of her parents. A second family moved from their home to the wife's parents' southside home, and then again to a north-side working-class, non-*barrio* area. Other variables confounded a neat delineation of the households. Rosalba, chosen for the study based on her enrollment in a class for 4-year-olds who were at risk, was cared for by her grandmother who lived in the *barrio*, but Rosalba actually lived on an acre of land with ducks, chickens, and rabbits. Additionally, her mother turned out to have a degree from the University of Arizona, even though she worked as a cashier at a small southside grocery store. Where could I classify her family? I had also hoped to get a fair number of Spanish-dominant households from the *barrio* sample. I had only one. The emergence of language patterns within the homes that was predicated on an infusion of evangelical Christian tapes, books, and discourse patterns was a further deviation. This was not the data set that I had hoped for. Yet, was it really so different from what I already knew?

I obviously had known of an influx of proselytizing among Latinos. I was well aware of high levels of English dominance among children in the local schools. I had long rejected ideas of a monolithic community or of a simplistic two-dimensional analysis based on class, education, or residential pattern. But because I needed a comparable set of household data, I had stripped my own subjectivity of any validity. I had begun to view the processes of everyday life as getting in the way of analyses, rather than being the heart of analyses. My primary question remained. Are there identifiable processes by which children are socialized through language in U.S. Mexican households? The next question that inevitably followed was more enigmatic: How can these processes be elucidated, taking into account the smorgasbord of households I was encountering?

As I contemplated the disjointed scenario before me, I attempted to come to grips with all of the facets I felt were involved. How could I devise neat theoretical constructs when the continuum of everyday life kept getting in my way? I was unaware at the time that it was precisely because of the fluidity of the field I was observing that I would glean one of my most significant insights.

I had come full circle in constructing a theoretical perspective. Alarmed that my subjectivity and in-member status was an impediment to unbiased research, I had opted to reject variation from the socially defined norm. Yet, my objective analysis had led me back to my original starting point: faced with the multiple perspectives of subordinated discourses.

I came away from my fieldwork experience changed in a fundamental way. I had experienced first-hand the fracturing of subjectivities, inter- and intra-personally. I had begun by stripping away my own life experiences in the quest for social science objectivism. I had found that objectivity was a facile construct, predicated on the dismissal of the nonnormative. Most important was the insight that I had gained about language. In studying language with predigested structures, we defeat the creative forces that it unleashes. Language reflects the ineffability of our being. Through language we define, and are defined by, ourselves and others. The recognition of raw effect of emotion on language, and of language on emotion, was one legacy of doing fieldwork in my own backyard.

I gleaned a second insight at the level of communicating with the house-holds I interviewed. Because these households were mediated by intersections of class, gender, religion, and other constructs, I found that language use crafted multiple identities. Our identity is not fixed and immutable, but is malleable and subject to our own choice. Language choice is often a marker of the particular identity we choose to adopt. Language is not simply something that stands outside of experience and refers to it; rather, we use language to create a particular order. The world we live in is built on the linguistic beliefs and practices of social groups and language builds our social identities. As Gloria Anzaldúa (1987) noted, "So, if you want to really hurt me, talk badly about my language. Ethnic identity is twin skin to linguistic identity—I am my language" (p. 59).

I also came away convinced that the affective dimension of language use must not be relegated to the unknowable and therefore discarded. Although the connection between language and affect has been referenced, it is often relegated to either grammatical markers of affect or to classroom techniques for producing language learners. The ineffable creative force of language to construct social worlds and personhood is a dimension that cannot be overlooked.

As a researcher who works with language, I need to remind myself regularly never to fall into the labyrinth of equating language with grammar, or with phonology, or as simply a means of getting things done with words. As I reflected on my earliest language experiences, I became aware that much of communication is extralinguistic . . . that communication involves much more than words. As I continue the process of self-reflection, I have come to accept self-questioning as an integral part of the development of a researcher. Because I work in my own community, I am aware that there is no one or correct interpretation to language data. Questioning the data, questioning the informants, questioning the methodology, and questioning oneself are not often represented in published sources. Data do not always neatly fall into place, and objective discourse often obscures the very processes we are attempting to document.

As I continue to straddle two systems as both language researcher and language producer, I have come full circle to my first and most basic insights on language: that its most powerful use is as a creative force—a creator of personhood, of domain, and of identity. These insights were wrested in opposition to academic and positivistic traditions that deprivilege experience, emotion, and subjectivity, and that cannot be extirpated from learning about language.

REFERENCE

Anzaldúa, G. (1987). *Borderlands-la frontera: The new mestiza*. San Francisco: Aunt Lute Books.

Credits